The American Experience in Vietnam

The American Experience in Vietnam

A Reader

Edited by

Grace Sevy

University of Oklahoma Press : Norman and London

Library of Congress Cataloging-in-Publication Data

The American experience in Vietnam : a reader / edited by Grace Sevy.
        p.   cm.
    ISBN 0-8061-2211-0 (alk. paper)
    1. Vietnamese Conflict, 1961-1975—United States.   2. United
States—History—1945.   I. Sevy, Grace, 1936-   .
DS558.A445   1989
959.704'3373—dc20   89-40222

For Sol

Contents

Acknowledgments   *page* ix
Introduction   xi
Part One   American Policy in Vietnam: Why Did We Get
   In? Why Did We Stay So Long?   3
"God's Country and American Know-How" (*Backfire*), by
   Loren Baritz   5
"Crisis, Commitment, and Counterrevolution, 1945–1952"
   (*America in Vietnam*), by Thomas McCormick   17
"Whose Immorality?" (*Why We Were in Vietnam*), by
   Norman Podhoretz   34
"How Could Vietnam Happen? An Autopsy" (*Atlantic
   Monthly*, April 1968), by James C. Thomson, Jr.   37
Part Two   A Different War: The Military in Vietnam   51
"A Different War" (*Long Time Passing*), by Myra
   MacPherson   53
"What the Vietnam Vets Can Teach Us" (*The Nation*,
   Nov. 27, 1982), by Peter Marin   75
"Cohesion and Disintegration in the American Army: An
   Alternative Perspective" (*Armed Forces and Society*, May
   1976), by Paul L. Savage and Richard A. Gabriel   86
"How Different Is the Military Today because of the
   Vietnam War?" (*Vietnam Reconsidered*), by Cecil B.
   Currey   99
Part Three   The Role of the Press: Was the Coverage of
   the War Fair?   105
"Vietnam 1954–1975" (*The First Casualty*), by Phillip
   Knightley   107

"How to Lose a War: Reflections of a Foreign
Correspondent" (*Encounter*, August 1981), by Robert
Elegant   138
"Once Again—Did the Press Lose Vietnam? A Veteran
Correspondent Takes on the New Revisionists"
(*Columbia Journalism Review*, Nov./Dec. 1983), by
Charles Mohr   143
"An Extreme Case" (*Big Story*), by Peter Braestrup   153
Part Four   The Antiwar Movement: Why Was There So
Much Opposition?   163
"The Impossible Victory: Vietnam" (*A People's History of
the United States*), by Howard Zinn   165
"Seizing History: What We Won and Lost at Home"
(*Mother Jones*, November 1983), by Todd Gitlin   183
"The Legacy of Choices" (*The Wounded Generation:
America after Vietnam*), by Sam Brown   195
"A Young Pacifist" (*Drawing the Line: The Political Essays
of Paul Goodman*), by Paul Goodman, edited by Taylor
Stoehr   204
"What Did You Do in the Class War, Daddy?" (*The
Washington Monthly*, October 1975), by James Fallows   214
"Why Protest?" (Address to Clergy and Laymen Concerned
about Vietnam, April 4, 1967), by Martin Luther King, Jr.   224
"Statement of Mr. John Kerry, Representing the Vietnam
Veterans Against the War" (Senate Foreign Relations
Committee, April 22, 1971)   233
Part Five   The Continuing Controversy: Coming to Terms
with a Confusing War   239
"American Guilt: An Interview with Richard Falk on
Vietnam" (*The Center Magazine*, Jan./Feb. 1974)   241
"Is American Guilt Justified?" (*The Center Magazine*, July/
Aug. 1979)   257
"On the Consequences of Vietnam" (*Harper's*, April 1985)   277
"Epilogue" (Reflections on the Wall: The Vietnam
Veterans Memorial), by James Quay, edited by Edward
Clinton Ezell   300
Notes on Contributors   303
Index   305

Acknowledgments

I wish to thank the people who have made contributions to this book. I am indebted to the authors and publishers who have granted permission to reprint the materials in this collection. Special thanks are due to my friends, relatives, and associates. LeRoy Votto gave me my first opportunity to teach Vietnam in his Recent America classes at the Urban School of San Francisco. Hubert Marshall sponsored my courses on the American experience in Vietnam at Stanford University. It was he who suggested that I put the selections on my reading list into one volume, and he has generously shared his knowledge and critical judgment with me. Saul Siegel, Winnie Siegel, and Rachelle Marshall have consistently given me invaluable support and assistance. My brother, Henry Schwartz, helped me find a good publisher. John Drayton, editor-in-chief, and Mildred Logan, associate editor, have been a pleasure to work with. Most of all, my husband, Sol Sevy, has given the solid encouragement and sustenance that have made it possible for me to do this work. This book is dedicated to him.

Introduction

The Vietnam War triggered a profound transformation in American political consciousness. It shattered the myths of American moral superiority and American military omnipotence. For more than twenty years, the United States tried to contain revolutionary change in a seemingly powerless Third World country fighting to free itself from foreign domination. We used sophisticated strategies of economic assistance and political manipulation, and we used raw military force, but we could not prevent a communist-led movement for national liberation from expelling the French and reunifying Vietnam.

The American disaster in Vietnam was a traumatic event in the lives of millions of Americans. The disparity between the official rhetoric of fighting for freedom and the disturbing reality of destroying the society we claimed to be saving tested our tolerance for dissonance and challenged our national self-image. It exploded our cherished illusion that morality and democracy are the guiding principles of American foreign policy. Proud and patriotic Americans lost faith in the wisdom and veracity of presidents and started thinking of their government in cynical ways. There was a general loss of trust in established authorities. During the height of our massive military intervention, the American political consensus on foreign policy was torn apart by bitter divisions of public opinion about how to end the longest war in American history. The violence of the war eventually worked its way back into American society as indignant protesters and outraged supporters of the war clashed in our streets. For the first time since the Civil War, the American social fabric began to disintegrate.

When the war finally came to an unsatisfactory end, we suppressed our feelings of shame, humiliation, and lost innocence and tried to get on with our lives. We closed our eyes to the devastating consequences of what we had done to Vietnam and what we had done to ourselves. Vietnam is an unresolved anxiety festering in our national unconscious, where it depresses our spirit and distorts our political thinking.

The prospect of another Vietnam in Central America, or some other Third World country, has become a national nightmare. The Iran-Contra fiasco is a direct result of President Reagan's refusal to accept the lessons of Vietnam as communicated to him by the American people. Reagan's obsession with reasserting the supremacy of American power abroad drove him to exceed his constitutional authority. When the sordid details of his private war were exposed to public scrutiny, America was humiliated again.

The post-Vietnam generation has grown up in a pessimistic political culture that is defensive about the meaning of America. Many of my students describe themselves as cynical; during my first years of teaching, I heard this at almost every class meeting. Others want desperately to believe in American virtue, "to dwell on the positive and create good feelings in the hearts of Americans." Still others call themselves idealists, but they often apologize for this stance so their peers will not automatically discount what they have to say as naïve and unrealistic. Most of my students never had confidence in the myth that "American arms and American aims were linked somehow to justice and morality."[1] When asked to write an essay on how we might restore a meaningful patriotism after Vietnam, almost all of them wishfully quote this specific line from a large selection of readings, but few of them have any specific notion of how to go about linking American aims to justice and morality.

When I started teaching at Stanford in 1985, students came into my classes contemptuous of public protest, having been brought up to view this form of political expression as useless and obnoxious. They identified protest with hippies, whom they regarded as the ultimate negative role model, and they criticized their few fellow students who did participate in political demonstrations as inauthentic faddists, fantasizing a rerun of the sixties.

This year my Stanford students seem different. Many of them admire political activists for their commitment and their perseverance, and some believe in public service. Perhaps they are the vanguard of a new post-Vietnam generation, although they too sense that the American corruption in Vietnam may be the source of the widespread cynicism in American culture at large. They are curious about the facts and opinions behind prevalent analogies comparing past U.S. policy in Vietnam with current U.S. policy in Central America. They have a vague, uncomfortable impression that Vietnam was some kind of terrible American failure that their elders are reluctant to discuss and afraid to repeat.

How did this happen to a righteous nation that had recently emerged from a great world war, not only victorious but the undisputed moral leader of the world?

This collection of excerpts and articles offers information, opinion, and insight with which to think through answers to this question. Young students, who know almost nothing about the war, and older Americans, who lived through the war but are still confused by the searing controversy surrounding it, can use these readings as a basis for understanding the complex political, social, and moral crises that traumatized the American body politic, year after year, for a decade.

This volume is organized as a supplement to three other books: a diplomatic history of U.S. involvement in Vietnam,[2] an oral history about the experiences of Americans who served in Vietnam,[3] and a cultural analysis of the war's effect on American conscience and consciousness.[4] For the past five years I have been using this combination of readings with considerable success in my classes on the American experience in Vietnam. It provides a solid foundation for class discussions, giving students a lively sense of what it felt like to be an American during those tumultuous and agonizing years.

I was moved to teach these classes by my own experience of disillusionment during the war years, which led me to think more deeply about issues of foreign policy. Subsequently, I conducted a study on the effects of disillusionment on Vietnam veterans, which, in turn, persuaded me to start teaching courses on Vietnam to high-school and college students. An almost unanimous finding in my interviews with veterans was their resentment about not having the information or the historical perspective with which to make an informed decision about whether or not to go to war. They went off to Vietnam in a rush of ignorance, arrogance, and patriotic pride, taking it for granted that they would be "winning the hearts and minds of the Vietnamese" in a glorious fight against "communist aggression."

If the United States is to avoid future Vietnams, we the people will have to know more about the facts of American foreign policy and be more assertive in influencing the decisions of our elected representatives. If we are serious about protecting our national security, we will have to learn how to move our nation in more life-sustaining directions. To do this, we need to educate ourselves about current world events and to view them in the light of our historical experience.

The following selections are geared to stimulate a thorough and thoughtful discussion of the American experience in Vietnam so that readers can begin to deal with the tragic consequences of our inter-vention in the Vietnamese War. The catastrophic experience of the Vietnamese people is not included here, because it is a vast and sepa-rate subject deserving a separate book.

GRACE SEVY

San Francisco, California
1988

NOTES

1. Morris Dickstein, *Gates of Eden: American Culture in the Sixties* (New York: Basic Books, 1977), pp.IX, 40, 271. Quoted in Walter Capps, *The Unfinished War: Vietnam and American Conscience* (Boston: Beacon, 1982), p. III.

2. George C. Herring, *America's Longest War: The United States in Vietnam 1950–1975* (New York: Knopf, 1979) is a thorough and compact history. Stanley Karnow, *Vietnam: A History* (New York: Viking, 1983) is a more exhaustive history.

3. Mark Baker, *Nam* (New York: Berkeley, 1981) has a sociological organization covering the different phases of the Vietnam experience in chronological order. Al Santoli, *Everything We Had* (New York: Ballantine, 1981) also covers the subject.

4. Walter Capps, *The Unfinished War: Vietnam and American Conscience* (Boston: Beacon, 1982).

The American Experience in Vietnam

*The hope for America's future
rests with a well-informed citizenry*

THOMAS JEFFERSON

Part One

AMERICAN POLICY IN VIETNAM: WHY DID WE GET IN? WHY DID WE STAY SO LONG?

The selections in this section provide background analyses to accompany the reading of a comprehensive diplomatic history of U.S. involvement in Vietnam.

Loren Baritz looks at the cultural elements that propelled us into Vietnam. He concentrates on our historical mind-set, our sense of moral and technological superiority that led us to assume that we knew what was best for Vietnam and that we had the power to impose our will on the Vietnamese.

Thomas McCormick offers an economic perspective on U.S. interest in Vietnam. He argues that American policy makers were trying to restore the balance within the world capitalist system after the dislocations of World War II. Their Cold War strategy was to secure Southeast Asia as a reliable trading partner for Japan, so that she would not accommodate her economy to that of Communist China.

Norman Podhoretz sees an altruistic explanation for U.S. intervention in Vietnam. He argues that our motivation was not selfish or self-interested: "We were there for the sake of an ideal," to save South Vietnam from Communism.

James Thomson focuses on why we persisted in Vietnam, despite years of failure and frustration. He provides insight into the policy-making process, the institutional and psychological inertia that prevented American war planners from seeing clearly and acting effectively.

God's Country and American Know-How

BY LOREN BARITZ

Americans were ignorant about the Vietnamese not because we were stupid, but because we believe certain things about ourselves. Those things necessarily distorted our vision and confused our minds in ways that made learning extraordinarily difficult. To understand our failure we must think about what it means to be an American.

The necessary text for understanding the condition of being an American is a single sentence written by Herman Melville in his novel *White Jacket:* "And we Americans are the peculiar, chosen people—the Israel of our time; we bear the ark of the liberties of the world."[1] This was not the last time this idea was expressed by Americans. It was at the center of thought of the men who brought us the Vietnam War. It was at the center of the most characteristic American myth.

This oldest and most important myth about America has an unusually specific origin. More than 350 years ago, while in mid-passage between England and the American wilderness, John Winthrop told the band of Puritans he was leading to a new and dangerous life that they were engaged in a voyage that God Himself not only approved, but in which He participated. The precise way that Brother Winthrop expressed himself echoes throughout the history of American life. He explained to his fellow travelers, "We shall find that the God of Israel is among us, when ten of us shall be able to resist a thousand of our enemies, when he shall make us a praise and glory, that men shall say of succeeding plantations [settlements]: the Lord make it like that of New England: for we must Consider that we shall be as a

Pp. 25–30, 33–34, 37–38, 41–46 from *Backfire: A History of How American Culture Led Us Into Vietnam* by Loren Baritz. Copyright © 1985 by Loren Baritz. By permission of William Morrow & Co.

City upon a Hill, the eyes of all people are upon us."[2] The myth of America as a city on a hill implies that America is a moral example to the rest of the world, a world that will presumably keep its attention riveted on us. It means that we are a Chosen People, each of whom, because of God's favor and presence, can smite one hundred of our heathen enemies hip and thigh.

The society Winthrop meant to establish in New England would do God's work, insofar as sinners could. America would become God's county. The Puritans would have understood this to mean that they were creating a nation of, by, and for the Lord. About two centuries later, the pioneers and the farmers who followed the Puritans translated God's country from civilization to the grandeur and nobility of nature, to virgin land, to the purple mountains' majesty. Relocating the country of God from civilization to nature was significant in many ways, but the conclusion that this New World is specially favored by the Lord not only endured but spread.

In countless ways Americans know in their gut—the only place myths can live—that we have been Chosen to lead the world in public morality and to instruct it in political virtue. We believe that our own domestic goodness results in strength adequate to destroy our opponents who, by definition, are enemies of virtue, freedom, and God. Over and over, the founding Puritans described their new settlement as a beacon in the darkness, a light whose radiance could keep Christian voyagers from crashing on the rocks, a light that could brighten the world. In his inaugural address John Kennedy said, "The energy, the faith, the devotion which we bring to this endeavor [defending freedom] will light our country and all who serve it—and the glow from that fire can truly light the world."[3] The city on a hill grew from its first tiny society to encompass the entire nation. As we will see, that is one of the reasons why we compelled ourselves to intervene in Vietnam.

An important part of the myth of America as the city on a hill has been lost as American power increased. John Winthrop intended that his tiny settlement should be only an example of rectitude to the cosmos. It could not have occurred to him that his small and weak band of saints should charge about the world to impose the One Right Way on others who were either too wicked, too stupid, or even too oppressed to follow his example. Because they also had domestic distractions, the early American Puritans could not even consider foreign adventures. In almost no time they had their hands full with a variety of local malefactors: Indians, witches, and, worst of all, shrewd Yankees who were more interested in catching fish than in catching the spirit of the Lord. Nathaniel Hawthorne, brooding about these Puritans, wrote that civilization begins by building a jail and a graveyard, but he was only two-thirds right. Within only two generations, the New England saints discovered that there was a brothel in Boston, the hub of the new and correct Christian order.

The New World settlement was puny, but the great ocean was a defensive moat that virtually prohibited an onslaught by foreign predators. The new Americans could therefore go about perfecting their society without distracting anxiety about alien and corrupting intrusions from Europe. This relative powerlessness coupled with defensive security meant that the city on a hill enjoyed a favorable "peculiar situation." It was peculiarly blessed because the decadent world could not come here, and we did not have to go there. The rest of the world, but especially Europe, with its frippery, pomp, and Catholicism, was thought to be morally leprous. This is what George Washington had in mind when he asked a series of rhetorical questions in his farewell address in 1796:

> Why forego the advantages of so peculiar a situation? Why quit our own to stand upon foreign ground? Why, by interweaving our destiny with that of any part of Europe, entangle our peace and prosperity in the toils of European ambition, rivalship, interest, humor, of caprice?[4]

This is also what Thomas Jefferson told his countrymen when he was inaugurated five years later. This enlightened and skeptical philosopher-President announced that this was a "chosen country" which had been "kindly separated by nature and a wide ocean from the exterminating havoc of one quarter of the globe." He said that the young nation could exult in its many blessings if it would only keep clear of foreign evil. His prescription was that America should have "entangling alliances with none."[5]

One final example of the unaggressive, unimperial interpretation of the myth is essential. The entire Adams family had a special affinity for old Winthrop. Perhaps it was that they grew up on the soil in which he was buried. On the Fourth of July, in 1821, John Quincy Adams gave a speech that captured every nuance of the already ancient myth. His speech could have been the text for the Vietnam War critics. He said that America's heart and prayers would always be extended to any free and independent part of the world. "But she goes not abroad in search of monsters to destroy." America, he said, hoped that freedom and independence would spread across the face of the earth. "She will recommend the general cause by the countenance of her voice, and by the benignant sympathy of her example." He said that the new nation understood that it should not actively intervene abroad even if such an adventure would be on the side of freedom because "she would involve herself beyond the power of extrication." It just might be possible for America to try to impose freedom elsewhere, to assist in the liberation of others. "She might," he said, "become the dictatress of the world. She would no longer be the ruler of her own spirit."[6]

In 1966, this speech was quoted by George F. Kennan, the thoughtful analyst of Soviet foreign affairs, to the Senate Foreign Relations Committee which was conducting hearings on the Vietnam War. Perhaps not knowing the myth, Mr. Kennan said that he was not sure what Mr. Adams had in mind when he spoke almost a century and a half earlier. But whatever it was, Mr. Kennan told the senators who were then worrying about Vietnam, "He spoke very directly and very pertinently to us here today."[7]

The myth of the city on a hill became the foundation for the ritualistic thinking of later generations of Americans. This myth helped to establish nationalistic orthodoxy in America. It began to set an American dogma, to fix the limits of thought for Americans about themselves and about the rest of the world, and offered a choice about the appropriate relationship between us and them.

The benevolence of our national motives, the absence of material gain in what we seek, the dedication to principle, and our impenetrable ignorance were all related to the original myth of America. It is temptingly easy to dismiss this as some quaint idea that perhaps once had some significance, but lost it in this more sophisticated, tough-minded, modern America. Arthur Schlesinger, Jr., a close aide to President Kennedy, thought otherwise. He was concerned about President Johnson's vastly ambitious plans to create a "Great Society for Asia." Whatever the President meant, according to Professor Schlesinger, such an idea

> . . . demands the confrontation of an issue deep in the historical consciousness of the United States: whether this country is a chosen people, uniquely righteous and wise, with a moral mission to all mankind . . . The ultimate choice is between messianism and maturity.[8]

The city myth should have collapsed during the war. The war should have taught us that we could not continue to play the role of moral adviser and moral enforcer to the world. After the shock of the assassinations, after the shock of Tet, after President Johnson gave up the presidency, after the riots, demonstrations, burned neighborhoods, and the rebellion of the young, it should have been difficult to sustain John Winthrop's optimism. It was not difficult for Robert

Kennedy who, after Senator Eugene McCarthy had demonstrated LBJ's vulnerability in New Hampshire, finally announced that he would run for the presidency himself. The language he used in his announcement speech proved that the myth was as alive and as virulent as it had ever been: <u>"At stake," Senator Kennedy said, "is not simply the leadership of our party, and even our own country, it is our right to the moral leadership of this planet."</u> [9] Members of his staff were horrified that he could use such language because they correctly believed that it reflected just the mind-set that had propelled us into Vietnam in the first place. He ignored their protests. This myth could survive in even the toughest of the contemporary, sophisticated, hard-driving politicians. Of course, he may have used this language only to persuade his listeners, to convince the gullible. But, even so, it showed that he believed that the myth was what they wanted to hear. In either case, the city on a hill continued to work its way. . . .

The myth of the city on a hill combined with <u>solipsism</u> in the assumptions about Vietnam made by the American war planners. In other words, we assumed that we had a superior moral claim to be in Vietnam, and because, despite their quite queer ways of doing things, the Vietnamese shared our values, they would applaud our intentions and embrace our physical presence. Thus, Vice-President Humphrey later acknowledged that all along we had been ignorant of Vietnam. He said that "to LBJ, the Mekong and the Pedernales were not that far apart." [10] Our claim to virtue was based on the often announced purity of our intentions. It was said, perhaps thousands of times, that all we wanted was freedom for other people, not land, not resources, and not domination.

<u>Because we believed that our intentions were virtuous, we could learn nothing from the French experience in Vietnam.</u> After all, they had fought only to maintain their Southeast Asian colonies and as imperialists deserved to lose. We assumed that this was why so mighty a European power lost the important battle of Dien Bien Phu to General Giap's ragged army. America's moral authority was so clear to us that we assumed that it also had to be clear to the Vietnamese. This self-righteousness was the clincher in the debate to intensify the conflict in Vietnam, according to George W. Ball, an undersecretary of state for Presidents Kennedy and Johnson. Washington's war planners, Mr. Ball said in 1973, had been captives of their own myths. [11] Another State Department official also hoped, after the fact, that Americans "will be knocked out of our grandiosity . . . [and] will see the self-righteous, illusory quality of that

* solipsism — theory that the self is the only thing that can be known & verified.

vision of ourselves offered by the high Washington official who said that while other nations have 'interests' the United States has 'a sense of responsibility.'" [12] Our power, according to this mentality, gives us responsibility, even though we may be reluctant to bear the burden. Other peoples' greed or selfishness gives them interests, even though they may not be strong enough to grab all they want.

Our grandiosity will, however, not be diminished so easily. At least since World War II, America's foreign affairs have been the affairs of Pygmalion*. We fall in love with what we create. We create a vision of the world made in what we think is our own image. We are proud of what we create because we are certain that our intentions are pure, our motives good, and our behavior virtuous. We know these things to be true because we believe that we are unique among the nations of the world in our collective idealism. . . .

Although the nationalists of the world all share a peoples' pride in who they are, a loyalty to place and language and culture, there are delicate but important differences. Because of its Puritan roots, it is not surprising that America's nationalism is more Protestant than that of other countries. It is more missionary in its impulses, more evangelical. It typically seeks to correct the way other people think rather than to establish its own physical dominion over them. It is, as it were, more committed to the Word, as befits serious Protestants, than other nationalisms.

One of the peculiarities of American Protestant nationalism, especially in its most aggressive mood, is its passion about ideas. What we want is to convert others to the truth as we understand it. We went to war in Vietnam in the name of ideas, of principles, of abstractions. Thus, President Johnson said in his inaugural, "We aspire to nothing that belongs to others." [13] And added in his important address at Johns Hopkins in April 1965: "Because we fight for values and we fight for principles, rather than territory or colonies, our patience and our determination are unending." [14] This is what we mean when we think of ourselves as idealists, magnanimous and moral. It is what cold warriors mean when they say over and over that we are engaged with the Soviet Union "in a competition of ideas." . . .

Tangled up in old myths, fearful of speaking plain English on the subject, the political conscience of many Americans must be troubled. There is bad faith in accepting the city myth of American uniqueness as if the myth can be freed from its integral Protestantism, almost always of a fundamentalist flavor. Conservatives have less need to launder the myth of its religion. Because liberals require a secular version of nationalism, and if they need or want to retain some sense of the unique republic, they are required to rest their

*Kings of Cyprus who [carved] + then fell in love a statue of a f, which Aphrodite brought to life as Galatea

case on a secular basis. Wilsonian idealism was the answer in the 1960s, as liberals argued that America was the only society capable of creating social justice and genuine democracy at home and abroad. These ideals merged with the cold war and persuaded the best of American liberals to bring us Vietnam.

In America, as elsewhere, elected officials are especially suscep-tible to the fundamental myths of nationalism because they must em-body them to get elected and act on them to govern. The vision of the world that suffused Mr. Wilson's Fourteen Points and League of Nations was also the vision of John Kennedy and his circle. They were pained by the knowledge that a people anywhere in the world struggled toward freedom but was frustrated by the imposition of force. So it was that John F. Kennedy's inspired inaugural address carried the burden of Woodrow Wilson's idealism, and also carried the deadly implication that America was again ready for war in the name of goodness.

President Kennedy's language must be understood in the light of what was just around the corner in Vietnam. He announced to the world, "We shall pay any price, bear any burden, meet any hard-ship, support any friend, oppose any foe to assure the survival and the success of liberty." He said that it was the rare destiny of his gen-eration to defend freedom when it was at its greatest risk. "I do not shrink from this responsibility—I welcome it."[15]

The difference between the two sons of the Commonwealth of Massachusetts, John Quincy Adams and John Fitzgerald Kennedy, was the difference between good wishes and war, but also the differ-ence between a tiny and isolated America and the world's most powerful nation. Presidents Wilson and Kennedy both fairly repre-sented American liberalism at its most restless and energetic. This was a liberalism that wanted, as President Wilson put it, to make the world safe for democracy, or as President Kennedy said, to defend "those human rights to which this nation has always been com-mitted, and to which we are committed today at home and around the world." JFK described this as "God's work."[16]

An important part of the reason we marched into Vietnam with our eyes fixed was liberalism's irrepressible need to be helpful to those less fortunate. But the decency of the impulse, as was the case with President Wilson, cannot hide the bloody eagerness to kill in the name of virtue. In 1981, James C. Thomson, an aide in the State Department and a member of the National Security Council under President Johnson, finally concluded that our Vietnamese interven-tion had been motivated by a national missionary impulse, a "need to do good to others." In a phrase that cannot be improved, he and others called this "sentimental imperialism." [17] The purity of intention and the horror of result is unfortunately the liberal's continuing burden.

American conservatives had it easier, largely because they believed in the actuality of evil. In his first public statement, President Eisenhower informed the American public, "The forces of good and evil are massed and armed and opposed as rarely before in history." For him the world struggle was not merely between conflicting ideologies. "Freedom is pitted against slavery; lightness against the dark." [18]

Conservatives in America are closer than liberals to the myth of the city on a hill because they are not embarrassed by public professions of religion. They are therefore somewhat less likely to ascribe American values and behavior to other cultures. This is so because of the conservatives' conviction that America is so much better—more moral, godly, wise, and especially rich—than other nations that they could not possibly resemble us. Thus, President Eisenhower announced that one of America's fixed principles was the refusal to "use our strength to try to impress upon another people our own cherished political and economic institutions." [19] The idea of uniqueness means, after all, that we are alone in the world.

Conservatives shared with liberals the conviction that America could act, and in Vietnam did act, with absolute altruism, as they believed only America could. Thinking of this war, President Nixon, another restless descendent of Mr. Wilson, declared that "never in history have men fought for less selfish motives—not for conquest, not for glory, but only for the right of a people far away to choose the kind of government they want." [20] This was especially attractive because in this case the kind of government presumably sought by this faraway people was opposed to Communism, our own enemy. It was therefore an integral part of the universal struggle between freedom and slavery, lightness and dark. As a result it was relatively easy for conservatives to think of Vietnam as a laboratory to test ways to block the spreading stain of political atheism.

Power is sometimes a problem for liberals and a solution for conservatives. When Senator Goldwater rattled America's many sabers in his presidential campaign of 1964, and when General Curtis LeMay wanted to bomb North Vietnam "back to the stone age," [21] they both made liberals cringe, partly from embarrassment, and partly because the liberals were appalled at the apparent cruelty. In the 1950s, Dr. Kissinger cleverly argued that the liberal embarrassment over power made its use, when necessary, even worse than it had to be. "Our feeling of guilt with respect to power," he wrote, "has caused us to transform all wars into crusades, and then to apply our power in the most absolute ways.''[22] Later, when he ran America's foreign policy, his own unambivalent endorsement of the use in Vietnam of enormous power inevitably raised the question of whether bloody crusades are caused only by the squeamishness of liberals or also by the callousness of conservatives.

Implicit in John Winthrop's formulation of the city myth was the idea that the new Americans could, because of their godliness, vanquish their numerically superior enemies. The idea that warriors, because of their virtue, could beat stronger opponents, is very ancient. Pericles spoke of it in his funeral oration to the Athenians. The Christian crusaders counted on it. *Jihad,* Islam's conception of a holy war, is based on it. The Samurai believed it. So did the Nazis.

In time, the history of America proved to Americans that we were militarily invincible. The Vietnam War Presidents naturally cringed at the thought that they could be the first to lose a war. After all, we had already beaten Indians, French, British (twice), Mexicans, Spaniards, Germans (twice), Italians, Japanese, Koreans, and Chinese. Until World War II, the nation necessarily had to rely on the presumed virtue, not the power, of American soldiers to carry the day, and the war. This was also the case in the South during our Civil War.

Starting in the eighteenth century, the nation of farmers began to industrialize. As the outcome of war increasingly came to depend on the ability to inject various forms of flying hardware into the enemy's body, victory increasingly depended on technology. The acceleration of industrialization in the late nineteenth century inevitably quickened the pace of technological evolution. By then no other power could match the Americans' ability to get organized, to commit resources to development, and to invent the gadgets that efficiently produced money in the marketplace, and, when necessary, death on the battlefield. The idea of Yankee ingenuity, American know-how, stretches back beyond the nineteenth century. Our admiration for the tinkerer whose new widget forms the basis of new industry is nowhere better shown than in our national reverence of Thomas Edison.

Joining the American sense of its moral superiority with its technological superiority was a marriage made in heaven, at least for American nationalists. We told ourselves that each advantage explained the other, that the success of our standard of living was a result of our virtue, and our virtue was a result of our wealth. Our riches, our technology, provided the strength that had earlier been missing, that once had forced us to rely only on our virtue. Now, as Hiroshima demonstrated conclusively, we could think of ourselves not only as morally superior, but as the most powerful nation in history. The inevitable offspring of this marriage of an idea with a weapon was the conviction that the United States could not be beaten in war—not by any nation, and not by any combination of nations. For that moment we thought that we could fight where, when, and how we wished, without risking failure. For that moment we thought that we could impose our will on the recalcitrant of the earth.

A great many Americans, in the period just before the war in Vietnam got hot, shared a circular belief that for most was probably not very well formed: America's technological supremacy was a symptom of its uniqueness, and technology made the nation militarily invincible. In 1983, the playwright Arthur Miller said, "I'm an American. I believe in technology. Until the mid-60s I never believed we could lose because we had technology." [23]

The memory of World War II concluding in a mushroom cloud was relatively fresh throughout the 1950s. It was unthinkable that America's military could ever fail to establish its supremacy on the battlefield, that the industrial, scientific, and technological strength of the nation would ever be insufficient for the purposes of war. It was almost as if Americans were technology. The American love affair with the automobile was at its most passionate in the 1950s, our well-equipped armies stopped the Chinese in Korea, for a moment our nuclear supremacy was taken for granted, and affluence for many white Americans seemed to be settling in as a way of life.

It is, of course, unfortunate that the forces of evil may be as strong as the forces of virtue. The Soviet Union exploded its first atomic bomb way ahead of what Americans thought was a likely schedule. This technology is not like others because even a weak bomb is devastating. Even if our bombs are better than theirs, they can still do us in. America's freedom of action after 1949 was not complete. President Eisenhower and John Foster Dulles, the Secretary of State, threatened "massive retaliation" against the Soviet Union if it stepped over the line. They knew, and we knew, that this threat was not entirely real, and that it freed the Soviets to engage in peripheral adventures because they correctly believed that we would not destroy the world over Korea, Berlin, Hungary, or Czechoslovakia.

Our policy had to become more flexible. We had to invent a theory that would allow us to fight on the edges without nuclear technology. This theory is called "limited war." Its premise is that we and the Soviets can wage little wars, and that each side will refrain from provoking the other to unlock the nuclear armory.

Ike threatened the Chinese, who at the time did not have the bomb, with nuclear war in Korea. JFK similarly threatened the Soviets, who had nuclear capability, over Cuba. But, although some military men thought about using nuclear weapons in Vietnam, the fundamental assumption of that war was to keep it limited, not to force either the Soviets or the Chinese, who now had their own sloppy bombs, to enter the war. Thus, we could impose our will on the recalcitrant of the earth if they did not have their own nuclear weapons, and if they could not compel the Soviets or the Chinese to force us to quit.

In Vietnam we had to find a technology to win without broadening the war. The nuclear stalemate reemphasized our need to find a more limited ground, to find, so to speak, a way to fight a domesticated war. We had to find a technology that would prevail locally, but not explode internationally. No assignment is too tough for the technological mentality. In fact, it was made to order for the technicians who were coming into their own throughout all of American life. This war gave them the opportunity to show what they could do. This was to be history's most technologically sophisticated war, most carefully analyzed and managed, using all of the latest wonders of managerial procedures and systems. It was made to order for bureaucracy.

James C. Thomson, who served both JFK and LBJ as an East Asia specialist, understood how the myths converged. He wrote of *"the rise of a new breed of American ideologues who see Vietnam as the ultimate test of their doctrine."* These new men were the new missionaries and had a trinitarian faith: in military power, technological superiority, and our altruistic idealism. They believed that the reality of American culture "provides us with the opportunity and obligation to ease the nations of the earth toward modernization and stability: toward a full-fledged *Pax Americana Technocratica.*"[24] For these parishioners in the church of the machine, Vietnam was the ideal laboratory.

NOTES

1. Herman Melville, *White Jacket* (London: Oxford University Press, 1924), p. 189.

2. John Winthrop, *Papers*, A. B. Forbes, ed. (Boston: Massachusetts Historical Society, 1931), Vol. II, p. 295.

3. John F. Kennedy, *Public Papers of the Presidents*, Jan. 20, 1961 (Washington, D.C.: G.P.O., 1962), p. 3.

4. Worthington Chauncey Ford, ed., *The Writings of George Washington* (New York: Putnam's Sons, 1889–93), Vol. XIII, p. 317.

5. Saul Padover, ed., *The Complete Jefferson* (New York: Irvington Publishers, 1943), pp. 385–86.

6. *The Vietnam Hearings* (New York: Random House, 1966), p. 115.

7. *Ibid.*

8. Arthur M. Schlesinger, Jr., *The Bitter Heritage* (Boston: Houghton Mifflin Co., 1967), p. 79.

9. David Halberstam, *The Best and the Brightest* (New York: Random House, 1972), p. 41.

10. Hubert Humphrey, "Building on the Past," in Anthony Lake, ed., *The Legacy of Vietnam* (New York: New York University Press, 1976), p. 358.

11. George W. Ball, "Have We Learned or Only Failed?" *The New York Times Magazine*, April 1, 1973, p. 13.

12. Walter H. Capps, *The Unfinished War* (Boston: Beacon Press, 1982), pp. 70–71.

13. Lyndon B. Johnson, *Public Papers of the Presidents*, Jan. 20, 1965 (Washington, D.C.: G.P.O., 1966), p. 73.

14. *Ibid.*, April 7, 1965, p. 172.

15. *Public Papers of the Presidents*, Jan. 20, 1961, pp. 1–3.

16. *Ibid.*

17. Fox Butterfield, "Vietnam is Not Over," *The New York Times*, Feb. 11, 1983, p. A14.

18. Dwight D. Eisenhower, *Public Papers of the Presidents*, Jan. 20, 1953 (Washington, D.C.: G.P.O., 1960), p. 4.

19. *Ibid.*, p. 5.

20. Richard Nixon, *Public Papers of the Presidents*, April 7, 1971 (Washington, D.C.: G.P.O., 1972), p. 525.

21. Halberstam, *Best and Brightest*, p. 462.

22. Henry A. Kissinger, *Nuclear Weapons and Foreign Policy* (New York: W. W. Norton & Co., 1957), p. 427.

23. "Lessons from a War," speech at conference *Vietnam Reconsidered*, University of Southern California, Feb. 9, 1983.

24. James C. Thomson, Jr., "How Could Vietnam Happen?" *The Atlantic*, April 1968, p. 53.

Crisis, Commitment, and Counterrevolution, 1945–1952

BY THOMAS McCORMICK

In August 1945, World War II jolted to its heart-stopping, nuclear end in Asia. Vietnam emerged with vivid memories of Japan's subordination and de facto replacement of French authority. The memories produced two lessons: Western colonialism was not omnipotent; and imperialism by any other name was still imperialism—even if Japan preferred to call it an "Asian Co-Prosperity Sphere." Vietnamese nationalism was the beneficiary of both insights, as the movement for an independent, Vietnamese nation topped that society's public agenda. In the movement's vanguard was the Vietminh organization, led by Ho Chi Minh of the Vietnamese Communist Party.

By definition, Vietnam could not act out its historic quest in isolation, for she was a dependent part of a modern world system almost five centuries in the making. At the *core* of that world system—dominating and benefitting—were the powerful, unified, industrial nations of Europe, North America, and Japan: the Trilateral bloc. At the *periphery* of that system—dominated and dependent—were weak, disunified, backward areas like Vietnam itself: the Third World. Marked by a complex, specialized division of international labor, the core-periphery relationships of the system rather resembled a global food chain of nations—each link part of a hierarchical structure among nations of dominance/subordination that tended to reproduce and perpetuate the whole. Vietnam was part of Indochina (along with Laos and Cambodia); Indochina, in turn, was just a portion of the vast Southeast Asia land peninsula (including Thailand, Burma, and Malaya); the peninsula, likewise, was integrally connected to the offshore archipelagoes of Indonesia and the Philippines, and the two together constituted the Southeast Asia region (or SEA as it is noted in American government sources). But even SEA was widely perceived as a functioning part of a larger Asian crescent, anchored by Japan at one end and extending, at the other, as far as India, perhaps as far as Iran and the Persian Gulf. Moreover, prior to World War II, almost all of these peripheral links had been colonial holdings—imperial extensions—of core countries: Britain, France, Holland, Japan, and the United States (the Philippines).

However small and remote, Vietnam was an organic part of this core-periphery structure. Implicitly then, this postwar world order placed certain constraints on the Vietnamese drive for autonomy. On the other hand, the system's capacity to sustain those constraints was seriously called into question by its own self-destructive tendencies. Demoralized by a decade of history's worst economic depression and devastated by six years of one of history's worse wars, the world of 1945 looked like a star on the downhill side of a nova. Therein entered America and its foreign policy—that fixer of universes; the new world once more entering the fray to redress the balance of the old. And that entrance was to set American and Vietnamese societies on a collision course that was to delay Vietnamese independence for three decades and culminate in America's longest and most debated war.

Even before Pearl Harbor and American entrance into World War II, American political and business leaders had largely agreed that two things were necessary to breathe life and energy back into the world system, and that only the United States had the insight and capacity to see them done. First, some political entity had to play the dual role of judge and policeman in the system; to arbitrate differences within the system and to enforce its decisions; to coordinate world affairs in the interests of the whole system, not its specific parts. Since the decline of British hegemony in the late nineteenth century, neither balance-of-power politics nor the League of Nations had successfully done the job. Now, American leaders felt both able and eager to take on the mantle of hegemony themselves, a *Pax Americana* to replace a *Pax Britannia*. Second, the chief task of hegemonic America was to restore economic expansiveness to a system racked and distorted by the Great Depression and ensuing war. A static or contracting economic pie not only threatened world capitalism (and American capitalism) with stagnation, but invited internal strife and aggression to redivide the zero-sum pie by force. Two world wars and three major revolutions made that abundantly clear.

From 1945 to 1949 the core countries of war-devastated Europe and Japan occupied center stage. In an international version of supply-side economics, America's major effort was to restore high levels of productivity—with minimal redundancy and maximum interdependence. The major obstacle was the imbalance within the world system. American capitalism was too strong and that of other core countries too weak—a disequilibrium most acutely demonstrated by the so-called Dollar Gap. Europe and Japan's disastrous balance of payments deficit created such a shortage of dollars that it retarded the level of intra-core trading. Moreover, it tempted them to resort to tariff and convertibility controls that would have retarded it even further. Without a large transfusion of American dollars, the world system seemed more destined to return to the depression of the 1930s than the "normalcy" of the 1920s. The Marshall Plan for Europe and the Special Offshore Procurement Program for Japan were the main American efforts to address this paradox of "progress and poverty."

Southeast Asia was initially of marginal importance to this reconstruction of the industrial core. Indeed, its importance was largely delineated by the impact that the European colonies there seemed to have upon the well-being of their colonizers. In the case of French Indochina, the well-being seemed largely measured in political and psychological terms. French self-esteem apparently required restoration of her overseas empire, and any frustration of that goal might undercut the tenuous stability of French domestic policies to the ultimate benefit of the French Left. Given American concern for France's pivotal role in European recovery, it seemed prudent to set aside America's marginal anticolonialism; refrain from erecting any barriers to French actions in Indochina; and indulge only in occasional sermonettes to the French about giving the "natives" more responsibilities. Indeed, that was the essence of American policy between 1946 and 1949 as France sought to reintegrate Indochina into the French empire in the face of determined opposition from the Vietminh.[1]

The escalation of the French military efforts to reassert colonial control, coupled with the move toward NATO and German rearmament, only reinforced the Eurocentricism of American policy. By 1949 the American ambassador to France believed that continuation of the war was "a severe strain on the French economy and diverted from the defense of Western Europe sizable quantities of French military equipment and personnel."[2] By early 1950 the French diversion of Marshall Plan aid to finance her Vietnam War became such a "great drain" that it "conflicted with her obligations under ECA bilateral [Marshall Plan] and North Atlantic and Brussels Pact [NATO]."[3] Moreover, it impeded French acceptance of German participation in a NATO multilateral army since "a considerable portion of the crack French troops [were] now in Indochina."[4] French leaders encouraged such American perceptions. In thinly veiled diplomatic blackmail, they warned, "Without outside help the future of Indo-China was black."[5] While American counterparts saw through the blackmail, they did accept much of the French analysis. So even before the first formalization of American aid in the spring of 1950, the United States looked the other way while France used surplus American military equipment and Marshall Plan dollars to fight and finance her war. Still, American aid was indirect, its commitment limited and cautious, and its sense of Indochina's importance ephemeral and contingent on France's role in Europe.

The watershed trauma in the last third of 1949 and the first third of 1950 profoundly altered the circumstances of the world system and triggered the curtain's rise on the first act of the long drama of America in Vietnam. What happened between Labor Day 1949 and May Day 1950 was no less than a structural crisis in the world system—a crisis exacerbated by the Cold War and the apparent Russian threat, but not caused by it. George Frost Kennan, chairman of the State Department's Policy Planning Staff (PPS), called attention to that crisis in an August 22 broadcast for CBS radio, which began by defining "the international situation" as in "transition from the immediate posthostilities era, with its short-term problems and demands, to a new stage of affairs which may endure for a long time and many aspects of which we may have to regard as normal." In discussing those new, long-term problems, he put his finger on the central failure of postwar efforts to reconstruct the system: "For it is one thing to produce; it is another thing to sell." The codifier of America's containment policy concluded by alerting his listeners to the "real urgency" of "this problem," and predicted that "coming discussions here in Washington will be devoted to the exploration of possible solutions."[6]

Two key facts produced the beehive of bureaucratic exploration that Kennan anticipated, and ultimately produced commitments at the highest levels by President Truman and Secretary of State Acheson—all with profound relevance for Southeast Asia. One was "the understanding of Congress and the people that the European Recovery Program [Marshall Plan] will be brought to a close in 1952"—and with no prospects for any continuation. The other was the awareness that the structural problem of imbalance in the system—"the problem of the dollar gap"—had not been solved; that "about a third of our exports is being financed by grants. At the end of ERP, European production will have been restored . . . but the problem of payment for American goods and services will remain." Secretary of State Acheson got to the nub of matters in his February 16, 1950, memorandum to the President:

> Put in its simplest terms, the problem is this: as ERP is reduced, and after its termination in 1952, how can Europe and other areas of the world obtain the dollars necessary to pay for a high level of United States exports, which is essential both to their own basic needs and to the well-being of the United States economy? This is the problem of the "dollar gap" in world trade.

The inner working papers of State Department study groups and the Committee of Economic Advisers abound with evidence of the high anxiety that attached to this "problem of crisis magnitude"; "the highest priority"; "the critical and far-reaching decisions of policy arising out of our economic relationships with the rest of the world"; or "the importance to the United States of a successful economic system among the free nations . . . even if it requires adjustments and sacrifices by particular economic groups in the United States in the interest of the nation as a whole."[7]

The structural crisis of 1949–50 produced a tripartite bureaucratic debate, and the ensuing trade-offs were to transform Southeast Asia from an area of marginal, ephemeral concern to one of fundamental, enduring importance. (1) The State Department mainstream, echoing the Council of Economic Advisers, argued that "When all is said and done, it is evident that if exports are to be maintained and there is to be curtailment in extraordinary assistance, the main burden of adjustment in our balance of payments must be accomplished by an increase in our imports of goods and services." (2) The newly emerged "recovery" bureaucracy (like ECA) predictably urged a continuation of their international pump-priming to Europe and expansion to Japan and the Third World via an Asian Marshall Plan and an enlargement of the Point Four program proposed by President Truman. (3) The Pentagon and the MDAP bureaucracy (Mutual Defense Assistance Program) pushed for a militarized version of international Keynesianism: a massive increase in American military spending that could be transferred to Europe either in "direct dollar assistance" or "in kind." Military aid as economic aid to "benefit both military production and the economic situation."[8] The proverbial two birds with one stone.

The militarized option, albeit with modification, largely prevailed.

It did so first because it was the only option that was politically viable. Congress showed no willingness to extend or expand foreign economic aid to confront the dollar gap, nor did it respond positively to State Department feelers about liberalizing access to the American market for foreign producers. The legislative branch, in its attitudes and its political constituency, tended to be more nationalistic, and little inclined to jeopardize home-market business and labor in the name of economic internationalism and the world system. But the political side of that congressional nationalism would and did respond positively to initiatives framed in terms of national security. It would vote to prime the military pump. Therein lay common ground. Nationalists and internationalists alike shared fears generated by the Communist triumph in China and, more especially, by the Russian acquisition of the atomic bomb. To be sure, the fears were of a different order. Nationalists focused on the enhanced possibility of direct military aggression by the U.S.S.R. Many internationalists, however, continued to believe that "Soviet history seems to be against military adventures which entail any risk." But they did fear that the Russian atomic bomb would reduce the credibility of the United States to protect and manage the world system, especially in the eyes of Europe and Japan.

The DOD-MDAP bureaucratic triumph found expression in the adoption of NSC 68 in April 1950. But that National Security Council document also was the product of some important tradeoffs with the Department of State (DOS) and the "recovery" bureaucracy. First, in proposing "to merge the U.S. organizations and appropriations for military assistance and for economic aid," Army Secretary Tracy Voorhees made clear "that the ECA organizations here and abroad should be the backbone of the combined agency."[9] The "recovery" bureaucracy would not be out of a job. Second, the defense bureaucracy had to address the crucial insight of DOS that "European production has been restored to the point at which the primary problem is now the need for *markets*." (Emphasis added.)[10] Since domestic politics inhibited access to the major capitalist market (the United States) and since Cold War politics—militarized and heated up—tightly restricted access to socialist markets (Russia and China), where were the markets to be had? Acheson and Kennan were right: that was the structural obstacle to equilibrium in the world system.

The answer, long proposed by area specialists in DOS itself, was the Third World: integrate periphery areas more thoroughly into the market economies of Europe and Japan. But how, when Third World poverty was so high and its productivity so low—"predominantly agricultural and their economies basically self-sufficient or noncomplementary at the *present level of their development?*" (Emphasis added.) In stable areas, it was argued that private investment and Point Four technical aid would suffice; the goal, after all, was not industrial development but increasing the productivity of raw materials and foodstuffs to supply core-country needs and purchase core-country manufactured products. But in areas of political instability and civil strife, "the first prerequisite to economic recovery . . . is, not increased production and exports, fiscal reform and economic cooperation as in Europe, but effective solutions for fundamental political and military conflicts which are stifling production and trade. Given these political solutions . . . economic recovery could be attained rapidly, and with relatively little capital expenditure. . . ."[11] The consensus equation was complete: a massive military buildup would not only contain Russia (and/or China), profit America, and provide a short-term solution to the Dollar Gap. It would also create the instrument (the oft-noted "military shield") to pacify and stabilize volatile but important areas of the Third World. And no area was more volatile or more important than Southeast Asia.

Indochina, with its French-Vietminh war, was most in need of pacification. But the rest of Southeast Asia was viewed as so weak and unstable that the National Security Council concluded in February 1950 that the "neighboring countries of Thailand and Burma could be expected to fall under Communist domination if Indochina were controlled by a Communist-dominated government. The balance of Southeast Asia would then be in grave hazard" (i.e., Malaya, the Philippines, and Indonesia).[12] This early version of the famous "falling dominoes" theory posited a regional indivisibility that endowed the Indochina conflict with an importance it otherwise would not have had. Save for its impact on France (and much of that counterproductive), Indochina was of little intrinsic importance or interest. But as perceived linchpin in the crescent that stretched between India and Japan, it was seen as vital. If the region as a whole—this collage of former European, American, and Japanese colonies—was to be reintegrated successfully into the world system, then some military or political solution to the Indochina war was crucial.

The American decision in early 1950 to play a committed and more active role in the Indochina pacification did not flow from direct American interests in the region. Save for the Philippines and, potentially, Indonesia, American economic and military interests were minimal. But power has its price as well as its profit, and American hegemonic leadership in the "free world" did dictate that the United States play surrogate for other core countries—for whom Southeast Asia was of considerable, direct importance. For its Marshall Plan partners in Europe, "Southeast Asia, especially Malaya and Indonesia, is the principal world source of natural rubber and tin . . . Indonesia a secondary source of petroleum . . . Malaya is the largest net dollar earner for the United Kingdom, and its loss would seriously aggravate the economic problems facing the UK." [13] The last factor was vital. Britain's financial-economic situation was perhaps more complex than any other European power. Her Malayan exports to the dollar bloc constituted her most productive short-term effort to ameliorate her dollar gap; indeed, the American government helped make it more productive by scaling down its synthetic rubber program and modifying its trade policy on tin imports. [14]

For Japan (and her American occupiers), Southeast Asia commanded even greater present and potential concern. It had "been clear, from the beginning of the occupation, that a revived Japanese foreign trade is an indispensable prerequisite to the reconstruction of a stable economy." The Acting Political Adviser in Japan summed it well in 1947:

> Foreign trade historically has been Japan's economic lifeblood. Before the war, Japan ranked fifth among the great nations of the world. With a population of over 70,000,000 living on the small, arable area afforded by the four main islands, and with relatively meager natural resources, Japan maintained herself in large part by importing raw materials, processing them, and exporting the finished products in exchange for food and additional raw materials. [15]

Moreover, "among the major problems facing the healthy development of Japanese commerce is the restriction of economic activities resulting from the unstable political situation in various countries of the Far East [China and SEA] which, rich in natural resources but poor in industry, would naturally be expected to complement Japan's economy by mutually beneficial trade." [16]

By 1947 continuing civil war in China led American leaders to give up on that country as America's postwar "doorman" in Asia, and to turn to Japan as the model of pro-capitalist modernization—Asia's "workshop." The resulting "reverse course" in United States occupation policy strongly supported the revival of heavy industry and its monopoly tendencies. That "workshop" economy approach only intensified the apparent Japanese need for markets and for less distant sources of food and raw materials. Where revolutionary China fit into this need was a matter of debate and concern among American leaders. Occasionally there were suggestions that Sino-Japanese trade might be a good thing—not simply for Japan, but perhaps to wean China herself away from the U.S.S.R. and thus sustain the American dream of an Open Door ("a lever of some utility in our efforts to bring changes within Communist China"). Perhaps reflective of that opinion, COCOM (the Coordinating Committee on Export Control), in 1949–50, exercised restraint in restricting trade with China save in strategic materials that might be transshipped to Russia. Still, the dominant opinion was that Japan ought not be allowed to play her "China card," and if that was to be so, the United States faced the responsibility and necessity of providing Japan an alternative source of markets and primary commodities. Secretary of State Dean Acheson put it crudely in his May 8, 1949, circular telegram to American embassies in ten Far Eastern countries that "Japs will either move toward sound friendly relations with non-Commie countries or into association with Commie system in Asia."[17]

The Acheson position led logically to an American strategy of regionalism—criticized by General MacArthur's occupation headquarters in Japan as "economically similar to those of pre-war Japan in its *Asiatic co-prosperity sphere* plans."[18] On January 10, 1950, the National Security Council (NSC 61) formally subscribed to the principle that "Japan's economic recovery depends upon keeping Communism out of Southeast Asia, promoting economic recovery there and in further developing these countries, together with Indonesia, the Philippines, Southern Korea and India as the *principal trading areas* for Japan." NSC 61, in conjunction with the Special Offshore Procurement Program, constituted a triangular arrangement for the U.S.-Japan-SEA. (1) American economic and military aid programs would be fused into one, directed jointly by DOS-SOS-ECA (the tripartite bureaucracy). (2) Save for some small Point 4 money, American dollar aid would be pumped into Japan rather than Southeast Asia itself. Offshore Procurement would eventually become the main pump-primer by subcontracting the production of military items (jeeps, trucks, uniforms, and the like) to Japanese industry (a key factor in the revival of the Japanese auto industry). (3) The burden of developing the food and raw material productivity of Southeast Asia would fall mainly on Japan—directly through technical aid and war reparations, indirectly through the demand stimulus of Japan's "workshop" market. The American market, with its demand for rubber, tin, and bauxite (especially in Indonesia and Malaya), would supplement that stimulus. Four months after NSC action, on the eve of President Truman's landmark commitment to the French in Indochina, the Economic and Scientific Staff Section in Tokyo completed a highly detailed projection study entitled "Japan's Export Potential" to Southeast Asia, and predicted that "exports to these countries will considerably exceed 50% of her total projected export trade" by 1955. Indonesia—considered by many Americans as the most important "domino" in the area—was projected as twice as important as any other SEA market. Significantly, French Indochina seemed to possess so little market potential that it ranked last in the country-by-country summary.[19]

This American intent to stabilize Southeast Asia and integrate it more systematically into the world system seemed to run counter to the dominant historical force in the area—that is, nationalism and Pan-Asianism. That movement grew out of and fed off of hostility to three phenomena. The most long-term was European and North American imperialism, which, for more than a half century, had colonized every SEA country save Siam (Thailand). The most recent was Japan's perversion of Pan-Asianism (Asia for Asians) into her own blatant imperialism during World War II. The most persistent was economic dependency: that is (in the eyes of a UN economic commission), "the economic insecurity and hazardous exposure of nations whose livelihood was dependent upon the export of raw materials" and, as consequence, the "grossly inferior position compared to predominantly industrialized nations." In short, the subordination to core countries—perceived in political, economic, and racial terms—and the drive to alleviate it and to achieve a real measure of national and regional autonomy. Now, in late in 1949 and early 1950, American policy seemed to embrace all three hate symbols of Southeast Asian nationalism: to support residual colonialism of the French in Indochina; to resurrect Japan's co-prosperity sphere but under American aegis; and to perpetuate the region's specialization in primary commodities in a "complementary relationship" with the industrial core.[20] Even as early as 1944, American diplomats in the area had warned the State Department that "there is much bitterness, whether justified or not, among leading and important Asiatics and colonial people toward 'white' imperial or colonial power. Propaganda associating the United States with such powers did not begin with this war and has not always fallen on barren soil."[21] Indeed, by 1950, the soil had produced a bumper crop. As one DOS official put it:

> In this connection, it is a fairly sound if unpleasant generalization to state that the U.S. is feared throughout the whole area, and much of

the fear is based upon the notion that our interest in the area origi- nates in large part from conscious programs of economic imperialism. Neither French nor Dutch imperialism is regarded by the sensitive and somewhat xenophobic native nationalism as a serious barrier to their ambitions. We, however, are regarded with considerable apprehension.[22]

American leaders were not insensitive to such apprehension; nor could they be and still succeed in their policy objectives. But the apparent contradictions between those objectives and SEA nationalism created a circle that somehow had to be squared. In a preview of later efforts, "Vietimization" of the Indochina war became the American solution to that problem in political geometry—a sort of pseudo-nationalism to legitimize French efforts. With American encouragement, France created native regimes in Cambodia, Laos, and Vietnam—the latter headed by former Emperor Bao Dai. While these puppet governments were granted nominal autonomy as "free states," the French continued to exercise real authority over them. France's move deceived no one—especially SEA countries like Thailand, who withheld diplomatic recognition of Bao Dai and the other regimes because of "repugnance voluntarily to recognize any regime which in their minds represents perpetuation of colonial rule."[23] In an effort to assuage such views and to facilitate stabilization, the United States did advise France to grant more substantive autonomy, to give some deference to the goal of eventual independence, and to create an indigenous army that would cooperate in the French pacification attempt. But since colonial powers are not known to fight wars with decolonization as their objective, France predictably declined the advice. And since in the American scheme of values, anticolonialism was a minor good alongside the major good or regional stabilization, American leaders perceived but one choice: bed down with France and Bao Dai and do one's best to make the *ménage à trois* look respectable.

One route to relative respectability is to rob one's adversaries of legitimacy. By dismissing European colonialism as dead or dying, and positing that Soviet-directed communism constituted the new imperialism of the postwar era, the United States attempted to define revolutionary communism as the archenemy of Southeast Asian nationalism, and anti-Communist "containment" as its firmest friend. But the empirical question remained: was the Vietminh wholly Communist-dominated, and even if so, was it or would it likely become a lackey for Soviet or Sino-Soviet international policy? Some American area specialists and intelligence people were clearly unsure. Those with

greater power were not. As early as May 1949, Secretary of State
Acheson dismissed the "question [of] whether Ho [was] as much
nationalist as Commie [as] irrelevant. All Stalinists in colonial areas
are nationalists."[24] The communist triumph in China only hardened the Secretary's view and led him to predict to the British ambassador in December that "there was likely to be early expansion
south and east beyond the borders of China." Chinese and Russian
recognition of the Vietminh a month later was all Acheson needed
to carry the day over any "doubting Thomases." Plane political geometry gave way to solid: circles squared within circles squared.
The choice of stabilization *at the expense* of area nationalism + the
rationalization of pseudo-nationalism + the legitimization of anti-
communism = the transformation of that choice into a policy *in behalf* of area nationalism.

Many of Southeast Asia's leaders—even staunch non-Commu-
nists—did not buy this example of the New Math. Filipino leader
Carlos Romulo, presiding head of the UN General Assembly, spoke
for many of them in a long, eloquent, and critical letter to Acheson
on March 2, 1950. Questioning not only policies but underlying
premises, Romulo concluded with the quintessential question. Noting recent Vietminh contact with Yugoslavia, he inquired:

> Suppose now that Vietnamese Communism should assume the shape
> of Titoism, would the United States still prefer a puppet Bao Dai to a
> Titoist Ho Chi-minh?

Acheson had, in fact, answered the question nearly a year earlier.
While acknowledging a Vietnamese Titoism as a "theoretical possibility," he thought the United States should explore it "only if every
other avenue closed."[25] The "puppet Bao Dai" was indeed preferable
to a "Titoist Ho Chi-minh," and for the simple reason that pseudo-
nationalism was less an obstacle to an Americanized coprosperity
sphere than the genuine article. In any case, Acheson declared the
issue moot on February 1, 1950, following Russian recognition of the
Vietminh regime. Ho, he declared, stood revealed "in his true colors
as the mortal enemy of native independence in Indochina."[26]

Acheson's public statement coincided to the day with completion
of a DOS "Problem Paper" on "Military Aid for Indochina." In essence, it recommended a dramatic reversal of past American policy
(epitomized earlier in PPS 51) that "we are powerless to bring about
a constructive solution of the explosive Indochinese situation"; that
neither a "French imperialism" nor "militant nationalism" were viable alternatives; and that moral suasion, aimed at reconciling both,

was the only available option.[27] A year after that Policy Planning Staff conclusion, the departmental "Working Group" determined that "significant developments" had radically altered the situation, and it made *THE* crucial recommendation:

> The United States should furnish military aid in support of the anti-Communist nationalist governments of Indochina, this aid to be tailored to meet deficiencies toward which the United States can make a unique contribution, *not including United States troops.* [Emphasis added.]

Two weeks later, the French Government formally requested immediate military aid and a commitment of "further military assistances . . . on a very much larger scale and for an *indeterminate period of time.*" (Emphasis added.) On February 27 the National Security Council approved the proposal of military aid in principle and ordered the Joint Chiefs of Staff to "prepare as a matter of priority a program of all practicable measures to protect United States security interests in Indochina."[28] After six weeks of labor, the JCS report—along with parallel reports from DOS—were submitted to NSC and the President. Finally, on May 1, 1950, President Truman gave new meaning to May Day by announcing the first installment of military and economic aid to bolster the French effort in Indochina.

The final two years of the Truman administration that followed saw that modest seed money of some $15,000,000 transformed into a multibillion-dollar investment that paid about 40 percent of the cost of France's war in Indochina by 1952—and it would continue to expand, not unlike the jungle growth of Vietnam itself. Three related factors prompted that quantum jump: the failure of French suppression in Indochina, the Korean War, and the continuing problems of the Japanese economy. The French failure is well known. French military fortunes plummeted in 1950, hitting a new low in the Vietminh victory at Cao Bung that cost France some 6,000 troops and a mountain of equipment and supplies. French resurgence in the Red River Delta area in early 1951 proved only temporary—prelude to France's worst defeat yet, near Hanoi in late 1951. By 1952, after two years of American military aid, the goal of pacification—as first step to stabilization—was as far away as ever.[29]

In itself, the French failure could as easily have negated the American investment as expanded it. Why throw good money after bad—especially when the French effort "will further deplete defenses of Western Europe without—so far as we can tell—solving the Indochina problem"? Or when the long-term consequence might find

America "completely committed to direct intervention. These situations, unfortunately, have a way of snowballing"?[30] But the other two factors stimulated the United States to protect its investment rather than liquidate it. The Korean War, for its part, compounded the volatility of Southeast Asia and dictated that only increased commitment had any chance of success. Interpreted as a Soviet venture rather than a civil war, Korea gave credence to the notion of Communist expansionism and the possibility that its tactics had moved from Cold War to military aggression. Given Acheson's earlier prediction of Communist expansion south and east from China, it now became increasingly plausible for his subordinates like Dean Rusk—then Assistant Secretary for Far Eastern Affairs—to predict in September 1950 "a probable communist offensive against Indochina in late September or early October . . . carried out by augmented Viet Minh forces" trained and supplied "from Communist China." Chinese entry into the Korean War, arguably done for defensive reasons, nonetheless reinforced a militarized perspective. As early as December 29, 1950, the Central Intelligence Agency made the first of many similar predictions to follow: "Direct intervention by Chinese Communist troops [in Indochina] may occur at any time. It may have already begun." Operating from similar premises, but unwilling and unable to take over the French role directly, the National Security Council (NSC 48/5) could only conclude in May 1951 that the United States should "continue to increase the military effectiveness of French units and the size and equipment of indigenous units," while also encouraging "internal autonomy and progressive social and economic reforms."[31] It was a feeble substitute for earlier PPS advice that France be pressured to promise full independence within a stated two-year period.

If the seeming lesson of Korea was that only enhanced American aid held out any hope for eventual stabilization, then the Japanese situation seemed to teach another one—that the stakes were too high not to make the attempt. General Matthew Ridgway, MacArthur's successor in Korea, summed those stakes up well in recounting a conversation with John Foster Dulles—later Secretary of State in the Eisenhower administration:

> Mr. Dulles then stated his view that the two major problems facing the United States in foreign relations were Japan and Germany, of which the former was much more difficult. The problem of weaving Germany into the economic, industrial and security fabric of Western civilization was infinitely easier than that of first bringing Japan into

that fabric, and then of keeping her there against the promises of Communism in contiguous Asia.[32]

In the short run, the Korean War eased the problem of Dulles' concern. Enlisting Japanese productivity to meet wartime needs, America's Special Procurement program pumped $860 million (1951) in military purchases into the Japanese economy, and canceled out the $700 million in Japan's dollar deficit resulting from her unfavorable balance of trade with the United States. But in 1952, American anxiety heightened again as its leaders confronted the question of what to do about a "Viable Economy of Japan" once the Korean War ended.[33] What would take the place of American military Keynesianism as a market for Japanese industrial production? The answer was the same as that given Kennan when he first posed the question in late 1949: Southeast Asia. High tariffs inhibited expansion of the American market; declining raw material productivity diminished the sterling bloc market. But "a way to break through is to bestow the purchasing power to Southeast Asian regions."[34]

In a lengthy report on "How to cope with the present dollar deficit of Japan?" the Economic and Scientific Bureau in Tokyo saw economic integration of Japan and SEA as the only viable supplement to a declining procurement operation. Noting that Japan already had a favorable balance of some $100 million with the area, the report argued that Japan could earn dollar exchange by export of its manufactured products to SEA, and reduce its imports of food and raw materials from the United States by substituting those from SEA. None of this could happen, however, unless something was done about political instability and low "purchasing power in these areas." American foreign policy would have to solve the former; "Japan's investment is the only way" to solve the latter.[35] The report's analysis was mirrored in NSC 124/2 (June 1952):

> In the long run the loss of Southeast Asia, especially Malaya and Indonesia, could result in such economic and political pressures in Japan as to make it extremely difficult to prevent Japan's eventual accommodation to the Soviet Bloc.[36]

The same concern largely motivated American negotiation of the Japanese Peace Treaty formally ending World War II. Designed to integrate Japan politically and to leave open the option of remilitarization, it also sought to facilitate the broadening of Japan's trade relations with her former SEA victims by bestowing upon her the legitimacy of a peace-loving nation. But before Japan—or anyone else—could profitably walk the commercial streets of Southeast Asia, those streets would first have to be made safe. Law and order—pacification and stabilization—was the indispensable prerequisite.

NOTES

Throughout the Notes section the abbreviation *FRUS* is used for *Foreign Relations of the United States*. PSA is used for Philippines and South Asia desk.

1. The authors wish to thank Professor George Kahin for his generosity in sharing parts of his forthcoming book on the Indochina conflict. The chapter on the post-war French phase was very useful.

2. George W. Perkins to Acheson, Oct. 22, 1949, *FRUS, 1949,* IV, p. 495.

3. U.S. Delegation/Tripartite Meeting to Secretary of State, Apr. 20, 1950, *FRUS, 1950,* III, p. 897.

4. Merchant to Mr. Lacy, July 19, 1950, Lot Files, PSA, Box 8, Folder, "Mutual Defense Assistance."

5. U.S. Delegation/Tripartite Meeting to Secretary of State, loc. cit.

6. Department of State, *Bulletin,* Sept. 5, 1949, pp. 323–24.

7. Acheson to Truman, Feb. 16, 1950, *FRUS, 1950,* I, pp. 834–40. Memorandum for Discussion, "Foreign Economic Policy," Jan. 14, 1950, George M. Elsey papers. Ibid., Memorandum for the President, "Development of Policy for Adjusting the Balance of Payments of the U.S.," Jan. 26, 1950, pp. 1–20.

8. Memorandum (Attachment), Secretary of State to the President, Feb. 16, 1950, *FRUS, 1950,* I, p. 839. Ibid., III, Bonestell to Ohly, March 20, 1950, pp. 36–40.

9. Tracy Voorhees, "Proposal for Strengthening Defense Without Increasing Appropriations," Apr. 5, 1950, Tracy S. Voorhees papers.

10. Stanley Andrews to Tracy Voorhees, "A Proposal to Correlate Economic Aid to Europe with Military Defense," May 29, 1950, Stanley Andrews papers. Ibid., Voorhees to Andrews, "Commentary," June 2, 1950.

11. Butterworth to Acting Secretary of State, Oct. 27, 1948, NARS—890.50/10-2748.

12. NSC 64, Feb. 27, 1950, *FRUS, 1950,* VI, p. 747.

13. NSC 124/2, June 25, 1952 [PPS Draft, March 27, 1952], *FRUS, 1952–1954,* XIII, p. 84. As the date indicates, NSC 124 (and the quote from it) was formulated in 1952. Its concerns for SEA raw materials—especially Malayan rubber exports as a British dollar-earner—was already part of the conventional wisdom by 1950. NSC 124 is used here because it is published and more readily accessible and verifiable to the readers. For more elaborate and developed analysis and documentation, see Andrew Rotter, "The Big Canvas," dss., Stanford University, 1981, Chs. 4 and 8.

14. Rotter, "The Big Canvas." The authors wish to thank Professor Rotter for his scholarly kindness and work in sharing copies of documents unearthed in his dissertation. That dissertation, when published, will be a major contribution to the growing historiography on the roots of American involvement in Southeast Asia.

15. Acting Political Adviser in Japan (Sebald) to Secretary of State, Sept. 16, 1947, *FRUS, 1947,* VI, p. 290.

16. Ibid., p. 292.

17. "U.S. Post-Treaty Policy Toward Japan," Apr. 23, 1952, PSA, Box 13. Acheson to "Certain Diplomatic Offices," May 8, 1949, *FRUS, 1949,* VII, pp. 736–37.

18. General Headquarters, Supreme Command for Allied Powers (SCAP), to Tracy Voorhees, Mar. 22, 1950, Record Group-9: DA CX MacArthur Archives.

19. For a highly sophisticated treatment of postwar Japan, the dollar gap, and the Southeast Asia region, see William Borden, *Pacific Alliance* (Madison, Wisc., 1984). The authors owe much to Mr. Borden, by way of a heavy intellectual debt as well as gratitude for his great labor and openness in making many of his documents available to us. His excellent book has relevance not only to America's early commitment in SEA, but to the global and regional framework in which it occurs.

20. Sherwood Fine to SCAP, Economic and Scientific Section, Nov. 9, 1949, Box 4, SEA, Tracy Voorhees papers.

21. Consul Max W. Bishop to Secretary of State, Nov. 21, 1944, 740.0011 P.W./ 11–1044.

22. PSA to Assistant Secretary of State for Far Eastern Affairs, Mar. 16, 1950, *FRUS, 1950*, VI, p. 62.

23. Ambassador in Thailand (Stanton) to Secretary of State, Jan. 19, 1950, *FRUS, 1950*, VI, p. 697.

24. Acheson to Consulate at Hanoi, May 20, 1949, *FRUS, 1949*, VII, pp. 29–30.

25. Secretary of State to Consulate at Hanoi, May 20, 1949, *FRUS, 1949*, VII, p. 29.

26. Public release, Secretary Acheson, Feb. 1, 1950, *FRUS, 1950*, VI, p. 711.

27. PPS 51, "Paper on United States Policy Toward Southeast Asia," Mar. 29, 1949, *FRUS, 1949*, VII, pp. 1129, 1132.

28. Chargé in France (Bohlen) to Secretary of State, Feb. 16, 1950, *FRUS, 1950*, VI, p. 734. Ibid., p. 745.

29. George C. Herring, *America's Longest War*, pp. 14–23. Good, short summary of 1951–52 period.

30. Ambassador in France (Bruce) to Secretary of State, Nov. 21, 1950, *FRUS, 1950*, VI, p. 930.

31. NSC 48/5, "U.S. Objectives, Policies and Courses of Action in Asia," May 17, 1951, *FRUS, 1951*, VI, p. 61.

32. Memo for Record, Ridgway Conference with Dulles and Sebald, Apr. 22, 1951, Matthew B. Ridgway papers.

33. Economic and Scientific Bureau, June 3, 1952, John Dower collection.

34. ESB, Feb. 2, 1952, Dower collection.

35. Loc. cit.

36. Draft Statement of Policy Proposed by NSC on "U.S. Objectives and Courses of Action with Respect to S.E. Asia," June 19, 1952, National Archives, unnumbered.

Whose Immorality?

BY NORMAN PODHORETZ

Why did the United States undertake these burdens and make these sacrifices in blood and treasure and domestic tranquility? What was in it for the United States? It was a question that plagued the antiwar movement from beginning to end because the answer was so hard to find. If the United States was simply acting the part of an imperialist aggressor in Vietnam, as many in the antiwar movement professed to believe, it was imperialism of a most peculiar kind. There were no raw materials to exploit in Vietnam, and there was no overriding strategic interest involved. To Franklin Roosevelt in 1941 Indochina had been important because it was close to the source of rubber and tin, but this was no longer an important consideration. Toward the end of the war, it was discovered that there was oil off the coast of Vietnam and antiwar radicals happily seized on this news as at last providing an explanation for the American presence there. But neither Kennedy nor Johnson knew about the oil, and even if they had, they would hardly have gone to war for its sake in those pre-OPEC days when oil from the Persian Gulf could be had at two dollars a barrel.

In the absence of an economic interpretation, a psychological version of the theory of imperialism was developed to answer the maddening question: *Why are we in Vietnam?* This theory held that the United States was in Vietnam because it had an urge to dominate— "to impose its national obsessions on the rest of the world," in the words of a piece in the *New York Review of Books*,[1] one of the leading centers of antiwar agitation within the intellectual community. But if so, the psychic profits were as illusory as the economic ones, for the war was doing even deeper damage to the national self-confidence than to the national economy.

Yet another variant of the psychological interpretation, proposed by the economist Robert L. Heilbroner, was that "the fear of losing our place in the sun, of finding ourselves at bay, . . . motivates a great deal of the anti-Communism on which so much of American foreign policy seems to be founded." This was especially so in such underdeveloped countries as Vietnam, where "the rise of Communism would signal the end of capitalism as the dominant world order, and would force the acknowledgment that America no longer constituted the model on which the future of world civilization would be mainly based." [2]

All these theories were developed out of a desperate need to find or invent selfish or self-interested motives for the American presence in Vietnam, the better to discredit it morally. In a different context, proponents of one or another of these theories—Senator Fulbright, for example—were not above trying to discredit the American presence politically by insisting that *no* national interest was being served by the war. This latter contention at least had the virtue of being closer to the truth than the former. For the truth was that the United States went into Vietnam for the sake not of its own direct interests in the ordinary sense but for the sake of an ideal. The intervention was a product of the Wilsonian side of the American character—the side that went to war in 1917 to "make the world safe for democracy" and that found its contemporary incarnations in the liberal internationalism of the 1940s and the liberal anti-Communism of the 1950s. One can characterize this impulse as naive; one can describe it, as Heilbroner does (and as can be done with any virtuous act), in terms that give it a subtly self-interested flavor. But there is no rationally defensible way in which it can be called immoral.

Why, then, were we in Vietnam? To say it once again: because we were trying to save the Southern half of that country from the evils of Communism. But was the war we fought to accomplish this purpose morally worse than Communism itself? Peter L. Berger, who at the time was involved with Clergy and Laymen Concerned About Vietnam (CALCAV), wrote in 1967: "All sorts of dire results might well follow a reduction or a withdrawal of the American engagement in Vietnam. Morally speaking, however, it is safe to assume that none of these could be worse than what is taking place right now." Unlike most of his fellow members of CALCAV, Berger would later repent of this statement. Writing in 1980, he would say of it: "Well, it was *not* safe to assume. . . . I was wrong and so were all those who thought as I did." For "contrary to what most members (including myself) of the antiwar movement expected, the peoples of Indochina have, since 1975, been subjected to suffering far worse than anything that was inflicted upon them by the United States and its allies."[3]

To be sure, the "bloodbath" that had been feared by supporters of the war did not occur—not in the precise form that had been anticipated. In contrast to what they did upon taking power in Hanoi in 1954 (when they murdered some 50,000 landlords), or what they did during their brief occupation of Hué during the Tet offensive of 1968 (when they massacred 3,000 civilians), the Communists did not stage mass executions in the newly conquered South. According to Nguyen Cong Hoan, who had been an NLF agent and then became a member of the National Assembly of the newly united Communist Vietnam before disillusionment drove him to escape in March 1977, there were more executions in the provinces than in the cities and the total number might well have reached into the tens of thousands. But as another fervent opponent of the war, the New York *Times* columnist Tom Wicker was forced to acknowledge, "what Vietnam has given us instead of a bloodbath [is] a vast tide of human misery in Southeast Asia—hundreds of thousands of homeless persons in United Nations camps, perhaps as many more dead in flight, tens of thousands of the most pitiable forcibly repatriated to Cambodia, no one knows how many adrift on the high seas or wandering the roads."[4]

NOTES

1. Jason Epstein, "The CIA and the Intellectuals," *New York Review of Books*, Apr. 20, 1967.

2. Robert L. Heilbroner, "Counterrevolutionary America," *Commentary*, Apr. 1967.

3. "Indochina and the American Conscience," *Commentary*, Feb. 1980.

4. Tom Wicker, New York *Times*, July 8, 1979. Quoted in Charles Horner, "America Five Years After Defeat," *Commentary*, Apr. 1980.

How Could Vietnam Happen?
AN AUTOPSY

BY JAMES C. THOMSON, JR.

As a case study in the making of foreign policy, the Vietnam War will fascinate historians and social scientists for many decades to come. One question that will certainly be asked: How did men of superior ability, sound training, and high ideals—American policy-makers of the 1960s—create such costly and divisive policy?

As one who watched the decision-making process in Washington from 1961 to 1966 under Presidents Kennedy and Johnson, I can suggest a preliminary answer. I can do so by briefly listing some of the factors that seemed to me to shape our Vietnam policy during my years as an East Asia specialist at the State Department and the White House. I shall deal largely with Washington as I saw or sensed it, and not with Saigon, where I have spent but a scant three days, in the entourage of the Vice President, or with other decision centers, the capitals of interested parties. Nor will I deal with other important parts of the record: Vietnam's history prior to 1961, for instance, or the overall course of America's relations with Vietnam.

Yet a first and central ingredient in these years of Vietnam decisions does involve history. The ingredient was _the legacy of the 1950s_—by which I mean the so-called "loss of China," the Korean War, and the Far East policy of Secretary of State Dulles.

This legacy had an institutional by-product for the Kennedy Administration: in 1961 the U.S. government's East Asian establishment was undoubtedly the most rigid and doctrinaire of Washington's regional divisions in foreign affairs. This was especially true at the Department of State, where the incoming Administration found the Bureau of Far Eastern Affairs the hardest nut to crack. It was a bureau that had been purged of its best China expertise, and of far-sighted, dispassionate men, as a result of McCarthyism. Its members were generally committed to one policy line: the close containment and isolation of mainland China, the harassment of "neutralist" nations which sought to avoid alignment with either Washington or Peking, and the maintenance of a network of alliances with anti-Communist client states on China's periphery.

Another aspect of the legacy was the special vulnerability and sensitivity of the new Democratic Administration on Far East policy issues. The memory of the McCarthy era was still very sharp, and Kennedy's margin of victory was too thin. The 1960 Offshore Islands TV debate between Kennedy and Nixon had shown the President-elect the perils of "fresh thinking." The Administration was inherently leery of moving too fast on Asia. As a result, the Far East Bureau (now the Bureau of East Asian and Pacific Affairs) was the last one to be overhauled. Not until Averell Harriman was brought in as Assistant Secretary in December, 1961, were significant personnel changes attempted, and it took Harriman several months to make a deep imprint on the bureau because of his necessary preoccupation with the Laos settlement. Once he did so, there was virtually no effort to bring back the purged or exiled East Asia experts.

There were other important by-products of this "legacy of the fifties":

The new Administration inherited and somewhat shared *a general perception of China-on-the-march*—a sense of China's vastness, its numbers, its belligerence; a revived sense, perhaps, of the Golden Horde. This was a perception fed by Chinese intervention in the Korean War (an intervention actually based on appallingly bad communications and mutual miscalculation on the part of Washington and Peking; but the careful unraveling of that tragedy, which scholars have accomplished, had not yet become part of the conventional wisdom).

The new Administration inherited and briefly accepted *a monolithic conception of the Communist bloc*. Despite much earlier predictions and reports by outside analysts, policy-makers did not begin to accept the reality and possible finality of the Sino-Soviet split until the first weeks of 1962. The inevitably corrosive impact of competing nationalisms on Communism was largely ignored.

The new Administration inherited and to some extent shared *the "domino theory" about Asia*. This theory resulted from profound ignorance of Asian history and hence ignorance of the radical differences among Asian nations and societies. It resulted from a blindness to the power and resilience of Asian nationalisms. (It may also have resulted from a subconscious sense that, since "all Asians look alike," all Asian nations will act alike.) As a theory, the domino fallacy was not merely inaccurate but also insulting to Asian nations; yet it has continued to this day to beguile men who should know better.

Finally, the legacy of the fifties was apparently compounded by an _uneasy sense of a worldwide Communist challenge_ to the new Administration after the Bay of Pigs fiasco. A first manifestation was the President's traumatic Vienna meeting with Khrushchev in June, 1961; then came the Berlin crisis of the summer. All this created an atmosphere in which President Kennedy undoubtedly felt under special pressure to show his nation's mettle in Vietnam—if the Vietnamese, unlike the people of Laos, were willing to fight.

In general, the legacy of the fifties shaped such early moves of the new Administration as the decisions to maintain a high-visibility SEATO (by sending the Secretary of State himself instead of some underling to its first meeting in 1961), to back away from diplomatic recognition of Mongolia in the summer of 1961, and most important, to expand U.S. military assistance to South Vietnam that winter on the basis of the much more tentative Eisenhower commitment. It should be added that the increased commitment to Vietnam was also fueled by a new breed of military strategists and academic social scientists (some of whom had entered the new Administration) who had developed theories of counterguerrilla warfare and were eager to see them put to the test. To some, "counterinsurgency" seemed a new panacea for coping with the world's instability.

So much for the legacy and the history. Any new Administration inherits both complicated problems and simplistic views of the world. But surely among the policy-makers of the Kennedy and Johnson Administrations there were men who would warn of the dangers of an open-ended commitment to the Vietnam quagmire?

This raises a central question, at the heart of the policy process: Where were the experts, the doubters, and the dissenters? Were they there at all, and if so, what happened to them?

The answer is complex but instructive.

In the first place, the American government was sorely _lacking in real Vietnam or Indochina expertise._ Originally treated as an adjunct of Embassy Paris, our Saigon embassy and the Vietnam Desk at State were largely staffed from 1954 onward by French-speaking Foreign Service personnel of narrowly European experience. Such diplomats were even more closely restricted than the normal embassy officer— by cast of mind as well as language—to contacts with Vietnam's French-speaking urban elites. For instance, Foreign Service lin-

guists in Portugal are able to speak with the peasantry if they get out
of Lisbon and choose to do so; not so the French speakers of Embassy Saigon.

In addition, the *shadow of the "loss of China"* distorted Vietnam
reporting. Career officers in the Department, and especially those in
the field, had not forgotten the fate of their World War II colleagues
who wrote in frankness from China and were later pilloried by Senate committees for critical comments on the Chinese Nationalists.
Candid reporting on the strengths of the Viet Cong and the weaknesses of the Diem government was inhibited by the memory. It was
also inhibited by some higher officials, notably Ambassador Nolting
in Saigon, who refused to sign off on such cables.

In due course, to be sure, some Vietnam talent was discovered or
developed. But a recurrent and increasingly important factor in the
decision-making process was *the banishment of real expertise*. Here the
 underlying cause was the "closed politics" of policy-making as issues
become hot: the more sensitive the issue, and the higher it rises in
the bureaucracy, the more completely the experts are excluded while
the harassed senior generalists take over (that is, the Secretaries, Un-
dersecretaries, and Presidential Assistants). The frantic skimming of
briefing papers in the back seats of limousines is no substitute for the
presence of specialists; furthermore, in times of crisis such papers
are deemed "too sensitive" even for review by the specialists. Another underlying cause of this banishment, as Vietnam became more
critical, was the replacement of the experts, who were generally and
increasingly pessimistic, by men described as "can-do guys," loyal
and energetic fixers unsoured by expertise. In early 1965, when I
confided my growing policy doubts to an older colleague on the NSC
staff, he assured me that the smartest thing both of us could do was
to "steer clear of the whole Vietnam mess"; the gentleman in question had the misfortune to be a "can-do guy," however, and is now
highly placed in Vietnam, under orders to solve the mess.

Despite the banishment of the experts, internal doubters and dissenters did indeed appear and persist. Yet as I watched the process,
such men were effectively neutralized by a subtle dynamic: *the domestication of dissenters.* Such "domestication" arose out of a twofold
clubbish need: on the one hand, the dissenter's desire to stay aboard;
and on the other hand, the nondissenter's conscience. Simply stated,
dissent, when recognized, was made to feel at home. On the lowest
possible scale of importance, I must confess my own considerable
sense of dignity and acceptance (both vital) when my senior White
House employer would refer to me as his "favorite dove." Far more
significant was the case of the former Undersecretary of State, George

Ball. Once Mr. Ball began to express doubts, he was warmly institutionalized: he was encouraged to become the inhouse devil's advocate on Vietnam. The upshot was inevitable: the process of escalation allowed for periodic requests to Mr. Ball to speak his piece; Ball felt good, I assume (he had fought for righteousness); the others felt good (they had given a full hearing to the dovish option); and there was minimal unpleasantness. The club remained intact; and it is of course possible that matters would have gotten worse faster if Mr. Ball had kept silent, or left before his final departure in the fall of 1966. There was also, of course, the case of the last institutionalized doubter, Bill Moyers. The President is said to have greeted his arrival at meetings with an affectionate, "Well, here comes Mr. Stop-the-Bombing . . ." Here again the dynamics of domesticated dissent sustained the relationship for a while.

A related point—and crucial, I suppose, to government at all times—was _the "effectiveness" trap,_ the trap that keeps men from speaking out, as clearly or often as they might, within the government. And it is the trap that keeps men from resigning in protest and airing their dissent outside the government. The most important asset that a man brings to bureaucratic life is his "effectiveness," a mysterious combination of training, style, and connections. The most ominous complaint that can be whispered of a bureaucrat is: "I'm afraid Charlie's beginning to lose his effectiveness." To preserve your effectiveness, you must decide where and when to fight the mainstream of policy; the opportunities range from pillow talk with your wife, to private drinks with your friends, to meetings with the Secretary of State or the President. The inclination to remain silent or to acquiesce in the presence of the great men—to live to fight another day, to give on this issue so that you can be "effective" on later issues—is overwhelming. Nor is it the tendency of youth alone; some of our most senior officials, men of wealth and fame, whose place in history is secure, have remained silent lest their connection with power be terminated. As for the disinclination to resign in protest: while not necessarily a Washington or even American specialty, it seems more true of a government in which ministers have no parliamentary backbench to which to retreat. In the absence of such a refuge, it is easy to rationalize the decision to stay aboard. By doing so, one may be able to prevent a few bad things from happening and perhaps even make a few good things happen. To exit is to lose even those marginal chances for "effectiveness."

Another factor must be noted: as the Vietnam controversy escalated at home, there developed _a preoccupation with Vietnam public relations as opposed to Vietnam policy-making_. And here, ironically, internal doubters and dissenters were heavily employed. For such men, by virtue of their own doubts, were often deemed best able to "massage" the doubting intelligentsia. My senior East Asia colleague at the White House, a brilliant and humane doubter who had dealt with Indochina since 1954, spent three quarters of his working days on Vietnam public relations: drafting presidential responses to letters from important critics, writing conciliatory language for presidential speeches, and meeting quite interminably with delegations of outraged Quakers, clergymen, academics, and housewives. His regular callers were the late A. J. Muste and Norman Thomas; mine were members of the Women's Strike for Peace. Our orders from above: keep them off the backs of busy policy-makers (who usually happened to be nondoubters). Incidentally, my most discouraging assignment in the realm of public relations was the preparation of a White House pamphlet entitled *Why Vietnam,* in September, 1965; in a gesture toward my conscience, I fought—and lost—a battle to have the title followed by a question mark.

Through a variety of procedures, both institutional and personal, doubt, dissent, and expertise were effectively neutralized in the making of policy. But what can be said of the men "in charge"? It is patently absurd to suggest that they produced such tragedy by intention and calculation. But it is neither absurd nor difficult to discern certain forces at work that caused decent and honorable men to do great harm.

Here I would stress the paramount role of *executive fatigue.* No factor seems to me more crucial and underrated in the making of foreign policy. The physical and emotional toll of executive responsibility in State, the Pentagon, the White House, and other executive agencies is enormous; that toll is of course compounded by extended service. Many of today's Vietnam policy-makers have been on the job for from four to seven years. Complaints may be few, and physical health may remain unimpaired, though emotional health is far harder to gauge. But what is most seriously eroded in the deadening process of fatigue is freshness of thought, imagination, a sense of possibility, a sense of priorities and perspective—those rare assets of a new Administration in its first year or two of office. The tired policy-maker becomes a prisoner of his own narrowed view of the world and his own clichéd rhetoric. He becomes irritable and defensive—short on sleep, short on family ties, short on patience. Such men make bad policy and then compound it. They have neither the time nor the temperament for new ideas or preventive diplomacy.

Below the level of the fatigued executives in the making of Vietnam policy was a widespread phenomenon: _the curator mentality_ in the Department of State. By this I mean the collective inertia produced by the bureaucrat's view of his job. At State, the average "desk officer" inherits from his predecessor our policy toward Country X; he regards it as his function to keep that policy intact—under glass, untampered with, and dusted—so that he may pass it on in two to four years to his successor. And such curatorial service generally merits promotion within the system. (Maintain the status quo, and you will stay out of trouble.) In some circumstances, the inertia bred by such an outlook can act as a brake against rash innovation. But on many issues, this inertia sustains the momentum of bad policy and unwise commitments—momentum that might otherwise have been resisted within the ranks. Clearly, Vietnam is such an issue.

To fatigue and inertia must be added the factor of internal confusion. Even among the "architects" of our Vietnam commitment, there has been persistent _confusion as to what type of war we were fighting_ and, as a direct consequence, _confusion as to how to end that war._ (The "credibility gap" is, in part, a reflection of such internal confusion.) Was it, for instance, a civil war, in which case counterinsurgency might suffice? Or was it a war of international aggression? (This might invoke SEATO or UN commitment.) Who was the aggressor—and the "real enemy"? The Viet Cong? Hanoi? Peking? Moscow? International Communism? Or maybe "Asian Communism"? Differing enemies dictated differing strategies and tactics. And confused throughout, in like fashion, was the question of American objectives; your objectives depended on whom you were fighting and why. I shall not forget my assignment from an Assistant Secretary of State in March, 1964: to draft a speech for Secretary McNamara which would, _inter alia_, once and for all dispose of the canard that the Vietnam conflict was a civil war. "But in some ways, of course," I mused, "it _is_ a civil war." "Don't play word games with me!" snapped the Assistant Secretary.

Similar confusion beset the concept of "negotiations"—anathema to much of official Washington from 1961 to 1965. Not until April, 1965, did "unconditional discussions" become respectable, via a presidential speech; even then the Secretary of State stressed privately to newsmen that nothing had changed, since "discussions" were by no means the same as "negotiations." Months later that issue was resolved. But it took even longer to obtain a fragile internal agreement that negotiations might include the Viet Cong as something other than an appendage to Hanoi's delegation. Given such confusion as to the whos and whys of our Vietnam commitment, it is not surprising, as Theodore Draper has written, that policy-makers find it so difficult to agree on how to end the war.

Of course, one force—a constant in the vortex of commitment—was that of _wishful thinking._ I partook of it myself at many times. I did so especially during Washington's struggle with Diem in the autumn of 1963 when some of us at State believed that for once, in dealing with a difficult client state, the U.S. government could use the leverage of our economic and military assistance to make good things happen, instead of being led around by the nose by men like Chiang Kai-shek and Syngman Rhee (and, in that particular instance, by Diem). If we could prove that point, I thought, and move into a new day, with or without Diem, then Vietnam was well worth the effort. Later came the wishful thinking of the air-strike planners in the late autumn of 1964; there were those who actually thought that after six weeks of air strikes, the North Vietnamese would come crawling to us to ask for peace talks. And what, someone asked in one of the meetings of the time, if they don't? The answer was that we would bomb for another four weeks, and that would do the trick. And a few weeks later came one instance of wishful thinking that was symptomatic of good men misled: in January, 1965, I encountered one of the very highest figures in the Administration at a dinner, drew him aside, and told him of my worries about the air-strike option. He told me that I really shouldn't worry; it was his conviction that before any such plans could be put into effect, a neutralist government would come to power in Saigon that would politely invite us out. And finally, there was the recurrent wishful thinking that sustained many of us through the trying months of 1965–1966 after the air strikes had begun: that surely, somehow, one way or another, we would "be in a conference in six months," and the escalatory spiral would be suspended. The basis of our hope: "It simply can't go on."

As a further influence on policy-makers I would cite the factor of _bureaucratic detachment._ By this I mean what at best might be termed the professional callousness of the surgeon (and indeed, medical lingo—the "surgical strike" for instance—seemed to crop up in the euphemisms of the times). In Washington the semantics of the military muted the reality of war for the civilian policy-makers. In quiet, air-conditioned, thick-carpeted rooms, such terms as "systematic pressure," "armed reconnaissance," "targets of opportunity," and even "body count" seemed to breed a sort of games-theory detachment. Most memorable to me was a moment in the late 1964 target planning when the question under discussion was how heavy our bombing should be, and how extensive our strafing, at some midpoint in the projected pattern of systematic pressure. An Assistant Secretary of State resolved the point in the following words: "It seems to me that our orchestration should be mainly violins, but with periodic touches of brass." Perhaps the biggest shock of my return to Cambridge, Massachusetts, was the realization that the young men, the flesh and blood I taught and saw on these university streets, were potentially some of the numbers on the charts of those faraway planners. In a curious sense, Cambridge is closer to this war than Washington.

There is an unprovable factor that relates to bureaucratic detachment: the ingredient of *cryptoracism.* I do not mean to imply any conscious contempt for Asian loss of life on the part of Washington officials. But I do mean to imply that bureaucratic detachment may well be compounded by a traditional Western sense that there are so many Asians, after all; that Asians have a fatalism about life and a disregard for its loss; that they are cruel and barbaric to their own people; and that they are very different from us (and all look alike?). And I *do* mean to imply that the upshot of such subliminal views is a subliminal question whether Asians, and particularly Asian peasants, and most particularly Asian Communists, are really people—like you and me. To put the matter another way: would we have pursued quite such policies—and quite such military tactics—if the Vietnamese were white?

It is impossible to write of Vietnam decision-making without writing about language. Throughout the conflict, words have been of paramount importance. I refer here to the impact of *rhetorical escalation* and to the *problem of oversell.* In an important sense, Vietnam has become of crucial significance to us *because we have said that it is of crucial significance.* (The issue obviously relates to the public relations preoccupation described earlier.)

The key here is domestic politics: the need to sell the American people, press, and Congress on support for an unpopular and costly war in which the objectives themselves have been in flux. To sell means to persuade, and to persuade means rhetoric. As the difficulties and costs have mounted, so has the definition of the stakes. This is not to say that rhetorical escalation is an orderly process; executive prose is the product of many writers, and some concepts— North Vietnamese infiltration, America's "national honor," Red China as the chief enemy—have entered the rhetoric only gradually and even sporadically. But there is an upward spiral nonetheless. And once you have *said* that the American Experiment itself stands or falls on the Vietnam outcome, you have thereby created a national stake far beyond any earlier stakes.

Crucial throughout the process of Vietnam decision-making was a conviction among many policy-makers: that Vietnam posed a _fundamental test of America's national will._ Time and again I was told by men reared in the tradition of Henry L. Stimson that all we needed was the will, and we would then prevail. Implicit in such a view, it seemed to me, was a curious assumption that Asians lacked will, or at least that in a contest between Asian and Anglo-Saxon wills, the non-Asians must prevail. A corollary to the persistent belief in will was a _fascination with power_ and an awe in the face of the power America possessed as no nation or civilization ever before. Those who doubted our role in Vietnam were said to shrink from the burdens of power, the obligations of power, the uses of power, the responsibility of power. By implication, such men were soft-headed and effete.

Finally, no discussion of the factors and forces at work on Vietnam policy-makers can ignore the central fact of _human ego investment._ Men who have participated in a decision develop a stake in that decision. As they participate in further, related decisions, their stake increases. It might have been possible to dissuade a man of strong self-confidence at an early stage of the ladder of decision; but it is infinitely harder at later stages since a change of mind there usually involves implicit or explicit repudiation of a chain of previous decisions.

To put it bluntly: at the heart of the Vietnam calamity is a group of able, dedicated men who have been regularly and repeatedly wrong—and whose standing with their contemporaries, and more important, with history, depends, as they see it, on being proven right. These are not men who can be asked to extricate themselves from error.

The various ingredients I have cited in the making of Vietnam policy have created a variety of results, most of them fairly obvious. Here are some that seem to me most central:

Throughout the conflict, there has been _persistent and repeated miscalculation_ by virtually all the actors, in high echelons and low, whether dove, hawk, or something else. To cite one simple example among many: in late 1964 and early 1965, some peace-seeking planners at State who strongly opposed the projected bombing of the North urged that, instead, American ground forces be sent to South Vietnam; this would, they said, increase our bargaining leverage against the North—our "chips"—and would give us something to negotiate about (the withdrawal of our forces) at an early peace conference. Simultaneously, the air-strike option was urged by many in the military who were dead set against American participation in "another land war in Asia"; they were joined by other civilian peace-seekers who wanted to bomb Hanoi into early negotiations. By late 1965, we had ended up with the worst of all worlds: ineffective and costly air strikes against the North, spiraling ground forces in the South, and no negotiations in sight.

Throughout the conflict as well, there has been _a steady give-in to pressures for a military solution and only minimal and sporadic efforts at a diplomatic and political solution. In_ part this resulted from the confusion (earlier cited) among the civilians—confusion regarding objectives and strategy. And in part this resulted from the self-enlarging nature of military investment. Once air strikes and particularly ground forces were introduced, our investment itself had transformed the original stakes. More air power was needed to protect the ground forces; and then more ground forces to protect the ground forces. And needless to say, the military mind develops its own momentum in the absence of clear guidelines from the civilians. Once asked to save South Vietnam, rather than to "advise" it, the American military could not but press for escalation. In addition, sad to report, assorted military constituencies, once involved in Vietnam, have had a series of cases to prove: for instance, the utility not only of air power (the Air Force) but of supercarrier-based air power (the Navy). Also, Vietnam policy has suffered from one ironic by-product of Secretary McNamara's establishment of civilian control at the Pentagon: in the face of such control, interservice rivalry has given way to a united front among the military—reflected in the new but recurrent phenomenon of JCS unanimity. In conjunction with traditional congressional allies (mostly Southern senators and representatives) such a united front would pose a formidable problem for any President.

Throughout the conflict, there have been _missed opportunities, large and small, to disengage ourselves from Vietnam on increasingly unpleasant but still acceptable terms._ Of the many moments from 1961 onward, I shall cite only one, the last and most important opportunity that was lost: in the summer of 1964 the President instructed his chief advisers to prepare for him as wide a range of Vietnam options as possible for postelection consideration and decision. He explicitly asked that all options be laid out. What happened next was, in effect, Lyndon Johnson's slow-motion Bay of Pigs. For the advisers so effectively converged on one single option—juxtaposed against two other, phony options (in effect, blowing up the world, or scuttle-

and-run)—that the President was confronted with unanimity for
bombing the North from all his trusted counselors. Had he been
more confident in foreign affairs, had he been deeply informed on
Vietnam and Southeast Asia, and had he raised some hard questions
that unanimity had submerged, this President could have used the
largest electoral mandate in history to de-escalate in Vietnam, in the
clear expectation that at the worst a neutralist government would
come to power in Saigon and politely invite us out. Today, many
lives and dollars later, such an alternative has become an elusive and
infinitely more expensive possibility.

In the course of these years, another result of Vietnam decision-
making has been *the abuse and distortion of history.* Vietnamese,
Southeast Asian, and Far Eastern history has been rewritten by our
policy-makers, and their spokesmen, to conform with the alleged necessity of our presence in Vietnam. Highly dubious analogies from
our experience elsewhere—the "Munich" sellout and "containment" from Europe, the Malayan insurgency and the Korean War
from Asia—have been imported in order to justify our actions. And
more recent events have been fitted to the Procrustean bed of Vietnam. Most notably, the change of power in Indonesia in 1965–1966
has been ascribed to our Vietnam presence; and virtually all progress
in the Pacific region—the rise of regionalism, new forms of cooperation, and mounting growth rates—has been similarly explained. The
Indonesian allegation is undoubtedly false (I tried to prove it, during
six months of careful investigation at the White House, and had to
confess failure); the regional allegation is patently unprovable in either direction (except, of course, for the clear fact that the economies
of both Japan and Korea have profited enormously from our Vietnam-
related procurement in these countries; but that is a costly and highly
dubious form of foreign aid).

There is a final result of Vietnam policy I would cite that holds
potential danger for the future of American foreign policy: *the rise of
a new breed of American ideologues who see Vietnam as the ultimate test
of their doctrine.* I have in mind those men in Washington who have
given a new life to the missionary impulse in American foreign relations: who believe that this nation, in this era, has received a threefold endowment that can transform the world. As they see it, that
endowment is composed of, first, our unsurpassed military might;
second, our clear technological supremacy; and third, our allegedly
invincible benevolence (our "altruism," our affluence, our lack of
territorial aspirations). Together, it is argued, this threefold endowment provides us with the opportunity and the obligation to ease the
nations of the earth toward modernization and stability: toward a

full-fledged *Pax Americana Technocratica*. In reaching toward this goal, Vietnam is viewed as the last and crucial test. Once we have succeeded there, the road ahead is clear. In a sense, these men are our counterpart to the visionaries of Communism's radical left: they are technocracy's own Maoists. They do not govern Washington today. But their doctrine rides high.

Long before I went into government, I was told a story about Henry L. Stimson that seemed to me pertinent during the years that I watched the Vietnam tragedy unfold—and participated in that tragedy. It seems to me more pertinent than ever as we move toward the election of 1968.

In his waning years Stimson was asked by an anxious questioner, "Mr. Secretary, how on earth can we ever bring peace to the world?" Stinson is said to have answered: "You begin by bringing to Washington a small handful of able men who believe that the achievement of peace is possible.

"You work them to the bone until they no longer believe that it is possible.

"And then you throw them out—and bring in a new bunch who believe that it is possible."

Part Two
A DIFFERENT WAR:
THE MILITARY IN VIETNAM

The selections in Part Two provide an analytical context to comple-ment the first-person narratives portrayed in an oral history covering the experiences of Americans who served in Vietnam.

Myra MacPherson systematically delineates the peculiar nature of the Vietnam War, comparing the experiences of the American men and women who went to Vietnam with those of their peers who did not go, and with the experiences of those who fought in World War II.

Peter Marin concentrates on the spiritual ordeal of Vietnam vet-erans after they returned home from a war that, in retrospect, many of them could not justify in their own minds. He compares the devel-opment of moral seriousness in veterans who are coming to terms with the irrevocable consequences of what they did in Vietnam with the moral indifference of American culture in general, which, until recently, has denied the war and denied recognition to the men and women who participated in it.

Paul L. Savage and Richard A. Gabriel offer a sociological analysis explaining the disintegration of the American army in Vietnam. They attribute this phenomenon to causes within the military struc-ture itself rather than to sociopolitical factors in American society at large. Their emphasis is on the character, integrity, and competence of the officer corps, and on the corrupting effects of a radical change in its leadership style.

Cecil B. Currey criticizes the current military establishment for blaming the politicians, the press, and the civilian population for what went wrong in Vietnam. Instead of coming to terms with their own mistakes, he sees them erasing the memory of Vietnam from their Command structure.

A Different War

BY MYRA MacPHERSON

It is difficult to understand the special problems of Vietnam veterans without knowing what made that war different. "War is hell" and "Killing is killing" are clichés certainly based on reality. After all, the horrors of combat in Erich Maria Remarque's *All Quiet on the Western Front* or Stephen Crane's *The Red Badge of Courage* or James Jones's *The Thin Red Line* find their parallels in the tales of Vietnam.

In many ways Vietnam veterans, repelled by the absurdity of dying in Vietnam, identified with the scaring recollections of those who fought in the senseless slaughters of World War I more than they ever did with their fathers of World War II: "What am I doing here? We don't take any land. We don't give it back. We just mutilate bodies. What the *fuck* are we doing here?" cried one GI in Vietnam. "We are indifferent. We are forlorn like children and experienced like old men. I believe we are lost," cried one soldier in *All Quiet on the Western Front*. In the woods of France several World War I German soldiers tried to comprehend why they were dying there— "What exactly is the war for?"—just as GIs in Vietnam would ask years later the same question.

There are, however, specific differences between Vietnam and other wars.

First, the antiwar element is paramount and cannot be stressed too often. It is the unique facet that colors every aspect of the Vietnam experience. In this past "decade of denial," veterans were the scapegoats. When they finally speak of coming home, they recount still wrenching memories. Whether successfully readjusted or troubled, hawk or dove, college graduate or high school dropout—they remember. The neighbors and relatives who did not want to listen. The people who moved away from them on planes. In a major study by Louis Harris in 1980, nearly half of the younger veterans (47 percent) recalled that when on leave they were not "always proud to wear my uniform to public places."[1] Even in Middle America, where anti-war stigma was missing, there were older men who would preach to them of wars they had *won*.

The problem was especially acute for the thousands—often high school or college dropouts—who returned from the horrors of war driven to succeed and who encountered ridiculing antiwar professors and nongoing peers on campuses. Now there is some meager measure of reconciliation; some who used to taunt them at Army camps and airports—the students deferred taunting those less privileged draftees or those who felt compelled to serve their country—admit guilt and shame. Still, those memories haunt veterans. In interviews with hundreds of veterans—from the most successful to the least well-adjusted—I have yet to find one who did not suffer rage, anger, and frustration at the way the country received them.

Above all, indifference, hostility, and denial allowed no catharsis for the veteran. That is why the phrase "No homecoming parade" is much more significant than the simple cliché it has become. Many veterans of past wars say they, too, were soon forgotten. As civilians began to ignore them, former soldiers viewed their homecoming as "Welcome our boys back" hollow claptrap. Yet they did, collectively, benefit from that returning warrior's welcome with its symbolic cleansing that offered both respect and expiation. From ancient times, there have been elaborate rituals for purifying and returning the warrior to society.

In the *Aeneid*, Virgil ascribes these words to Aeneas:

In me it is not fit, holy things to bear,
Red as I am with slaughter and new from war,
Til in some stream I cleanse
The guilt of dire debate and blood in battle spilt.

American Navajo Indians have long recognized the need to cleanse the warrior. After battle, they paid homage to their enemies and made reconciliation with their spirits. American Indian veterans in World War II went through such tribal rituals.

Ticker tape parades and the generous GI Bills of the past were forms of absolving the soldier of anything he may have done in the course of battle, as well as signs of societal commitment, the recognition that "You did it for your country."

All of this was absent after Vietnam. Societal indifference was a form of punishment instead; this was symbolized in the punitive attitude toward everything from meager GI benefits to unconcern for Vet Centers or Agent Orange studies. "In past wars, symbolically, through cleansing acts, society *shared* the blame and responsibility by saying, 'We sent you off to do this for us.' Victory banners, medals, and parades were ways of recognizing the tasks they did in the country's name. Vietnam was not 'in our name,'" said Jack Smith, an ex-marine and psychologist. "The responsibility and blame was left on the heads of the guys who fought it. They were left to sort out who was responsible for what."

Sharing has not been easy for those who protested our involvement and felt it was not "their war." But that is what veterans and those who work with Vietnam's delayed stress victims feel must be achieved to reach that catharsis. "They want the country to say, 'God, it was a mess—but we can acknowledge that and then go on,'" said Smith.

Going on is what it is all about for the survivors of Vietnam, the majority of whom have adjusted successfully, have found pride and strength in their service, no matter what their feelings on the war. Most are understanding of the estimated 500,000 to 700,000 still suffering from delayed stress.

The Vietnam Veterans Memorial, dedicated in November 1982, was not only to honor the dead but for the living, "for the guy who has been stigmatized and needs that cleansing," said Hubert Brucker, standing by the wall one spring day in 1983. A former Army lieutenant, Brucker saw heavy fighting at Dak To in 1967. He cannot forget a final, horrific farewell to men who had been his friends. "We were there three days, couldn't get the helicopters in. The bodies were rotting in the sun. They got this cargo net. There must have been thirty bodies. As the cargo net swung back and forth, fluid and blood sprayed down from the sky. Arms and legs were falling out. . . ." Some would have combat veterans keep such nightmares to themselves. But wars are not marble monuments and dress uniforms. For Brucker, as well as many others, being forced to hide those memories by an unsympathetic public took its toll. Now a successful businessman, Brucker said, "Some of us have made it, but a lot haven't."

It was not just the homecoming that caused problems for many veterans. Revisionists and veterans who supported the war do not like to hear of the many veterans who feel a guilt about Vietnam, but one VA study shows that 33 percent of the younger veterans (those in the

Vietnam Generation age group) expressed a sense of shame or guilt about Vietnam—at the same time expressing pride in their individual performance. The study concluded that the representation of veterans as being consumed by guilt is a myth—pointing out that two thirds reject the statement "It is shameful what my country did to the Vietnamese people." However, when you study _only_ the young, who comprise the Vietnam Generation, the numbers change dramatically. Only 7 percent of the older veterans said they were not always proud to wear their uniforms while home on leave, as opposed to nearly half of the younger veterans.

Similarly, younger veterans far more often expressed guilt or shame—33 percent to 16 percent, respectively. The study concluded that "A sense of guilt or shame about Vietnam is fairly common among younger veterans. It seems highly unlikely that similar attitudes would be found among veterans of any of America's earlier wars."[2]

Another major point differentiates Vietnam from past wars. Vietnam-era veterans of the Vietnam Generation, now in their thirties, "are decidedly negative in their assessment of American involvement in the Vietnam conflict," concluded a major 1980 study. However, "above age forty-four [in 1980] a clear majority of Vietnam-era veterans believe that their country did the right thing in getting involved in the fighting in Vietnam." Moreover, the difference in generational attitudes carries over in how they regard their own service. While 90 percent of Vietnam-era veterans say they are glad to have served their country, that number drops sharply to 64 percent among men in the Vietnam Generation. An ambivalence and sense of duty courses through these answers however. No matter how they felt about the war, two thirds of Vietnam veterans who were in the war zone said they would serve again.[3]

"If my own postwar experiences and those of other veterans I've talked to are typical, the main unresolved problem is guilt, a triple burden of guilt," wrote Phil Caputo, author of _A Rumor of War_. "There is the guilt all soldiers feel for having broken the taboo against killing, a guilt as old as war itself. Add to this the soldier's sense of shame for having fought in actions that resulted, indirectly or directly, in the deaths of civilians. Then pile on top of that an attitude of social opprobrium, an attitude that made the fighting men feel personally morally responsible for the war, and you get your proverbial walking time bomb. . . ."[4]

Other veterans, who felt the war was right or did not participate in acts that bothered them, do not manifest such guilt reactions—but they can feel stress nonetheless. As one psychiatrist and veterans' counselor said, "*Antiwar* veterans are troubled because they experienced Vietnam as an atrocity and believe they did terrible things to the Vietnamese for no good reason. *Pro-war* veterans feel that our government and our military betrayed them for cynical purposes by sending them over there and not letting them win."

In considering both the generation gap of the 1960s and the sense of profound patriotism that prompted many to enlist, the timing of Vietnam must be stressed. In many ways the young men of that generation were destined to be marked by their fathers' World War II memories. The war of their fathers was history's anomaly; America's one black-and-white, good-versus-evil war of the twentieth century. And it was *the war* that touched and motivated the Vietnam soldier, the war they heard about from infancy, not the more recent, murkier, and far less glamorous Korea. Had Vietnam come later—had the fathers of a Vietnam Generation been *Korean* veterans—perhaps that reflexive blind patriotism would have been less strong. Conversely, many young men who chose not to go to Vietnam had to battle the heartbreak and anger of fathers who remembered a time of simpler choices, when you went to war without question. Only years later would some reconcile with their sons, recognizing in retrospect that Vietnam was different.

Lines of combat were blurred. It was a war of intense guerrilla fighting, as well as major battles with NVA forces, but seldom conventional frontline maneuvers. Veterans themselves go through a litmus test of who was and wasn't in combat. Purists scoff at the cushy world of Saigon posts, while some who were in base camps argue that without front lines all were adversely affected by the fear of attack.

"Complete safety was always relative in Vietnam and therefore combat paranoia was endemic," comments Clark Smith in *Strangers at Home*. Others argue that less than one out of three who served in the war zone saw action. Yet another study theorizes the opposite: "Exposure to at least moderate levels of combat was the rule, not the exception, in Vietnam."[5]

Being in the rear was no protection against rocket attacks or emotional wounds. To this day, nurses and medics remain shattered by their memories of the dead and dying and wounded. Men who served as grim accountants of the dead in graves registration and never fired a shot were profoundly affected by their nightmare task of filing the dead.

For the combat solider, relentless guerrilla warfare caused isolation and months of jungle combat with an unseen enemy. Above all, the soldier did not know who the enemy was. The farmer by day was the soldier by night; the smiling mamasan was often a Viet Cong sympathizer. Soldiers in the field lived in a constant state of nervousness. No civilian could be trusted.

In heavily Viet Cong-controlled territory, killing civilians was hardly unique; many, including children, were armed enemies. The dehumanizing endemic to warfare had begun in boot camp when GIs were taught to "waste gooks and dinks."

In order to make civilian death acceptable, "the mere gook syndrome" prevailed. Phrases were invented to take the place of death. Instead of someone being killed, he was "wasted." (This inventiveness is common in war. In *All Quiet on the Western Front:* "When a man dies, then we say he has nipped off his turd. That keeps us from going mad; as long as we take it that way, we maintain our own resistance.")

In World War II it was Japs and Nips; in World War I it was Huns and Krauts. When an enemy was "wasted" in Vietnam, he or she was "merely a gook anyway." After seeing buddies led into ambush by villagers, after seeing them slaughtered, many soldiers retaliated. *Breaker Morant*, the brilliant Australian film about the Boer War, in its way does more to explain Vietnam warfare than an overblown extravaganza such as *Apocalypse Now*.

"It's a new kind of war, for a new century," says Australian officer, Harry ("Breaker") Morant, just before he is executed for killing civilians who had mutilated his best friend. Boers invented a new word for the men and women civilians wearing no uniforms, who stealthily and persistently fought the enemy: "commando." "They are people from small towns, they shoot at us from paddocks. Some of them are women, some of them are children, and some of them are missionaries," says Morant.

The rules of war did not apply: "We fought the Boer the way *he* fought us."

Sixty-five years later, the same issues as those in *Breaker Morant* were examined at many trials of Vietnam soldiers: in a remote guerrilla war, where the enemy wears no uniform and plays by no rules, where ambiguous orders come from desk-bound officers remote to the realities of that kind of warfare, where does combat end and murder begin?

Seventy-one Americans were convicted of murdering Vietnamese noncombatants. Thousands more tell of having to fire on villages or of not being sure who they killed. The most extreme case was that of Lieutenant William Calley, convicted of systematically rounding up civilians and gunning them down by the score. Many veterans insist

My Lai was an aberration, others say it was not. Other cases were more ambiguous, conflicting, and, ultimately, heartbreaking for many of the young grunts who were, truly, "following orders."

Another difference was the attitude of the public toward Vietnam's carnage. Daily television coverage was in stark contrast to the highly censored coverage of World War II. For example, the first published photo of a dead American World War II soldier was not until 1944— a warrior face down in the sands of New Guinea. In this war, Americans were treated to pictures of Vietnam marines of the "Zippo brigades" torching hooches, sending out napalm's fiery flare. Many Americans, viewing such grisly realities of war from the remoteness of their living rooms, concluded that the men in Vietnam were somehow morbidly different from those warriors of the past. This is, of course, untrue.

Americans, steeped in the worst of Vietnam's war—the atrocity trials, the hamlets leveled—knew far less about the marines, for example, who risked their lives to help Viet Cong-surrounded villagers.

The hatreds of war are difficult to understand when viewed from the safe morality of civilian life. Listen to Anne M. Auger, a former nurse in Vietnam: "The only time I've ever felt hate and rage enough to murder was when I was expected to treat an injured NVA [North Vietnamese Army soldier] who had just *killed* several GIs. I couldn't go near him, or touch him, or treat him because I knew without a doubt that I'd put my hands around his throat and *strangle* him. This intense emotion scared me to death." Now, a decade later, she says, "I'm *still* scared of experiencing it again. I had tremendously conflicting thoughts: 1. I *hate* this man. 2. I want to *kill* him. 3. I'm scared of these overwhelming and almost uncontrollable feelings. 4. I am a nurse: I vowed to help *all* sick people. 5. I must be worthless as a nurse because I can't bring myself to help this patient—and worthless as a human being because I want to kill another."

This from a good Catholic young woman.

"War changes men's natures," says the lawyer, pleading for the three soldiers in *Breaker Morant.* "The barbarities of war are seldom committed by abnormal men. The tragedy of war is these barbarous acts are committed by normal men in abnormal situations. . . ."

Off the field of battle, back home, soldiers have time to reflect. After World War II, sleepless nights and doubts came to young men once taught "Thou shalt not kill."

However, public attitude played a major role in expunging traumatic memories. Dr. Jack Ewalt, the VA's chief psychiatrist, counseled World War II veterans. They spoke of nightmares, of bombing

villages and knowing they had killed civilians. Dresden and countless lesser horrors lingered. But everyone was telling them that they
were heroes. Buying them beers at the club or tavern. Small town car
dealers saved the best cars "for the boys when they came home."
Pretty young women were hugging them in the streets. If they ever
hinted that they might have done something wrong "over there,"
they were bathed in the approval of home. Ewalt marks this as a
major, significant difference for Vietnam veterans. "Those poor
suckers were taught to fight and then yelled at for it."

Unrelieved combat was another significant difference. In World War
II, the Marine "Battle Cry" Division was in the South Pacific for
three years—but in combat a total of six weeks. Tarawa was described as a seventy-nine-hour, brutal, mad moment in history. But
those who made it out, as James Webb, author of *Fields of Fire*, said,
"could go down to Australia. They could get drunk, get laid, could
refurbish, could become human beings again." (In Europe, however, some troops spent long periods of time under battle conditions.) In Vietnam, although some soldiers saw almost no action,
many in the Marine Corps operated continually—often in the field
for eighty days at a time.[6]

*A major anger comes from the betrayal veterans feel at the government
for the kind of war they were asked to fight—a war of "attrition" with no
fixed goals for winning.* Hills were taken at great cost of lives and then
abandoned. There were free-fire zones where you could kill everything—and zones where you couldn't kill at all.

In San Diego, Larry refuses to give his last name. He skirts every
issue, plays verbal games for hours. Then at 2 A.M. he pounds at my
hotel door to tell me he is sorry and then disappears again. Larry is
brilliant, with two master's degrees collected since his return from
Vietnam. He can talk in scholarly flights of fancy with the former
chaplain who works with him at San Diego's Vet Center. Yet he is
able to sustain only marginal jobs, such as selling fish or being
a short-order chef. Larry never removes his dark sunglasses. "I'm
getting better," he says with a soft smile. "I used to wear hats all
the time."

After much patient waiting, there is, finally, one small break-
through to Larry's feelings. He talks of Khe Sanh and how the Marines took it and held it for days and how friends were killed there.
"And *then* they *abandoned* it. *Those fuckers abandoned it!* We took it,
we won it, we died there, and then those fuckers abandoned it.
That's what our lives meant to our government."

Disillusionment with the country's leaders runs deep. In one
major study, 76 percent of the Vietnam veterans agreed that "Our

political leaders in Washington deliberately misled the American people about the way the war in Vietnam was going."

Above all, body counts became a perverted measurement for victory. They were often inflated, faked, or served as an incentive for further, needless killing. The common saying was: "If it's dead, it's VC."

Vietnam grunts and groundpounders tell terrible, demoralizing stories: about officers pushing for success in the form of more body counts, of charging on when there were no goals anyone could possibly understand.

Jack McCloskey, a wounded and decorated veteran leader of the San Francisco Vet Center, says that body counts haunt veterans to this day. "They would set up competition. The company that came in with the biggest body count would be given in-country R and R or an extra case of beer. Now, if you're telling a nineteen-year-old kid it's okay to waste people and he will be *rewarded* for it, what do you think *that* does to his psyche?" Over there it was orders. Now, years later, they're reflecting on it.

The warriors of Vietnam were among America's youngest. The average age was 19 as opposed to 25.8 for World War II.[7] "What did I need with shaving equipment?" wondered one marine when they handed it out at the Marine Corps Recruit Depot at Paris Island. "I was only seventeen. I didn't have hair under my *arms,* let alone my face."

Psychiatrists and sociologists who have studied the Vietnam veteran see their youth as fundamental to understanding why many feel emotionally bereft. At a time when they should have been freeing themselves from parents, making career choices and early attempts at sexual intimacy, learning about *themselves,* adolescence essentially stopped for them. Teenage warriors in Vietnam were denied that "psychological moratorium" of adolescence; the unreal reality of war halted a natural progression of youth to manhood. "Forming a coherent sense of ego identity" at this point is "paramount" to that growth, wrote Dr. John P. Wilson, one of the foremost authorities on Vietnam veterans.[8]

There are precedents, of course, for sending the young. The Civil War, as it raged on, took youths barely out of grammar school—and other countries, ravaged by battles on their own soil, have also had their "War of Children." Remarque, in *All Quiet on the Western Front,* tells of the unspoken thoughts of Paul, saying farewell to his mother on his last leave.

"Ah! Mother, Mother! You still think I am a child—why can I not put my head in your lap and weep? Why have I always to be strong and self-controlled? I would like to weep and be comforted too, in-

deed, I am little more than a child; in the wardrobe still hang short,
boy's trousers—it is such a little time ago, why is it over?"

Paul of 1918 and the teenagers of Vietnam were kindred youths.
*Something new was tried in Vietnam—fighting the war in one-year
hitches, creating "short-timer's mentality."* Various phrases were invented for the remaining length of time in the country. A "one-digit
midget" was so "short" that he had anything under ten days left.

The idea behind the one-year tour was to make fighting in Vietnam more palatable.

World War II soldiers, once assigned to a fighting unit, could look
forward to release from danger only through death or wounds or,
hopefully, a cessation of war. This resulted in a sensation of "end-
lessness" and "hopelessness" so depressing and widespread in its
effects that it eventually prompted the high command to institute
fixed one-year terms of combat battle. Thus began the controversial
"Vietnam Year."[9]

While some World War II veterans called Vietnam soldiers "candy
asses," sissies fighting one-year hitches, the experiment proved disastrous in many cases. The prospect of leaving as your year came to
an end created enormous tension and fear. Soldiers would do anything to keep from fighting in their final days. Leaving created both
joy at going home and a conflicting "survival guilt" as buddies were
left behind.

*This was the first war in which drugs were plentiful—especially in the
later stages.* Keegan writes that alcohol has long been "an inseparable
part both of preparation for battle and of combat itself. Alcohol . . .
depresses the self-protective reflexes and so induces the appearance
and feeling of courage. Other drugs reproduce this effect, notably
marijuana; the American Army's widespread addiction to it in Vietnam, deeply troubling though it was to the conscience of the nation,
may therefore be seen, if not as a natural, certainly as a time-honored
response to the uncertainties with which battle racks the soldiers."

James sits in the Coolbreezes restaurant, just a few blocks from the
Congress that long ignored special legislation to aid Vietnam veterans. He is seeking help at the Vet Center across the street. "I
wasn't on nothin' when I went there, but in Vietnam you had a
choice: getting high on hard drugs or hard liquor. Heroin was plentiful, falling out of trees. You see someone get blown away and, hey,
you smoke some OJs [Opium Joints, of very strong quality] and,
hey, man, that's cool."

Many came home addicted—including the all American farm boy.
A Harris survey in 1971 showed 26 percent of Vietnam veterans had

used drugs after returning from the war, about 7 percent had used heroin or cocaine, about 5 percent had used heroin. Some 325,000 Vietnam-era veterans had taken heroin since being discharged. One New York City Mayor's Office for Veterans Action estimate: between 30,000 and 45,000 Vietnam veterans in New York are heroin addicts. Of those who saw heavy combat, 24 percent have been incarcerated for a crime, often drug-connected. While some went to Vietnam from backgrounds of violence, many returned from Vietnam changed for the worse, vainly trying to support a drug habit. The voice of a white veteran: "Where did I get hooked? Nam. Why Nam? Cheap stuff, good stuff. Why Nam? I'll give you one word: 'despair.' Now that's a big word, it's damn near the biggest word I know. I got hooked for jollies, to ward off the despair."[10]

It was a loner's war of isolated, private little battles, companies and squads, platoons and five-man teams. No Ikes. No Pattons. "A dirty little war," the saying goes. And it was a loner's return. Unlike other wars, they came home not on troop ships where they could wind down, decompress, be together. They went alone and came home alone. And with the mindwrenching suddenness of jet-age from here-to-there, from Nam to the world.

From firefight to front porch in thirty-six hours. After all these years, many veterans still shudder at the unbelievable suddenness of it all. "I was killing gooks in the Delta and seventy-two hours later I'm in bed with my wife—and she wonders why I was 'different,'" says one warrant officer. No one bothered to examine the incredible psychological trauma this jet return to civilization often created.

And so they came home. Some were eager to embrace the antiwar movement of their peers, growing their hair as fast as they could. Others were driven to make up for lost time. Some were "still in Saigon"; one veteran, an eventual Walpole Prison inmate, recalls bivouacking in fatigues and boonie hats and combat boots with his veteran friends in a Boston park, unable to move on from their nomadic killing days in Vietnam. Some truly put it all to rest, as if Vietnam was some distant thing that happened to them. Others appeared to have put it all behind, only to erupt in anger or violence years later.

An insidious erosion of self-confidence began for men and women in their early twenties who had been given enormous responsibility beyond their years: captains of companies in charge of the life and death of comrades; college dropout intelligence officers handling networks of agents with the skill of those many years their senior;

nurses in emergency rooms who literally became assistant doctors in terrible on-the-job crisis training; medics who learned much about medicine and death and dying.

In many, the confidence to cope in the most difficult of situations was born in Vietnam. In other wars such skills were rewarded on return. The Vietnam veteran found that to many doing the hiring his experience was as meaningless as the war. A former helicopter pilot and successful lawyer today recalls a prospective boss who asked him to take off his coat—to see if there were any needle tracks on his arm. An intelligence officer who got his master's degree on return couldn't get a job, so he tended bar in Washington where he would slip his résumé to influential customers. They all advised him—especially State Department officials—to X out Vietnam. A medic whose emergency room experience more than qualified him for a stateside hospital job was turned down as soon as the administrator learned he picked up his skills in Vietnam. "I could see in his eyes that I wouldn't get the job when I *admitted* I had been in Vietnam," he said. "It was all accusatory." A nurse who had saved many lives—had operating room authority beyond her years—came back to the rank and file of the Walter Reed Army Medical Center and was given bedpan duty. For years many veterans were underemployed, working at jobs far beneath their capabilities.

While there is nothing new to ex-soldiers' complaints about being left behind or overlooked, Vietnam, once again, was different in its "we-they" confrontational nature of postwar competiveness. Vietnam veterans comprised such a definite minority of their peers that they were both isolated and alienated from the mainstream of their generation who stayed behind.

Time blurs how completely the two themes—the war and the antiwar movement—dominated the media in those days. One group not explaining the war was Vietnam veterans. An overwhelming number told the public *nothing* on their return. Not even their parents and close friends.

Their very silence, in fact, profoundly told much about that war and our government's policy. It was a war that was "psychologically illegitimate," to use the term of Dr. Robert Lifton, who wrote one of the first studies of returned Vietnam veterans.

When they did speak out, the two earliest voices came from opposite ends of the political spectrum. The POWs who returned with tales of torture remained for the most part steadfast to our involvement in Vietnam and became accidental heroes in a war that crowned very few. The other group came to the Capitol in 1971 to fling their medals, to protest—Vietnam Veterans Against the War. America learned from this remarkable demonstration. *For the first time in this country's history, men who fought a war marched to demand its halt.* More than 1,000 came. They were mostly the grunts of that war. They spoke of a corrupt South Vietnamese regime, of lack of support by the South Vietnamese Army, of obliterating villages in order to "save" them, of the falsification and glorification of body counts. Many came in wheelchairs and on crutches. Still, they were denounced as fakes by the same Administration that would be disgraced a few years later by Watergate.

They ripped the myths away and many did not want to hear. "My parents told me that if I turned in my medals that they never wanted anything more to do with me," wrote one VVAW member. "That's not an easy thing to take. I still love my parents."[11]

They were dismissed by many—including hawkish veterans—as a fraction of a minority. Yet, years later, I have heard the same views from many veterans who never joined a group but sat silently, only to speak out finally, a decade later. On the other hand, those who supported the war felt that the media didn't want *their* voices. "Early in 1970, I still thought what we were doing was right. I would go on talk shows and no one wanted me to talk like that," said Chuck Hagel. Men like Hagel feel that the media only wanted veterans who would recant.

For years the traditional veterans service organizations wanted nothing to do with Vietnam veterans who had lost their war. In turn, the young band of veteran rebels ridiculed the VFW and American Legion beer drinkers as a bunch of "puss guts."

"The very words 'American Legion' make many of us shudder," wrote Tim O'Brien in 1974. "A place to go to play bingo, to wallow in pride and self-congratulation. But we have no victories to celebrate till we die; we did not win; *our* war, it is said, was not a just war. We are loners. Loners and losers."

Today 750,000 Vietnam-era veterans belong to the 2.7 million-member American Legion and over 500,000 to the 1.9 million-member VFW. The recent dramatic turnabout in attitude by the traditional service organizations is looked on with a cynicism endemic to many Vietnam veterans. "I know why they want us, why they're wooing the hell out of us," says Angel Almedina, who runs a Manhattan Vet Center. "It's because the old farts are all dying out—and they need the money for dues."

A turning point for veterans began in January 1981 as they watched the nation's extravagant euphoria over the return of the fifty-two hostages from the American Embassy in Teheran. Suddenly, all over the country, veterans were expressing rage at the contrast between the hostage homecoming and the silence and hostility that greeted them a decade earlier.

"The return of the hostages stands as the single most important event to benefit Vietnam veterans," contends Robert Muller, a paralyzed former Marine lieutenant and director of Vietnam Veterans of America.

Veterans' adverse reaction to the hostage homecoming welcome startled a complacent country into recalling the *non*homecoming Vietnam veterans experienced. And enough time has passed so that people were able to begin listening. They found that the inequities in treatment of the Vietnam veteran were outrageous.

Many of the minorities and unskilled, promised a trade by the Army, face chronic unemployment today. Wounded veterans were saved in the field often to live a half-life at home; unemployment for them was more than 20 percent. GIs returned when times were hard and jobs scarce. "Veterans' preference" was often not enforced and even then was being challenged as unfair to women by feminists. For Vietnam veterans, because of inflation, the GI Bill was greatly inferior to that for World War II and Korean veterans.

There is a pervasive myth that Vietnam veterans are crybabies, asking for special programs—such as readjustment counseling centers—not afforded past GIs. But, in fact, there was extensive treatment available for World War II GIs who returned with war neuroses. Congress eagerly passed laws after World War II providing psychiatric counseling, both federally administered and community-based.

By contrast, Vietnam veterans sought help for years. It took Congress a full decade after they had returned to fund a handful of readjustment centers—and this is in an era when psychiatric help is widely recognized and practiced.

After Vietnam, Congress, mirroring the public's attitude, treated the veterans' special needs with consummate indifference. Once again, the divided generation played a major part in that response. World War II veterans often capitalized on their war records to win elective offices. However, the vast majority of congressional members who comprise the Vietnam Generation were the ones who *didn't* go. In 1981, of the eighty-two members born since 1942, only a handful had any service. Just five saw combat. (A half-dozen more joined them in 1982 when they were elected to the House.) For years there was no Vietnam veteran constituency pushing for readjustment counseling or Agent Orange studies.

A few years ago, Agent Orange was so unfamiliar to most that when veterans complained of lack of treatment for symptoms allegedly caused by the defoliant that rained on Vietnam some thought they were saying, "Asian Orange." After years of ignoring the issue, in a turnabout, Congress unanimously passed a bill in 1981 calling for preferential treatment in the VA of those who feel they are Agent Orange victims. (The "Catch-22"—there always seems to be one—is that the VA had next to nothing in the way of treatment and is staffed with people who resist the idea that there are any problems due to Agent Orange exposure.) Today Agent Orange remains an incendiary issue that the government prefers to duck.

In 1974 the Educational Testing Service, Princeton, New Jersey, reported that our national newspapers—and the editors and journalists who staff them—had decided that veterans did not make "good copy." One Washington editor said, "Veterans are not sexy. Who cares?" In 1946 popular magazines printed over 500 articles about veterans. In 1972 they printed fewer than 50.

Books on Vietnam were not selling in the seventies. This was not unique. For example, the great literary outpourings about World War I—moving and enduring accounts of man confronting death in battle—did not come until a full decade following the war. It is perhaps only at a distance that people can read of such horror.

Still, there may be another reason why the Vietnam veteran was generally buried by the mass media. Most Vietnam Generation reporters and writers in the mid-seventies were not the ones who went. I have known editors, whose sons went to Harvard and protested the war, totally unconcerned with stories about veterans. Today there are the beginnings of change. Both the public and the press seem to want to understand better what the veteran is all about. And more and more veterans are moving into positions of power in business, politics, and the media.

Today, as veterans are becoming more vocal, more listened to, there is one disturbing backlash. In their attempts to deny, to prove that they have no problems or to *remove* themselves from any taint, some veterans vociferously attack other Vietnam veterans who seek psychological help or remain antiwar.

As just one example of how statistics are used by groups to prove differing points of view about veterans, conservative members of Vietnam Veterans Leadership Program (VVLP), who seek to change the image of veterans and cast Vietnam as a noble cause, emphasize that two thirds of the men who served in Vietnam enlisted. That figure is misleading. Studies and individual interviews show that time and again, men enlisted *after* they were drafted or with the draft breathing down their neck, in the hopes of getting a better assignment.

The VVLP also contends that volunteers accounted for 77 percent of combat deaths in Vietnam. If they take the *Army* statistics alone— without adding the Marines, more than 90 percent of whom en- listed—the view drastically changes. In 1969 Army draftees were killed in Vietnam at nearly double the rate of nondraftee enlisted men. Draftees comprised 88 percent of infantry riflemen in 1969, while first-term regular Army men comprised 10 percent. The re- maining 2 percent were career Army men. Over five years in which Americans were engaged in combat through March 1970, draftee ca- sualties ran 130 per 1,000 as compared to nondraftee casualty rates of 84 per 1,000. At that time, William K. Brehm, Assistant Secretary of the Army for Manpower and Reserve Affairs, said, "We couldn't come anywhere near the 5,000-man level [of men with hard-core combat skills] a month without the draft." [12]

Today the media are blamed—for sensationalizing, distorting, or wanting to make veterans a new pitiable crowd. One veteran railed in a letter to the editor about the "liberals" whose "intent is to turn us into another welfare constituency. Your best bet, pity the vet. 'We are heroes' only if we express our guilt."

Veterans shrewdly point out that many of the psychiatric and sociological studies of veterans are conducted by men their age who didn't go. Some do have an antiwar bias to protect that undoubtedly skews some of their findings. "The men who fought in Vietnam are being looked upon as victims, often by the very sort of people who reviled them—liberal columnists, actors and actresses, academics, the usual crowd who need some oppressed group to pity and cham- pion," wrote Caputo. "Unfortunately, some veterans are falling into this sentimental trap. Having been denied the laurels due victorious heroes, they are clutching at the sprigs of sympathy offered the vic- tim. . . . Most veterans, though, reject this course." [13]

While I understand the anger that Caputo, a Marine combat vet- eran, feels, I think he is painting an incorrect picture of America's response to veterans. If anything, I see not pity but still far too much indifference.

In 1980 a survey on public attitudes toward the Vietnam War con- ducted by Louis Harris and Associates indicated overwhelming pub- lic support for veterans. The public felt the war was a decided mistake, but did not hold the warriors responsible for either the war or its consequences. What is more, the public's feeling toward those who actually served in Vietnam was, after the fact, "especially warm"—and *on a par with their feelings toward veterans of World War II and Korea.* Asked to name the two or three most important aspects of the war on Americans, 33 percent cite harm done to veterans. The most striking of the public's *volunteered* statements about the effects of the war focus on the price paid by veterans. There is a high level of concern, in terms of both direct effects (death and disability) and indirect effects (being badly treated by the rest of society and having employment, psychological and family problems). Blacks are much more likely than whites to cite concerns for veterans (44 percent to 32 percent), as are women more likely to than men (37 percent to 28 percent). Researchers detected a growing sympathy for veterans. Thus, while 49 percent of the public felt in 1971 that "Veterans were made suckers, having to risk their lives in the wrong war in the wrong place at the wrong time," that number jumped to fully 64 percent in 1980.[14]

Veterans may bristle at people having "sympathy" for them or feeling they were "made suckers" in a war that went bad, but there is little indication that these attitudes translate into "pity."

However, giving lip service to concern in an attitude survey does not translate on a large scale into active support for veterans' programs or benefits.

America needs to cure itself of the post-Vietnam syndrome—so often attributed only to veterans. The way to do that is by "reconciling the schism created by the war," writes Caputo. That schism he sees between "moral conviction, as represented by those who *resisted* the war—and service, as represented by those who *fought* it."

That goal cannot be met by reopening the "tired old Vietnam debate between right and left. . . . President Reagan's attempts to conceal the ugliness of the war under the cloak of a 'noble cause' are as suspect as the left's attempts to present it as a crime on a par with the Nazi invasion of Poland."[15]

His point is a good one. However, I have found in countless interviews that it is important for everyone to walk through his beliefs on that war—not for the sake of debate but for catharsis. Only then can they better understand one another.

Ideological and political arguments are more than just historical musings for most veterans. They go to the heart of their sense of alienation or, at least, separation from others.

Both veterans and the American public-at-large strongly cling to the comforting view that we could have won but that "Our troops were asked to fight in a war which our political leaders in Washington could not let them win." Forty-seven percent of the public agree—and 72 percent of the Vietnam-era veterans do. Moreover, of those who saw heavy combat, the number jumps to 82 percent. The country and the veterans remain deeply divided on this central issue, however. Some 37 percent of Vietnam veterans believe that they were asked to fight in a war we could *never* win. (The American public percentage is roughly the same, 38 percent.)[16]

Today, as the country turns more to the right, as hundreds of billions are being spent on what many analysts view as useless weaponry, right-wing revisionists are trying to turn Vietnam into a "noble cause." Some veterans scoff at the idea: "You can't sell bullshit twice." Others feel revisionism has considerable appeal to a country still licking its wounds. We seem to be a nation overly willing to forget—even as we barely take the time to try to comprehend our last sad little war.

Vietnam and its generation are too important for the country to ignore. Vietnam was a turning point. Reverberations of Vietnam will be felt by society for the next fifty years, as the Vietnam Generation moves, once again, into a position of prominence. By sheer numbers alone, they will move on to become tomorrow's leaders and followers. They, of course, present no single voice, but they are a large voting bloc; politicians who can capture their majority will derive a strength in numbers.

"The shaping experiences for this next generation of American leaders were the civil rights struggle and the war in Vietnam—or, more precisely, the effort to end the war in Vietnam," wrote David Broder in *The Changing of the Guard*. Broder theorized that tomorrow's leaders were forged largely in the antiwar movement. Veterans feel—and rightly so—that they have been unwisely overlooked in such a judgment. Already there have been battles for political appointments between nongoers and veterans. A Senate hearing over the appointment of Tom Pauken, now director of Action, is a case in point. Pauken, a Vietnam veteran, was in Army intelligence. There was a legitimate question as to whether a former intelligence officer should run the agency that oversees the Peace Corps—long vociferous in its attempts to protect itself from any CIA involvement. However, Pauken and his forces charged that his antagonists were "antisoldier." The other side—composed of Senate assistants of the same age who had *not* done any service—scoffed "Hogwash." However, the "we-they" antagonisms were palpable. After all these years, both sides had difficulty understanding the realities of the Vietnam years that the other tried to describe.

How this generation is going to play out is an imponderable, however, worth exploring. The questions are many. As the country turns more to the right politically and militaristically, what role do the Vietnam veterans play? The VFW and American Legion of the past have long pushed right-wing causes. Will the Vietnam veteran, as he grows older, be different than those of past wars? Will the divisions ever heal?

At least for now there seems to be one legacy. America's upper middle class did not fight the Vietnam War. Its working class may be tomorrow's defectors. The lessons of Vietnam veterans—unemployment, psychological problems, health problems—are cruel, a far greater deterrent, some believe, than any incentives the government can push for signing up a whole new generation for the next big one.

Many of today's skeptics, concerning United States involvement in other countries, are Vietnam veterans and their families. Efforts to reinstate the draft, our huge defense budget, military advisers in Central America, marines dying in Lebanon and Grenada, hard-line attitudes toward Russia, talk of "winnable" nuclear wars make the lessons of Vietnam as current as tomorrow's headlines. This time the disaffection may well come from the blue-collar world. Middle-class parents of teenage children, facing unrest in the world, may not have the less privileged bailing them out the next time—no matter how "immoral" the next conflict might seem. A draft would surely have to be more equitable than the last.

Working-class youths now share a cynicism with their Harvard counterparts. A shiny silver-and-blue Air Force recruitment poster hangs on a subway wall in working-class Dorchester. The poster is as marred by graffiti as those outside Harvard Yard. JOIN THE AIR FORCE AND SEE THE WORLD beckons the slogan. Across it, in black, is scrawled: AND DIE YOUNG. Already, nearly half a million young men have not registered for the draft—a felony that could mean five years in prison or a fine of $10,000. And 25,000 who have registered have signed a declaration that they will apply for conscientious objector status if a draft is enacted according to antidraft groups. A federal survey of high school seniors in 1981 revealed that 30 percent would try to avoid compulsory military or civilian service if drafted. By 1984, however, the Reagan era had produced a new enthusiasm for the military. Still, that legacy of the sixties—a fear that tomorrow's youth may be asked to fight another unfortunate war like Vietnam— makes many veterans cautious. They relay that caution to their younger brothers and nephews. They regard themselves—and are— among the most patriotic of American patriots. But what many have said signals not the death of that patriotism in their hearts and minds but the death of *blind* patriotism.

The Vietnam War will not go away. Veterans are moving from their sackcloth-and-ashes victim status toward a new militancy. It takes on bizarre forms at times: the bikers, arms ladened with tattoos, in camouflage fatigues, shouting in Senate hearings for their rights in 1981, were tragicomic.

They invoked memories of the most outrageous black militants of the sixties. They were almost ineffective and an embarrassment to those veterans who had made constructive legislative change through years of hard, quiet work. A quiet militancy shows in Vietnam veterans who have made it in the professional world and are now forming networks to further advance other veterans.

It showed in the contentiousness of the air traffic controllers' strike in 1981. One negotiator pointed out that PATCO's ranks were filled with Vietnam veterans. "These veterans were militant to begin with," the labor official said. "Most of them are combat veterans. They have longer hair, they wear Levi's. They think nothing of confronting their supervisors." Vietnam is a big part of their attitude today, he contends, "the bad treatment they got, the unpopular war. They're the ones pushing guys like me into the line."

At first blush, the militant Vietnam veteran often seems an anomaly. His vaguely counterculture attire—the mustache, the beard, the hair over the collar—belies, in some cases, a conservative political ideology. Meanwhile, those who never had to go through basic training have moved into establishment Brooks Brothers suits and sport haircuts in that crisp 1930s look.

Government and management in the future are probably going to have to deal with this Vietnam veteran phenomenon—as they test the waters and fight for what they feel is their due in the aftermath of Vietnam.

As the baby boom children grow into their early forties, the grab for bigger and better brass rings will escalate. Some observers predict that misunderstandings and hostilities left over from the sixties may give that competition a cutting edge. Many a veteran, for example, feels a deep satisfaction at besting some yesteryear draft dodger in today's job market.

Ron Simon, a lawyer who now works for veterans' benefits, went to Harvard, protested the war, but came from a working-class background. "I had a lot of resentment against those rich kids." He feels that attitudes still fall along class lines. "There are a lot of sixties' radical chic protesters who are corporate junkies, sitting out in the suburbs, smoking dope and still thinking they are radical because they opposed Vietnam. A lot of their identity is tied up in that, as if they are somehow 'different' from all the other achievers. They're *conservative* on every issue, for Christ's sake, but they've got this vague identity with the 'oppressed people,' left over from the sixties. I think they have a guilt, but they hide it and still hate veterans—or have a continuing distaste for them."

The divisions are not necessarily divisions of animus. Rancor has faded on both sides. For some the division lies solely in the fact that they experienced a vastly different adolescence. They have been denied shared memories. This is, to some extent, true in all wars. A World War II clerk in the Pentagon certainly had no commonality of experience with a marine on Iwo Jima, but there was a shared common goal.

There are all kinds of permutations of friendship today; draft dodgers and veterans are roommates, women who protested the war are married to veterans. A cultural affinity and shared attitude comes with being a part of the same generation—until Vietnam surfaces and then old differences collide.

Some nongoers say they feel embarrassed and awkward about talking to veterans. Yet, in my experience, even veterans who believed they were mistreated or that we could have won seek no revenge.

Veterans, for the most part, simply want to be recognized as having made great personal sacrifices in good faith. That is definitely one quality they share with veterans of previous wars. Acknowledging it is long overdue.

NOTES

1. *Myths and Realities. A Study of Attitudes Toward Vietman Era Veterans.* Reprinted by the Veterans Administration, July 1980.

2. Ibid.

3. Ibid.

4. *Playboy.* January 1982.

5. *Myths and Realities.* Seventy-seven percent of those who served in Vietnam *saw* Americans wounded or killed; 43 percent of those in Vietnam killed or thought they had killed someone; 23 percent of those veterans suffered war-related wounds. Furthermore, the study states that these statistics obviously "understate the actual impact of combat on those troops who fought in Vietnam. Only the survivors are represented in this sample."

6. Horne, A. D., ed. *The Wounded Generation, America After Vietnam.* A Washington *Post* Book. Englewood Cliffs, New Jersey: Prentice-Hall, 1981.

7. U.S. Army official statistics, Division of the Office of Comptroller of the Army.

8. Figley, Charles, and Leventman, Seymour, eds. *Strangers at Home.* New York: Praeger, 1980.

9. Keegan, John. *The Face of Battle.* New York: Viking Press, 1976.

10. *Playboy.* January 1982.
11. Kerry, John. *The New Soldier.* New York: MacMillan, 1971.
12. *National Journal.* August 15, 1970.
13. *Playboy.* January 1982.
14. *Myths and Realities.*
15. *Playboy.* January 1982.
16. *Myths and Realities.*

What the Vietnam Vets Can Teach Us

BY PETER MARIN

The dedication of the Vietnam veterans' memorial on the Washington Mall two weeks ago aroused the familiar controversies about its design and its cultural and political functions, echoing many of the points of view about the war that remain among us. There is very little one can say about the monument itself. Its clean lines demand contemplation rather than patriotism or veneration, and perhaps no one can argue with that; but they do very little to remind Americans about the actual nature of the Vietnam War—the horrors and corruption, the moral culpability and negligence, the excesses—or about their own country.

One cannot be surprised by that, of course. Roland Barthes pointed out long ago that a culture's myths serve two functions at once: they commemorate the past but also disguise it, they make it both more and less than it was, they erode history and with it the palpable truths of specific human action and its consequences. It is much the same with monuments or memorials. These are the material ways societies mythologize the past, making it a part of memory rather than thought, an object of sentiment rather than sentience. The Vietnam memorial is no exception, and the fact that we do the same thing in America makes us no worse than anyone else; one can hardly expect images of napalmed children and weeping parents to remind us of what the war was really like. And it is true, too, that there are so many veterans currently in one sort of distress or another that one ought not to be overly scrupulous about anything that may, like the memorial, alleviate it.

Reprinted from *The Nation*, November 27, 1982, by permission. Copyright ©1982 *The Nation* magazine/The Nation Company, Inc.

And yet, having said that, one must say something more. It would be unfortunate for us all, including the veterans, if the memorial had the effect of closing the door on the past or trying to heal the wounds left behind—as if, in the words of a veteran I met recently, "everything was all right now, all hunky-dory, we're all friends again and all that shit, and the war itself will be forgotten." For we have not, as a people, really come to terms with the moral questions raised by the war or understood the lessons it ought to have taught us. And we have not begun to come to terms with what the vets are only now, as the war gradually recedes into the past, beginning to learn about themselves and can perhaps teach the rest of us.

That is why it seems to me important not to worry too much about the memorial's design, nor even to concentrate on the horrors of war and the plight of the vets, but rather to reflect upon the knowledge and wisdom that at least a few men have begun in private to mine from the war. I cannot speak here about all vets, or even most of them, so I will concentrate on the men I met this September in Rochester at the first New York State convention of the Vietnam Veterans of America, which I was invited to attend because of what I had previously written about veterans. Technically, what I have to say applies only to the 300 or so vets at the convention, and obviously it is not true of all vets. The V.V.A. as an organization is rather radical, or at least its leaders and several of its chapters are, but even among its members there are many different attitudes toward the past: many of the men are antiwar and antigovernment, but many others believe (or try to believe) that the war was necessary and just and their own roles justifiable. Yet whatever their differences, they have certain characteristics in common; and I have met enough other vets to know that there must be countless others like them scattered across the country, and that what I saw in Rochester must be going on elsewhere.

What impresses me most about the vets I know is the sensibility that has emerged among them in recent years: a particular kind of moral seriousness which is unusual in America, one which is deepened and defined by the fact that it has emerged from a direct confrontation not only with the capacity of others for violence and brutality but also with their own culpability, their sense of their own capacity for error and excess. Precisely the same kinds of experiences that have produced in some vets the complex constellations of panic from which they seem unable to recover have engendered in others an awareness of moral complexity and human tragedy unlike anything one is likely to find elsewhere in America today.

It is this underlying seriousness, I think, that accounts, among other effects, for the ways these veterans treat one another. Whatever their behavior—and it is often skeptical, joking, an affectionate roughhousing—there remains an undercurrent of easygoing and generous concern, or care, or what one might even call (how one hesitates to use the word) love.

I remember two instances of it in particular. The first was a talk given by Gary Beikirch, a Medal of Honor winner who is now president of the Genesee Valley V.V.A. chapter. He described his sense of isolation and humiliation in the years after the war, somehow intensified by the medal he had gotten (so much for the dream that "appreciation" will make the vets feel better). And then he talked about what it had been like to make tentative contact with the vets in the Rochester group and to discover among them the camaraderie he needed. What he described was a kind of healing similar to that which some vets in outreach programs and "rap" groups have provided for one another.

The second occasion was the appearance, at the start of the final night's dinner, of a black vet who had apparently walked in off the street uninvited with his wife and child in tow. He made his way to the microphone and, while brandishing a baseball bat, began to speak: "I ain't here to make trouble, I don't wanna *have* any trouble, but I gotta tell you, I need help. I got a wife, a kid, I got no job, I don't belong anywhere, there's no one will give me any help. . . ." The vets to a man had been tensed for trouble, but now, suddenly, two or three came up to him and led him to a table and invited his wife and child to join them, and he became part of their group. And at the microphone Bobby Muller, the national V.V.A. head, whose turn it was to speak, smiled and said from his wheelchair: "Listen, bro, you're gonna come to our big convention next year in Washington, you hear me? But that's a big one, so bring more than a baseball bat. You'll need your heavy artillery."

These are vets who have, quite literally, brought one another back from the dead, often saved one another from suicide. Their relationships are full of a tenderness and generosity that is rare among American men—at least in public. (Sometimes they themselves are blissfully unaware of it; at others, when they notice it, they seem astonished.) I cannot remember seeing anything like it save among black college students in the late 1960s or among civil rights workers and elderly blacks in the South or—oddly enough—among the members of a fraternity to which I belonged in the 1950s, who seemed, beyond all rhetoric, to be genuinely brotherly toward one another.

It is this capacity for generosity, this kind of learned concern, which colors their moral sensibility, as if there were still at work in them a moral yearning or innocence that had somehow been deepened, rather than destroyed, by the war. A few days after I came home from my stay with the vets, a friend asked me: "Well, what is it they really want?" And I said, without thinking, "Justice." That is what they want, but it is not justice for themselves—though they would like that too. They simply want justice to *exist*, for there to be justice in the world: some moral order, a moral order maintained by other men and women one can trust. Their yearning is made all the more poignant by the fact that they still do not understand that if justice is to exist, they will have to be the ones who *create* rather than receive it. They do not yet—not *yet*—see it as their own work, not because they are lazy, but simply because it is not a role they associate with themselves. Like most Americans, they do not have a sense of themselves as makers and sustainers of moral values, even though, without knowing it, that is what many of them have become.

I remember how, at the closing banquet, the vets rose and applauded each speaker, moved by the sentiments they heard. There came a moment when a former South Vietnamese major, attending the convention uninvited, came up to the dais to offer a plaque to Gary Beikirch. He said that someday the vets would have to return to Vietnam to finish the job they had started but had been forced to stop. Without thinking, on cue, the whole room stood and applauded, the vets and their wives and friends and guests. Yet it was obviously not a sentiment most of them really shared, and later they laughed sheepishly about their enthusiasm. What it revealed was how susceptible the vets are—as, in a sense we all are—to rhetoric and ritual and what the moment seems to demand. It is, paradoxically, the vets' yearning for goodness, for something to believe, which fuels their desire for justice but also makes them vulnerable to rhetoric and ritual, just as it did long ago when they went off to war.

One must remember: these were the good children. Several of them had fathers who served in World War II and passed on to them a sense of obligation and a belief in the glory of war. Many others—a surprising number, in fact—were Catholics who were inspired at an early age by John Kennedy's call to "ask what you can do for your country"; in fighting Communism (one must not forget how rigorously at the time American Catholicism was intent on confronting Communism everywhere), they would satisfy not only their parents, teachers and priests but also God and the Pope and the President— all at once. They were, in short, those whose faith in their elders, and in American myths and the American order of things, was so strong, so innocent, that war seemed beyond all doubt a good thing, a form of virtue.

And largely because their belief was so strong at the start—not only in the war but in all authority—their disillusionment and subsequent sense of loss were much stronger. One is tempted to call this an "orphan effect." They were cut off from any sustaining world. Church, state, parents, politicians, Army officers—all the hierarchical sources of moral truth and authority dissolved around them during the war, leaving them exposed without consolation to the stark facts of human culpability and brutality. I remember a remark I heard a vet make a year or two ago. He had said that he wondered if the Vietnamese people would ever forgive him for what he did. When someone asked whether he worried about God forgiving him, he answered, "*My* problem is that I haven't yet learned how to forgive *God*."

When I am asked, as I often am, why the Vietnam War so much affected—and so adversely affected—these young men, I am always surprised by the question, because the answers seem to me so obvious.

In the first place, it is probable that all wars have devastating effects upon the men they use—and these were not men when they fought but adolescents, averaging just about 19 years of age. It is hard to believe that something similar to what the soldiers in Vietnam felt was not felt by the men involved in the pointless horrors of trench warfare in World War I; and I cannot help thinking about what one vet told me in Rochester about his father and World War II:

"He never talked much about it except for the usual glorious things, about service to the country and becoming a man. But every year, on New Year's Day, he would lock himself into his den and get dead drunk. He never explained why he did it, but I think now he was remembering the war and mourning. Once, just once, after I got back from Nam, he asked me what it was like, and then he began talking about his war and what he had seen and how it had felt, the killing and the death, and he didn't really feel very much different about it than I did about Nam. It was simply that he had kept it to himself."

For another thing, although what happened to many men in Vietnam did happen to other men in other wars, the cumulative psychological effects were much greater. War, to be sure, is hell, but the effects of this one were compounded by its specific characteristics, as witnessed by the fact that a higher percentage of veterans emerged from this war with psychological disturbances than, as far as we know, from any previous war. (Without question, the rate of suicide and attempted suicide is higher among Vietnam vets than among those of other wars.) Moreover, the attention paid to the damages wrought upon the veterans by this war has been much greater than in the past.

There are other elements that make the Vietnam War different from and even worse than other wars. Even now most Americans do not realize the extent to which it was marked by arbitrary killing and the murder of civilians—out of either official policy or the casual, recreational or simply half-mad behavior of individual men apparently subject to neither internal nor external constraint. It was a war in which innocents became fair game and in which our soldiers—who went to war convinced they were saviors and guardians of freedom—found themselves perceived by the civilian population as intruders, conquerors and even murderers. Their military leaders at several levels of command proved to be venal, dishonest or stupid, and everywhere around them flourished forms of American corruption and vice—black-marketeering, profiteering, thievery—which most of them had never seen close up before. It was a bad war fought for all the wrong reasons and in all the wrong ways, and one could hardly avoid seeing that after being in it for a short while. All of the death, and all of the risk, and even all of the camaraderie and bravery that mark the lives of soldiers anywhere, even those engaged in wrong causes—all of that was rendered meaningless and unnecessary because the war itself was so obviously a bad one.

And there is, finally, one other reason for the Vietnam vets' special pain: we have, as a people, and largely without knowing it, shifted our attitudes toward war, outgrowing the ease with which we may once have accepted violence. Cultures *do* grow up; just as certain moral attitudes can atrophy, others can develop. Many Americans are no longer able to accept without question or horror the nature of war; indeed, it may well be that in future wars (save for the most obviously self-defensive) many combatants will feel, afterward, what the vets now feel about Vietnam. In short, the vets may be experiencing, as their *individual* pain, the half-conscious tensions and confusions that Americans, as a society, now bring to violence and war.

Therefore, more than veterans of any other wars past, what these men have been forced to confront is *their own capacity for error;* they understand that whatever they experienced—the horror, the terror—has its roots and complements in their own weaknesses and mistakes. For them, all conversation about human error or evil is a conversation about themselves; they are pushed past smug ideology and the condemnation of others to an examination of the world that is an examination of self. They know there is no easy relation between one's self-image and the consequences of one's actions. They know too that whatever truths one holds at any given moment will turn out to be if not mistaken then at least incomplete, and that often one's opponents or antagonists will turn out to have been more right than one thought and probably as serious in intention as oneself. Because they cannot easily divide the world into two camps, and because they cannot easily claim virtue while ascribing evil to others, they inhabit a moral realm more complex than the one in which most others live. They know that a moral life means an acknowledgment of guilt as well as a claim to virtue, and they have learned—oh, hardest lesson of all—to judge their own actions in terms of their irrevocable consequences to others.

This sense of moral complexity seems to me to put to shame much of the rhetoric and ethical carelessness that marks America's political life. On both the left and the right, there is a puritanical zealousness attached to almost every position, a moral provincialism in the midst of which people become magically assured of their own virtue and their opponents' culpability and knavery, no matter what the issue or how complicated the questions involved. It hardly matters whether one is speaking to a conservative who favors abortion or a liberal who opposes it, to a proponent of nuclear energy or someone against it. People seem to believe beyond all question that they speak somehow for God and Truth, and that anyone who holds a different view is not only wrong but also less humane, less human, allied with the Devil. Moral hysteria and smugness triumph on every side; Jane Fonda's liberal heroines in film after film are as hollowly virtuous, as unmitigatedly pure, as John Wayne's heroes ever were. The complexities and ironies of truth and half truth and the ambiguities of moral experience are crushed under the weight of assurance and attitudinizing. One has the feeling that the Jacobins reign supreme and that one's own side, in power, would be no more humane or generous than the side to which it is opposed.

Not so with the vets—that is what I love about them.

But this moral depth, this seriousness, may well go to waste—that is what is most poignant about it. The vets for the most part remain so isolated, so locked into their own pain, that there are few avenues for what is within them to make its way into the larger world, or be sustained and refined by the larger world. If someone somewhere would take the trouble to draw forth from the veterans what it is they feel, think and know, or to convince them to speak, all of us would be better off.

It is probably true, as Karl Jaspers pointed out almost four decades ago in talking to the German people about guilt, that people
can look closely at their own moral guilt only when others around
them are willing to consider *their* lives in the same way. This is precisely what the vets have been denied, and therefore their seriousness—which ought to afford them entrance into the larger world,
connecting them to all those others who have thought about and suffered similar things—does not. They cannot locate men or women
willing to take them as seriously as they take the questions that
plague them.

That is what seems so wasteful, and there is something almost un-
forgivable about it. I have seen similar kinds of waste over and over
in America during the past several decades: among children, whose
sense of community and fair play is allowed to atrophy or is conscien-
tiously discouraged; in universities, where the best and deepest yearnings of students go unacknowledged or untapped; even in literature,
where, with very few exceptions, the capacities for generosity and
concern which abound unrecognized in most men and women have
gone unexamined. But for this to happen to the vets is perhaps the
greatest waste of all, since, in many of them, so much understanding
has so obviously emerged from their experience.

What astonishes me is that this situation is being ignored by the
American intellectual community, even by those whose resistance to
the war was based on moral principles and doubts. The quandaries
of the vets, and their pain—a pain they bear for the rest of the nation
that now refuses to confront it—certainly demand the attention of
intelligent men and women. And their quandaries and pain also provide the best subject I know—the most real, the most immediate—
for the kind of moral speculation and self-investigation one would
have expected to see in the wake of the war.

But most of the intellectuals concerned with the war have largely
ignored the vets; Robert Jay Lifton and Gloria Emerson are the only
intellectuals I know who have made the effort to contact them directly and help them think through their condition. And effort is
what it takes, because the lines between American castes are so
clearly drawn, and our acquiescence to them so nearly complete, that
there is no natural way for vets and intellectuals to come together.
There is, in effect, a set of social pass-book laws at work—not overt,
of course, but implicit, so deeply internalized and so much taken for
granted that we never notice it.

Friends tell me that the vets are probably better off because of
this, since most intellectuals are so limited in understanding and
generosity. Perhaps that is true; it may well be that the intellectuals I

am talking about exist only in my mind. Still, as limited as the intellectual world may be, there are people within it whose intelligence and understanding of moral issues would, if coupled with generosity and compassion, be of immense use to the vets. Robert Coles is one, for instance, and Arthur Miller, John Seeley and I. F. Stone are others. A few hours with any one of these men might save some vets months and months of agonizing.

The fact that such contacts are not often made results in a double loss. The first loss is to the vets themselves. I often find myself telling them that they are not likely to find anywhere the kinds of help they want or need, and that whatever moral wisdom America gains from the war will result from their efforts and theirs alone. But the fact that I tell them they must do it on their own does not mean that I believe they will be able to do it. Without someone to listen to them, many vets may not accept their right or responsibility to speak openly about moral questions.

Gloria Emerson points out that the vets are hampered in this re gard as much by their sense of class as by anything else, and she is probably right. Most vets went into the Army right out of high school and were not the kids who would have gone to college—not the "good" colleges, anyway. They were taught by American institutions to remain mute, to refrain from turning into words what they know or feel. They have, still, in relation to "experts" and intellectuals and academics the odd combination of disdain and exaggerated awe that they had in the Army in relation to authority. They were schooled systematically to doubt the authenticity of their own perceptions and sensibilities; they do not think they have the right to speak; they do not know the tricks of the intellectual and public trades; and they do not think that what they say will make much difference.

Most important, the vets lack, because they cannot reach those who might provide it, a *context* for what they feel. They have little sense of the ways in which their suffering is like the suffering of others, so they feel more separated and idiosyncratic than they really are. What many of the vets felt when they returned from Vietnam, for instance, was different in intensity but not in kind from what many returning Peace Corps workers felt: both found the surface of American life surrealistically absurd, somehow less than fully human, not worthy of the seriousness they knew within themselves. And much of what the vets suffer is attendant to *all* those who live on the margins of society, free of its dominant myths; and this, after all, is something about which some writers and artists know.

Beyond that, most of the vets, though confronted by the deepest philosophical questions, have little knowledge of philosophy or of the great and grave human texts in which over centuries other men and women have created a tradition of concern. The greatest thinkers about guilt, for instance, have been theologians and novelists. Sophocles, Kierkegaard, Conrad in *The Heart of Darkness*, Dostoyevsky in *Crime and Punishment* and Tolstoy in *War and Peace* have all placed at the very heart of human existence the issues that plague the vets.

The vets' suffering, in sum, has in fact brought them closer to the heart of their culture than anything else might have done, but how can they know that, and, knowing it, how can they make use of it? For most of them, the deep seriousness visited upon them, which ought to make them feel more fully human, has merely served to isolate them and to make them feel like monsters and pariahs rather than men.

The other losers are the intellectuals themselves, because much of what the vets have to say would be of use to those who took the time to listen. What confronts the vets, after all, is the same moral landscape that confronts us all, a set of ambiguities, confusions and inadequacies that run through our culture from top to bottom. I remember once describing to a woman friend, a writer, how it was the vets felt. "But that's it, that's it exactly," she said. "That's how I felt having my abortions, after the abortions. The same sense of significance and meaning. The same sense of isolation—no one on either side of the question to understand how I felt. The difficulty in straightening it out in my mind, the loneliness of having no one who would forgive me and also understand my refusal to forgive myself."

The vets' difficulty in coming to terms with their own past, coupled with their refusal to put it aside, their stubbornness in clinging to its inchoate power, is not very different from the even more hidden yearnings and sorrows of many Americans about many things— yearnings and sorrows for which we no longer have a usable language, and which no longer form (as they once would have) the center of our conversations about what it means to be human.

What is more, the vets' loss of the myths that ordinarily protect people from the truth has brought them face to face with several problems that beleaguer almost all those who approach value from a secular position: the difficulty of dealing with questions of good and evil in the absence of divine, absolute and binding powers or systems. We have learned by now—or we should have—that humans kill just as easily in God's absence as they do in his name, and that the secularization of value, which people believed a hundred years ago might set them free of ignorance and superstition, leads along its own paths to ignorance and superstition. To be absolutely honest, *none* of us who are secular thinkers have anything more than the tatters of past certainty to offer in regard to establishing and sustaining morality, or increasing kindness in men and women and justice in the world. These questions, which plague the vets, ought to plague every thinking man and woman, and none of us can afford to ignore the vets' experience.

In the end, what we owe the dead (whether our own or the Vietnamese), what we owe the vets and what we owe ourselves is the same thing: the resumption of the recurrent conversation about moral values, the sources and meaning of conscience, and the roots of human generosity, solidarity and community. If the Vietnam memorial manages to remind us that this is what is missing and what must be begun, that is fine. If not, then it will become—no matter how moving or lovely—simply another means by which, in the name of memory, we destroy the past.

Cohesion and Disintegration in the American Army
AN ALTERNATIVE PERSPECTIVE

BY PAUL L. SAVAGE AND RICHARD A. GABRIEL

INTRODUCTION

If societies can be compared in their political systems, they should be comparable in the management of their war making. More importantly, the performance of their military forces can be cross-evaluated respecting cohesion, discipline, and professional leadership. Toward the end of the Viet Nam war, the U.S. Army exhibited clear indicators of disintegration under what appear to be conditions of relatively minimal combat stress.

The purpose of this analysis is to examine indicators of disintegration, together with some historical comparisons, all in the context of socio-military processes which simultaneously appear to affect military cohesion in the U.S. Army. These processes are:

1. *The replacement of a traditional "gladiatorial" officer stereotype with the managerial combat nonparticipant, where efficiency instead of "honor" becomes the performance standard.* The managerial disposition undermines, it seems to us, the sense of military honor. Inasmuch as the latter is involved with "profitless" personal sacrifice, a managerial "commander" may tend to see his troops as a resource base of potential career survival and profitability, not as a moral charge upon his honor and duty rested in reciprocal trust and self-sacrifice.[1]

2. *A radical inflation of officer strengths.* Where the officer percentage of Army strength during World War II and in Korea reached 7% and 9% respectively, by the end of the Viet Nam war officers constituted approximately 15% of total strength. There is further evidence

Reprinted from *Armed Forces and Society*, Vol. 2 No. 3, May 1976, by permission. Copyright ©1976 by *Armed Forces and Society*.

that with the swelling in the officer corps, a corresponding decline in quality occurred.

3. *Destruction of primary military groups.* Military units whose first task is combat resist disintegration principally because of the integrity of the primary military unit—the squad, platoon, or company. The American Army since World War II has experienced a progressive reduction of primary group cohesion until the Viet Nam war, where it may be said it ceased to exist at all. The proximate cause of primary group destruction was the rotation system.

We suggest two interrelated hypotheses:

(1) The United States Army underwent a progressive disintegration and finally an accelerating one over an approximate period, 1961–1971, and that to a significant degree the disintegrative process operated independently of sociopolitical factors in the larger American society.

(2) The disintegration of the Army, together with the dissolution of primary group cohesion, is directly related to the loss of officer professionalism expressed in the pervasive phenomenon of "managerial careerism."

It is, perhaps, useful to define cohesion and disintegration; by defining one, the other follows, since they are reciprocals. Disintegration of a military organization is the emergence of conditions which make effective operations impossible. These conditions are desertion, mutiny, assassination of leaders, and other phenomena at odds with discipline, such as drug usage. Cohesion is assurance that a military unit will attempt to perform its assigned orders or charged mission, irrespective of the situation. Victory or defeat is not a condition of measurement.

It is our contention that a condition of cohesion or disintegration in a military structure is by and large a function of circumstances generated within the military structure. This is to suggest that such factors as the decline in professionalism and the military ethos are more likely to be responsible for disintegration than are factors operant in the society at large. This does not deny, of course, that there are linkages between the larger society and its military structure, for clearly such linkages do exist. With regard to Viet Nam, for example, such linkages were evident in the adoption of a rotation policy designed to avoid a total war footing, the isolation of elites in colleges which acted to reduce the high-quality pool of potential officers, and the obvious restrictions placed upon military operations as a result of domestic political considerations. Yet while we do not imply that military structures are totally independent of wider societal forces, we suggest that other forces internal to the military structure—such as a developed sense of professionalism and an honored military ethic—are far more crucial in determining the degree of cohesion that an army will manifest under stress.

To illustrate the process of military disintegration, historical comparisons are essential. The first comparison is that of the German historical model, an army that maintained its cohesion under enormous pressures even during final defeat in World War II. The German model is appropriate for two reasons. It is a product of western civilization, exhibiting more commonalities with other western armies than differences. In this regard one can point to similarities in organizational and value structures, belief systems rested in patriotism, and conscription based in citizen mass armies.[2] The second reason is that the cohesion of the German Army has been studied in some detail using empirical data.[3]

The German Officer Corps and the Burden of Sacrifice

Despite repeated catastrophes, the Wehrmacht remained so cohesive that it fought effectively until eventually overrun. And indeed, never did it surrender after the fashion of World War I. German speed, discipline, and efficiency in the attack combined with determined, relentless, and methodical resistance over thousands of miles have been attributed to a multitude of generalities including nationalism, National Socialist ideology, and "inherent militarism." Little of the available evidence reveals these factors as important, or indeed that any special *external* sociopolitical factors acted as major influences on military cohesion. Indeed the cohesion of the German Army "was sustained only to a very slight extent by the National Socialist political convictions of German soldiers . . . and that more important in the motivation of the determined resistance of the German soldier was the ready satisfaction of certain primary personality demands afforded by the social organization of the army."[4] German battlefield cohesion related directly to the individual soldier's personal reinforcement due to interactions of esteem and respect with his primary group—squad, platoon, and company—and to his perceptions of his immediate officers and NCOs as men of honor eminently deserving of respect, who in turn cared for their men.[5] German Army officers were very carefully selected and virtually all had education superior to the average German. Moreover, the high selection standards for German officers were maintained throughout the war.[6]

When restrictive standards are combined with very high casualties, the result inevitably is the severe contraction of an officer corps—especially one insisting on rigorous qualification. In 1939, the German Field Army contained 81,314 officers and 2,741,064 enlisted men. Officers constituted 2.96% of total fighting strength; for the German Army as a whole, the figure was 2.86%. The officer/enlisted ratio was 1 : 34.[7]

German officers clearly suffered losses in much higher proportion than their share of the force strength: that is, 2.86% of officers absorbed 3.5% of the number killed. The German Army lost 1,709,739 men killed in action including 59,965 officers. 30.8% of the German officer corps was killed in action as against 26.1% of the enlisted ranks.[8]

In Germany, military rank and social status overlapped extensively, as did the indicators of sacrifice. Europeans keep track of their nobility by way of such references as the *Almanach de Gotha*. Germans, being the researchers they are, have accounted, in part, for the losses of their noble class in World War II. One source lists 8,284 German noblemen; of these, 4,690 were lost in action, or 56.6% of those listed.[9] Noblemen tended to enter the officer corps, and these high losses are similar to the losses of the officer corps itself, but 25.8% higher. It seems evident that, in some measure, the attitude of deference and respect the German soldier showed his social and military superiors was merited in turn by the willingness of his "betters" to assume the costs of status.

Certainly, a main cohesive factor of the primary group, namely the company, in the German Army was the sense of responsibility and performance of duty demonstrated by German officers. Concern by German officers for their soldiers was, in turn, reciprocated by their men, reinforcing the unit cohesion that remained high in the German Army to the end.[10] To some extent then, military cohesion is a function of the quality of the officer corps, its skill, dedication, and readiness to sacrifice.

The readiness of German officers to lead was apparent to the German soldier; however, this capacity for leadership did not hinge upon a dedication to the "cause"—Nazi ideology or even nationalism.[11] This point is the heart of the Shils and Janowitz study already cited. Such findings, of course, contravene the conventional wisdom which tends to lay military disintegration at the feet of a society badly fragmented. However, in all German field operations, one found a readiness by officers to undertake an inordinate share of risk and to regard any insulation of officers from the risks of battle as dishonorable, regardless of prevailing civil societal disharmony.[12]

The fighting qualities of the German Army in large measure can be attributed to the quality of its leadership. The leadership remained, throughout the war, at a very low percentage of total strength, even declining to half of authorized strength at the end. The Germans, therefore, may have achieved a type of optimum leadership quotient, relying on high quality and low numbers of officers. Officer visibility to the German soldier was apparently maintained at a level sufficient to meet the need on the soldiers' part to be cared for by their officer leaders yet not overwhelmingly through an excessive "visibility of brass." Senior officers, while remote from enlisted ranks and rarely interfering in detail with smaller commands, nonetheless bore a substantial share of sacrifice as the data show and as German soldiers were aware; the front-line soldier knew his officers would remain with him "even unto death." Equal assumption of the burden of sacrifice and death, perceived by German officers as both necessary and right, was not the case with American senior officers in Viet Nam. Indeed, quite the opposite situation occurred.

To be sure, other factors affected military cohesion: the sense of Germany besieged, the traditional deference of a subject-oriented culture, a belief that military service was an honor, some secondary influence in Hitler as a father image, and fear of the security police. But all of these remained far less important than the primary group and its respected leadership. An important additional element adding to cohesion in the German Army was the German policy of rotating divisions out of the line for reconstitution of primary groups.[13] Contrarily, American policy in all recent wars has been to maintain units in combat for protracted periods, keeping them filled by the replacement stream, and, in effect, considerably reducing the maintenance of primary group ties in American units and, hence, unit cohesion.[14]

The German historical model during World War II emerges as one of high military professionalism and cohesion. The cement of the German Army was the sense of the soldier as belonging, of deferring to and admiring immediate leaders who could be counted on to accept sacrifice far beyond what was demanded of the ordinary soldier. Using even these minimal measures of cohesive professionalism the American Army offers an interesting study in contrast. . . .

The American Officer Corps

Armies in large measure are products of their leadership: good leadership, dedication, integrity, and competence bring military cohesion. Conversely, bad leadership seems intimately associated with disintegration: a high desertion rate might be explainable, even a mutiny or two, but when desertion, fragging, mutiny, and drug addiction come together in staggering proportions in a short four or five years, oversimplified references to permissive societies and national "fragmentation" because of unpopular wars will not suffice as credible explanations.[15] Knowing well that the heroin racket destroying their forces was operated by their high-ranking Vietnamese allies, in collusion with higher American authorities, not a single senior officer in Viet Nam protested or resigned over the situation. Indeed, there seem to have been no protest resignations by generals for any reason at all while the United States Army was literally coming apart as an effective combat mechanism. Why did all of this occur and in this war alone? To what degree can the officer corps be faulted? How effective were leadership efforts to build primary groups and strengthen morale? How willing was the leadership to share the burden of combat and death by exposing itself to the same hazards as the line soldiers? The answers to these questions certainly would aid in an understanding of the process of disintegration which occurred in the American Army in Viet Nam.

One of the first factors concerning the Army officer corps is its large numbers. Until 1918, the officer corps averaged about 5.3% of the total strength of the Army. In the thirties, officer percentages varied between 7% and 9%. At the end of World War II, officers accounted for 7.7% of the strength, minus Army Air Force strength. . . . The expansion of the officer corps . . . stabilized at about 11% in the sixties, fell to an average of 9% from 1965 to 1967, and then rose to almost 15% of total strength in 1972, a ratio of one officer for every 5.7 enlisted men. Compared to World War II the number of officers had increased by almost 100%. Even compared to 1965, the beginning of the large Viet Nam build-up, officers increased from 9.4% of total strength to 15.0%—an increase of 59.9%. . . . Expanding signs of disintegration seem to be associated with the extreme expansion of the officer corps to levels unknown in the Army. The German Army, we know, was historically "underofficered." Most armies by American standards are underofficered as, indeed, was the French Army in Indo-China.

Where factors external to the military system cannot clearly be tied to military disintegration, internal factors may have the greatest bearing on disintegration during Viet Nam. Some of the principal internal but generally widespread military conditions linked to disintegration, in association with other influences discussed earlier, appear below:

(1) Relative to their number, the American Army officers did not share the combat burden imposed on their men. Indeed, the total number of enlisted men in the front lines was only a small share

of all forces. In 1968, at the height of the build-up, fewer than 80,000 combat troops could be put into battle against a maximum strength of 543,000 in Viet Nam.

(2) The tactical nature of the war and its logistical configuration created a circular rather than linear system; that is, large numbers of officers and men, of mostly noncombat specialties, were in base areas. Accordingly, combat troops were exposed to large numbers of high-ranking officers with conspicuously greater privileges and immunity from harm, this more so than in any previous war.

(3) High-ranking officers were associated with a career system that was manifestly corrupt. Inevitably, troops lost respect for leaders who, acutely aware of drug traffic and profiteering, did little to eliminate these unethical and personally gainful practices.

These conditions focus more on the officer corps than on the Army as a whole, and in particular as the overburden of officers may have affected the enlisted ranks in terms of military cohesion. Thus the remainder of this study will address each of these conditions as they are seen to be indicators, and perhaps even causes, of disintegration in the American Army in Viet Nam. . . .

The Environmental and Operational Milieu

Over some 11 years (1961–1971) of the Viet Nam war we observed that the officer corps swelled to historically high numbers. At the same time the higher quality pool that might have been available for officer recruitment sought a haven in universities and colleges, which themselves became centers of opposition to the war. ROTC became increasingly unpopular and dried up as a source of leadership. We know from available data that the level of college graduates serving in the Army fell drastically during Viet Nam. The final effect of the quality of officer produced by the need to accept officers of low qualifications remains to be examined. That some connection exists between disintegration and a low-quality officer corps appears evident from the data.

Under ordinary circumstances the lowered quality of the officer corps and their inordinate numbers might only marginally have affected operations and discipline. In Korea and World War II, the direct exposure by enlisted men to officers, and especially senior officers, was strictly limited. Basic training involved, primarily, noncommissioned officers and a few company grade commissioned officers. The same condition existed during combat, however protracted. Indeed, the more protracted the battle and the higher the officer losses, the less were officers encountered on the enlisted man's "perception horizon."

In Viet Nam, conditions were radically different. Aggravating the conspicuous differences in the privileges of rank was the rotation policy employed for officers when combat service became necessary. Officers often served in their (combat) commands for approximately six months of 13. Enlisted men normally had to remain in a combat situation for the entire tour.[16] It cannot have escaped the troops that the central concern of such a policy was career advancement ("ticket punching") and not the pursuit of "duty and honor," much less the stress on the traditional image of a commander dedicated to the care of his men. Together with the general rotation system, even more frequent changes in command only increased turbulence in morale and discipline, and the placement of inexperienced commanders with experienced units—the former always attempting to demonstrate their competence as a means of career advancement often by ill-advised tactics or policy changes—created more turbulence. Troops could hardly build much of a level of respect for their officers in this limited time or under such circumstances. And if troop regard for their officers is important to cohesion, then in a situation which does not permit such regard to develop, given both the shortness of time and the conduct of the officers, primary group cohesion cannot but be affected.

Another probable factor destroying cohesion was the excessive burden of battle placed upon draftees. . . . Both absolutely and proportionately Army draftees in Viet Nam became casualties in greater numbers than did volunteers—"lifers." One of the reasons contributing to this condition was the institutional arrangement created by the Army. Volunteers usually received far more consideration in a choice of schooling—almost inevitably noncombat. Further, it was possible in Viet Nam to get out of the "bush" by reenlisting for a longer term and, perhaps, an extension of tour in Viet Nam. The reward for reenlistment amounted to an assurance of a noncombat assignment. By opting for the professional army one could get out of combat; the hostility of the draftee for the "lifer" is then evident and understandable.

Some of the Army higher leadership, recognizing indicators of disintegration, extend a certain *apologia pro vitis nostris*. One argument heard frequently is that rapid changes in society; the dilution of traditional values; and the rejection of home, family, country, and duty in the nation generally, and among the young specifically, are at fault. This forces the Army to bear the burden of coping with youth poorly socialized by parents or with youth who are self-indulgent, hostile to legitimate authority, and indifferent to the national interest. It is the burden of this analysis that such an argument is open to serious question.

First, sociological and historical research reveal that military systems can persist in disciplined and effective form long after the societies that gave them birth have undergone vast changes. The disciplinary ethos of the Roman legion persisted far past the decay of Roman society and well into the period of "barbarization" of the Roman Army. Additionally, the Prussian tradition persevered through multiple regimes and wars until 1945. Accordingly, there appears no causal relationship between the quality of an army and the quality of its society.

Second, the permissive youth who reject the notions of duty, discipline, and sacrifice tend to be concentrated largely in the middle and upper strata who, for a variety of reasons, have been protected from the draft. Privileged classes are not typical of the enlisted combat soldier. Enlisted combat ranks tend, on the contrary, to be filled by lower-middle and working-class strata, groups lacking the affluence permitting either the luxuries of "dropping out" or finding insulated security from the draft at a university or college. Accordingly, the social population of Army combat units in Viet Nam was not radically different from the enlisted social types populating armies in western nations for centuries, i.e., rural yeomen and urban working classes. This, therefore, leaves no other implication than that the military subsystem and its leadership had to be at fault when the Viet Nam armies lost coherence and began to disintegrate.

Unit cohesion and traditional discipline were destroyed in Viet Nam because of the military subsystem itself. Past studies on the American Army reveal that, in conflict, the unit of cohesion tends to be the squad. During the Korean War, the primary group contracted to the "buddy" system. By the time of Viet Nam, the buddy system had been destroyed. The results have been that the field army in Viet Nam was substantially made of military isolates which constituted *noyaus* far more than a "society."[17] Under these circumstances, discipline obviously became increasingly difficult to maintain.

If soldiers committed to Viet Nam combat were forced to function in a progressively unstructured social and military millieu, as this analysis implies, then the lack of effective leadership would only compound the factors leading to disintegration. In the nature of the draft, the burden of battle rested not only upon draftees but also upon enlistees from the lower socioeconomic strata of the country.

Men of this social order are often stereotyped as persons subject to impulses of immediate gratification, sudden urges toward violence, and a higher incidence of inability to adapt to military life. If men of these dispositions are placed in a situation where their leaders seem undeserving of respect and where enforcement of traditional and severe discipline is absent, then the incidence of hostile acts by its own troops against the military system and its symbols will increase. Concurrently, if the military system can not, or will not, provide a set of constraining values that serve as guides to behavior, then the tendency to insubordination will be further reenforced.

Senior officers who directed the war in Viet Nam can argue, it is said with some legitimacy, that opportunities for their frequent participation in battle, and thus direct leadership, were relatively limited.[18] Controlling the movement of hundreds or thousands of squad, platoon, and company-sized units; the continuous operation of multiple and complex communications; and problems of supply, transport, and evacuation may have required the presence of senior officers at command centers in base camps rather than in battle, so as to ensure "rational" command control. If this argument be admitted, Viet Nam operations were not consistent with large numbers of generals and colonels intruding their physical presence upon the battle in progress. In this view, the immediate and junior commander on the ground is the best judge of action and therefore requires a high degree of tactical autonomy; a constant presence of senior officers would then tend to inhibit decision-making and to slow tactical reactions unacceptably. In the first place, the war in Viet Nam was one tied intimately to politics, and especially the political culture of the Viet Nam population whose freedom from communist influence was one of the political objectives of the war. Accordingly, by the terms of these conditions of the war, *all* operations should have been subject to intense high command supervision in order to ensure that the violence employed was moderated commensurate with political warfare. By this rubric of political warfare, small unit commanders should not have been permitted to follow the formal doctrines of conventional warfare which dictate tactical autonomy. Instead, all lower level combat commanders ideally should have demonstrated high competence in counterguerilla tactics, while being at the same time closely controlled according to a strict overall counterguerilla policy. However, neither their military training nor their education prepared American troops for this challenge. The lower levels of the army in Viet Nam were indeed amateurs in a "Peoples War," due to the rotation system which limited the vast bulk of forces to 13-month tours, with much the same thing being true of officers at all levels. Clearly, no great expertise could be developed in guerilla warfare by such men.

Given this picture of the war as reasonably accurate, there was a need for the continual presence of highly sophisticated senior officers in action, not merely attempting to lead from helicopters or visiting from time to time the various base camps. The evidence is that the war was not adequately supervised by senior ranks in such a manner as to conduct the war by rules initially laid down by the Army itself. The rules of which we speak are those declaiming, "winning the hearts and minds. . . . ," "unconventional warfare," "civic action," and the like. In time, the absence of senior officers from actual battle cannot have escaped the attention of the troops engaged. Insofar as the perceptions of troops toward the war (any war) are conditioned by the military system, visible symbols of the system are necessary to morale. Recall, however, that because of the base system, senior officers were highly visible in noncombat areas. It can be assumed that the idea spread that the generals and colonels not only absented themselves from battle, as their minor losses show, but that they, by their actual behavior, cared little about what the troops did so long as the "forms" were observed (body counts, status reports, reports of "victories"). Why should one then be surprised at a rising incidence of "My Lais"? The eventual breakdown of discipline and respect simply cannot be treated with surprise or amazement.

[There is] clear evidence of a decline of officer quality. . . . Between 1960 and 1970, Army ROTC recruitment declined over 60%; consequently, the strength of the active officer corps between 1960 and 1972 increased by 57%. Evidently, the Army had difficulty not only replacing its own losses from discharge, but in finding the numbers necessary to fill the expansion pressured by a "felt" need for an ever larger officer corps. However, it is expecting too much to believe that the complexities of the war in Viet Nam could have been coped with by such men. The argument advanced by the Army is that such numbers of officers had to be obtained even if quality were sacrificed (anent the case of Lt. Calley). Yet, historical experience dictates otherwise, as the examples of well-led German and French military forces show. A large army, skillfully led by a small number of dedicated, competent officers, exhibiting a concrete sense of the military ethic, is always more cohesive than a vast mass of poor officers and badly handled troops. All evidence points to the fact that disintegration in the Army relates directly to the character, integrity, and competence of the officer corps. Nothing in the available data shows any connection between disintegration and such external factors as the "permissive society," fragmenting ideologies, or a "nation being torn apart."

NOTES

1. "Because the military establishment is managerially oriented, the gap between the heroic leader and the military manager has also narrowed. . . . The technologist is likely to be most concerned with the means, the manager with the purpose of military policy. . . . Presently the military academies are deeply concerned with whether they can adequately present an image of a 'whole man', who, realistically, is both a modern heroic leader and a military manager." Morris Janowitz, *The Professional Soldier* (New York: Free Press, 1971), p. 425. It may be that the disintegration of the U.S. Army is associated with the rise of the managerials and their extreme displacement of Janowitz's "heroic" images, i.e., men seeking privilege and displacing men of honor.

2. The general staff organization of the American Army, like that of many other western armies, is a variation of the Prussian system of command and staff. American field regulations governing the conduct of armies in the field are derived also from Prussian influence. For example, see Leon Friedman, ed., *The Law of War*, Vol. 1 (New York: Random House, 1972), pp. xv–xviii.

3. Edward A. Shils and Morris Janowitz, "Cohesion and Disintegration in the German Wehrmacht in World War II," Public Opinion Quarterly 12 (1948): 280–315.

4. Ibid., p. 281.

5. Ibid., pp. 284, 287, 295–297. In addition to the usual esteem held by German soldiers for their immediate leaders, primary group cohesion was further strengthened by a "hard core" which had a "gratifying adolescence under National Socialism" (p. 286). Even this small hard core was oriented toward the military and not toward politics.

6. Ibid., p. 299.

7. Burkhardt Mueller-Hillebrand, *Das Heer 1933–1945, Band III, Der Zweifrontenkrieg* (Frankfurt am Main: Verlag E. S. Mittler & Son, 1969), pp. 248–266.

8. If the average German officer's risk of being killed was far higher than that of his men's, the losses of field grade leadership were even greater. Of 675 general officers in the German Army list, 223 were killed in action (33%). See Josef Folttman and Hans Moeller-Witten, *Opfergang der Generale* (Berlin: Verlag Bernard und Graefe, 1959), p. 85.

9. Dr. Matthias Graf Von Schmettow, *Gedenkbuch des Deutschen Adels* (Limburg a.d. Lahn: C. A. Starke Verlag, 1967), p. x. No similar study exists on American "elites." In any case, the Brahminates of Boston and Virginia do not seem to appear too often in the casualty lists—and clearly not in the Viet Nam war casualty lists.

10. Other data support the sense of duty and cohesion in the German Army. One example was the very low desertion rate. See Shils and Janowitz, "Cohesion and Disintegration . . ." p. 285. Mueller-Hillebrand notes that only 2,600 men were listed as actual deserters in the total Wehrmacht (*Das Heer*, p. 262).

11. See Paul Carell, *Scorched Earth* (New York: Ballantine, 1971), pp. 596–597. In July 1944, the German Central Army Group was virtually destroyed with 28 of 38 German divisions being put out of action. Thirty-one of 47 general officers commanding were lost, approximately 7% of the general officers in the German Army. A sharply illustrative and autobiographical account of small unit warfare and the cohesion of German combat units is Guy Sajer, *The Forgotten Soldier* (New York: Harper and Row, 1971). This account stresses the regard German soldiers had for their officers,

especially at the company level. See Shils and Janowitz, "Cohesion and Disintegration . . ." p. 298.

12. The Germans, as with all armies, had their "bombproofs": civilians with assimilated ranks, paper generals whose rank was acquired by politics, SS rear area administrators, Nazi party hacks in ornate uniforms, concentration camp officials. All these were regarded by combat soldiers with contempt. See Sajer, *The Forgotten Soldier* or any standard work on *SS Einsatzgruppen*.

13. Shils and Janowitz, "Cohesion and Disintegration . . ." pp. 287–288.

14. American combat replacement policies have produced combat units composed of men who do not know each other. The phenomenon of units of strangers is, of course, greater after protracted combat than before. Still, the practice of treating the American soldier as a "component" instead of as a member of a group tends to create a mass army instead of one composed of cohesive units. See Morris Janowitz and Roger Little, eds., *Sociology and the Military Establishment* (New York: Russell Sage Foundation, 1965), pp. 82–83.

15. Those so inclined are invited to read in the reports of congressional hearings the weak replies given by generals to questions by senators and representatives about fraggings, mutinies, desertion, and drugs; and they may reflect upon the prolonged unwillingness of the Congress to conduct detailed inquiries as to why such expensive armed systems were allowed to disintegrate. As an example, see Nomination of Robert R. Froehlke: Hearing, pp. 220–251.

16. The decision to adopt the one-year rotation policy was not purely military, so the Army cannot be held totally responsible. Rather, it was the inevitable result of a politically devised policy of refusing to mobilize the country for war. The Army thus faced the problem of how to command an army without being able to utilize its officers on tours extending "for the duration." They adopted the policy of frequent rotation based on "equity," the expectation that all officers would serve at least one tour. In this sense, the rotation policy was imposed upon the military. Still, the effect of the rotation policy can be exaggerated. The one-year tour was also military policy in Korea during the combat phase, but disintegration indicators were not evident among American units in Korea.

17. See Moskos, *The American Enlisted Man*, pp. 7, 24, 30. See also Little, "Deterioration of Military Work Groups."

18. This argument was made in a personal letter from a senior officer of the United States Army. The same letter justified the discriminatory distribution of losses among RAs and draftees by arguing that enlisted men represent a better long-term investment for the Army and their training should not be wasted.

How Different is the Military Today Because of the Vietnam War?

BY CECIL B. CURREY

Did the military win or lose in Vietnam? The answer obviously depends upon the one giving the response. Three years after the collapse of South Vietnam, Gen. William Childs Westmoreland announced that "militarily we were successful . . . we didn't lose a single battle above company level."[1] Retired Marine officer, combat veteran, author of *The Betrayal*, William R. Corson writes of the military's "debacle in Vietnam."[2] Viet vet Joseph A. Rehyansky, writing in *The National Review,* proudly points out that the army "brought the enemy to its knees by the end of 1972."[3] Maj. Harlan Jencks, army reservist and expert on the Far East, describes Vietnam as "our most disastrous war."[4] Maj. Gen. John R. Galvin proclaims that when our army was withdrawn from Vietnam by the government, it was standing firmly on its own feet. "No one," he writes, "brought the American army to its knees."[5] Prof. Paul Savage, long-time army reserve officer and coauthor of *Crisis in Command,* judges that our army was defeated in Vietnam "by an unkempt, undersized, ill-equipped . . . force of jungle fighters."[6]

Whether one believes that America won or lost the military struggle in Vietnam, even sanguine patriots and army leaders admit that this longest of the nation's wars was complex and that it was "an event we must reconsider with objectivity and care."[7] The army, however, has not yet become serious about such a restudy. There have been no official gatherings within the military—publicized or private—to ponder that late conflict and to gather from it lessons applicable to future combat actions. This dereliction has persisted despite warnings even from within the military that "With all its many wars within wars, like Chinese boxes, Vietnam may be prototypical of what the future holds for us." An exhaustive and accurate analysis of the army's performance there is essential if it is to better prepare itself for the next war. Yet, the army refuses to make "any kind of solid, objective study" of the Vietnam era.[8]

I maintained in a recent book that many of the army's problems were self-imposed; they did not grow out of civilian dictates. At least one military prolocutor, using words reminiscent of my own, warns that "the American military must stop blaming politicians for inhibiting tactical success in the war and must instead study carefully the . . . lessons that are there to be learned."[9]

Precedents exist for such an effort. After World War II, although many of those responsible for directing its battles were either still on active duty or else very much in people's memories, the army's Office of Military History brought together 210 scholars who wrote our official history of the Second World War. The resulting "Green Book" series was meticulous in detail and often analytic. After Korea, that same office produced another series of official studies analyzing that police action.

At present, the U.S. Army Center for Military History has only ten people working on twenty-three projected volumes covering the Vietnam conflict; although it has been nine years since our troops were pulled out of Indochina, none have yet been published. The primary reason for such a lackluster performance can only be military reluctance over having its Vietnam leadership subjected to careful scrutiny. General Galvin rightly criticizes this inaction. Writing in *Parameters: The Journal of the U.S. Army War College,* he notes that there is an urgency facing the army to learn how to respond to similar military confrontations. "We lack an answer to the question, *What was Vietnam, in its essence, as an American military experience?* Even if we wanted to, we could not turn away from the answer to that question."[10]

Our army does indeed want to turn away from that answer; to close its eyes to the black days of Vietnam; to move *tabula rasa*–like into the future. Those who must be counted upon to solve our army's problems were themselves deeply involved in command decisions during Vietnam. They need diagnosis, either from within or without. They have not yet been persuaded to entertain ideas suggesting institutional changes or structural reform. Troubled by spears cast by Vietnam War critics, their usual reaction has been hostile.

Col. David Hackworth, one of our most decorated officers in Vietnam, retired in frustration when his advice and criticisms were continually ignored. Lt. Col. Anthony (*Soldiers*) Herbert was forced into retirement after he accused two of his superiors of covering up war crimes. The "fact sheet" produced on him by the Pentagon contained base *ad hominem* arguments. Lt. Col. Edward L. (*Death of an Army*) King is dismissed as one who began to question the war only when he got orders transferring him to Vietnam from a cushy Fort McNair desk job. Lt. Col. William R. (*The Betrayal*) Corson only narrowly avoided a court-martial because of his book, and the decision not to prosecute was made reluctantly after no breaches of security could be found in the manuscript. William L. Hauser, a West-Pointer with twenty-five years of service, retired only as a colonel despite a distinguished record. Author of *America's Army in Crisis*, which contained mild criticism of the military in Vietnam, Hauser may now appreciate the 1823 comment of Gouvion Saint-Cyr, the French field marshal who said, "I will remove from the promotion list the name of any officer I find on the title page of a book." Richard Gabriel and Paul Savage, coauthors of *Crisis in Command*, have been dismissed as part-time soldiers and ivory-tower academics, despite the force of their words. My own book, *Self-Destruction*, was denigrated as the effort of a part-time reservist and a "damn chaplain who never set foot in Vietnam."

Perhaps as a consequence, the army faces today the same predicament it faced in Vietnam. Gen. Maxwell Davenport Taylor described it well. "We didn't know the enemy, we didn't know our allies, and we didn't know ourselves." No wonder we faced failure then and have learned precious little since."

One of the army's most tragic failures, which underlay and underscored so many other mistakes, has been described by an infantry officer who spent long years in Vietnam. "We were in a war that was a contest for people's minds. Their support was essential if we were to build institutions and organizations capable of regularizing functional behavioral patterns, of getting people active around local issues. In such a contest, there was an obvious correlation between our use of inordinate firepower in response to stimuli that had little to do with the outcome of the war, and the loss of legitimacy for our own government and for the ones we supported in Vietnam. When foreigners kill a lot of the wrong people—noncombatants—they hand the enemy free propaganda. The foe doesn't even have to make up its own. We ourselves created the necessary adverse feelings." [12]

The U.S. military unfortunately thought of Vietnam as a conflict to be won by firepower, by killing the enemy. It never understood that its actions only strengthened the opposition. It ignored persistent suggestions and criticism from dozens of its own mid-level officers, such as Colonels Hackworth and Hauser, Lieutenant Colonels Donald B. Vought, Carl F. Bernard, Jean Sauvageot, and many others.

Even in the midst of that war, the army looked upon its involvement in Vietnam as something of an aberration, unpleasant and temporary, to be borne stoically only for so long as it was necessary to be there. Combat in Southeast Asia did not call for any major reshaping of procedures, nor for any important rethinking of tactics, strategy, organization, equipment. Only minor tinkering was necessary to cope with the irregular warriors, the Viet-cong and their North Vietnamese allies. The *real* enemy was the Soviet Union and its satellite cohorts.

"We do not," suggests the author of a recent article, "care to dwell on insurgencies that make up in moral ambiguity what they lack of the decisiveness attributed to conventional war. . . . This penchant is unfortunate, for [they] have much to tell us about how we fight and with what effect."[13] These words well describe the army's attitude, then and now. At its service schools during the Vietnam era, officer students learned not about infrastructures and cadres and people's wars, but about motorized divisions and electromagnetic pulses and echeloned attacks. Those same subjects are emphasized today.

One officer recalls that "As a career course student at [the infantry school at] Fort Benning in 1973, I was shocked to hear an instructor begin a class . . . with, 'Now that the Vietnam experience is behind us.' Nineteen seventy-three! He was stating an army policy that was never officially promulgated but was known by every serving officer: the U.S. Army consciously and actively is trying to erase the whole painful episode from its institutional memory. In its place there is only the semi-official myth that if it hadn't been for the cowardice and caprice of civilian populations, we could have won with more of the same—more firepower, more troops, more of the bullheaded brutality that was in fact so utterly self-defeating. That myth, and the army's refusal to remember the truth, means we are condemned to relive the past the next time we get involved in a 'people's war of national liberation.'"[14]

Another army officer has put it more succinctly: "Our army's penchant for forgetting nasty tropical wars is well known."[15] . . .

Those who brought us Vietnam, and who there produced the army's self-destruction, remain in control of our military apparatus and its doctrines. They are not eager to have their records subjected to public scrutiny or to admit that they made inept mistakes; not willing to admit that their own incompetence caused subsequent and consequent grave damage to the army—wounds so severe that a staff member at the Command and General Staff College once exclaimed to me that "the U.S. Army was in bad—in horrible—shape in seventy-three. My God, man, it was almost unusable because of the Vietnamese experience. . . . We didn't have a unit . . . that really was usable at all. . . ."[16] Even those who lead our military establishment today would admit, if pressed, that commanders are responsible for *everything* within their commands—both achievements and failures.

Armies in wartime function effectively and efficiently only so long as their "primary groups" do not suffer from rapid personnel changes; only so long as their members feel a "sense of the regiment, esprit, unit tradition and memories, of *legio nostra patria*, of immediate, known, trusted, and approachable commanders,"[17] and only so long as they are well trained. All these factors were repudiated by those in charge of the Vietnam-era army.

NOTES

1. Associated Press wire service story, 30 April 1978.

2. Letter, Lt. Col. William R. Corson, U.S.M.C. (Ret.), to the author, 6 April 1981.

3. Major Joseph A. Rehyansky, "Divergent Views on the Problems of the Volunteer Armed Forces with One Point in Common," *National Review*, Vol. 33, No. 6 (April 3, 1981), pp. 367–68.

4. Manuscript copy of review of *Self-Destruction* supplied by Harlan Jencks to the author.

5. John R. Galvin, *Parameters: The Journal of the U.S. Army War College*, Vol. 11, No. 1 (March, 1981), p. 18.

6. Paul Savage, "Cincinnatus Recidivus: A Review Essay" (discussing *Self-Destruction*), *The Nation*, 232 (February 21, 1981), p. 214.

7. Galvin, *op cit.*, pp. 16–17.

8. *Ibid.*, 15, 15, 17

9. *Ibid.*, 17.

10. *Ibid.*, p. 18.

11. These words were recalled for me by Corson, *op. cit.*

12. Taped interview made in August 1977, Washington, D.C., during research for my *Self-Destruction: The Disintegration and Decay of the United States Army in the Vietnam Era* (New York, W. W. Norton, 1981).

13. Maj. Andrew J. Bacevich, Jr., "Disagreeable Work: Pacifying the Moros, 1903–1906." *Military Review*, Vol. 62, No. 6 (June, 1982), p. 50.

14. Jencks, *op. cit.*

15. Bacevich, *op. cit.*

16. Currey, *op. cit.*, p. 166.

17. Savage, *op. cit.*, p. 213, and Savage, "Patterns of Excellence, Patterns of Decay," *Reviews in American History*, Vol. 9, No. 4 (December, 1981), p. 560.

Part Three
THE ROLE OF THE PRESS:
WAS THE COVERAGE OF THE WAR FAIR?

A stubborn controversy left over from the war still provokes angry debate. That controversy is examined in Part Three. Did the press prejudice the attitudes of the American people and thereby exert undue influence on the outcome of the war?

Phillip Knightley presents an historical analysis depicting the twenty-year evolution of Vietnam press coverage. Formal censorship was never imposed on news reporting, but escalating antagonism developed between the press and the government over what kind of information should be given to the American people. The government wanted the press to report the war as partisans for the American cause. Members of the Vietnam press corps, by and large, interpreted their responsibility differently. They did their best to inform their readers of the situation in Vietnam as they saw it with their own eyes.

Robert Elegant presents his reasons for claiming that the defeat of South Vietnam can be largely blamed on his fellow journalists. He asserts that the war was not lost on the battlefield in Vietnam but in Washington, where political pressures built up by the media blocked continuing U.S. support for the South Vietnamese government.

Charles Mohr defends the performance of the press corps, refuting revisionist claims that willful misrepresentations by reporters during the Tet Offensive caused a massive erosion of public backing for the war. He contends that the American people were shocked into a new level of awareness about the actual situation in Vietnam when they were confronted with the discrepancy between General Westmoreland's optimistic reports and the dramatic reality of the enemy's actual military capability.

Peter Braestrup offers insight into the special susceptibilities and limitations of modern American journalism as they affected the coverage of Tet. He discusses why he thinks the media performed unsatisfactorily and enumerates the peculiar political, military, and psychological circumstances that combined to influence the way the war was covered.

Vietnam 1954–1975

BY PHILLIP KNIGHTLEY

At the end of the Second World War, in order to help rehabilitate the Western alliance, the United States decided to support France in her efforts to cling to her former colonies in Indo-China. By 1950, the rise of Mao Tse-tung in China and the outbreak of the Korean War had, in Washington's eyes, turned the Cold War into a global ideological struggle. In 1954, following the French defeat at Dien Bien Phu, Vietnam was divided between a Communist North, under Ho Chi Minh, and a non-Communist South, under Ngo Dinh Diem. The United States, as part of its policy of containing China, supported Diem, and the first of 200 military advisers left for South Vietnam. This act was to cause the United States to be inexorably drawn into the most traumatic war in its history. However, the events in Vietnam that followed the arrival of the advisers received only modest attention in the American press. There were few experts on the area, and most articles, in the period from 1954 to 1960, concentrated on the Communist menace and the need for greater American involvement. "Battered and shunted about by the war," wrote Leo Cherne in *Look* magazine on January 25, 1955, the South Vietnamese "are too weary to resist the Reds without us." Diem, later to be recognized as one of the most corrupt leaders in Asia, was hailed by *Newsweek* as "one of Asia's ablest leaders" and by *Time* as "doughty little Diem."[1]

It was only after the revolt of army paratroopers in Saigon in November 1960, when some 400 civilians were killed before the rebels were overcome, that the American press showed the first signs of interest in what was really going on in Vietnam. The *New York Times* sent out a veteran war correspondent, Homer Bigart, formerly with the *Herald Tribune,* who joined a tiny corps of full-time reporters in Saigon. The others were Malcolm Browne of the Associated Press, Ray Herndon of the UPI, Nicholas Turner of Reuters, and Pierre Chauvet of Agence France Presse. *Time* had Jim Wilde as a stringer (a part-time correspondent), and François Sully, a Frenchman, who had been living in Vietnam for thirteen years, was a stringer for *Newsweek.* No British daily newspaper had a full-time correspondent there at this stage. A major story would bring in correspondents like Richard Hughes of the *Sunday Times,* Frank Robertson of the *Daily Telegraph,* Dennis Bloodworth of the *Observer,* Denis Warner, who represented various Australian and American newspapers, and other special correspondents, from Tokyo, Bangkok, Hong Kong, Singapore, or even as far afield as Melbourne. But, to the discredit of the world's press, the fact remains that in the crucial years of Diem's decline, with American involvement growing steadily, the only daily newspaper with a full-time correspondent in Saigon was the *New York Times.* The rest relied for their day-by-day coverage on the four news agency men.

These correspondents had a difficult task. To begin with, they were accredited by the Diem government, which saw no reason why it should allow foreign correspondents to write stories critical of its performance. If the correspondents did so, the Diem regime called them spies and Communists, and did its best to censor their copy and, by intimidation, prevent them from repeating the offence. The United States Military Assistance Advisory Group (MAAG) was desperately trying to conceal the full extent of American participation in the war against the Vietcong, and it tried to make the correspondents accomplices in this deception. The correspondents were depressed about it. "[We] seem to be regarded by the American mission as tools of our foreign policy," wrote Homer Bigart in the *New York Times'* house magazine. "Those who baulk are apt to find it a bit lonely, for they are likely to be distrusted and shunned by American and Vietnam officials."[2] Malcolm Browne of the AP decided to put his experiences on public record. He sent in a dispatch complaining that United States officials had concealed from correspondents the extent to which American servicemen were performing combat duties, and his story appeared in, among other newspapers, the *New York Times,* on March 24, 1962.

Diem's government reacted swiftly. At that stage, it did not move against Browne. Instead, it issued expulsion orders against Sully, the *Newsweek* stringer, because of his stories about Diem's corruption and ineptness, and against Bigart for the general tone of his reporting, and in particular for a story he had written about members of a Michigan State University group, who had expressed disgust at the corruption they had encountered.* The expulsion orders were withdrawn when the State Department, alarmed at the uproar that seemed likely to result, put pressure on the United States Mission in Saigon, which in turn put pressure on Diem. But, clearly, matters could not go on like this, and so the State Department arranged for John Mecklin, *Time's* bureau chief in San Francisco, to have leave for government service, and sent him to Saigon to straighten out the press problem, or the "press mess," as it was known in the mission.

Mecklin had an unenviable job. The basic difficulty was that the mission in Saigon had to keep to the line being given out in Washington, namely, that the American advisers *were* only advisers, that the United States was not actively involved in the war, and that Diem, although a little shaky in his interpretation of democracy, was coming along fine. So, although members of the mission knew the truth about the United States' involvement and about the real nature of the Diem regime, they had to lie to the correspondents. They did not tell "really big falsehoods," Mecklin said, but only "endless little ones." But the correspondents knew they were being told lies, and were given to storming into the offices of the United States Information Service to make it clear that they knew. The only way out for the American officials was to claim that this deception on the American public was necessary, that the Communists had to be stopped, that the United States had "put all its chips on Diem," and to appeal to the correspondents' patriotism not to damage the national interest.

This appeal failed. The American military authorities were bewildered. Correspondents had been patriotic in the Second World War. They had been on side in Korea. What was wrong in Vietnam? "So you're Browne," said Admiral Harry D. Felt, meeting the Associated Press man at a press conference in Saigon. "Why don't you get on the team?" Mecklin was bitter. "In Vietnam," he wrote later, in *Mission in Torment*, "a major American policy was wrecked, in part, by unadorned reporting of what was going on."[3] So it is clear that American correspondents were doing their best, during this period, to inform their readers of the true situation in Vietnam. Unfortunately, they were not as successful as they could have been. In the early years of the American involvement, the administration misled Washington correspondents to such an extent that many an editor, unable to reconcile what his man in Saigon was reporting with what his man in Washington told him, preferred to use the official version.

---

* The group had been sent to advise Diem's police force on administrative matters.

John Shaw, a *Time* correspondent in Vietnam (now *Time's* bureau chief in Moscow), says, "For years the press corps in Vietnam was undermined by the White House and the Pentagon. Many American editors ignored what their correspondents in Vietnam were telling them in favor of the Washington version. Yet the Pentagon Papers proved to the hilt that what the correspondents in Saigon had been sending was true."[4]

Perhaps the editors and the Washington correspondents can be excused, on the grounds that President Kennedy's administration itself did everything in its power to ensure that the existence of a real war in Vietnam was kept from the American people, as witness the notorious Cable 1006 from the State Department to its information service in Saigon. This cable warned against providing transport for correspondents on military missions that might result in the correspondents' producing undesirable stories, and it ordered that they be told that any criticism of Diem's regime would make it difficult for the United States to maintain friendly relations with the South Vietnamese government. Assistant Secretary of State Robert Manning went to Vietnam for an on-the-spot survey of the press situation, to try to do something, as he reported, about "the long-standing desire of the United States government to see the American involvement minimized, even represented as something less in reality than it is."[5]

The little corps of correspondents was not co-operative. The smallness of the group and their vulnerability made them stick together, so that, as official sources became closed to them, they could co-operate in pooling what information they could gather. The war was still a leisurely, almost unreal one, something like the phoney-war period in Europe in 1939–40. The correspondents could take a taxi from Saigon in the morning, drive down Route 4 to the Mekong Delta, lunch at a river-bank French seafood restaurant on four courses and three wines, go on to discuss the military situation with a South Vietnamese army officer, and be back in Saigon before dusk; after dark the roads belonged to the Vietcong. The group of full-time correspondents was still so small in 1963 that when they met for lunch, on most days at Brodards, in Tu-do Street, they were all comfortably accommodated at one table.

But interest in Vietnam began to grow. British correspondents, hampered by none of the political difficulties that beset their American colleagues, began to sense the real story there. Richard Hughes wrote bluntly in the *Sunday Times*, as early as March 4, 1962, that the United States military intervention in South Vietnam "has already passed the point where aid can be distinguished from involvement," and the following week Nicholas Turner of Reuters spelt out just what this involvement meant, catching Washington out in a direct lie. "The official United States position . . . has been that American forces are not taking part in combat missions in South Vietnam, except when their role as advisors brings them under fire," Turner wrote. "A Vietnamese communiqué last Sunday said that about sixty communist guerrillas were killed by attacks by the Vietnamese air force. In fact, careful checking shows that only the co-pilots of the aircraft were Vietnamese. The pilots were Americans."[6] While American newspapers were describing "Operation Sunrise" as a trial resettlement programme, Bruce Rothwell of the *Daily Mail* wrote that whole villages were being burnt down and thousands of peasants forcibly resettled in camps, which had a minimum of barbed wire, "to avoid a concentration camp atmosphere."[7] When the United States Secretary of Defense, Robert McNamara, was quoted in America as saying that he was "tremendously encouraged" by what he had seen in Vietnam, Denis Warner was writing in the *Daily Telegraph* that the Vietcong dominated three-fifths of the land area and about one-third of the population. Dennis Bloodworth of the *Observer* forecast the failure of the strategic-hamlet operation and was sceptical about the possibility of defeating the Vietcong. In *The Times* of London, John White explained one reason why the American army was not averse to further involvement in Vietnam: "South Vietnam is the only part of the world where the Pentagon's training manuals can be put to the test under conditions of real warfare. In this tropical Salisbury Plain [a British army training area] new techniques are being developed of 'counter-insurgency.'"[8]

American correspondents wrote stories like these at their own risk. François Sully wrote an article for *Newsweek* on August 22, 1962, headed VIETNAM: THE UNPLEASANT TRUTH. It said that the war was "a losing proposition" and quoted the historian Bernard Fall as saying that Diem's government was inadequate and the Americans inept at teaching the South Vietnamese army. Diem's regime issued an expulsion order against Sully twelve days after the article appeared, and, despite protests from other correspondents, the order was enforced and Sully had to leave Vietnam. A few weeks later, NBC's South-East Asia correspondent was also expelled—for remarking to a fellow correspondent that an interview with Diem was a waste of time.

Over the next six months, relations between the correspondents, on the one hand, and the American mission and the Diem regime, on the other, deteriorated rapidly. In January 1963 the first significant battle of the war took place. At Ap Bac, in the northern Mekong

Delta, a clash between an armoured column of the South Vietnamese army's Seventh Division and a small force of Vietcong turned into a shambles. Three American advisers were killed trying to lead reluctant Vietnamese troops into action; the Vietnamese shelled their own men and narrowly missed American Brigadier-General Robert H. York; 100 Vietnamese troops were killed and five American helicopters were shot down. It was a humiliating defeat, rubbed with salt when David Halberstam, who had succeeded Homer Bigart as correspondent for the *New York Times*, Browne of the Associated Press, Neil Sheehan of United Press International, and Turner of Reuters wrote stories quoting one of the United States advisers, Lieutenant-Colonel John Vann, on how well the Vietcong had fought and how cowardly the South Vietnamese troops had been—an assessment that did little to help Colonel Vann's military career.

The correspondents learned the following month what the American mission thought of this sort of reporting. Mecklin, asked to write a memorandum on the press problem in Vietnam, was blunt. He described the correspondents as inexperienced and unsophisticated, and their reporting as "irresponsible" and "sensationalized." Someone leaked a copy of the memorandum to the correspondents, who digested it but, probably correctly, did nothing about it. They no longer had to rely on official sources for information—because there were now many people who were unhappy at the way things were going in Vietnam and who were only too ready to tell the correspondents what they knew.

One such source was the Buddhist community, particularly after Diem's troops fired on Buddhist demonstrators in May 1963. On June 9, the Buddhists told the correspondents that something important would happen that day. This advance information enabled Browne to be on the spot—with his camera—when a monk, Thich Quang Duc, immolated himself while his brother monks threw themselves in front of fire engines to prevent the firemen from halting the suicide. Browne photographed it all and quickly got the pictures and his story on the AP wire to the United States. The pictures became front-page news around the world, and, in many cases for the first time, readers began to wonder what was happening in Vietnam.

Diem's reaction was to accuse Browne of bribing the Buddhist monks to murder their fellow monk. The American mission's reaction was to try to freeze the few official sources that still remained open to correspondents—not an easy task, because the press corps was now a tight, united, and formidable group. Diem's secret police tapped their telephones, monitored their Telex machines, planted agents in their offices, and tried to follow them in the streets. But, by using visitors, airline employees, and even friendly military personnel as couriers, the correspondents continued to get out the story as they saw it. So, having failed to manage the media at the source, Kennedy's administration went higher up the editorial ladder.

In the United States, pressure on editors to "get on the team" had begun after François Sully's expulsion from Saigon in September 1962. *Newsweek* was bombarded with official complaints about Sully's negative attitude, and in particular about his description of Diem's sister-in-law, the notorious Madame Nhu, as a "detested" figure in Vietnam. *Newsweek* buckled under the onslaught and sent one of its columnists, Kenneth Crawford, a Roman Catholic liberal, for a fresh appreciation of the Saigon Scene. On December 10, *Newsweek* ran a cover story about Diem's regime praising his strategy and referring to Madame Nhu as that "beautiful and strong-willed woman."

Now it was *Time's* turn to join the team. In August 1963, Charles Mohr, the magazine's chief correspondent in South-East Asia, and Merton Perry, who had been a *Time* stringer in Saigon since 1962, wrote, at the request of the head office, a long story on the Saigon correspondents and their battle with the American mission and an even longer round-up of the war situation. The latter began: "The war in Vietnam is being lost." When it appeared in *Time*, this line had disappeared. Things were going well in Vietnam, the article said, and "government troops are fighting better than ever." The article on the Saigon press corps did not appear, but on September 20 another article was published. It was a vicious attack on the correspondents, and it began: "For all the light it shed, the news that U.S. newspaper readers got from Saigon might just as well have been printed in Vietnamese." The article accused the correspondents of pooling "their convictions, information, misinformation and grievances," of becoming themselves "a part of Vietnam's confusion," and of producing material that was "prone to distortions."

It transpired that the Saigon press corps had made some powerful enemies. Marguerite Higgins, the *New York Herald Tribune's* correspondent, who, after her spell as a war correspondent in Korea, had married General William Hall, of the United States Air Force, had visited Vietnam in the summer of 1963 and had been unable to understand the attitude of correspondents like Mohr, Halberstam, and Sheehan. "Reporters here would like to see us lose the war to prove they are right," she wrote. Otto Fuerbringer, then the managing editor of *Time*, agreed, and had discarded the original Mohr-Perry article. He had then called a *Time* writer to his office and dictated the outline of an article to replace it. When the article appeared, *Time's* chief of correspondents, Richard Clurman, who had tried to have it stopped, called Mohr to placate him. Mohr said that unless he could have equal space to reply personally to Fuerbringer's story, he would resign. *Time* would not agree to this, so Mohr and Perry went.

Washington kept up the pressure. News reports from Vietnam, said Pierre Salinger, the White House press secretary, were emotional and inaccurate.* A stream of highly regarded reporters and special writers went out to Vietnam, including several Second World War correspondents, and the columnist Joseph Alsop. All decided that the war was going well. Frank Conniff, a Hearst writer, blamed the pessimistic reporting on American editors. The fact that young reporters, most of them in their twenties, had been assigned to report an involved story reflected little credit on the prescience of their employers, he wrote. President Kennedy felt the same way, and he tried to get rid of his particular bête noire, David Halberstam, by asking the *New York Times'* publisher, "Punch" Sulzberger, to reassign him. Sulzberger not only refused to do so, but also cancelled a two-week holiday Halberstam was about to take, in case it should appear that the *Times* had yielded to Kennedy's pressure.[9] So the impression of these early years of Vietnam is of courageous and skilled correspondents fighting a long and determined action for the right to report the war as they saw it.

There is only one flaw in this: the correspondents were not questioning the American intervention itself, but only its effectiveness. Most correspondents, despite what Washington thought about them, were just as interested in seeing the United States win the war as was the Pentagon.† What the correspondents questioned was not American policy, but the tactics used to implement that policy, in particular the backing of Diem as the "white hope" of Vietnam. "We would have liked nothing better than to believe that the war was going well, and that it would eventually be won," Halberstam wrote later. "But it was impossible to believe these things without denying the evi-

---

* Salinger's attitude on what the press should be told can be judged from an admiring note by McGeorge Bundy, Kennedy's national security adviser, that was found in Kennedy's official White House papers. As quoted in *The Times* of August 3, 1971, Bundy had written in the margin of a communiqué prepared by Salinger: "Champion . . . a communiqué should say nothing, in such a way as to fool the press without deceiving them."
† Mohr's commitment was such that, back in Vietnam for the *New York Times*, he took part, armed with an M-16, in the American retaking of Hué Citadel after the Tet offensive.

dence of our senses." [10] Mohr was embarrassed when he found that his stand against *Time* had made him something of an anti-war hero. "Everyone thought I left because I was against the war. I just thought it wasn't working. I didn't come to think of it as immoral until the very end." [11]

Sheehan said he had arrived in Vietnam convinced that what the United States was doing was correct—helping the non-Communist Vietnamese to "build a viable and independent nation state and defeat a communist insurgency that would subject them to a dour tyranny." [12] When he left in 1966, to become the *New York Times'* man at the Pentagon (where he broke the great story of the Ellsberg-Pentagon Papers), he still hoped that even if the United States should be unable to score a clearcut victory, as in 1945, "yet we may well prevail." True, Sheehan wondered whether any nation had the right to inflict suffering on another for its own ends, and he hoped that it would not be necessary to do so again, but after three years in Vietnam he was—like most of the correspondents—basically still a partisan for the American cause.

In August 1964, General William Westmoreland took over command of the rapidly increasing American forces in Vietnam, the first land-based jets arrived, and the United States Seventh Fleet was patrolling international waters off North Vietnam, where it exchanged shots with Northern gunboats. Navy jets bombed selected targets in the North, amidst international uproar, and the United States set out down the rocky road to full-scale war.

It became a war like no other, a war with no front line, no easily identifiable enemy, no simply explained cause, no clearly designated villain on whom to focus the nation's hate, no menace to the homeland, no need for general sacrifice, and, therefore, no nation-wide fervour of patriotism. It was a vicious war, in a tiny, distant, devastated, and backward nation, against what Bernard Kalb of CBS described as "the most faceless foe in our history." It was a war in which military success had to be measured in numbers—numbers of incidents, of destruction, defection, weapons lost, weapons captured, villagers relocated, areas searched, areas cleared, and that new American statistic, the body count—until only computers became capable of digesting and understanding it all, and machines took over decisions on life and death. It was a war in which, as the desperate quest for a solution intensified, a new expedient would be mooted, rejected as almost inconceivable, accepted, and then dismissed as inadequate. In this manner, the whole awesome range of American military technology—short only of a nuclear strike or the sowing of a biological plague—was steadily brought to bear on an Asian peasant nation.

At each stage of this escalation, the United States tried either flatly to deny what it was doing or to minimise the effects or to conceal the results behind a torrent of questionable statistics, a bewildering range of euphemisms, and a vocabulary of specially created words that debased the English language. To its credit, it did not attempt to solve the problem by imposing censorship. Instead, it mounted a public relations campaign, under highly professional direction, to get over its version of the war.

Photographers from the smaller American papers were brought across for short conducted tours. Transport was provided for correspondents from Europe and Asia—"so they can see for themselves and get a first hand acquaintance with the facts." United States Information Service agencies throughout the world were told to encourage correspondents to come to Vietnam. If they needed money, the American government did its best to provide it, and up to the end of 1966 about thirty-five non-American correspondents were assisted to visit Vietnam in this questionable way.[13] The pitfalls were obvious. Richard West, a British free-lance journalist, who paid his own fare to Vietnam, wrote in the *New Statesman:* "Even those who come at their newspaper's expense are likely to be overwhelmed by the help and hospitality they receive from the American propaganda machine. . . . [They] are bound to be grateful. Moreover, they feel a natural sympathy for the pleasant and long suffering GIs. In consequence, there is a danger of their becoming simply a part of the military propaganda machine."[14] American correspondents were subjected to repeated appeals to their patriotism and the national interest. "When you speak to the American people," Vice President Hubert Humphrey told correspondents in Chu Lai in November 1967, "give the benefit of the doubt to our side. . . . We're in this together."[15] And Dean Rusk said at a background briefing in February 1968, just after the Tet offensive: "There gets to be a point when the question is, whose side are you on? Now I'm the Secretary of State of the United States and I'm on our side."[16]

The danger Richard West saw was real, as was the pressure on American correspondents. Yet—and it must be said at this stage, so as to put the later criticism into perspective—things did not work out that way. Some correspondents became part of the military propaganda machine, and "got on side," but, largely thanks to those who did not, the whole story of the Vietnam War all came out in the end. Some of it could have been told earlier than it was, some of it was told not by war correspondents but by determined reporters at home, some of it was told first outside the United States and then belatedly picked up by American papers, and some of it was told by correspondents who risked life and reputation to report from the other side. The administration's policy proved self-defeating. By making every facet of the war unusually accessible to any correspondent who turned up in Saigon, it lost control of the situation. When there were eventually nearly 700 war correspondents in South Vietnam, it became inevitable that some of them would refuse to accept the official line at face value and would get out into the field to see things for themselves. So when Barry Zorthian, the public relations chief for the United States Embassy, complained that he had not been able to get over to the American public the real story, his self-reproach was unjustified. The real story finally *did* get over, and it toppled a president, split the country, and caused Americans to make a serious reappraisal of the basic nature of their nation.

British correspondents were better placed to write about Vietnam than were their American colleagues—just as, later, Americans were better placed to write the truth about Northern Ireland. But the British press seemed reluctant to get deeply involved. *The Times* would send a man only infrequently and—until the paper's change of ownership in 1967—would never allow him to stay long enough, a criticism equally valid for the *Observer*. The *Sunday Times* sent someone only at long intervals, the *Daily Mail* hardly ever, the *Guardian* only seldom. The *Daily Telegraph* had the most regular coverage. However, John Draw, the *Daily Telegraph* correspondent in Saigon who reported events leading up to the retreat of the South Vietnamese army in March–April 1975, was actually Captain Nguyen Ngoc Phach, aide to the chief of staff of the South Vietnamese army. With the exception of the *Telegraph* and *The Times,* both of which aimed at producing a daily record of the war, British papers tended to give news coverage to Vietnam only when the war flared up. The *Daily Express* is an example of this. The *Daily Mirror,* like the *Express,* had a man in Saigon at frequent intervals, but from 1966, when the *Mirror* decided that it was against the war, it also sent feature writer John Pilger, once or twice a year, to write his own very personal view of the war.

Pilger's attitude was that Vietnam was a new type of war, "impossible to cover without becoming part of it yourself, and when you become part of it you have to decide where you stand."[17] Pilger made his stand clear in a series of articles on what the war was doing to Vietnamese civilians, which the *Sunday Mirror* launched with the front-page headline HOW CAN BRITAIN SUPPORT A WAR LIKE THIS?

When Pilger's Vietnam reporting won two major British awards, his critics said his work was emotional and anti-American. He replied that it was anti-war, rather than anti-American, and that the charge of emotional reporting usually came from correspondents who had been so long exposed to the war that their compassion had been deadened.

British magazines relied for their Vietnam coverage mostly on freelance journalists and photographers, who visited Vietnam for short periods. Although these correspondents were usually not as well informed about the war as the resident men, they did have the advantage of a fresh eye for some of the stranger facets. In 1964, Brian Moynahan, a free-lance writer, interviewed Nguyen Cao Ky, then a not-so-well-known South Vietnamese air force officer, and was so struck by Ky's political views that he took careful note of them for a story. "People ask me who my heroes are," Moynahan quoted Ky as saying. "I have only one hero—Hitler. . . . We need four or five Hitlers in Vietnam." When Ky became premier the following year, Moynahan dug out his earlier story and sold it to the *Sunday Mirror,* which displayed it prominently.[18] At first, no American newspaper picked up the story, but then the *New York Times* carried a report from its office in London quoting the United States Embassy there as saying not only that Ky had never made such a statement about Hitler, but also that he denied ever having spoken to Moynahan. Unfortunately for the embassy and for the *New York Times,* the very day that this report appeared Ky repeated the statement almost verbatim to the Reuters and BBC correspondents in Saigon.

Neither British nor American correspondents did very well in writing about the unimaginable scale of corruption in Vietnam, perhaps because few correspondents could claim to be completely untainted themselves. Most of them changed dollars and pounds on the black market, and many bought stolen army goods, although one British correspondent said he felt things were going a little too far when a United States army captain called on him in his hotel room, within hours of his arrival in Saigon, to ask whether he wanted to buy liquor, clothing, luggage, cameras, or electrical goods. In fact, as Murray Sayle, in 1967 the correspondent for the *Sunday Times* of London, wrote: "Economic activity in the South has practically ceased, except for the war; Saigon is a vast brothel; between the Americans who are trying more or less sincerely to promote a copy of their society on Vietnamese soil, and the mass of the population who are to be 'reconstructed,' stand the fat cats of Saigon."[19]

When the full story of the pilfering, theft, hijacking, bribery, smuggling, extortion, and black-market dealings finally emerged—mainly through United States Senate hearings in Washington and, in the case of opium-smuggling, in a series of articles by John Hughes in the *Christian Science Monitor*[20]—the facts were staggering. In one South Vietnam black market, at Qui Nhon, thousands of cases of army C rations, liquor, clothing, television sets, washing machines, and weapons and ammunition worth an unbelievable $11 million changed hands *each month*. Vietnamese dealers offered to supply anything from a heavy-duty truck or an armoured personnel carrier to a helicopter. One American sub-contractor lost through pilfering, over a one-year period, $118 million worth of goods. In 1967, half a million tons of imported American rice simply disappeared. Black-market currency transactions were estimated to run to some $360 million a year. The Central Intelligence Agency allowed Laotian generals to use its private airline, Air America, to smuggle opium. The United States Army's own police force, the Criminal Investigation Division, accused its senior officer, Major-General Carl C. Turner, of refusing to permit it to investigate the dealings of a network of sergeants who personally profited from their operation of clubs for servicemen at army bases.* And, finally, in the three fiscal years 1968–70, $1.7 billion authorized for the Saigon government pacification programme was, according to the General Accounting Office, lost without trace.[21]

Most correspondents considered corruption stories peripheral to the war itself. It seemed to many of them more important to devote their time to the army or the Marine Corps, to attach themselves to a unit going into action and to write about it, usually in simple Second World War terms. When the first Marines landed at Da Nang in 1965, American reporters spent weeks writing about leathernecks "storming ashore," whereas they had walked up the beaches unopposed. Almost any action produced emotive comparisons—"the biggest since Inchon," "the second biggest since Normandy." This sort of reporting—mostly by veteran correspondents—injected a new feeling of badly needed confidence in victory, and was the model the United States authorities wished all correspondents would follow.

Jim G. Lucas of the Scripps-Howard group is an example of this type of correspondent. Lucas, a Marine Corps combat correspondent at Guadalcanal, Iwo Jima, and Tarawa, has eight battle stars,

* The General, who retired in 1969, later had his Distinguished Service Medal revoked by the army.

the Bronze Star, the Presidential Unit Citation, and the Distinguished Service Award of the Marine Corps League. He was not very impressed with the other correspondents in Vietnam when he first went there, in 1964: "In the six months I lived in the Delta I was the only correspondent regularly assigned to—working and living with—combat troops." He wrote about the mud in the Mekong Delta, the conversation of GIs, the bravery of the Marines, the smell of cordite, and companionship under fire, in short, snappy sentences interlaced with simple war philosophy: "You know it's war when you see a young man dead. Young men court danger as they court women, and for much the same reasons . . . secretly each wants to be a hero, in the finest and best sense of the word, and there's nothing wrong with that, because quiet heroism is the stuff of war." [22]

Some of the correspondents, like Frank Harvey, were fascinated by the technical aspects of the war. Harvey went to Vietnam and wrote a long article for *Flying Magazine* in 1966, which he later expanded into a book. Harvey lived and flew with the Americans piloting the wide range of aircraft involved in the air war in Vietnam, and he described how they operated and what they felt about the war. "Ninety per cent gave me roughly the same answer, 'We have to stop Communism and we'd rather do it here in Vietnam than on the coast of California.' One F-4 fighter-bomber pilot in Danang told me he thought we should start at the DMZ and kill every man, woman and child in North Vietnam." [23] Like Lucas, Harvey saw the war in straightforward terms: "The United States is presently a world leader and I believe we intend to keep it that way. . . . We are prepared to fight, if necessary, to hold onto what we've got and get more. In Vietnam. In South America. Anywhere." [24]

Reporting like this had been quite adequate in the Second World War, where the issues were more clearly discernible. Vietnam was a new kind of war and required a new kind of war correspondent. It was an interdisciplinary war, where complex political issues intruded on the military aspects, where battle success was necessary but where battle success alone was insufficient, a war where unwarranted optimism, propaganda, and news management could deeply obscure the issue. Ward Just of the *Washington Post*, a compassionate and conscientious correspondent, summed it up in this story: "'You will never be any more clear-headed than you are right now,' an American major told a reporter driving in from Tansonnhut airport thirty minutes after his arrival in Vietnam. And the major, according to the reporter, has so far been right." [25]

Assessing the coverage of Vietnam, it seems clear that a primary requisite for this new war was for the correspondent to find some way of protecting his compassion. John Shaw has said, "Things which shocked you when you first went there, six weeks later shocked you no more. It became easier to let horrifying things slide over you. There was lots of cynicism and you could get very hard after a while." [26]

For American correspondents, Vietnam required the courage to face squarely the racist nature of the war and the effect this racism had on their fellow countrymen. It was no accident that the most damning indictments of this important aspect of the war did not come from American correspondents.

All governments realize that to wage war successfully their troops must learn to dehumanise the enemy. The simplest way to achieve this is to inflame nationalistic or racist feelings, or both. Thus, American racism, which had first been aroused on a national scale in the Second World War and then revived in Korea, reached a peak in Vietnam. But Vietnam was an insurgency war. The enemy was physically indistinguishable from the ally. Racist hate directed at Charlie Cong the enemy made no provision for exempting those Vietnamese that the United States had intervened to save. In motivating the GI to fight by appealing to his racist feelings, the United States military discovered that it had liberated an emotion over which it was to lose control. Sartre has written that American racism—anti-Negro, anti-Mexican, anti-Asian—is "a fundamental fact which goes very deep and which existed, potentially, or in fact, long before the Vietnam war."

In Vietnam, racism became a patriotic virtue. *All* Vietnamese became "dinks," "slopes," "slants," or "gooks," and the only good one was a dead one. So the Americans killed them when it was clear that they were Vietcong. "I shot up a Charlie in the paddies today," Frank Harvey quotes an American helicopter pilot as saying. "I ran that little mother all over the place hosing him with guns, but somehow or other we just didn't hit him. Finally, he turned on us and stood there facing us with his rifle. We really busted his ass then. Blew him up like a toy balloon." [27]

And they killed them when it was clear they were not Vietcong. A British free-lance photographer, Philip Jones Griffiths, went out with a platoon from the First Cavalry. The GIs were nervous and opened fire on the first farmer they saw. They missed. Jones Griffiths wrote: "The next farmer was not so lucky. Soon he lay dying among the ripening rice in a corner or the paddy field, the back of his skull blown away. He was somehow conscious, making a whimpering sound and trying to squeeze his eyes more tightly shut. He never spoke and died with the fingers of his left hand clenching his testicles so tightly they could not be undone. 'Got him in the balls, knew I hit him,' cried the boy from Kansas, until someone took him to one side and explained that they do that to relieve the pain elsewhere." [28]

The Americans mutilated bodies. One colonel wanted the hearts cut out of dead Vietcong to feed to his dog. Heads were cut off, arranged in rows, and a lighted cigarette pushed into each mouth. Ears were strung together like beads. Parts of Vietnamese bodies were kept as trophies; skulls were a favourite, and the then Colonel George Patton III—"I do like to see the arms and legs fly"—carried one about at his farewell party. [29] The Americans photographed dead Vietnamese as if they were game trophies—a smiling Marine with his foot on the chest of the nearest corpse or holding a severed ear or two—or, in the case of a dead Vietcong girl, without her pyjama pants and with her legs raised stiffly in the air. The Twenty-fifth Infantry Division left a "visiting card," a torn-off shoulder patch of the division's emblem, stuffed in the mouth of the Vietnamese they killed. Other divisions had similar practices.

Killing Vietnamese became almost mundane, almost like a movie in which the Americans were the cowboys and the Vietnamese the Indians. "Batchelor squeezes off a careful shot. The Marines around him cheer. 'Holy Jesus! You see that? Just like the movies. The guy sagged, then just kinda slowly slid down holding on to the doorway.'"—Ian Adams, in *Maclean's Magazine*, February 1968. Captain Lynn A. Carlson, who flew a Cobra helicopter gunship out of Pleiku, used to drop specially printed visiting cards over his target areas. The cards read: "Congratulations. You have been killed through the courtesy of the 361st. Yours truly, Pink Panther 20." On the reverse side were various messages: "Call us for death and destruction night and day." Or, "The Lord giveth and the 20mm [cannon] taketh away. Killing is our business and business is good." [30]

Carlson clearly enjoyed his work. He was not alone in this. The late Nicholas Tomalin of the *Sunday Times* of London spent an afternoon, in June 1966, with General James F. Hollingsworth, and wrote about it in an article headed THE GENERAL GOES ZAPPING CHARLIE CONG. It began: "After a light lunch last Wednesday, General James F. Hollingsworth, of the US 'Big Red I' Division took off in his personal helicopter and killed more Vietnamese than any of the troops he was commanding." Tomalin described how the helicopter covered the landscape beside Routes 13 and 16 while the General blazed away with his personal M-16 carbine at any Vietnamese seen running for cover. He concluded with Hollingsworth's saying: "There's no better way to fight than goin' out to shoot VCs. An' there's nothing I love better than killin' Cong. No, sir."[31] Set beside examples such as this, the fact that many helicopter pilots referred to their missions as "turkey shoots" was not surprising.

However, the attitude of some of the army chaplains remains bewildering. Those at Phu Cat air base went around in a jeep on which was inscribed, in bold white letters, "The God Squad."[32] A Marine who had taken some horrifying photographs after an operation on the Cua Viet River became worried about the morality of having done so and asked his chaplain for advice. Michael Herr reported, in *Esquire* in April 1970, that all the chaplain did was to tell the Marine that it was forgivable. He then put the pictures in his drawer and kept them. James Fox, an American writer based in London, met a Cobra pilot who planned to become a Lutheran missionary when he left Vietnam. Fox asked the pilot whether he felt any conflict between his religion and his gunship work. "Oh you oughta been here with Father Dodge," the pilot replied. "He always used to say, the faster you get 'em the quicker their souls get to heaven. I feel I'm killing to spare souls."[33]

Some of this side of the war appeared in American newspapers and magazines, but not without difficulty. General Hollingsworth's "Cong-zapping" activities were known to American correspondents before Nicholas Tomalin wrote his story—"Jeez, I'm so glad you was along," the General said. "I've been written up time and time again back in the States for shootin' up VCs, but no one's been along with me like you before." Yet when Tomalin's graphic account was passed to the *Washington Post*, the *Post* refused to publish it.[34] It eventually appeared in the *San Francisco Chronicle* and was read into the *Congressional Record*, along with an official explanation from the United States Army. In short, until the My Lai massacre story, American coverage was weak on the racist and brutalising nature of the war and on the way Americans treated the Vietnamese.

Herr offered one explanation in his *Esquire* article. A soldier from the First Infantry Division had just said that he believed that Americans treated the Vietnamese like animals. "You know what we do to animals . . . kill 'em and hurt 'em and beat on 'em, so's we can train 'em. Shit, we don't treat the Dinks no different than that." Herr wrote: "We knew that he was telling the truth. . . . We mentioned it later to some people who'd been at the Pacification briefings, someone from the [*New York*] *Times* and someone from the AP and they both agreed that the kid from the Big Red One has said more about the Hearts and Minds Programme than they'd heard in over an hour of statistics, but their bureaus could not use his story, they wanted Ambassador Komer's, and they got it and you got it."*

Perhaps the case of Martha Gellhorn deterred correspondents from writing this side of the war. Miss Gellhorn, a famous, experienced, and respected war correspondent (Spain, China, Finland, Britain, Italy, France, Germany), went to Vietnam in 1966–67 as a free-lance. Taking from the indoctrination lecture read to United States troops on their arrival in Vietnam the sentence "To really and truly and finally win this war we must . . . win the hearts and minds of the *people* of South Vietnam," she determined to see whether this central tenet of American doctrine was in fact being carried out. First, she visited Qui Nhon provincial hospital, where a team of dedicated New Zealand doctors and nurses was caring for wounded noncombatants, "under conditions suitable for the Crimean war." She reached the conclusion that

> we, unintentionally, are killing and wounding three or four times more people than the Vietcong do, so we are told, on purpose. We are not maniacs and monsters, but our planes range the sky all day and all night, and our artillery is lavish and we have much more deadly stuff to kill with. The people are there on the ground, sometimes destroyed by accident, sometimes destroyed because Vietcong are reported to be among them. This is indeed a new kind of war, as the indoctrination lecture stated, and we had better find a new way to fight it. Hearts and minds, after all, live in bodies.

Miss Gellhorn then went to an orphanage in Saigon, where Catholic nuns, desperate for funds to keep their institution going under the stress of new demands, wrote their first and only letter to the U.S. AID (Agency for International Development)—which that year had a budget of $700 million—asking for money to build a rain-water cistern. The letter was not answered. "The [South Vietnamese] Ministry of Social Welfare predicts an average of 2,000 more orphans every month," Miss Gellhorn wrote. "Is it not strange that we count and proclaim only military casualties? These lonely waifs of war should be listed as wounded, and wounded forever." In her final article Miss Gellhorn described a refugee camp, "a dump heap," where just a few of the million or more Vietnamese made refugee *in the previous two years* were housed.

> These peasants had survived the Vietcong since 1957, on whatever terms hostile or friendly, and the war however it came to them. But

---

* Robert Komer was the deputy ambassador in charge of pacification, and his story was of how well the programme was progressing.

they cannot survive our bombs. Even the Catholic refugees did not leave their hamlets until the bombs fell. We are uprooting the people from the lovely land where they have lived for generations; and the uprooted are given not bread but a stone. Is this an honourable way for a great nation to fight a war 8,000 miles from its safe homeland?

No newspaper in the United States would publish the series of articles. "Everywhere I was told that they were too tough for American readers." Eventually, the *St. Louis Post-Dispatch* took the two mildest ones. Miss Gellhorn had to turn to Britain to get all five published. They appeared in the *Guardian*,[35] and ended Miss Gellhorn's career as a war correspondent in Vietnam. When she applied for a visa to return there, her request was refused. She tried over the years since then, applying at various South Vietnamese embassies around the world, and was refused every time. "It appears I am on some sort of black list and I will not be allowed to report from South Vietnam again."[36]

Philip Jones Griffiths, one of the few photographers to concentrate on portraying what the war did to Vietnamese civilians, had great difficulty in finding an outlet for his work in the United States. "I was told time after time that my photographs were too harrowing for the American market."[37] When, eventually, a book of his photographs, *Vietnam Inc.*, was published in the United States, the South Vietnamese government banned his return to Saigon.

It was the racist nature of the fighting, the treating of the Vietnamese "like animals," that led inevitably to My Lai, and it was the reluctance of correspondents to report this racist and atrocious nature of the war that caused the My Lai story to be revealed not by a war correspondent, but by an alert newspaper reporter back in the United States—a major indictment of the coverage of the war.

What happened at My Lai is now well known. C Company, First Battalion, Twentieth Infantry, Eleventh Brigade, Americal Division, entered the village of My Lai on March 16, 1968, and killed between ninety and 130 men, women, and children. Acting, the men said later, under orders from the platoon commander, Lieutenant William L. Calley, Jr., they gathered the villagers into groups and "wasted" them with automatic-weapon fire. Anyone who survived was then picked off. "A really tiny kid—he had only a shirt on—nothing else . . . came over to the people and held the hand of one of the dead. One of the GIs behind me dropped into a kneeling position thirty metres from this kid and killed him with a single shot."[38]

A little over a year later, Ronald Ridenhour, a former door-gunner in a helicopter, who had heard about the massacre at My Lai from various members of C Company, mailed, from his home in Phoenix, Arizona, thirty letters setting out everything he had heard about My Lai and listing the names of people who had given him the information. The letters went to President Nixon, to various military authorities, and to senators and congressmen who, Ridenhour thought, might be able to exert some sort of pressure on the army to compel it to take action. Most of them never replied, but Congressman Morris Udall, a liberal from Arizona, telephoned to say that he would do everything in his power to see that the matter was investigated. The army began a full-scale investigation on April 23, 1969, and in September, only days before he was due to be discharged from the army, Lieutenant Calley was charged with the murder of 109 "Oriental human beings" (the number was later reduced to 102).

This fact was made public in a small item, of fewer than a hundred words, put out from Fort Benning, Georgia, by the Associated Press on September 6. The item did not say how many murders Calley had been charged with, and it gave no indication of the circumstances. It is not surprising, therefore, that not a single newspaper or broadcasting station called the AP to ask for more information.[39] In fact, the item passed completely unnoticed—the *New York Times*, on September 8, put it at the bottom of page 38—and that might have been the end of the matter had it not been for a free-lance reporter called Seymour Hersh.

Hersh, then aged thirty-two, had covered the Pentagon in 1966–67 for the Associated Press, but had hated it—"just one lie after another"—and had left. On October 22—six weeks after the first story about Calley and the murder charge—a contact of Hersh's, a lawyer called Geoff Cowan, said to him, "The army is trying to court-martial some guy in secret for killing seventy-five Vietnamese civilians." It took Hersh two days and twenty-five telephone calls to find out that the civilians numbered 109, and to sense that the story warranted a lot more effort and would require more money than he had. He telephoned Jim Boyd, of the Fund for Investigative Journalism, in Washington, and was promised $1,000. He then flew to Fort Benning and, after an amazing run-around, finally found Calley and on November 11 interviewed him at length. The problem now was where to publish the story. *Life* turned it down, even though it had earlier heard much the same version from Ridenhour. *Look* said that its publication delay was too long. So Hersh turned to a little-known Washington agency, the Dispatch News Service, started only a few months earlier by his neighbor, David Obst, aged twenty-three. Obst telephoned some fifty newspapers, offering the story for $100 if it was used. Subsequently, thirty-six of the fifty—including *The Times* of London, the *San Francisco Chronicle*, the *Boston Globe*, and the *St. Louis Post-Dispatch*—ran the story. It was first printed on November 13. On the same day, the *New York Times*, which had started working on the story six days earlier, ran its own account of My Lai, written by one of its reporters, Bob Smith.

Then, amazingly, the story appeared to die. Throughout the following week, when My Lai was a leading story in British and continental newspapers, it was still on an inside page in the *Washington Post*, and in other newspapers it was given less play than Apollo 12 or Vice President Spiro Agnew's attack on the liberal press. It was revived when the Dispatch News Service sent out Hersh's second story, interviews with members of C Company, and it really made headlines on November 20, when the *Cleveland Plain Dealer* carried photographs of the massacre taken by an army photographer, Ronald L. Haeberle, who had been in My Lai with Calley and C Company, and who had settled in Cleveland after leaving the army. The photographs were a harrowing record. One showed a boy of about seven lying on a pathway with protective arms around a smaller boy, who had been shot but was still alive. Then, according to Haeberle, the GIs had moved in and shot both of them dead. But even now, in spite of Haeberle's detailed account of how he had taken the photographs, and in spite of the evidence of the photographs themselves, obstacles were still put in the way of their world-wide publication.

The first objection came from David Duncan, a photographer who had taken war pictures during the Second World War, in Korea, and in Vietnam. Duncan had been to Vietnam for *Life*. There, his series on the fighting at Con Thieu "Inside the Cone of Fire"—had won him the Overseas Press Club's Robert Capa Gold Medal. Duncan, who was in Cleveland promoting his latest book, saw an early edition of the *Plain Dealer*, called the newspaper, said he believed the photographs were phoney, and begged the paper to stop the presses in the national interest: "You're doing a disservice to America." The *Plain Dealer* had been uneasy about the authenticity of Haeberle's photographs and had done all it could to check them. Duncan's telephone call went to the night managing editor, a tough home-town newspaperman, who was not impressed by Duncan's arguments and so got rid of him as politely as he could.[40]

Then, negotiations to sell the photographs nearly foundered. *Life*, having offered $100,000 for world rights, became worried in case it should appear in America that the magazine was acting as "brokers for massacre pictures." The *New York Times* did not want to be "in the position of buying massacre pictures," but it was prepared to help to sell them.[41] The Japanese made a modest offer of $500, and when this was declined they announced that they would simply copy the photographs from the *Plain Dealer*, "because it will take thirty years in the Japanese courts for the [copyright] case to come to trial."* The *New York Post* broke the deadlock in the United States by copying the *Plain Dealer's* pictures, on the ground that Haeberle's copyright was dubious because he was an army photographer and on duty at the time he took the photographs; therefore, the photographs were United States government property, and, since they had been published, they were in the public domain. As newspapers from all over the world began to carry the pictures, Haeberle quickly settled for $50,000 from *Life*.

The following week, the outcry in the United States grew rapidly, until, three weeks after Hersh's original story had appeared, *Time*, in its issue of December 5, and *Newsweek*, in its issue of December 8, carried major stories on My Lai. *Time* called it "an American tragedy." *Newsweek* used the headline A SINGLE INCIDENT IN A BRUTAL WAR SHOCKS THE AMERICAN CONSCIENCE. Paul Meadlo, a C Company soldier who had participated in the attack at My Lai, "sold" by Hersh and the Dispatch News Agency to CBS for $10,000, appeared on television to say he was sorry for what he had done. His mother, who appeared with him, blamed the army. "I sent them a good boy," she said, "and they made him a murderer." The United States wallowed in weeks of conscience-searching.

Suddenly, nearly every war correspondent who had been in Vietnam had an atrocity story to tell. *Time's* correspondent Frank McCulloch had had nothing to say about atrocities when, in December 1967, he had written a farewell assessment of Vietnam after covering the war for four years.[42] Now, McCulloch recalled having seen men pushed from aeroplanes, shot with their hands tied behind their backs, and drowned because they refused to answer questions. He recalled having seen Americal Division troops unleash a Doberman pinscher dog on an old man suspected of being a Vietcong and watch it tear the man from head to belly. *Time's* correspondent Burt Pines related the case of a sergeant on patrol who shouted, "A three day pass for whoever gets that gook." After a moment's hesitation, most of the patrol opened up with their M-16s, ripping an old man, as well as the child he was carrying, into pieces.[43]

If there were atrocities before My Lai, why did not correspondents write about them at the time? And if the answer proves to be

---

* The Japanese did copy the pictures, and they were more widely circulated in Japan than in any other country, including the United States.

that they did but that no one would publish them, then why was it suddenly possible to publish the story of My Lai? The word "atrocity" requires careful handling, but it can be argued that My Lai was *not* an atrocity—at least, if it is argued that an atrocity is taken to be something freakish, something quite apart from the normal events coming before and after it. My Lai, on the contrary, was an un-usually pure example of the nature of the war in Vietnam and de-parted little—if at all—from common American practice.

There were events equally horrifying before My Lai, and massacres on a larger scale occurred afterwards. The war in Vietnam was an unusually frustrating one. The fact that the Americans were able to destroy the enemy's country and yet were not able to win was something new to their experience, and they sought desperately to cope. The destruction of villages and the relocation of the inhabi-tants in operations like "Cedar Falls"—chillingly described, in July 1967, in "The Village of Ben Suc," a fine piece of war reporting by *The New Yorker's* correspondent Jonathan Schell—only helped to expose the shortcomings of the American military conduct of the war. In particular, the use of raw young soldiers, on a fixed period of service, bewildered by the faceless nature of the enemy, and encour-aged to regard the Vietnamese as less than human, made an event such as My Lai highly likely to occur. The system of evaluating the progress of the war in terms of a body count, which rewarded indi-viduals, units, and whole brigades on the basis of how many Viet-cong they had killed, made it inevitable. A Vietnamese taken pris-oner might turn out to be an innocent civilian. A Vietnamese shot dead became a Vietcong killed in action.

With no moral restraints against "wasting" Vietnamese, in fact with incentives to do so, and with the understandable desire, above all, to stay alive, the American soldier in Vietnam ended up commit-ting acts that the nation believed impossible. "Some people think that the Japanese committed atrocities, that the Germans committed atrocities, that the Russians committed atrocities, but that the Ameri-cans don't commit atrocities," Colonel Robert Rheault, a former commander of the United States Special Forces in Vietnam, said just after My Lai. "Well, this just isn't so. American troops are as ca-pable as any other of committing atrocities."[44]

My Lai removed inhibitions on talking about the nature of the Vietnam War. Ex-soldiers appeared on television to confess to having shot children. Others, in hearings conducted by the National Com-mittee for a Citizens Commission of Inquiry on United States War Crimes in Vietnam, told of rape, the machine-gunning of women and children in fields, torture, and murder. Lieutenant-Colonel Anthony

Herbert, the most-decorated American soldier of the Korean War, a battalion commander of the elite 173rd Airborne Brigade, claimed he had reported seeing a United States lieutenant allow a South Vietnamese soldier to slit a woman's throat while her child clung screaming to her leg. Colonel Herbert alleged that when he made his report, his superiors told him to mind his own business.[45]

It emerged that some incidents had actually been reported at the time, and had passed with little or no notice. John Shaw of *Time*, for example, had reported as early as 1965 that "the marines have begun to kill prisoners, embittered perhaps by a recent incident; they wounded two Vietcong in an ambush, took them to a field hospital, where navy doctors expended twelve hours and several hundred pounds of invaluable ice in saving them. Then the South Vietnamese army claimed the prisoners, took them up in a helicopter, and pushed them out the hatch."[46] A Japanese photographer, Akihiko Okamura, had published photographs of the water torture of Vietcong suspects in 1964.[47] And, unless it should appear that only the South Vietnamese soldiers were guilty of atrocities, in July 1967 *Newsweek*, complimenting the United States forces on their restraint in the use of terror, in contrast with the methods of the Vietcong, said that fewer than a dozen American atrocities had been reported and verified in the course of the war.

But, before My Lai, anyone seeking evidence of the nature of the Vietnam War need only have consulted official records. The writer Norman Poirier used the files of the judge-advocate-general of the navy, in Washington, to compile a story of how a squad of nine Marines gang-raped a young Vietnamese mother at Xuan Ngoc on the night of September 23, 1966, and gunned down her entire family— herself, her husband, her two children, and her sister. When the Marines returned in the morning to make the carnage look like an engagement with the Vietcong, they found that one of the children, a five-year-old girl, was still alive, and so one of the Marines stood over the child "and with his M14 rifle bashed its brains in." They were exposed by the recovery of the mother, who had been left for dead, were arrested and tried, and six of them were convicted. Poirier's account of the incident appeared in *Esquire* in August 1969—*three months before* the story of My Lai broke. Despite the fact that *Esquire* sent proofs to the major American newspapers, to promote the article, it created hardly a ripple of interest.

Daniel Lang, in his book *Casualties of War*,[48] which was based on court files, tells of a patrol of five United States soldiers, operating in the Central Highlands, who abducted a young Vietnamese girl. Four of them raped her, and then ripped her belly open and blew her head off. The fifth soldier reported the incident, and proceedings were initiated against the others, who, after some reluctance on the part of the army, were brought to trial, then retried, and sentenced to rather light terms of imprisonment. Lang's book was reviewed in *Newsweek* in the very issue that was devoted to the My Lai story. The reviewer wrote: "The brutal killing of a Vietnamese civilian . . . should not in itself, surprise us . . . after all, no one seriously informed about the war in Vietnam believes that U.S. body counts have not included a number of civilians all along."

Correspondents in Vietnam were well aware of this. As proof, there is the manner in which they were able to recall, after the My Lai story broke, incidents they themselves had witnessed, and I have spoken to some who agree that the killing of Vietnamese civilians was a well-known fact. They did not write this, because the killing of civilians was not unusual either on a small or on a large scale, and because their public, certainly in the United States (as Poirier's *Esquire* article showed), was not ready to listen. In August 1965, CBS showed a harrowing documentary on the nature of the war in Vietnam. It depicted United States Marines turning their flamethrowers on a village south of the Da Nang air base. Vietnamese children and elderly couples were shown pleading for their homes to be spared. In all, 150 homes were leveled in retaliation for a short burst of gunfire from the village. After the broadcast, CBS's switchboard was jammed with calls from viewers attacking the film as a piece of Communist propaganda abetting the enemy's cause, a viewer reaction that must have made CBS think twice about using films of a similar sort again.

Philip Jones Griffiths, the British photo-journalist, accompanied a unit of the Americal Division on a mission in Quang Ngai in September 1967. The Americans approached a fortified village called Red Mountain, not far from Mo Duc, and lost two men in a grenade exchange. Several armed Vietcong were killed, the village occupied, and about fifteen women and children rounded up and herded together. The Americans withdrew, and the captain called in an artillery strike. As Jones Griffiths remembers: "I said to the captain, 'Hey, what about those civilians? They'll be killed.' The captain looked straight at me and said, 'What civilians?'" If one asks Jones Griffiths why he did not write about this incident—he had photographed the women and children huddled together, just before they were killed by the artillery strike—he replies: "If I had gone back to Saigon and into one of the agencies and had said, 'I've got a story about Americans killing Vietnamese civilians,' they would have said, 'So what's new?' It was horrible, but certainly not exceptional, and it just wasn't news."[49]

Neil Sheehan of the *New York Times*, a fine political reporter and military analyst, defended the correspondents' attitude in his newspaper in 1971. "I had never read the laws governing the conduct of war, although I had watched the war for three years in Vietnam and had written about it for five. . . . The Army Field Manual says that it is illegal to attack hospitals. We routinely bombed and shelled them. The destruction of Vietcong and North Vietnamese army hospitals in the South Vietnamese countryside was announced at the daily press briefings, the Five o'Clock Follies, by American military spokesmen in Saigon. . . . Looking back, one realizes that the war crimes issue was always present." Sheehan described the ravaging of five fishing hamlets on the coast of Quang Ngai by United States destroyers and bombers, which killed, he estimated, as many as 600 Vietnamese civilians. "Making peasants pay so dearly for the presence of guerillas in their hamlets, regardless of whether they sympathised with the Vietcong, seemed unnecessarily brutal and politically counter-productive to me. When I wrote my story, however, it did not occur to me that I had discovered a possible war crime." [50]

Peter Arnett, a correspondent for the Associated Press, agrees with Sheehan and goes further—that even if he had known he was witnessing a war crime, he would not have described it as such, because that would have been making a judgement, and as a correspondent for the AP he dealt in facts, not judgements.* "I accompanied Neil Sheehan on some of those military operations he wrote about; I watched hooches burning down; I saw the civilian dead. I did not write about war crimes either. We took pictures of those burning buildings, we told of the civilian dead and how they died, but we didn't make judgements because we were witnesses, and, like witnesses to robbery, accident, or murder, surely it was not for us to be judge and jury." [51]

So the My Lai massacre was revealed because it was written not by a war correspondent on the spot, but by a reporter back in the United States who was capable of being shocked by it, and because he wrote the story at a moment when, for a variety of reasons, the American public was prepared to read, believe, and accept it. Foremost among these reasons was the change in attitude in the United States brought about by the 1968 Tet offensive. Throughout 1967, the army in Viet-

* This was true of most of the American correspondents. They did not consider it their job to speculate on the morality of the war. It was in direct contrast to the attitude of the American correspondents in the Spanish Civil War, who had considered it their job to do exactly that.

nam and the Pentagon in Washington had led the public to believe
that victory was just around the corner. Then, on January 31, 1968,
the Vietcong and the North Vietnamese launched a major offensive
throughout South Vietnam. A commando squad of Vietcong succeeded in getting briefly into the compound of the United States Embassy in Saigon, the former imperial city of Hué was occupied for
twenty-five days, and nearly every town, city, and major military installation came under fire.

It is now clear that the attack on the United States Embassy was
inflated beyond its military significance and that the Tet offensive as
a whole was such a military disaster for the Vietcong that they never
really recovered. But it was also a traumatic shock to the American
public. The attack on the embassy was given extensive television
coverage and became, for many Americans, the first battle of the war
that was immediately understandable. It showed the Vietcong, supposedly on their last legs, attacking the heart of the American presence in South Vietnam. How was this possible? As Walter Cronkite,
the CBS Evening News anchor man said when he read the news
agency tapes in the CBS newsroom in New York, "What the hell is
going on? I thought we were winning the war." Or, as the *Washington Daily News* demanded, WHERE WERE WE? WHERE ARE WE?

Coming, as it did, just before the first primaries in a presidential
election year, the Tet offensive caught the administration at its weak-
est politically, and dealt a powerful blow to its sagging credibility.
When Senator Eugene McCarthy, running on a peace platform, won
the New Hampshire primary, President Johnson was faced with
an extremely difficult situation. He resolved it by announcing, on
March 31, that he would not run for a second term and that he was
prepared "to move immediately toward peace through negotiations." Yet the new President, Richard Nixon, seemed just as determined to carry on the war, which had become the longest in the nation's history, and which, by late in 1969, had cost the United States
more than 300,000 dead and wounded. A political and emotional climate was created in which more and more Americans were prepared
to believe that the war had long ceased to be a just cause. At this
moment My Lai emerged. It provided the basis for an examination
of America's motives, of the nature of the war, and of the national
conscience, and a concrete moral reason for withdrawal from it. My
Lai made it clear that the cost of continuing in Vietnam was too high.
From then on, the question of getting out was one of timing and no
longer one of principle.

Unfortunately, My Lai had two unexpected repercussions. From
this moment on, the media, especially in the United States, decided

that the war was all but over. The amount of space and time devoted
to it began to decline. The number of correspondents accredited by
MACV (Military Assistance Command, Vietnam) in Saigon provides
some measure of this loss of interest. In 1968, at the height of the Tet
offensive, there were 637 accredited correspondents; in 1969, 467; in
1970, 392; in 1971, 355; in 1972, 295. By mid-1974, only thirty-five
correspondents remained, mostly American and Japanese.* All the
correspondents I have spoken with who were in Vietnam during this
period remarked that it became noticeably more difficult, from 1969
on, to get their stories used. ABC and NBC both told their Saigon
staffs and free-lancers in that year that the story would now be the
negotiations in Paris and that film footage from Vietnam should be
angled to the withdrawal of the American forces.[52]

This suggests a serious misjudgement on the part of editors and
television producers, for the period 1969–73 saw major escalations
and changes in the war. Two other countries, Laos and Cambodia,
became involved, there was a stepping up of bombing operations by
the United States, in highly controversial circumstances, and there
was the creation of some 3 million more refugees. Anthony Lewis of
the *New York Times*, one of the few correspondents to draw attention
to this, complained, in April 1971, that "as Americans are told by
their government that the war is winding down, the number of Vietnamese, Cambodians, and Laotians being killed and maimed and
made homeless is at a record high level. In 1971, more civilians are
being killed and wounded in the three countries and more made
refugees than at any time in history. Most of those casualties are
caused, and people made refugees, by American and Allied military
activity."[53] So, at a time when the most damage of the war was being
inflicted on Indo-China, the news coverage was at its worst, because
editors and producers had decided that the ground war was virtually
over and that, with the steady withdrawal of United States troops
under way, public interest had declined. The second unfortunate result was that those editors and producers decided that there was no
further interest in American atrocity stories. One example will illustrate both points.

In November 1971, Kevin Buckley, *Newsweek's* bureau chief in
Saigon, and Alec Shimkin, a *Newsweek* reporter, were working on
the history of the war. Buckley, who was on his second spell in Vietnam, had long been interested in the level of civilian casualties and

* The exception to the loss of interest appeared to be the *New York Times*. In the first
half of 1972 it had eight men on the Vietnam story, more on a war story than at any
time since the Second World War.

hoped one day to find documented evidence on which to base a story. He decided that while he and Shimkin were going through the files the bureau had accumulated over the years, they would look out for possible leads on this subject. In due course Shimkin came across an old MACV handout that set them after the story. It was a report on a campaign in late 1968 in which the United States forces claimed that 11,000 of the enemy had been killed in action and 700 weapons captured. The discrepancy between the number of enemy dead and the number of weapons captured seemed amazing. Had there really been only one gun for every fifteen Vietcong? Or had all those killed not been soldiers? Buckley and Shimkin made a few tentative enquiries and quickly realised that there must have been something seriously wrong with the operation. "MACV began volunteering lies about it and I realized that we were on to something," Buckley has recalled. "We dropped everything else and spent two and a half months on it."

What the *Newsweek* men had uncovered was the result of "Operation Speedy Express," part of an "accelerated pacification programme" that ran from December 1968 through May 1969 in the former Vietcong stronghold of Kien Hoa, in the Mekong Delta. During the operation, thousands of civilians had been killed by the United States Army's notorious Ninth Infantry Division. This division was reported by the Associated Press, in December 1969, to pride itself "on killing a hundred Vietcong a day every day." The AP noted, however, that innocent Vietnamese civilians were sometimes included in the totals. Buckley and Shimkin examined the records of "Speedy Express," interviewed pacification officials, talked with participants in the fighting, and combed through hospital records. They travelled throughout Kien Hoa on foot, by jeep, in boats, and by raft, talking to the people—Shimkin spoke fluent Vietnamese. One American official they spoke to estimated that, of the 11,000 Vietnamese who had been killed, 5,000 would have been non-combatants. As his researches progressed, Buckley kept *Newsweek* informed. "We had all the material to make a big prize-winning investigation. No one had ever documented civilian casualties so thoroughly and harshly. I told New York it was not another My Lai. There were no GIs face-to-face with Vietnamese babies. But this was killing on a much larger scale. This was policy. This was the stuff the war had been made of."

Buckley sent in the story in January 1972, and was disappointed when the foreign editor, Edward Klein, wrote saying that he wanted to brood on the best way of using it. Buckley sent a barrage of cables asking for some indication of when the story would run, but received no answer. "I just couldn't understand it. I considered quitting, but then my tour of duty was over and I went on a long vacation." In New York, Buckley resumed his efforts to get the story into *Newsweek*. "I felt like the mad inventor in the patent office. Everyone kept saying, 'You're much too upset. It's not that important.' I said that if they were not going to use the story then I wanted to free-lance it. They said no, because it would look as if *Newsweek* had been too timid to run it. At last I got a reason out of the editor, Kermit Lansner. He told me that it would be a gratuitous attack on the administration at this point to do another story on civilian deaths after the press had given the army and Washington such a hard time over My Lai."

On June 19, 1972, nearly six months after Buckley had written the story, *Newsweek* reversed its decision and ran it, under the heading PACIFICATION'S DEADLY PRICE. Buckley says, "It was savagely cut, but it still made the point. There was a flurry of low-level Congressional interest and then it faded. The Pentagon reaction was totally deceitful, so I pressed *Newsweek* to run a second piece. I wanted to expose the Pentagon's defense and demolish a letter to the editor from Robert Komer, the deputy ambassador who had been in charge of pacification until November 1968. But *Newsweek* refused to carry a second article and I was allowed only a tiny rebuttal to Komer. Looking back, what I remember most vividly was that the editor seemed to view the story not only with indifference but with utter boredom." *[54]

NOTES

1. *Newsweek*, June 29, 1960; *Time*, November 21, 1960.
2. *Times Talk*, April 1962.
3. John Mecklin, *Mission in Torment* (New York: Doubleday, 1965), p. xii.
4. Interview with John Shaw.
5. James Aronson, *The Press and the Cold War* (Indianapolis: Bobbs-Merrill, 1970), p. 182.
6. *Daily Telegraph*, March 10, 1962.
7. *Daily Mail*, February 16, 1963.
8. *The Times*, January 21, 1963.
9. David Halberstam, *The Making of a Quagmire* (London: Bodley Head, 1965), p. 268.
10. Aronson, p. 216.
11. Nora Ephron, "The War Followers," *New York Magazine*, November 12, 1973.
12. *New York Times Magazine*, October 9, 1966.
13. Hearings of U.S. Senate Committee on Foreign Relations, August 17, 1966.
14. *New Statesman*, September 23, 1966.

* Two letters to *Newsweek* asking for its version of this affair were not answered.

15. Aronson, p. 233.
16. Don Oberdorfer, *Tet* (New York: Doubleday, 1971; Avon edition, 1972), p. 381.
17. Interview with John Pilger.
18. Interview with Brian Moynahan.
19. *London Sunday Times*, November 26, 1967.
20. *Christian Science Monitor*, May 29–June 30, 1970.
21. *Sunday Times*, October 19 and October 10, 1971; *The Times*, July 12, 1971.
22. J. Lucas, *Dateline Vietnam* (New York: Award Books, 1967), p. 15.
23. F. Harvey, *Air War Vietnam* (New York: Bantam, 1967), p. 115.
24. Harvey, p. 184.
25. *Washington Post*, February 23, 1966.
26. Interview with John Shaw.
27. Harvey, p. 104.
28. P. Jones Griffiths, *Vietnam Inc.* (New York: Macmillan, 1971), p. 60.
29. Jones Griffiths, p. 62.
30. *Sunday Times Magazine*, June 25, 1972.
31. *Sunday Times*, June 5, 1966.
32. Major Anthony J. Asterita, APO San Francisco, "Humor in Uniform," *Reader's Digest*, April 1970.
33. *Sunday Times Magazine*, June 25, 1972.
34. Interview with Nicholas Tomalin.
35. *Guardian*, September 1966.
36. Interview with Martha Gellhorn.
37. Interview with Philip Jones Griffiths.
38. *Time*, December 5, 1969.
39. AP general manager Wes Gallagher, quoted in *Time*, December 5, 1969.
40. J. Eszterhas, "The Selling of the My Lai Massacre," *Evergreen Review*, October 1971.
41. Eszterhas.
42. *Life*, December 15, 1967.
43. *Time*, December 5, 1969.
44. Robert Rheault quoted in UPI feature "GIs Forget Enemy Is Human," *The News*, Mexico City, April 11, 1970.
45. Anthony Herbert in television interview, London, July 1, 1971.
46. *Time*, August 6, 1965.
47. *Daily Telegraph Magazine*, September 25, 1964.
48. Daniel Lang, *Casualties of War* (New York: McGraw-Hill, 1969).
49. Interview with Jones Griffiths.
50. *Sunday Telegraph*, April 4, 1971.
51. Address at Pennsylvania Press Conference, May 15, 1971.
52. J. Epstein, *News from Nowhere* (New York: Random House, 1973), pp. 17, 250.
53. *New York Times* news service, April 2, 1971.
54. Letter from Kevin Buckley to author, March 7, 1974; interview with Buckley.

How to Lose a War
REFLECTIONS OF A FOREIGN CORRESPONDENT

BY ROBERT ELEGANT

In the early 1960s, when the Viet Nam War became a big story, most foreign correspondents assigned to cover the story wrote primarily to win the approbation of the crowd, above all their own crowd. As a result, in my view, the self-proving system of reporting they created became ever further detached from political and military realities because it instinctively concentrated on its own self-justification. The American press, naturally dominant in an "American war," somehow felt obliged to be less objective than partisan, to take sides, for it was inspired by the *engagé* "investigative" reporting that burgeoned in the United States in these impassioned years. The press was instinctively "agin the government"—and, at least reflexively, for Saigon's enemies.

During the latter half of the fifteen-year American involvement in Viet Nam, the media became the primary battlefield. Illusory events reported *by* the press as well as real events *within* the press corps were more decisive than the clash of arms or the contention of ideologies. For the first time in modern history, the outcome of a war was determined not on the battlefield but on the printed page and, above all, on the television screen. Looking back coolly, I believe it can be said (surprising as it may still sound) that South Vietnamese and American forces actually won the limited military struggle. They virtually crushed the Viet Cong in the South, the "native" guerillas who were directed, reinforced, and equipped from Hanoi; and thereafter they threw back the invasion by regular North Vietnamese divisions. Nonetheless, the war was finally lost to the invaders *after* the U.S. disengagement because the political pressures built up by the media had made it quite impossible for Washington to maintain even the minimal material and moral support that would have enabled the Saigon regime to continue effective resistance. . . .

THE BROTHERHOOD

In my own personal experience most correspondents *wanted* to talk chiefly to other correspondents to confirm their own *mythical* vision of the war. Even newcomers were precommitted, as the American jargon has it, to the collective position most of their colleagues had already taken. What I can only call surrealistic reporting constantly fed on itself, and did not diminish thereby, but swelled into ever more grotesque shapes. I found the process equally reprehensible for being in no small part unwitting. . . .

Most correspondents were isolated from the Vietnamese by ignorance of their language and culture, as well as by a measure of race estrangement. Most were isolated from the quixotic American Army establishment, itself often as confused as they themselves were, by their moralistic attitudes and their political prejudices. It was inevitable, in the circumstances, that they came to write, in the first instance, for each other. . . .

After each other, correspondents wrote to win the approbation of their editors, who controlled their professional lives and who were closely linked with the intellectual community at home. The consensus of that third circle, the domestic intelligentsia, derived largely from correspondents' reports and in turn served to determine the nature of those reports. If dispatches did not accord with that consensus, approbation was withheld. Only in the last instance did correspondents address themselves to the general public, the mass of lay readers and viewers. . . .

The Cloud of Unknowing

It was my impression that most correspondents were, in one respect, very much like the ambitious soldiers they derided. A tour in Vietnam was almost essential to promotion for a U.S. Regular Army officer; and a combat command was the best road to rapid advancement. Covering the biggest continuing story in the world was not absolutely essential to a correspondent's rise, but it was an invaluable cachet. Quick careers were made by spectacular reporting of the obvious fact that men, women, and children were being killed; fame or at least notoriety rewarded the correspondent who became part of the action—rather than a mere observer—by influencing events directly.

Journalists, particularly those serving in television, were therefore, like soldiers, "rotated" to Vietnam. Few were given time to develop the knowledge, and indeed the intellectual instincts, necessary
to report the war in the round. Only a few remained "in country" for
years, though the experienced Far Eastern correspondents visited
regularly from Hong King, Singapore, and Tokyo. Not surprisingly,
one found that most reporting veered farther and farther from the
fundamental political, economic, and military realities of the war, for
these were usually *not* spectacular. Reporting Vietnam became a
closed, self-generating system sustained largely by the acclaim the
participants lavished on each other in almost equal measure to the
opprobrium they heaped on "the Establishment," a fashionable and
vulnerable target . . .

MEDIA'S KEY ROLE

However, the media have been rather coy; they have not declared
that they played a *key* role in the conflict. They have not proudly
trumpeted Hanoi's repeated expressions of gratitude to the mass
media of the non-Communist world, although Hanoi has indeed affirmed that it could not have won "without the Western press." The
Western press appears either unaware of the direct connection between cause (its reporting) and effect (the Western defeat in Viet
Nam), or strangely reluctant to proclaim that the pen and the camera proved decisively mightier than the bayonet and ultra-modern
weapons.

Nor have the media dwelt upon the glaring inconsistency between
the expectation they raised of peaceful, prosperous development
after Saigon's collapse and the present post-war circumstances in
Indochina. . . .

Any searching analysis of fundamental premises has remained as
unthinkable to "the critics" as it was during the fighting. They have
remained committed to the proposition that the American role in
Indochina was totally reprehensible and inexcusable, while the North
Vietnamese role—and, by extension, the roles of the Khmer Rouge
in Cambodia and the Pathet Lao in Laos—was righteous, magnanimous, and just. Even the growing number who finally deplored the
repressive consequences of the totalitarian victory could not bring
themselves to re-examine the premises that led them to contribute so
decisively to those victories. Thus William Shawcross, before his
sententious book, *Sideshow*, wrote of the Communists' reshaping of
Cambodian society: "The process is atrociously brutal." Although
"the Khmer people are suffering horribly under their new rules,"
this is how Shawcross unhesitatingly assigned the ultimate blame:

They have suffered every day of the last six years—ever since the beginning of one of the most destructive foreign policies the United States has ever pursued: the "Nixon-Kissinger doctrine" in its purest form. . . .

Most correspondents on the scene were not quite as vehement. But they were moved by the same conviction of American guilt, which was so fixed that it resisted all the evidence pointing to a much more complex reality. Employed in the service of that crusading fervor was, for the first time, the most emotionally moving medium of all.

Television, its thrusting and simplistic character shaping its message, was most shocking because it was most immediate. The Viet Nam War was a presence in homes throughout the world. Who could seriously doubt the veracity of so plausible and so moving a witness in one's own living room?

At any given moment, a million images were available to the camera's lens in Saigon alone—and hundreds of millions throughout Indochina. But TV crews naturally preferred the most dramatic. That, after all, was their business—show business. It was not news to film farmers peacefully tilling their rice fields though it might have been argued that nothing happening was news when the American public had been led to believe that almost every Vietnamese farmer was regularly threatened by the Viet Cong, constantly imperiled by battle, and rarely safe from indiscriminate U.S. bombing.

A few hard, documented instances. A burning village was news, even though it was a deserted village used in a Marine training exercise—even though the television correspondent had handed his Zippo lighter to a non-commissioned officer with the suggestion that he set fire to an abandoned house. American soldiers cutting ears off a Viet Cong corpse was news—even if the cameraman had offered the soldiers his knife and "dared" them to take those grisly souvenirs. . . .

THE REASONS WHY

The main question persists. Why was the press—whether in favor of official policy at the beginning or vehemently against the war at the end—so superficial and so biased?

Chief among many reasons was, I believe, the politicization of correspondents by the constantly intensifying clamor over Viet Nam in Europe and America. Amateur (and professional) propagandists served both sides of the question, but the champions of Hanoi were spectacularly more effective. They created an atmosphere of high pressure that made it exceedingly difficult to be objective. . . .

A NAIVE EXPECTATION

Many newcomers were shocked to find that American and Vietnamese briefing officers did not always tell them the truth even about a minor tactical situation. Despite their pose of professional skepticism, in their naivete they expected those officers to tell not merely the truth but the *whole* truth. Far from feeling the deep mistrust of officialdom they affected, the newcomers were dismayed by the briefing officers' inability (or unwillingness) to confide in them unreservedly. Older correspondents did not expect candor from briefing officers. They had learned several wars earlier that the interests of the press and the interests of the military did not normally coincide. They also knew that the briefing officers were themselves often uninformed—concerned, perhaps sometimes excessively, for military secrecy—and resentful of correspondents' badgering. . . .

Official deceit was thus exacerbated by incompetent journalism. While complaining about the press, many U.S. officials, who knew they were fighting "a media war," sought to manipulate—rather than inform—correspondents. But they were not skilled at manipulation. While complaining about the government's duplicity, many editors assigned correspondents who were not qualified to fill a normal foreign post, much less to thread the labyrinthine complexities of the Indochina War. Some editors told their correspondents what they wanted, while many correspondents had made up their own minds before they arrived "in country." . . .

Beyond the pressures exerted upon them, most correspondents—serving six-month to two-year tours—were woefully ignorant of the setting of the conflict. Some strove diligently to remedy that crippling deficiency by reading widely and interviewing avidly. Many lacked the time or the inclination to do so—or any real awareness of how crippling their ignorance was to them professionally. . . .

Despite their own numerous and grave faults, the South Vietnamese were, first and last, decisively defeated in Washington, New York, London, and Paris. Those media defeats made inevitable their subsequent defeat on the battlefield. Indochina was not perhaps the first major conflict to be won by psychological warfare. But it was probably the first to be lost by psychological warfare conducted at such great physical distance from the actual fields of battle—and so far from the peoples whose fate was determined by the outcome of the conflict.

Once Again—Did the Press Lose Vietnam?

A VETERAN CORRESPONDENT TAKES ON THE NEW REVISIONISTS

BY CHARLES MOHR

At about 3 A.M., January 31, 1968, reporters sleeping in hotels and apartments near Saigon's Lam Son square were awakened by the sound of multiple explosions and heavy small arms fire. Such sounds were not especially unusual, but the volume was. I dressed and left my hotel, but was waved back by a jeepload of nearly hysterical American military police shouting, "Get off the streets, we're under attack." After going up to the hotel roof for a few minutes and watching tracer fire over large areas of the city, I again left the hotel and trotted a couple of blocks to the Associated Press office, which was manned twenty-four hours a day. There I learned that fighting was reportedly taking place in many areas of the city, including near the gates of the Vietnamese Presidential Palace. (Reports of attacks on South Vietnamese provincial and district capitals also began to come in. In an apparent misunderstanding of their orders, the Viet Cong had attacked seven towns the night before.) Even more startling was word that the United States embassy was under attack; my friend Peter Arnett of the AP was checking it out. The Tet, or lunar new year, truce proclaimed by the South Vietnamese government had come to a noisy end.

At first light a small group of reporters and cameramen was huddled with military police at the corner of Hai Ba Trung and Thong Nhat streets near the entrance of the walled United States embassy. A Viet Cong sapper squad had gotten onto the embassy grounds, and some were still alive and holding out. One of the M.P. sergeants told us that the V.C. were also in the chancery building. We heard M.P. radio traffic making the same statement. As it turned out, the report was not true.

Reprinted from *Columbia Journalism Review*, Nov/Dec 1983. ©

As U.S. Army helicopters landed one at a time on the embassy roof and discharged a platoon of riflemen from the 101st Airborne division, another friend, Mert Perry of *Newsweek,* said, "Do you realize we are watching American troops assault our own embassy?"

By about 9 A.M. the embassy compound had been retaken; a talk with the U.S. Mission Coordinator, George Jacobson, who had been trapped in a villa in the compound, had provided a vivid, partly eyewitness, story; and I was at a typewriter banging it out. I was also already slightly behind normal deadline.

In a mixture of journalistic conservatism and sloppiness I waited until the sixteenth paragraph of the story before writing that some of the attackers were "said" to have held lower floors of the chancery building for several hours.

Six hours had elapsed.

THE TEST OF TET

I hope to make several points with the above narrative.

In early 1982, another journalist wrote: "It is charged the American press turned an enemy defeat into a political victory for North Vietnam by concentrating on one brief and unsuccessful Communist action, the attack on the United States embassy." He added that this "emphasis, it is argued, reinforced pressure at home for a negotiated settlement." A number of neoconservative essayists, New Right polemicists, and other Vietnam revisionists, to whom I shall return, have made similar arguments, as part of a larger framework of complaint about Vietnam War journalism.

As I hope to make clear in this article, I believe the performance of the news media during the Tet offensive—and, indeed, throughout the entire course of the Vietnam War—is open to legitimate criticism. It is also worthy of some praise. But let the criticism be legitimate. Some of the criticism of Vietnam war correspondents, it appears, has not been based on a careful re-examination of the journalistic product.

At 9 A.M. on January 31 the Vietnam press corps was in no position to declare a result, victory or otherwise, in the Tet offensive (we were not even calling it that yet), a complex event that was to continue for many weeks of intense combat. We had not yet had breakfast on the first day of what was to be a prolonged adventure; we had not yet even had a formal news briefing by Military Assistance Command Vietnam on the situation in Saigon and in South Vietnam as a whole. But by then we knew that much of Saigon was overrun by Viet Cong, and that many towns had also been overrun, although most government and U.S. military compounds in the towns were holding out.

No professional, serious journalist could have ignored the embassy attack. Not many overplayed it; there was no significant overemphasis on it. My own story was a sidebar to the main war roundup which another *New York Times* reporter, because of the time difference between Saigon and New York, had written the night before, and which he was updating on deadline that morning.

By 9 A.M. of the first day of the offensive the reporters were essentially finished with the embassy story. The next day I corrected in *The New York Times* the deplorable error about the Viet Cong having been in the chancery (an error made by all news organizations, as far as I know, but unfortunately not corrected by all). And I subsequently wrote a couple of other stories about embassy security when facts on that subject that were embarrassing to the U.S. Mission came to light. But I and other reporters did not give the embassy attack prolonged, obsessive coverage while ignoring the subsequent course of battle. If some failed to report Viet Cong losses adequately in subsequent weeks, this was not a consequence of their having reported a six-hour attack by a nineteen-man sapper squad. The thesis that there was such a connection is only one of scores of myths about Vietnam journalism that, together, constitute a larger and pernicious myth.

More is at stake in this debate than wounded journalistic egos.

Almost twenty-two years have elapsed since the administration of John F. Kennedy involved the United States in what was called "combat support" in South Vietnam, a concept that brought thousands of military advisers and hundreds of helicopters to assist in the prosecution of a proxy war. Less than four years later it had become a real war for United States combat troops.

The ultimate failure (I have chosen that word with care   United States troops were never defeated militarily and, until very late in the war, no sizable South Vietnamese unit ever broke, was overrun, or defected) of that enterprise became undeniable by April of 1975, when Saigon fell to North Vietnamese troops. So painful was the Vietnam experience that both the U.S. Army and civilians seemed to want to put Vietnam out of memory.

In the last few years, however, there has been a resurgence of interest in the war. A number of historical treatments and analytical discussions of the conflict have been published. Even a controversy about the design of the emotionally moving Vietnam memorial in Washington aroused controversy about the way the war was fought, the way it was supported or obstructed by Congress and the public—

and the way it was reported by American journalists. The ambitious public television series *Vietnam: A Television History*, which is being broadcast this autumn, will almost certainly increase the interest of adults who had tended to expunge Vietnam from their memories and to interest people too young to have experienced or understood the war.

Unfortunately, much of the discussion of the war has involved a kind of revisionist "history" which, in fact, comes from people who are not historians and who are not using historical methods.

This does not apply to such careful work as *Vietnam: A History*, Stanley Karnow's recently published history of the war (he was also chief correspondent of *A Television History*.) Nor does it apply to Peter Braestrup's *Big Story*, a lengthy study of how journalism covered the Tet offensive. Braestrup, who himself was an able Vietnam correspondent and a witness to Tet, may have annoyed some of his colleagues with his thesis that Tet was such an "extreme" event and reportorial challenge that it simply overwhelmed the Vietnam press corps. But Braestrup first carefully reread the journalistic record: the product. He then reprinted most of it. If his thesis is thought debatable, or only disagreeable, by some, it at least rests on a foundation of evidence. Being reminded of what we said, and did not say, proves in some cases to be embarrassing. It is less troubling, however, than the surly critiques of the polemicists.

Notable among the critics, writing and speaking with varying degrees of bitterness and coherence, have been the editorial page of *The Wall Street Journal*, Robert S. Elegant (a former *Los Angeles Times* reporter), William F. Buckley, John P. Roche, Walt W. Rostow, William C. Westmoreland, Richard M. Nixon, and Henry A. Kissinger. This is not meant to be a full list, nor do I intend to focus my rebuttal specifically on those I have named. Certain of these critics have also constructed a pontoon bridge from the Vietnam quagmire to Central America by contending that reporters now covering Central America are falling into the same bad habits the critics attribute to the reporters who covered Vietnam.

Some of these critics have drawn conclusions that bear little relation to the actual conduct of mainstream journalists for major news organizations in the years 1961 to 1975. Some of their conclusions also reflect an astonishing misrepresentation, or at least misunderstanding, of the nature of the war. This can be especially disturbing when it comes from former civilian officials who helped to manage and prosecute the war. There is also confusion about the manner in which events actually unfolded, the problems of Vietnam war correspondence, and what the journalists *actually* said and wrote.

THE MAKING OF A MYTH

Although I like to argue that wars are not lost in the newspapers (or in television broadcasts), the revisionist argument goes far toward making that claim. In some cases it is flatly made. The core of the complaint is complicated, and not always quite coherent. Although to answer the critics it is necessary to discuss the entire course of the war, it is also convenient to focus on Tet.

One element of the revisionist argument is that Tet was not only a "victory" for the U.S.-South Vietnamese coalition, but that this was clearly and unmistakably true, and that willful misrepresentation by reporters caused a collapse of United States domestic morale in the first days of the offensive.

Certainly, massive erosion both of domestic American public support for the war, and of public confidence in the country's policy-makers, did eventually follow the Tet offensive.* Such erosion was already well advanced among the members of the antiwar movement. But, in its magnitude, the loss of support among the general public to some extent genuinely surprised me and a number of other "veteran" Vietnam war correspondents. The revisionists ascribe the erosion to hysterical reporting from Vietnam; my own belief is that it was the result of strong public shock following the highly optimistic public claims of progress by American officials in the fall of 1967. A few journalists lost their composure, but most Vietnam correspondents did not. I and most others, even in the earliest hours of the offensive, did not believe that the enemy was going to "win" a military victory, capture the Saigon post office, and bayonet us and the allied high command in our beds. No fair reading of the body of news stories produced in early 1968 will sustain that myth.

I did not share the sentiments of Senator John Stennis, who said a few days after the Tet kickoff that it was "embarrassing" and "humiliating" to the United States. But I could sympathize with him. Like Arthur Krock of *The New York Times* in 1963 at the time of the battle of Ap Bac, Stennis had tended to support—and for all I know, believe—the official optimism, and now felt betrayed.

In *Big Story*, Braestrup wrote that the press "emphasized the political and psychological effects" of the enemy attacks. (So poisonous was domestic feeling at that time that the mere use of the word "enemy" to describe men who were killing American troops usually drew angry letters. And when, at the end of the three-week battle for

---

*In the latest edition of his book, Braestrup cites poll data which casts strong doubt on the assertion that early Tet reports from Vietnam caused a significant loss of support for the war among the general public.

the ancient imperial capital of Hue, I wrote of the "liberation" of Hue, one reader angrily denounced me for doing so.) Braestrup's argument, it seems to me, was far more true of stories written in the United States than of those filed by relatively objective reporters in Vietnam, who did not believe it was their job to assess political effects in the United States, but who did speculate about the V.C.'s desire for psychological victory.

Like many other journalists in Vietnam, I assumed and wrote, early in the offensive, that it was logical to believe that North Vietnam and the Viet Cong were seeking a psychological victory, since it was difficult to believe that they seriously thought they could achieve an actual military victory by pitting a nationwide assault force estimated at about 35,000 men against a force of more than one million regular United States and South Vietnamese troops.* This was not a political or ideological notion, but the conclusion of a reporter who had begun to gain some military sophistication.

There followed an irony, or perhaps a paradox. Senior officials of the U.S. Mission Vietnam came to dislike it that a reporter for an influential paper was writing that the enemy had probably not sought a military victory, even though the reporter did so because he believed that the possibility of success had been so inherently remote. Subjectively, the argument that the V.C. had sought, but had been denied, a purely military victory became very attractive to the officials. And objectively, captured documents indicated that the communist leadership had really believed in the concept of a "general uprising" by the South Vietnamese civilian population that could bring about both the collapse of the Saigon government and the forced evacuation of American troops. Some American officials, whose intellectual honesty was respected by the reporters, then met at length with some of us to argue the thesis that the Vietnamese communists had indeed believed in the general uprising and had sought not "merely" the destruction of an already frayed domestic American support for the war, but a clear-cut military victory. The relationship between the journalists and these unquestionably honest members of the official mission was never as hostile or adversarial as some revisionists have painted it. Most of the reporters, including me, came to accept the general-uprising theory and to describe it in news stories.

---

*It subsequently also seemed absurd when MACV in the first few days claimed that more than 30,000 V.C. had been killed in action.

WERE OFFICIAL VIEWS MUFFLED?

This suggests several other significant elements in the discussion of the role and performance of journalists over the long haul in Vietnam. As early as late 1961, when the great Homer Bigart arrived in Vietnam for *The New York Times,* a degree of tension developed between some officials and most of the then tiny press corps. These differences, however, were not over the "morality" of the war or the desirability of winning (a concept not easy to define, then or later). Essentially, the dispute involved optimism versus pessimism, growing out of conflicting views about the way the war was being prosecuted and about the viability of the South Vietnamese government in a revolutionary conflict.

This debate was not essentially, as some seem to believe, a quarrel between the press and U.S. officials in Vietnam. It was, rather, a quarrel between factions within the U.S. Mission. For the most part, field advisers closest to the action and to the Vietnamese took the pessimistic view. Some of the more senior officials in Saigon, who were reporting to Washington on the progress of the programs they were themselves administering, were publicly and persistently optimistic. The reporters quickly became aware of this dispute because brilliant younger field officials and officers, as exemplified by the late John Paul Vann, increasingly turned to the journalists. The reporters did not invent the somber information that sometimes appeared in their stories. Nor did they relentlessly emphasize it.

One of the persistent myths about Vietnam journalism is that the copy was deeply colored by ideology, that it was loaded with strong advocacy, and that it muffled the voice and views of officialdom. Again, this misrepresents the actual news product. Much of it was cautious and bland—probably, in retrospect, too bland. For practical reasons, journalists always reported the claims, appraisals, and statements of the senior officials who asserted that "progress" was being made. These stories almost always got prominent play. At many points in the war, progress *was* being made and many journalists could see and agree that this was taking place. Less often, and seldom in shrill tones, correspondents also reported the countervailing views of Americans who were eager to place greater pressure on the South Vietnamese for better management of their war. It is mostly the latter stories that the revisionists and embittered officials, now retired, seem to remember today.

There is also the persistent argument that, because of television, Vietnam "was the first war that came into people's living rooms" and that TV coverage caused a fatal revulsion for the war. Several aspects of this argument fascinate me. It is often advanced by pro-war people who suggest that "seeing" the war did not bother them, but that other Americans could not be expected to withstand such a shock to the emotions. It also seems to reflect how isolated and safe America has been for most of its history. Most wars literally, not merely photographically, go through people's living rooms. The awesome casualty lists of World War I, the London Blitz, the stark still photography of World War II have never seemed to me to be less psychologically important than Vietnam TV coverage.

Rereading the Tet coverage, I am struck by how much space and emphasis were given to claims of "victory" when they were made. But, as we shall see, officials spent much of that period not claiming victory, but warning of harder fighting ahead and ominous enemy threats.

A VICTORY CONCEALED?

The most serious charge made by the revisionists, and one of the most frequently repeated, is that the Vietnam press corps failed to report an allied victory at Tet and, indeed, concealed its existence. There were, unquestionably, flaws in the purely military coverage; and not all of them were sins of omission. But in its raw form the charge does not seem to hold up.

I believe that Tet represented a serious *tactical* defeat for the Viet Cong and their North Vietnamese superiors. But this did not ultimately constitute a strategic victory for South Vietnam. That should be obvious. It is also argued that Tet shattered, nearly destroyed, the indigenous guerrillas and forced North Vietnam to continue the war with its own regular army troops. This was to a large extent true; but it was also what almost all serious journalists reported (though anyone who was around at the time of the 1973 "truce" quickly learned that there were still many Viet Cong in the countryside five years later).

In early January of 1969, I wrote a story, which was printed on the front page of the *Times*, that began: "After days of overoptimism, false starts, half-completed programs and lost opportunities, the allied forces in Vietnam appear to be making major progress against the enemy." The story also said that officials with reputations for intellectual honesty and skepticism "believe they see a drastic decline in the fighting quality and political abilities of the Viet Cong guerrillas and modest improvements in South Vietnamese and American prosecution of the war. Taken together, these may have broken the stalemate of previous years." (The story also contained plenty of qualifications and warnings that great problems persisted.)

Did the story come too late, as I suspect some revisionists would argue? Perhaps. But, although I was proud of my willingness to follow my reporting to any conclusions to which that reporting led, the real point today is that the story turned out to be essentially wrong. It appeared in print just before Nixon and Kissinger took office. They adopted a policy of "Vietnamization" of the war. And although the pace of American withdrawal seemed too slow to many people in this country, it seemed fatally rapid to some journalists in Vietnam. Then, in 1973, Kissinger signed a peace treaty that left some 140,000 regular North Vietnamese troops on South Vietnamese soil. Together, these steps guaranteed ultimate collapse. The stalemate of previous years was broken, but in an entirely different way.

As for the argument that the reporters were much too slow to accept the concept of at least a purely military victory at Tet, re-examination of the record is again revealing. Claims of victory were faithfully reported, often on the front page; apparently, Congress and the public were no longer so willing to believe. In the meantime, officers and officials in Vietnam kept warning that "second wave" attacks were likely, that the enemy was still full of fight. I and some other reporters tended journalistically to declare the battle for Saigon over within a few days—and we kept being fooled. Space will permit only a small sample of hundreds of incidents. On February 21, 123 troops were killed in heavy fighting at the city line. On March 4, forty-eight Americans were killed in an ambush near the airport. On March 12, General Westmorland predicted "very heavy fighting" in the northern provinces. On May 5, the "second wave" struck and the notorious police chief, General Loan, was seriously wounded on a downtown bridge. Casualties soared. (Shortly thereafter several journalists were killed in the Cholon section, an American armed helicopter accidentally killed the mayor of Saigon in an airstrike against Communist troops not far from downtown, and, during a spooky jeep reconnaissance of the city, Arnett and I discovered the bodies of several Korean reporters executed by V.C. at a gasoline service station.) In one two-week period in May, more than 1,100 American troops were killed in action, the worst losses in any such a period in the entire war.

The revisionists often suggest that the journalists failed to take into account the heavy enemy losses; in fact, the reporters in Vietnam did report that the Viet Cong were suffering staggering casualties. In any case, I doubt that the journalists can be accused of concealing a transparently clear allied victory—one which did not seem so clear until autumn, even to officials. Only in the post-war era have they tried to rehabilitate their reputations with such assertions.

OF TRUST AND DISTRUST

As both its practitioners and critics should recognize, journalism is an imperfect instrument. The Vietnam reporters were far from blameless. Some stateside editors and executives also failed, both early and late, to assign enough staffers, or any staffers, to the story. The Vietnam press corps was woefully short on language skills (the reporters now covering Central America seem to me better equipped, both linguistically and intellectually, for their assignment). Many were not sophisticated militarily, and too many posed as ordinance experts, ready to pronounce on the caliber of an incoming shell.

Before and after Tet, the story did often tend to overwhelm the essentially conventional journalistic methods we employed. Much went unreported, although this may have been unavoidable in a sprawling nation of forty-four provinces and scores of allied divisions and brigades.

Granted that much went unreported, that factual errors were not rare, that sometimes we were too argumentative and skeptical (although much of the time we were far too gullible), that we spent too much time covering American troops and too little with the South Vietnamese. Still, in a broad sense, the coverage seems sound in retrospect. Not only ultimately, but also at each major milestone of the war, the weight of serious reporting corresponds quite closely to the historical record. Revisionists seem to fault correspondents for distrusting the version of events propounded by the most optimistic senior officials in Vietnam. But what if the correspondents had believed that version and had been guided by it in carrying out their assignment? In that case, the reporters' reputations, which are not unblemished, would be irredeemably tarnished.

An Extreme Case

BY PETER BRAESTRUP

In overall terms, the performance by the major American television
and print news organizations during February and March 1968 constitutes an extreme case.

Rarely has contemporary crisis-journalism turned out, in retrospect, to have veered so widely from reality. Essentially, the dominant themes of the words and film from Vietnam (rebroadcast in
commentary, editorials, and much political rhetoric at home) added
up to a portrait of defeat for the allies. Historians, on the contrary,
have concluded that the Tet offensive resulted in a severe military-
political setback for Hanoi in the South. To have portrayed such
a setback for one side as a defeat for the other—in a major crisis
abroad—cannot be counted as a triumph for American journalism.

Why did the media perform so unsatisfactorily? I have come to
this general conclusion: The special circumstances of Tet impacted
to a rare degree on modern American journalism's special susceptibilities and limitations. This peculiar conjuncture overwhelmed reporters, commentators, and their superiors alike. And it could happen again.

In most American foreign policy crises since World War II, there
have been objective factors that assuaged journalistic needs and
curbed journalistic excess. One thinks in particular of the 1962 Cuban
missile crisis and Hanoi's 1972 offensive, the latter a far stronger military effort than Tet. In both cases, 1962 and 1972, there were perceived forewarnings of trouble, a well-defined geographical arena, a
widely shared sense of the relative strengths and capabilities of the
opposing sides, a conventional confrontation remote from journal-

From *Big Story*, Abridged Edition. Copyright ©1983 by Peter Braestrup. Reprinted
by permission of Yale University Press, New Haven and London.

istic havens, and a coherent Presidential response. None of these reassuring elements was fully present at Tet-1968.

In Vietnam, the sudden penetration of downtown Saigon by Vietcong sapper teams impacted personally on correspondents' lives.
The geographical dispersion of the concurrent communist attacks
elsewhere in the country led to uncertainty among newsmen about
the enemy's intent, strength, and degree of success in the countryside. Journalists' unfamiliarity both with the South Vietnamese
and with the relative military capabilities of each side increased this
uncertainty.

Inevitably, then, the overall pattern of events in Vietnam in February 1968 was for a time obscure. But commentators and many reporters did not wait. By the time the fog of war began to lift later that
month, the collective emanations of the major media were producing
a kind of continuous black fog of their own, a vague conventional
"disaster" image, which few newsmen attempted to reexamine and
which few news managers at home sought to question. Indeed, in the
case of *Newsweek*, NBC, and CBS, and of photo displays by others,
the disaster theme seemed to be exploited for its own sake. The journalistic fog had thinned to a patchy haze by the time of President
Johnson's March 31 speech, but it had not been penetrated by a cold,
retrospective light. The record was not set straight. The hasty assumptions and judgments of February and early March were simply
allowed to stand.

Indeed, Charles Mohr of the New York *Times* recalled, in a 1971
letter to the author, that when he wrote a piece later in 1968 analyzing the outcome of the Tet attacks as a setback to Hanoi, he received
letters from *Times* readers expressing surprise and disbelief.

In late 1968, according to Edward J. Epstein, an NBC field producer named Jack Fern suggested to Robert J. Northshield a three-
part series showing that Tet had indeed been a military victory for
America and that the media had exaggerated greatly the view that it
was a defeat for South Vietnam. The idea was rejected because,
Northshield (an NBC News producer) said later, Tet was already established "in the public's mind as a defeat, and therefore it was an
American defeat." [1]

Was this thematic persistence due to a sudden seizure of "antiwar"
feeling among newsmen, an ideological media conspiracy against
Johnson Administration war policy?

One must rely for the answer on contemporary impressions and
interviews obtained 18 months to two years after the fact—when
time and a new set of perceptions had clouded memories. What
seems fairly clear is that, in January 1968, there was little optimism

among newsmen, as among congressmen, with regard to the Vietnam venture. Many, as we have indicated, were simply skeptical of any success; a few were hostile to the military and sympathetic to the academicians and senators active in the peace movement; others hoped for a negotiated settlement. Hawks were few, except on *Time*. Outspoken doves were rare, except on the *Times*. At CBS and NBC, it appears, there was both impatience with the war's length and revulsion at its horrors. In Vietnam, there was little conversation about war policy; instead, newsmen exchanged anecdotes about the war's various aspects. Overall, there seems to have been no ideological consensus *prior* to Tet that could serve as an explanation for media treatment of the crisis.

It is true that, after the attacks broke, *Newsweek* became explicit in its political stance, citing the "utter inadequacy" of Administration war policy and calling for a negotiated settlement. (We have seen that that magazine's Vietnam news coverage was more negative than that of the other print media.) However, *Newsweek's* editors may have been equally concerned about keeping up with political fashion, with the much more vocal antiwar opinion, with the pessimism of Walter Cronkite and the New York *Times's* editorial page.*

Thus, out of his own experience, and interviews with his colleagues, this writer is convinced that ideology, per se, played a relatively minor role in the media treatment of the Tet crisis. The big problems lay elsewhere, and persist to this day.

Yet, downgrading the ideological factor in Tet media coverage—a factor so heavily stressed by Nixon Administration spokesmen in 1969–72 in their attacks on the "Eastern establishment press"—should not be taken to mean that newsmen, especially those in Washington and New York, were neutral with respect to the Johnson Administration. They were suspicious and resentful, on personal-professional grounds. As was noted at the beginning of this study, the credibility among newsmen of President Johnson, Secretary McNamara, and senior officialdom by 1968 was low. Johnson, starting with his first public budget discussions in 1964, had gained a reputation in Washington for manipulation and half-truths. The public utterances of generals and civilian officials alike concerning the war had seldom been distinguished by brutal candor. And Tet, as we have noted, came after an Administration propaganda campaign

---

* At an editorial meeting around March 1, Oberdorfer noted, "One of the editors expressed the fear that *Newsweek* would be the last to speak instead of being the pacesetter it aspired to be." (*Tet!*, p. 274.) *Newsweek* was quick off the mark during Hanoi's Easter offensive in 1972, prematurely invoking "the specter of defeat" in early May.

intended to shore up support for a long-term limited-war policy that embraced neither a decisive military strategy nor a plausible diplomatic ending. The policy satisfied neither hawks nor doves. Yet, this 1967 "progress" campaign had, in effect, made implicit promises that no unpleasant surprises were in store.

Although they voiced misgivings, newsmen in Vietnam (or Washington) could not *prove* in 1967 that the Administration's professed optimism was overblown. They had to report what the Administration said. But there was an underlying journalistic resentment, especially in Washington, at being thus used, and, when the crisis came, Johnson was not given the benefit of the doubt, as Presidents usually are. As several Washington reporters later noted, the primary reaction of many newsmen in the capital after Tet was to indulge in retribution for prior manipulation by the Administration.[2] Thus, while formal ideology did not heavily flavor media treatment of Tet, to a rare degree the initial coverage reflected subjective reactions by newsmen—not only to the sights and circumstances of Tet itself, but also to the Administration's past conduct.

This coverage was also shaped by habit and convention. The press, and, most strikingly, television news since the early 1960s, have sought "themes" and "story lines" to routinize major developments and to make events intelligible. "Keep it simple," is the deskman's warning to reporters, as much for his own sake as for the reader's. Election campaigns are portrayed as horse races (with front runners and dark horses); votes on major issues in Congress are often defined as "defeats" or "victories" for the President; and, for a long time in the 1950s and 1960s, local struggles in Africa and Latin America were simplified as contests between "procommunists" and "anticommunists." These ingrained professional habits left newsmen ill-equipped to cope with the unusual ambiguities and uncertainties surrounding Tet. In Washington, the assault on the U.S. Embassy in Saigon came as a crisis piled on top of another (apparent) crisis—the dramatic seizure of the *Pueblo* by the North Koreans— which had preoccupied news managers for a week. Moreover, as we have noted, President Johnson *did not seize the initiative* in terms of information or decision-making; and although Washington newsmen do not like to admit it, their dependence on the White House for a "news agenda" and a "frame of reference," especially in crisis, is considerable. When the President is vague, or delegates the discussion of bad news to subordinates (as Johnson largely did at Tet), without demonstrably responding to the crisis himself, the government seems incoherent, the future filled with uncertainty.

We have seen that in Vietnam, too, the circumstances for newsmen were at first ambiguous and uncertain. There was the personally
threatening combat in Saigon, the looming drama of Khe Sanh, the
destructive urban battle in Hue. There were the fragmentary reports
of action in other towns and cities. And there was Westmoreland
himself predicting a second wave. To newsmen accustomed to the
relatively brief, localized rural battles that characterized the war until Tet, the very persistence of communist effort in Saigon, Hue, and
Khe Sanh and along the highways was unsettling. The fate of the
initially inaccessible countryside, the state of the long-neglected
ARVN (suddenly a key actor), the intentions and capabilities of the
foe were all question marks throughout much of February. . . .

In retrospect, after all is said and done, the problem for the major
bureaus in Vietnam was not lack of *opportunity* to piece together the
overall picture and dispel some confusion as time went on. It lay in
their initial reactions to the Tet crisis, and in the subsequent preoccupation of most reporters and their managers with more compelling matters, such as Khe Sanh and upcoming enemy moves.

Faced with ambiguities and uncertainty, the major bureaus in
Saigon, for the most part, reacted in two ways. The first generalized
tendency was to follow standard Vietnam operating procedure, which
in turn was conditioned by standard perceptions of "news." For
newspapers and AP and UPI, this meant mining and processing the
most dramatic elements out of the daily communiqués and briefings
in Saigon. For everyone, it meant deploying reporters to the most
dramatic action elsewhere. This approach throughout an episodic
war had yielded both "hard news" and vivid human-interest "features" for print, and a steady flow of filmed vignettes, oftentimes
film clichés, for television. The tendency to head for "the action"
(which noticeably faded among newsmen in Saigon in later years)
was by no means universal in 1965–68. But it was common to the
reporters most respected by their peers. Going to "the action" served
the obvious professional requirements of seeing and experiencing the
war one had been sent to cover; and it sustained a proud tradition in
U.S. journalism. In the case of television, it also satisfied superiors'
demands for GI combat stories. On another level, it legitimized (or
seemed to legitimize) a newsman's claim to speak with authority on
the war; it gave him a certain status. And the risks of brief exposure
to danger justified his relative comfort amid so much courage and
suffering.

Most newsmen in Vietnam, in their late twenties and thirties,
sought the opportunity to witness a prolonged life-and-death drama

of major importance to America. But their time horizons were short. Their focus was narrow. By temperament or training they were not "experts," systematic researchers, writers skilled in synthesis; they were adventurers and, to some extent, voyeurs; at their best they were also shrewd observers and interrogators, and perceptive tellers of tales. To them and their superiors, the inherent drama—and importance—of Saigon, Hue, and Khe Sanh were compelling, and obviously "news." And the concentration of journalistic manpower on these dramatic but isolated stories insured that they were treated at home as the significant "news." What else was worthy of sustained firsthand attention was less obvious; and the media in Vietnam committed major sins of omission as time went on.

The second generalized reaction by the major news bureaus in Saigon was in keeping with the more ambitious, more "intellectual" journalism of the late 1950s and 1960s. It was to "explain" or "interpret" what had happened and, implicitly or explicitly, to forecast the future, especially as the fighting at Hue and Khe Sanh dragged on.

The wire services were relatively constrained in this regard; in passing, to enliven their war wrap-ups, they dwelled on the possibilities of renewed anti-cities attacks or the prospect of a second Dienbienphu at Khe Sanh. Far less constrained were *Time,* and especially *Newsweek,* where "projecting the story" was a standard technique. And on television, similar projection was used to lend added "significance" to reporters' comments (e.g., "The war is no closer to an end tonight than it was this morning").

On the *Times* and, more markedly, the *Post,* some license had been given since the early 1950s to ordinary reporters (as opposed to columnists, whose independence was generally accepted) to "explain" events within the confines of conventional hard-news stories. Here, selected opinions and interpretations were often vaguely attributed to anonymous "officials," "insiders," "observers," or "senior officers," as in *Time* or *Newsweek.* Greater freedom was allowed to reporters when they wrote under the rubric of "news analysis" or "commentary." Foreign correspondents, faced with the task of explaining far-off events to American readers, were allowed the most leeway. They often went beyond observable events, attributed information, and quoted opinion to interpret developments on their own authority.

Such interpretative reporting had long been characteristic of the *Post's* Washington coverage, occasionally to the point, in the early 1960s, where the analysis got more space and "play" than the hard news being analyzed. "News analysis" came to the *Times* in the 1950s, with James Reston among the first practitioners. The form caused early misgivings on the paper despite Reston's reputation for finding the facts, taking no sides, and eschewing the temptation to supply all the answers. But such fears eased. By Tet-1968, news analysis by *Times* reporters, especially in the Sunday "News of the Week in Review" section, was commonplace.

In the careful hands of Reston, Hanson Baldwin, Edwin Dale (the *Times* economist), and a few other specialists, the technique added considerably to reader understanding of complex matters. But no comparable competence existed among newsmen with regard to Vietnam. Indeed, as we have noted, both the war's circumstances and the media's own various organizational incentives worked against the acquisition of such competence in Vietnam (and Washington). Moreover, the problem in February 1968 for all would-be news analysts was that the Tet battlefields provided an insufficient "data base" from which to draw broad independent conclusions or to "project the story" in many areas. "Herd journalism" and the news focus on enemy threats and localized fighting in Saigon, Hue, and Khe Sanh— however important those battles might be—left many other crucial matters unexplored firsthand. Yet, the very existence of great uncertainty, added to the subjective responses noted earlier, appears to have impelled editors to publish, and reporters (and pundits) to compose, "analyses" of the crisis that would fill the vacuum. It proved a serious lapse of self-discipline. As we have seen, most analyses were the hasty reactions of the half-informed. Fewer than 15 percent of the *Times* and *Post* items about Vietnam were in explicit "commentary" categories, yet this segment of the coverage, often prominently displayed and "rebroadcast," accounted for a disproportionate share of both papers' sins of commission. And the "projection-analysis" technique, used so heavily on television and in *Newsweek*, produced more pervasive distortions.

These two immediate professional responses by major Vietnam news bureaus and their superiors back home—a focus of firsthand reporting on a few dramatic events, plus undisciplined "analysis" and "projection"—underlay the overall failure of the press and TV to cope with the formidable circumstances of February–March 1968. As often happens, these initial journalistic reactions set the tone and supplied the themes assigned to the crisis over the entire period.

The chronically short attention span of the media—four to six weeks in 1968—insured a feast-and-famine flow of information, aggravated by space and time limitations. As is usually the case in crisis, most space and "play" went to the Tet story early, when the least solid information was available. There was no institutional system within the media for keeping track of what the public had been told, no internal priority on updating initial impressions. As usual, the few catch-up or corrective stories later on were buried on back pages. This practice in turn gave Saigon correspondents little incentive to produce such stories. . . .

The result was that the media tended to leave the shock and confusion of early February, *as then perceived,* "fixed" as the final impression of Tet, and thus as a framework for news judgment and public debate at home. At Tet, the press shouted that the patient was dying, then weeks later began to whisper that he somehow seemed to be recovering—whispers apparently not heard amid the clamorous domestic reaction to the initial shouts.

There is little disagreement among historians or even journalists that the dramatic Tet surprises of late January were indeed shocking—to official Washington and the public at home, and to the U.S. Embassy and the Presidential Palace in Saigon, to say nothing of urban South Vietnamese and U.S. newsmen caught in the fighting. But drama or shock does not automatically mean a decisive turn of events, in this case "defeat" or "demoralization" on the ground. At Tet, the media managers hastily assumed it did, and led their readers to do the same. A mind-set—most obvious in the selection of page-one stories, TV film, and newspaper photographs—quickly developed: Tet was a *disaster,* not only for the highly visible 10 percent of the South Vietnamese population caught up in the urban fighting, but, actually or imminently, for the allied armies, the pacification effort, the Thieu government. Tet, belying the Johnson Administration's "progress" campaign, *thereby* showed that the war was being "lost." Tet proved that the North Vietnamese were the "winners" and their foes the "losers." Tet was a triumph for the wily Giap—in South Vietnam.

Was anything other than allied "defeat" discernible to newsmen in February–March 1968 on the ground? The answer is: Yes, starting in late February. Earlier, the newsmen in Saigon called into question MACV's hasty cumulative totals of enemy losses, and noted contradictions between the first optimistic communiqués and the realities at Hue and on Saigon's outskirts. They were skeptical of Ambassador Bunker's early (but ultimately accurate) accounting of enemy failures (no procommunist uprising, few ARVN defections). But they neglected to echo General Weyand's sensible warning in early February that it was premature to add up the final Tet score, good or bad; and, with the "disaster" mind-set, they pressed officials for predictions of future enemy initiatives—forgetting to keep posted on what was already happening as February ended.

Yet, after the recapture of Hue on February 24, the manpower was available, at least in the larger bureaus (AP, UPI, *Time*, the networks, the *Times*), to travel about for a systematic "second look." Moreover, the reporters were enormously helped by freedom from censorship—a freedom not enjoyed by their counterparts in both World Wars and Korea, or in coverage of the Arab-Israeli wars. Thanks to official cooperation and U.S. air mobility, they had unprecedented access to the battlefield. And they had facilities for relatively rapid transmission of film and prose. By March 1, it would have been possible to observe and to report that: (1) enemy military pressure had slackened, except at Khe Sanh; (2) the fighting was shifting back to the countryside; (3) ARVN, despite its 50 percent strength level and some extraordinarily incompetent senior leadership, had held together and fought back; (4) pacification, although hit hard, was not "dead"; and (5), amid many problems and much human suffering, urban recovery was beginning here and there. In short, it was a mixed picture, but clearly neither a military nor a psychological "disaster."

Time made a good effort to catch up. The other big organizations did not. Most of the scattered *Post* and *Times* catch-up stories—dealing with localized recovery—missed page one and landed inside the paper. In mid-March, *Newsweek*, CBS, and NBC were still portraying North Vietnamese troops as holding the "initiative," if only because of a fixation with Khe Sanh. Drama was perpetuated at the expense of information.

Competition did not make for more sophisticated journalism. The fierce rivalry between UPI and AP (with the outcomes judged on the basis of clients' choices of competing agency stories) and among networks (judged on the basis of news program audience "ratings") did not lead to breadth of coverage, and hence to a comprehensive countrywide portrait of a countrywide war. It led, as often happens, to clustering of rival newsmen at the same places, so that each agency "matched" the other on the same story. The wire services put out Saigon war wrap-ups competing for "impact" back home. Competition between NBC and CBS seemed at times a contest over who could shout the same words more loudly.

But in other media, where short-range competitive success was harder to quantify—and where *Time* and the *Times* clearly outgunned their putative rivals in Vietnam—the pressures were less severe, and duplication less frequent. Indeed, in terms of *staff*-written reports from Vietnam outside Saigon, the *Times* and *Post* overlapped relatively little after the first three weeks of February.

Traditional American journalistic skills—notably in reporting what can be seen or heard—served the print media well at Da Nang, Hue, in the Delta, and in some of the Saigon street fighting. AP's John Wheeler and others reported accurately from Khe Sanh, especially during the early stages of the siege of that base. But the newsmen, by and large, did not *see* very much of the countrywide Tet offensive or its aftermath. There were many gaps in their information (as in that initially available to officialdom). Yet, most news managers at home were apparently willing, even eager, to supply their audiences with quick, imaginative descriptions of the strategy of the "wily Giap," the psychological impact of Tet on South Vietnamese morale, the future of the Thieu regime, the "death throes" of pacification, the enemy's "awesome" weaponry—all mostly based on guesswork and secondhand sources in Saigon or Washington.

Most important, throughout Tet, the great bulk of the wire-service output actually used by U.S. newspapers (and its refined versions in network scripts) and of the newspapers' page-one Vietnam material did not come from eyewitness reports. It was secondhand or thirdhand information—reprocessed, as we have seen, several times over.

NOTES

1. See Epstein's *Between Fact and Fiction* (Vintage: 1975), p. 255.

2. In the spring of 1970, a similar overreaction occurred after the U.S.-South Vietnamese "incursions" into Cambodia. The limited ground operations against communist base areas were preceded by high-level State Department assurances that no such actions were contemplated. They were accompanied by a television speech by President Nixon who exaggerated their real scope and objectives and thereby contributed further to media alarmism and public alarm. Washington *Post* ombudsman Richard Harwood, in a January 26, 1971, memo to the editors, noted that "following the events of last spring a couple of our summer interns examined our Cambodia coverage—foreign and domestic. They concluded that it was one-sided and unfair [to the Nixon Administration]." He followed with a plea for the *Post* to "use the naked facts if at all possible and to use them with precision" in future coverage of Cambodian fighting. See Laura Langley Babb, ed., *Of the Press, by the Press, for the Press (and Others, Too)* (Washington, D.C.: Washington *Post* Co., 1974).

Part Four
THE ANTIWAR MOVEMENT:
WHY WAS THERE SO MUCH OPPOSITION?

The excerpts and articles in this section offer a view of the war from the perspective of Americans who opposed it and resisted it in one way or another. It is designed to give the reader a lively sense of who these people were, where they came from, why they could not go along with the war, and what they did about it. This section is much longer than Part Two, on those who went to war, because there is no comprehensive oral history on the antiwar movement to accompany this reader.

In a short historical passage, Howard Zinn emphasizes the demographics of the antiwar movement and the bold acts of individuals who took risks with their lives in their efforts to stop the war.

Todd Gitlin analyzes the effects of the antiwar movement, which he argues was "the most successful movement against a shooting war in history."

Sam Brown discusses his personal history in the antiwar movement, his idealistic intentions, the moral choices he made, and his retrospective view of the Vietnam generation.

Paul Goodman offers insight into the pacifist strain of the antiwar movement through his portrait of his son.

In an address to Clergy and Laity Concerned about Vietnam, Martin Luther King, Jr. discloses his reasons for coming out against the war, despite strong pressures to remain silent.

James Fallows reflects on the social implications of his decision to evade the draft by deliberately flunking his physical.

In his statement before the Senate Foreign Relations Committee, John Kerry speaks for Vietnam Veterans Against the War who had come to Washington as a group to petition their elected representatives to end the war.

The Impossible Victory
VIETNAM

BY HOWARD ZINN

Some of the first signs of opposition in the United States to the Vietnam war came out of the civil rights movement—perhaps because the experience of black people with the government led them to distrust any claim that it was fighting for freedom. On the very day that Lyndon Johnson was telling the nation in early August 1964 about the Gulf of Tonkin incident, and announcing the bombing of North Vietnam, black and white activists were gathering near Philadelphia, Mississippi, at a memorial service for the three civil rights workers killed there that summer. One of the speakers pointed bitterly to Johnson's use of force in Asia, comparing it with the violence used against blacks in Mississippi.

In mid-1965, in McComb, Mississippi, young blacks who had just learned that a classmate of theirs was killed in Vietnam distributed a leaflet:

> No Mississippi Negroes should be fighting in Viet Nam for the White man's freedom, until all the Negro People are free in Mississippi.
>
> Negro boys should not honor the draft here in Mississippi. Mothers should encourage their sons not to go. . . .
>
> No one has a right to ask us to risk our lives and kill other Colored People in Santo Domingo and Viet Nam, so that the White American can get richer.

When Secretary of Defense Robert McNamara visited Mississippi and praised Senator John Stennis, a prominent racist, as a "man of very genuine greatness," white and black students marched in protest, with placards saying "In Memory of the Burned Children of Vietnam."

The Student Nonviolent Coordinating Committee declared in early 1966 that "the United States is pursuing an aggressive policy in violation of international law" and called for withdrawal from Vietnam. That summer, six members of SNCC were arrested for an invasion of an induction center in Atlanta. They were convicted and sentenced to several years in prison. Around the same time, Julian Bond, a SNCC activist who had just been elected to the Georgia House of Representatives, spoke out against the war and the draft, and the House voted that he not be seated because his statements violated the Selective Service Act and "tend to bring discredit to the House." The Supreme Court restored Bond to his seat, saying he had the right to free expression under the First Amendment.

One of the great sports figures of the nation, Muhammad Ali, the black boxer and heavyweight champion, refused to serve in what he called a "white man's war"; boxing authorities took away his title as champion. Martin Luther King, Jr., spoke out in 1967 at Riverside Church in New York:

> Somehow this madness must cease. We must stop now. I speak as a child of God and brother to the suffering poor of Vietnam. I speak for those whose land is being laid waste, whose homes are being destroyed, whose culture is being subverted. I speak for the poor of America who are paying the double price of smashed hopes at home and death and corruption in Vietnam. I speak as a citizen of the world, for the world as it stands aghast at the path we have taken. I speak as an American to the leaders of my own nation. The great initiative in this war is ours. The initiative to stop it must be ours.

Young men began to refuse to register for the draft, refused to be inducted if called. As early as May 1964 the slogan "We Won't Go" was widely publicized. Some who had registered began publicly burning their draft cards to protest the war. One, David O'Brien, burned his draft card in South Boston; he was convicted, and the Supreme Court overruled his argument that this was a protected form of free expression. In October of 1967 there were organized draft-card "turn-ins" all over the country; in San Francisco alone, three hundred draft cards were returned to the government. Just before a huge demonstration at the Pentagon that month, a sack of collected draft cards was presented to the Justice Department.

By mid-1965, 380 prosecutions were begun against men refusing to be inducted; by mid-1968 that figure was up to 3,305. At the end of 1969, there were 33,960 delinquents nationwide.

In May 1969 the Oakland induction center, where draftees reported from all of northern California, reported that of 4,400 men ordered to report for induction, 2,400 did not show up. In the first quarter of 1970 the Selective Service system, for the first time, could not meet its quota.

A Boston University graduate student in history, Philip Supina, wrote on May 1, 1968, to his draft board in Tucson, Arizona:

> I am enclosing the order for me to report for my pre-induction physical exam for the armed forces. I have absolutely no intention to report for that exam, or for induction, or to aid in any way the American war effort against the people of Vietnam. . . .

He ended his letter by quoting the Spanish philosopher Miguel Unamuno, who during the Spanish Civil War said: "Sometimes to be Silent is to Lie." Supina was convicted and sentenced to four years in prison.

Early in the war, there had been two separate incidents, barely noticed by most Americans. On November 2, 1965, in front of the Pentagon in Washington, as thousands of employees were streaming out of the building in the late afternoon, Norman Morrison, a thirty-two-year-old pacifist, father of three, stood below the third-floor windows of Secretary of Defense Robert McNamara, doused himself with kerosene, and set himself afire, giving up his life in protest against the war. Also that year, in Detroit, an eighty-two-year-old woman named Alice Herz burned herself to death to make a statement against the horror of Indochina.

A remarkable change in sentiment took place. In the early 1965, when the bombing of North Vietnam began, a hundred people gathered on the Boston Common to voice their indignation. On October 15, 1969, the number of people assembled on the Boston Common to protest the war was 100,000. Perhaps 2 million people across the nation gathered that day in towns and villages that had never seen an antiwar meeting.

In the summer of 1965, a few hundred people had gathered in Washington to march in protest against the war: the first in line, historian Staughton Lynd, SNCC organizer Bob Moses, and long-time pacifist David Dellinger, were splattered with red paint by hecklers. But by 1970, the Washington peace rallies were drawing hundreds of thousands of people. In 1971, twenty thousand came to Washington to commit civil disobedience, trying to tie up Washington traffic to express their revulsion against the killing still going on in Vietnam. Fourteen thousand of them were arrested, the largest mass arrest in American history.

Hundreds of volunteers in the Peace Corps spoke out against the war. In Chile, ninety-two volunteers defied the Peace Corps director and issued a circular denouncing the war. Eight hundred former members of the Corps issued a statement of protest against what was happening in Vietnam.

The poet Robert Lowell, invited to a White House function, refused to come. Arthur Miller, also invited, sent a telegram to the White House: "When the guns boom, the arts die." Singer Eartha Kitt was invited to a luncheon on the White House lawn and shocked all those present by speaking out, in the presence of the President's wife, against the war. A teenager, called to the White House to accept a prize, came and criticized the war. In Hollywood, local artists erected a 60-foot Tower of Protest on Sunset Boulevard. At the National Book Award ceremonies in New York, fifty authors and publishers walked out on a speech by Vice-President Humphrey in a display of anger at his role in the war.

In London, two young Americans gate-crashed the American ambassador's elegant Fourth of July reception and called out a toast: "To all the dead and dying in Vietnam." They were carried out by guards. In the Pacific Ocean, two young American seamen hijacked an American munitions ship to divert its load of bombs from airbases in Thailand. For four days they took command of the ship and its crew, taking amphetamine pills to stay awake until the ship reached Cambodian waters. The Associated Press reported in late 1972, from York, Pennsylvania: "Five antiwar activists were arrested by the state police today for allegedly sabotaging railroad equipment near a factory that makes bomb casings used in the Vietnam war."

Middle-class and professional people unaccustomed to activism began to speak up. In May 1970, the *New York Times* reported from Washington: "1000 'ESTABLISHMENT' LAWYERS JOIN WAR PROTEST." Corporations began to wonder whether the war was going to hurt their long-range business interests; the *Wall Street Journal* began criticizing the continuation of the war.

As the war became more and more unpopular, people in or close to the government began to break out of the circle of assent. The most dramatic instance was the case of Daniel Ellsberg.

Ellsberg was a Harvard-trained economist, a former marine officer, employed by the RAND Corporation, which did special, often secret research for the U.S. government. Ellsberg helped write the

Department of Defense history of the war in Vietnam, and then decided to make the top-secret document public, with the aid of his friend, Anthony Russo, a former RAND Corporation man. The two had met in Saigon, where both had been affected, in different experiences, by direct sight of the war, and had become powerfully indignant at what the United States was doing to the people of Vietnam.

Ellsberg and Russo spent night after night, after hours, at a friend's advertising agency, duplicating the 7,000-page document. Then Ellsberg gave copies to various Congressmen and to the *New York Times.* In June 1971 the *Times* began printing selections from what came to be known as the *Pentagon Papers.* It created a national sensation.

The Nixon administration tried to get the Supreme Court to stop further publication, but the Court said this was "prior restraint" of the freedom of the press and thus unconstitutional. The government then indicted Ellsberg and Russo for violating the Espionage Act by releasing classified documents to unauthorized people; they faced long terms in prison if convicted. The judge, however, called off the trial during the jury deliberations, because the Watergate events unfolding at the time, revealed unfair practices by the prosecution.

Ellsberg, by his bold act, had broken with the usual tactic of dissidents inside the government who bided their time and kept their opinions to themselves, hoping for small changes in policy. A colleague urged him not to leave the government because there he had "access," saying "Don't cut yourself off. Don't cut your throat." Ellsberg replied: "Life exists outside the Executive Branch."

The antiwar movement, early in its growth, found a strange, new constituency: priests and nuns of the Catholic Church. Some of them had been aroused by the civil rights movement, others by their experiences in Latin America, where they saw poverty and injustice under governments supported by the United States. In the fall of 1967, Father Philip Berrigan (a Josephite priest who was a veteran of World War II), joined by artist Tom Lewis and friends David Eberhardt and James Mengel, went to the office of a draft board in Baltimore, Maryland, drenched the draft records with blood, and waited to be arrested. They were put on trial and sentenced to prison terms of two to six years.

The following May, Philip Berrigan—out on bail in the Baltimore case—was joined in a second action by his brother Daniel, a Jesuit priest who had visited North Vietnam and seen the effects of U.S. bombing. They and seven other people went into a draft board office in Catonsville, Maryland, removed records, and set them afire outside in the presence of reporters and onlookers. They were convicted and sentenced to prison, and became famous as the "Catonsville Nine." Dan Berrigan wrote a "Meditation" at the time of the Catonsville incident:

> Our apologies, good friends, for the fracture of good order, the burning of paper instead of children, the angering of the orderlies in the front parlor of the charnel house. We could not, so help us God, do otherwise. . . . We say: killing is disorder, life and gentleness and community and unselfishness is the only order we recognize. For the sake of that order, we risk our liberty, our good name. The time is past when good men can remain silent, when obedience can segregate men from public risk, when the poor can die without defense.

When his appeals had been exhausted, and he was supposed to go to prison, Daniel Berrigan disappeared. While the FBI searched for him, he showed up at an Easter festival at Cornell University, where he had been teaching. With dozens of FBI men looking for him in the crowd, he suddenly appeared on stage. Then the lights went out, he hid inside a giant figure of the Bread and Puppet Theatre which was on stage, was carried out to a truck, and escaped to a nearby farmhouse. He stayed underground for four months, writing poems, issuing statements, giving secret interviews, appearing suddenly in a Philadelphia church to give a sermon and then disappearing again, baffling the FBI, until an informer's interception of a letter disclosed his whereabouts and he was captured and imprisoned.

The one woman among the Catonsville Nine, Mary Moylan, a former nun, also refused to surrender to the FBI. She was never found. Writing from underground, she reflected on her experience and how she came to it:

> . . . We had all known we were going to jail, so we all had our toothbrushes. I was just exhausted. I took my little box of clothes and stuck it under the cot and climbed into bed. Now all the women in the Baltimore County jail were black—I think there was only one white. The women were waking me up and saying, "Aren't you going to cry?" I said, "What about?" They said, "You're in jail." And I said, "Yeah, I knew I'd be here." . . .
>
> I was sleeping between two of these women, and every morning I'd wake up and they'd be leaning on their elbows watching me. They'd say, "You slept all night." And they couldn't believe it. They were good. We had good times. . . .
>
> I suppose the political turning point in my life came while I was in Uganda. I was there when American planes were bombing the Congo, and we were very close to the Congo border. The planes came over

and bombed two villages in Uganda. . . . Where the hell did the American planes come in?

Later I was in Dar Es Salaam and Chou En-lai came to town. The American Embassy sent out letters saying that no Americans were to be on the street, because this was a dirty Communist leader; but I decided this was a man who was making history and I wanted to see him. . . .

When I came home from Africa I moved to Washington, and had to deal with the scene there and the insanity and brutality of the cops and the type of life that was led by most of the citizens of that city— 70 percent black. . . .

And then Vietnam, and the napalm and the defoliants, and the bombings. . . .

I got involved with the women's movement about a year ago. . . .

At the time of Catonsville, going to jail made sense to me, partially because of the black scene—so many blacks forever filling the jails. . . . I don't think it's a valid tactic anymore. . . . I don't want to see people marching off to jail with smiles on their faces. I just don't want them going. The Seventies are going to be very difficult, and I don't want to waste the sisters and brothers we have by marching them off to jail and having mystical experiences or whatever they're going to have. . . .

The effect of the war and of the bold action of some priests and nuns was to crack the traditional conservatism of the Catholic community. On Moratorium Day 1969, at the Newton College of the Sacred Heart near Boston, a sanctuary of bucolic quiet and political silence, the great front door of the college displayed a huge painted red fist. At Boston College, a Catholic institution, six thousand people gathered that evening in the gymnasium to denounce the war.

Students were heavily involved in the early protests against the war. A survey by the Urban Research Corporation, for the first six months of 1969 only, and for only 232 of the nation's two thousand institutions of higher education, showed that at least 215,000 students had participated in campus protests, that 3,652 had been arrested, that 956 had been suspended or expelled. Even in the high schools, in the late sixties, there were five hundred underground newspapers. At the Brown University commencement in 1969, two-thirds of the graduating class turned their backs when Henry Kissinger stood up to address them.

The climax of protest came in the spring of 1970 when President Nixon ordered the invasion of Cambodia. At Kent State University in Ohio, on May 4, when students gathered to demonstrate against the war, National Guardsmen fired into the crowd. Four students were killed. One was paralyzed for life. Students at four hundred colleges and universities went on strike in protest. It was the first general student strike in the history of the United States. During that school year of 1969–1970, the FBI listed 1,785 student demonstrations, including the occupation of 313 buildings.

The commencement day ceremonies after the Kent State killings were unlike any the nation had ever seen. From Amherst, Massachusetts, came this newspaper report:

> The 100th Commencement of the University of Massachusetts yesterday was a protest, a call for peace.
>
> The roll of the funeral drum set the beat for 2600 young men and women marching "in fear, in despair and in frustration."
>
> Red fists of protest, white peace symbols, and blue doves were stenciled on black academic gowns, and nearly every other senior wore an armband representing a plea for peace.

Student protests against the ROTC (Reserve Officers Training Program) resulted in the canceling of those programs in over forty colleges and universities. In 1966, 191,749 college students enrolled in ROTC. By 1973, the number was 72,459. The ROTC was depended on to supply half the officers in Vietnam. In September 1973, for the sixth straight month, the ROTC could not fulfill its quota. One army official said: "I just hope we don't get into another war, because if we do, I doubt we could fight it."

The publicity given to the student protests created the impression that the opposition to the war came mostly from middle-class intellectuals. When some construction workers in New York attacked student demonstrators, the news was played up in the national media. However, a number of elections in American cities, including those where mostly blue-collar workers lived, showed that antiwar sentiment was strong in the working classes. For instance, in Dearborn, Michigan, an automobile manufacturing town, a poll as early as 1967 showed 41 percent of the population favored withdrawal from the Vietnam war. In 1970, in two counties in California where petitioners placed the issue on the ballot—San Francisco County and Marin County—referenda asking withdrawal of the U.S. forces from Vietnam received a majority vote.

In late 1970, when a Gallup poll presented the statement: "The United States should withdraw all troops from Vietnam by the end of next year," 65 percent of those questioned said, "Yes." In Madison, Wisconsin, in the spring of 1971, a resolution calling for an immediate withdrawal of U.S. forces from Southeast Asia won by 31,000 to 16,000 (in 1968 such a resolution had lost).

But the most surprising data were in a survey made by the University of Michigan. This showed that, throughout the Vietnam war, Americans with only a grade school education were much stronger for withdrawal from the war than Americans with a college education. In June 1966, of people with a college education, 27 percent were for immediate withdrawal from Vietnam; of people with only a grade school education, 41 percent were for immediate withdrawal. By September 1970, both groups were more antiwar: 47 percent of the college-educated were for withdrawal, and 61 percent of grade school graduates.

There is more evidence of the same kind. In an article in *American Sociological Review* (June 1968), Richard F. Hamilton found in his survey of public opinion: "Preferences for 'tough' policy alternatives are most frequent among the following groups, the highly educated, high status occupations, those with high incomes, younger persons, and those paying much attention to newspapers and magazines." And a political scientist, Harlan Hahn, doing a study of various city referenda on Vietnam, found support for withdrawal from Vietnam highest in groups of lower socioeconomic status. He also found that the regular polls, based on samplings, underestimated the opposition to the war among lower-class people.

All this was part of a general change in the entire population of the country. In August of 1965, 61 percent of the population thought the American involvement in Vietnam was not wrong. By May 1971 it was exactly reversed; 61 percent thought our involvement *was* wrong. Bruce Andrews, a Harvard student of public opinion, found that the people most opposed to the war were people over fifty, blacks, and women. He also noted that a study in the spring of 1964, when Vietnam was a minor issue in the newspapers, showed that 53 percent of college-educated people were willing to send troops to Vietnam, but only 33 percent of grade school-educated people were so willing.

It seems that the media, themselves controlled by higher-education, higher-income people who were more aggressive in foreign policy, tended to give the erroneous impression that working-class people were superpatriots for the war. Lewis Lipsitz, in a mid-1968 survey of poor blacks and whites in the South, paraphrased an attitude he found typical: "The only way to help the poor man is to get out of that war in Vietnam. . . . These taxes—high taxes—it's going over yonder to kill people with and I don't see no cause in it."

The capacity for independent judgement among ordinary Americans is probably best shown by the swift development of antiwar feeling among American GIs—volunteers and draftees who came mostly from lower-income groups. There had been, earlier in American history, instances of soldiers' disaffection from the war: isolated mutinies in the Revolutionary War, refusal of reenlistment in the midst of hostilities in the Mexican war, desertion and conscientious objection in World War I and World War II. But Vietnam produced opposition by soldiers and veterans on a scale, and with a fervor, never seen before.

It began with isolated protests. As early as June 1965, Richard Steinke, a West Point graduate in Vietnam, refused to board an aircraft taking him to a remote Vietnamese village. "The Vietnamese war," he said, "is not worth a single American life." Steinke was court-martialed and dismissed from the service. The following year, three army privates, one black, one Puerto Rican, one Lithuanian-Italian—all poor—refused to embark for Vietnam, denouncing the war as "immoral, illegal, and unjust." They were court-martialed and imprisoned.

In early 1967, Captain Howard Levy, an army doctor at Fort Jackson, South Carolina, refused to teach Green Berets, a Special Forces elite in the military. He said they were "murderers of women and children" and "killers of peasants." He was court-martialed on the ground that he was trying to promote disaffection among enlisted men by his statements. The colonel who presided at the trial said: "The truth of the statements is not an issue in this case." Levy was convicted and sentenced to prison.

The individual acts multiplied: A black private in Oakland refused to board a troop plane to Vietnam, although he faced eleven years at hard labor. A navy nurse, Lieutenant Susan Schnall, was court-martialed for marching in a peace demonstration while in uniform, and for dropping antiwar leaflets from a plane on navy installations. In Norfolk, Virginia, a sailor refused to train fighter pilots because he said the war was immoral. An army lieutenant was arrested in Washington, D.C., in early 1968 for picketing the White House with a sign that said: "120,000 American Casualties—Why?" Two black marines, George Daniels and William Harvey, were given long prison sentences (Daniels, six years, Harvey, ten years, both later reduced) for talking to other black marines against the war.

As the war went on, desertions from the armed forces mounted. Thousands went to Western Europe—France, Sweden, Holland. Most deserters crossed into Canada; some estimates were 50,000, others 100,000. Some stayed in the United States. A few openly defied the military authorities by taking "sanctuary" in churches, where, surrounded by antiwar friends and sympathizers, they waited for capture and court-martial. At Boston University, a thousand students kept vigil for five days and nights in the chapel, supporting an eighteen-year-old deserter, Ray Kroll.

Kroll's story was a common one. He had been inveigled into joining the army; he came from a poor family, was brought into court, charged with drunkenness, and given the choice of prison or enlistment. He enlisted. And then he began to think about the nature of the war.

On a Sunday morning, federal agents showed up at the Boston University chapel, stomped their way through aisles clogged with students, smashed down doors, and took Kroll away. From the stockade, he wrote back to friends: "I ain't gonna kill; it's against my will. . . ." A friend he had made at the chapel brought him books, and he noted a saying he had found in one of them: "What we have done will not be lost to all Eternity. Everything ripens at its time and becomes fruit at its hour."

The GI antiwar movement became more organized. Near Fort Jackson, South Carolina, the first "GI coffeehouse" was set up, a place where soldiers could get coffee and doughnuts, find antiwar literature, and talk freely with others. It was called the UFO, and lasted for several years before it was declared a "public nuisance" and closed by court action. But other GI coffeehouses sprang up in half a dozen other places across the country. An antiwar "bookstore" was opened near Fort Devens, Massachusetts, and another one at the Newport, Rhode Island, naval base.

Underground newspapers sprang up at military bases across the country; by 1970 more than fifty were circulating. Among them: *About Face* in Los Angeles; *Fed Up!* in Tacoma, Washington; *Short Times* at Fort Jackson; *Vietnam GI* in Chicago; *Graffiti* in Heidelberg, Germany; *Bragg Briefs* in North Carolina; *Last Harass* at Fort Gordon, Georgia; *Helping Hand* at Mountain Home Air Base, Idaho. These newspapers printed antiwar articles, gave news about the harassment of GIs and practical advice on the legal rights of servicemen, told how to resist military domination.

Mixed with feeling against the war was resentment at the cruelty, the dehumanization, of military life. In the army prisons, the stockades, this was especially true. In 1968, at the Presidio stockade in California, a guard shot to death an emotionally disturbed prisoner for walking away from a work detail. Twenty-seven prisoners then sat down and refused to work, singing "We Shall Overcome." They were court-martialed, found guilty of mutiny, and sentenced to terms of up to fourteen years, later reduced after much public attention and protest.

The dissidence spread to the war front itself. When the great Moratorium Day demonstrations were taking place in October 1969 in the United States, some GIs in Vietnam wore black armbands to show their support. A news photographer reported that in a platoon on patrol near Da Nang, about half of the men were wearing black armbands. One soldier stationed at Cu Chi wrote to a friend on October 26, 1970, that separate companies had been set up for men refusing to go into the field to fight. "It's no big thing here anymore to refuse to go." The French newspaper *Le Monde* reported that in four months, 109 soldiers of the first air cavalry division were charged with refusal to fight. "A common sight," the correspondent for *Le Monde* wrote, "is the black soldier, with his left fist clenched in defiance of a war he has never considered his own."

Wallace Terry, a black American reporter for *Time* magazine, taped conversations with hundreds of black soldiers; he found bitterness against army racism, disgust with the war, generally low morale. More and more cases of "fragging" were reported in Vietnam— incidents where servicemen rolled fragmentation bombs under the tents of officers who were ordering them into combat, or against whom they had other grievances. The Pentagon reported 209 fraggings in Vietnam in 1970 alone.

Veterans back from Vietnam formed a group called Vietnam Veterans Against the War. In December 1970, hundreds of them went to Detroit to what was called the "Winter Soldier" investigations, to testify publicly about atrocities they had participated in or seen in Vietnam, committed by Americans against Vietnamese. In April 1971 more than a thousand of them went to Washington, D.C., to demonstrate against the war. One by one, they went up to a wire fence around the Capitol, threw over the fence the medals they had won in Vietnam, and made brief statements about the war, sometimes emotionally, sometimes in icy, bitter calm.

In the summer of 1970, twenty-eight commissioned officers of the military, including some veterans of Vietnam, saying they represented about 250 other officers, announced formation of the Concerned Officers Movement against the war. During the fierce bombings of Hanoi and Haiphong, around Christmas 1972, came the first defiance of B-52 pilots who refused to fly those missions.

On June 3, 1973, the *New York Times* reported dropouts among West Point cadets. Officials there, the reporter wrote, "linked the rate to an affluent, less disciplined, skeptical, and questioning generation and to the anti-military mood that a small radical minority and the Vietnam war had created."

But most of the antiwar action came from ordinary GIs, and most of these came from lower-income groups—white, black, Native American, Chinese.

A twenty-year-old New York City Chinese-American named Sam Choy enlisted at seventeen in the army, was sent to Vietnam, was made a cook, and found himself the target of abuse by fellow GIs, who called him "Chink" and "gook" (the term for the Vietnamese) and said he looked like the enemy. One day he took a rifle and fired warning shots at his tormenters. "By this time I was near the perimeter of the base and was thinking of joining the Viet Cong; at least they would trust me."

Choy was taken by military police, beaten, court-martialed, sentenced to eighteen months of hard labor at Fort Leavenworth. "They beat me up every day, like a time clock." He ended his interview with a New York Chinatown newspaper saying: "One thing: I want to tell all the Chinese kids that the army made me sick. They made me so sick that I can't stand it."

A dispatch from Phu Bai in April 1972 said the fifty GIs out of 142 men in the company refused to go on patrol, crying: "This isn't our war!" The *New York Times* on July 14, 1973, reported that American prisoners of war in Vietnam, ordered by officers in the POW camp to stop cooperating with the enemy, shouted back: "Who's the enemy?" They formed a peace committee in the camp, and a sergeant on the committee later recalled his march from capture to the POW camp:

> Until we got to the first camp, we didn't see a village intact; they were all destroyed. I sat down and put myself in the middle and asked myself: Is this right or wrong? Is it right to destroy villages? Is it right to kill people en masse? After a while it just got to me.

Pentagon officials in Washington and navy spokesmen in San Diego announced, after the United States withdrew its troops from Vietnam in 1973, that the navy was going to purge itself of "undesirables"—and that these included as many as six thousand men in the Pacific fleet, "a substantial proportion of them black." All together, about 700,000 GIs had received less than honorable discharges. In the year 1973, one of every five discharges was "less than honorable," indicating something less than dutiful obedience to the military. By 1971, 177 of every 1,000 American soldiers were listed as "absent without leave," some of them three or four times. Deserters doubled from 47,000 in 1967 to 89,000 in 1971.

One of those who stayed, fought, but then turned against the war was Ron Kovic. His father worked in a supermarket on Long Island.

In 1963, at the age of seventeen, he enlisted in the marines. Two years later, in Vietnam, at the age of nineteen, his spine was shattered by shellfire. Paralyzed from the waist down, he was put in a wheelchair. Back in the States, he observed the brutal treatment of wounded veterans in the veterans' hospitals, thought more and more about the war, and joined the Vietnam Veterans Against the War. He went to demonstrations to speak against the war. One evening he heard actor Donald Sutherland read from the post-World War I novel by Dalton Trumbo, *Johnny Got His Gun*, about a soldier whose limbs and face were shot away by gunfire, a thinking torso who invented a way of communicating with the outside world and then beat out a message so powerful it could not be heard without trembling.

> Sutherland began to read the passage and something I will never forget swept over me. It was as if someone was speaking for everything I ever went through in the hospital. . . . I began to shake and I remember there were tears in my eyes.

Kovic demonstrated against the war, and was arrested. He tells his story in *Born on the Fourth of July:*

> They help me back into the chair and take me to another part of the prison building to be booked.
> "What's your name?" the officer behind the desk says.
> "Ron Kovic," I say. "Occupation, Vietnam veteran against the war."
> "What?" he says sarcastically, looking down at me.
> "I'm a Vietnam veteran against the war," I almost shout back.
> "You should have died over there," he says. He turns to his assistant. "I'd like to take this guy and throw him off the roof."
> They fingerprint me and take my picture and put me in a cell. I have begun to wet my pants like a little baby. The tube has slipped out during my examination by the doctor. I try to fall asleep but even though I am exhausted, the anger is alive in me like a huge hot stone in my chest. I lean my head up against the wall and listen to the toilets flush again and again.

Kovic and the other veterans drove to Miami to the Republican National Convention in 1972, went into the Convention Hall, wheeled themselves down the aisles, and as Nixon began his acceptance speech shouted, "Stop the bombing! Stop the war!" Delegates cursed them: "Traitor!" and Secret Service men hustled them out of the hall.

In the fall of 1973, with no victory in sight and North Vietnamese troops entrenched in various parts of the South, the United States agreed to accept a settlement that would withdraw American troops and leave the revolutionary troops where they were, until a new elected government would be set up including Communist and non-Communist elements. But the Saigon government refused to agree, and the United States decided to make one final attempt to bludgeon the North Vietnamese into submission. It sent waves of B-52s over Hanoi and Haiphong, destroying homes and hospitals, killing unknown numbers of civilians. The attack did not work. Many of the B-52s were shot down, there was angry protest all over the world—and Kissinger went back to Paris and signed very much the same peace agreement that had been agreed on before.

The United States withdrew its forces, continuing to give aid to the Saigon government, but when the North Vietnamese launched attacks in early 1975 against the major cities in South Vietnam, the government collapsed. In late April 1975, North Vietnamese troops entered Saigon. The American embassy staff fled, along with many Vietnamese who feared Communist rule, and the long war in Vietnam was over. Saigon was renamed Ho Chi Minh City, and both parts of Vietnam were unified as the Democratic Republic of Vietnam.

Traditional history portrays the end of wars as coming from the initiatives of leaders—negotiations in Paris or Brussels or Geneva or Versailles—just as it often finds the coming of war a response to the demand of "the people." The Vietnam war gave clear evidence that at least for that war (making one wonder about the others) the political leaders were the last to take steps to end the war—"the people" were far ahead. The President was always far behind. The Supreme Court silently turned away from cases challenging the Constitutionality of the war. Congress was years behind public opinion.

In the spring of 1971, syndicated columnists Rowland Evans and Robert Novak, two firm supporters of the war, wrote regretfully of a "sudden outbreak of anti-war emotionalism" in the House of Representatives, and said: "The anti-war animosities now suddenly so pervasive among House Democrats are viewed by Administration backers as less anti-Nixon than as a response to constituent pressures."

It was only after the intervention in Cambodia ended, and only after the nationwide campus uproar over that invasion, that Congress passed a resolution declaring that American troops should not be sent into Cambodia without its approval. And it was not until late 1973, when American troops had finally been removed from Vietnam, that Congress passed a bill limiting the power of the President to make war without congressional consent; even there, in that "War Powers Resolution," the President could make war for sixty days on his own without a congressional declaration.

The administration tried to persuade the American people that the war was ending because of its decision to negotiate a peace—not because it was losing the war, not because of the powerful antiwar movement in the United States. But the government's own secret memoranda all through the war testify to its sensitivity at each stage about "public opinion" in the United States and abroad. The data is in the *Pentagon Papers*.

In June of 1964, top American military and State Department officials, including Ambassador Henry Cabot Lodge, met in Honolulu. "Rusk stated that public opinion on our SEA policy was badly divided and that, therefore, the President needed an affirmation of support." Diem had been replaced by a general named Khanh. The Pentagon historians write: "Upon his return to Saigon on June 5 Ambassador Lodge went straight from the airport to call on General Khanh . . . the main thrust of his talk with Khanh was to hint that the United States government would in the immediate future be preparing U.S. public opinion for actions against North Vietnam." Two months later came the Gulf of Tonkin affair.

On April 2, 1965, a memo from CIA director John McCone suggested that the bombing of North Vietnam be increased because it was "not sufficiently severe" to change North Vietnam's policy. "On the other hand . . . we can expect increasing pressure to stop the bombing . . . from various elements of the American public, from the press, the United Nations and world opinion." The U.S. should try for a fast knockout before this opinion could build up, McCone said.

Assistant Secretary of Defense John McNaughton's memo of early 1966 suggested destruction of locks and dams to create mass starvation, because "strikes at population targets" would "create a counterproductive wave of revulsion abroad and at home." In May 1967, the Pentagon historians write: "McNaughton was also very deeply concerned about the breadth and intensity of public unrest and dissatisfaction with the war . . . especially with young people, the underprivileged, the intelligentsia and the women." McNaughton worried: "Will the move to call up 20,000 Reserves . . . polarize opinion to the extent that the 'doves' in the United states will get out of hand—massive refusals to serve, or to fight, or to cooperate, or worse?" He warned:

> There may be a limit beyond which many Americans and much of the world will not permit the United States to go. The picture of the world's greatest superpower killing or seriously injuring 1000 non-combatants a week, while trying to pound a tiny backward nation into submission, on an issue whose merits are hotly disputed, is not a pretty one. It could conceivably produce a costly distortion in the American national consciousness.

That "costly distortion" seems to have taken place by the spring of 1968, when, with the sudden and scary Tet offensive of the National Liberation Front, Westmoreland asked President Johnson to send him 200,000 more troops on top of the 525,000 already there. Johnson asked a small group of "action officers" in the Pentagon to advise him on this. They studied the situation and concluded that 200,000 troops would totally Americanize the war and would not strengthen the Saigon government because: "The Saigon leadership shows no signs of a willingness—let alone an ability—to attract the necessary loyalty or support of the people." Furthermore, the report said, sending troops would mean mobilizing reserves, increasing the military budget. There would be more U.S. casualties, more taxes. And:

This growing disaffection accompanied as it certainly will be, by increased defiance of the draft and growing unrest in the cities because of the belief that we are neglecting domestic problems, runs great risks of provoking a domestic crisis of unprecedented proportions.

The "growing unrest in the cities" must have been a reference to the black uprisings that had taken place in 1967—and showed the link, whether blacks deliberately made it or not—between the war abroad and poverty at home.

The evidence from the *Pentagon Papers* is clear—that Johnson's decision in the spring of 1968 to turn down Westmoreland's request, to slow down for the first time the escalation of the war, to diminish the bombing, to go to the conference table, was influenced to a great extent by the actions Americans had taken in demonstrating their opposition to the war.

When Nixon took office, he too tried to persuade the public that protest would not affect him. But he almost went berserk when one lone pacifist picketed the White House. The frenzy of Nixon's actions against dissidents—plans for burglaries, wiretapping, mail openings—suggests the importance of the antiwar movement in the minds of national leaders.

One sign that the ideas of the antiwar movement had taken hold in the American public was that juries became more reluctant to convict antiwar protesters, and local judges too were treating them differently. In Washington, by 1971, judges were dismissing charges against demonstrators in cases where two years before they almost certainly would have been sent to jail. The antiwar groups who had raided draft boards—the Baltimore Four, the Catonsville Nine, the Milwaukee Fourteen, the Boston Five, and more—were receiving lighter sentences for the same crimes.

The last group of draft board raiders, the "Camden 28," were priests, nuns, and laypeople who raided a draft board in Camden, New Jersey, in August 1971. It was essentially what the Baltimore Four had done four years earlier, when all were convicted and Phil Berrigan got six years in prison. But in this instance, the Camden defendants were acquitted by the jury on all counts. When the verdict was in, one of the jurors, a fifty-three-year-old black taxi driver from Atlantic City named Samuel Braithwaite, who had spent eleven years in the army, left a letter for the defendants:

> To you, the clerical physicians with your God-given talents, I say, well done. Well done for trying to heal the sick irresponsible men, men who were chosen by the people to govern and lead them. These men, who failed the people, by raining death and destruction on a hapless country. . . . You went out to do your part while your brothers remained in their ivory towers watching . . . and hopefully some day in the near future, peace and harmony may reign to people of all nations.

That was in May of 1973. The American troops were leaving Vietnam. C. L. Sulzberger, the *New York Times* correspondent (a man close to the government), wrote: "The U.S. emerges as the big loser and history books must admit this. . . . We lost the war in the Mississippi valley, not the Mekong valley. Successive American governments were never able to muster the necessary mass support at home."

In fact, the United States had lost the war in both the Mekong Valley and the Mississippi Valley. It was the first clear defeat to the global American empire formed after World War II. It was administered by revolutionary peasants abroad, and by an astonishing movement of protest at home.

Back on September 26, 1969, President Richard Nixon, noting the growing antiwar activity all over the country, announced that "under no circumstance will I be affected whatever by it." But nine years later, in his *Memoirs,* he admitted that the antiwar movement caused him to drop plans for an intensification of the war: "Although publicly I continued to ignore the raging antiwar controversy. . . . I knew, however, that after all the protests and the Moratorium, American public opinion would be seriously divided by any military escalation of the war." It was a rare presidential admission of the power of public protest.

From a long-range viewpoint, something perhaps even more important had happened. The rebellion at home was spreading beyond the issue of war in Vietnam.

Seizing History

WHAT WE WON AND LOST AT HOME

BY TODD GITLIN

As my generation teeters uneasily between late youth and early middle age, and American expeditionary forces are launched toward new wars in the Third World, a good number of my old political buddies are wondering whether the antiwar passions of the 1960s were worth the effort. The Vietnam War dragged on and on, after all, and in the end, didn't Khmer Rouge genocide and Vietnamese authoritarianism discredit our hopes? Prompted by once-over-lightly media treatments of the era, today's campus inactivists also seem to believe that the '60s demonstrated conclusively that you can't change history to match your ideals. So why go to the trouble of letting tainted politics interfere with the rigors of preparing for the law boards?

Meanwhile, it's the so-called conservatives, neo- and paleo , who give the antiwar movement credit. They firmly believe that the country was seized during the '60s by a "new class" of overeducated left intellectuals, tantrum-throwing students, media liberals, uppity minorities, feminists, hedonists, homosexuals and assorted bleeding hearts, who not only succeeded in trashing tradition, standards, the family and all natural hierarchy, but also broke the back of national security, leveling America's just position in the world and costing us an achievable and noble victory in Vietnam. They have spent the past ten years trying to figure out how to recapture lost terrain from the barbarians. And they are haunted by the specter of revived antiwar activity—for good reason. For despite their paranoid exaggerations and their self-serving refusal to acknowledge just how much ideological ground they have already reconquered, they know in

Reprinted from *Mother Jones*, November 1983, by permission. Copyright © 1983 by Mother Jones.

their bones what many veterans of the '60s don't know or have forgotten: that the movement against the Vietnam War was history's most successful movement against a shooting war.

Not that there's much reason for unqualified self-congratulation. The napalm no longer falls on Vietnam, but the country still lives under dictatorship, on a perpetual war footing. Moreover, while the movement counted heavily in American politics, much of the leadership, eventually, wasn't satisfied simply to be against the war. Feeling either futile or giddy, they finally wanted a revolution, and came to define success accordingly. Those who persisted in that course made themselves irrelevant to the politics of the '70s and '80s. If the movement was effective, a less insular and more sophisticated movement might have been all the more so. To understand both the achievement and the limits, to learn lessons apropos impending wars, we have to look carefully at the movement's effects on the war and, with equal care, at the war's effects on the movement.

Already, the passing of time shrouds the '60s; the end is confounded with the beginning, the consequences with the causes; the all-important sequence of events is obscured. Our collective memory, such as it is, rests on a few disjointed images snatched out of order. For example, I was shocked in 1975 when the most sophisticated student in a class I was teaching at the University of California, Santa Cruz, said to me one day, "You were in SDS, right?" Right, I said. "That was the Weathermen, right?" How could I explain easily that the Weathermen were one of the factions that *ended* Students for a Democratic Society, exploded its ten-year history? (As an early leader of SDS I had fervently opposed them, in fact.)

The media and popular lore have dwelt on the lurid, easily pigeonholed images of 1968–71, as if they encompassed and defined the whole of "The '60s" in living color once and for all: the flags of the National Liberation Front of South Vietnam flying at antiwar demonstrations, singled out by TV cameras however outnumbered they were by American flags; window-trashers and rock-throwers, however outnumbered they were by peaceful marchers; the bombings and torchings of ROTC buildings; and the lethal explosions of the Weather Underground townhouse and the University of Wisconsin Army Mathematics Research Center in 1970.

To fathom the antiwar movement, though, we have to go back to 1964–65, when the Johnson administration committed itself to the war. In September 1964, while Lyndon Johnson was campaigning for peace votes with the slogan "We seek no wider war," American gunboats just offshore North Vietnam provoked an attack by the North Vietnamese, and a gullible Senate gave Johnson a carte blanche resolution that was to supply the questionable legal basis for years of subsequent escalation. The political climate of that moment is measured by the fact that the dissenting votes numbered a grand total of two—Wayne Morse and Ernest Gruening. That Christmas, Students for a Democratic Society, with all of a few hundred active members, presumptuously called for a demonstration against the war, to be held in Washington, D.C., in April. In February, Johnson began the systematic bombing of North Vietnam. In March came the first campus teach-ins against the war, and in April more than 25,000 marched in Washington—the majority dressed in jackets, ties, skirts. During the fall of 1965 there were the first coordinated demonstrations across the country, some of them more militant (a few symbolic attempts to block troop trains); there were a few widely publicized draft card burnings and a national media hysteria about a nonexistent SDS plan to disrupt the draft. Within the next 18 months, some leaders of the civil rights movement began denouncing the war—first the militants of the Student Nonviolent Coordinating Committee, then the Reverend Dr. Martin Luther King, Jr. There were attempts to get antiwar measures onto local ballots and to carry the war issue into professional associations.

With the number of American troops steadily swelling to almost the half-million mark and the bombing continuing mercilessly, antiwar militancy—still nonviolent—grew apace. In October 1967 there were vast mobilizations at the Pentagon and in Oakland, California, where, for the first time, armed troops and riot-control police wreaked havoc on active nonviolence. Only in 1968, after the assassinations of Martin Luther King and Robert F. Kennedy, did significant numbers of antiwar people murmur about the need for violence to raise the political cost of the war at home. There were also the first activities by government *agents provocateurs*.

We don't know nearly enough, and are not collectively curious enough, about government provocation. But one item may suggest how tantalizing this subject should be for a new generation of researchers. In August 1968, a few thousand demonstrators went out into the streets of Chicago. The tear-gas clouds and media spotlights during the Democratic convention polarized public opinion and established a new threshold for militancy while fatally discrediting the Democrats. Who were these protesters? According to army intelligence documents pried loose by CBS News ten years later, "About one demonstrator in six was an undercover agent." As flag-burning and cop-provoking increased, the movement became open territory for tough-talking infiltrators. With glacial slowness, information seeps into the light; but out famous investigative press—busy now uncovering the startling news that the KGB tries to influence anti-nuclear politics in Europe—is largely uninterested in this ancient history.

In any event, to gauge the effects of the movement as a whole, we might begin by asking what would have happened if the war had gone on without any material public opposition. Suppose, in other words, that without a movement in the streets there had been only a passive and ambiguous dissent in the polls as the American body-count mounted. Suppose also a numbed and passive Congress. Suppose, that is, a war very much like the Korean War.

What would have kept the war from escalating even more intensely than it actually did, with more ordnance and more troops producing more devastation, more refugees, more death? There were, of course, other forces working against the war: the economic drain; the breakdown of military discipline (inspired in a curious way by the movement); and the political mainstream's sense of the war's futility. But the North Vietnamese and the NLF were prepared to suffer huge casualties indefinitely rather than surrender. And once "Vietnamization" had changed the color of the corpses, the United States could have withdrawn its combat troops and still continued the air war for years without producing massive disgruntlement, for the bomber missions cost relatively few American lives. Support would likely have grown for the military's designs to press the war to the screaming limits of military technology in order to maintain an anti-Communist South Vietnam, indefinitely, at all costs.

Concrete evidence of the movement's influence was hard to come by. So much so, in fact, that, day to day, many movement people felt we were accomplishing next to nothing. After all, although the worst escalations *might* be averted or postponed at any given moment, this was abstract surmise; concretely, the bombs kept falling, and successive administrations weren't handing out public prizes for tying their hands.

Meanwhile, public opinion after the Tet offensive of early 1968 was ambiguous. It registered the growing conviction that the war was a mistake and a futility, coupled with the desire to "get it all over with" by any means possible, including bombing. This was the combination that Nixon brilliantly exploited to win the presidency in 1968, with vague references to a secret plan to end the war. So emerged the movement's desperate cycle of trying to raise the stakes, double or nothing—more fury and more violence—especially when the media dutifully played their part by amplifying the most flamboyant gestures of antiwar theatre.

Nonetheless, evidence is coming to light that the movement had a direct veto power over war escalations at a number of points. David Halberstam tells us in *The Best and the Brightest*, for example, that in late 1966 the military was already urging President Johnson to bomb Hanoi and Haiphong, to block the harbor and, in Halberstam's words, to "[take] apart the industrial capacity of both cities." "How long [will] it take," Johnson lamented, "[for] five hundred thousand angry Americans to climb that White House wall . . . and lynch their president if he does something like that?" "Which ended for a time," Halberstam writes, "the plan to bomb Hanoi and Haiphong."

Despite their denials at the time, Nixon administration officials were no less sensitive to the actual and potential political threat of movement protest. Early in the first Nixon administration, for example, during a lull in demonstrations—so writes Henry Kissinger in *White House Years*—Secretary of Defense Melvin Laird argued against the secret bombing of Cambodia for fear of "[waking] the dormant beast of public protest." At another point, Kissinger refers to "the hammer of antiwar pressure" as a factor that he and Nixon could never ignore.

The denials were, at times, actually a backhanded index of the movement's real influence. Unbeknownst to the movement, its greatest impact was exerted just when it felt most desperate. In the summer of 1969, while withdrawing some ground troops amidst great fanfare, Nixon and Kissinger decided on a "November ultimatum" to Hanoi. Either Hanoi would accommodate to Nixon's bargaining terms by November 1, or Nixon would launch an unprecedented new assault, including, as Seymour Hersh writes in *The Price of Power*, "the massive bombing of Hanoi, Haiphong and other key areas in North Vietnam; the mining of harbors and rivers; the bombing of the dike system; a ground invasion of North Vietnam; the destruction—possibly with nuclear devices—of the main north-south passes along the Ho Chi Minh Trail; and the bombing of North Vietnam's main railroad links with China." For a full month, in utter secrecy, Nixon kept American B-52s on full nuclear alert—the first such alert since the Cuban missile crisis.

Some White House staff members objected to the November ultimatum plans on military grounds, but by Nixon's own account, antiwar demonstrations were central to his decision not to go ahead with this blockbuster escalation. The massive October 15 Moratorium, and the promise of more of the same on November 15, convinced Nixon (as he wrote later) that "after all the protests and the

Moratorium, American public opinion would be seriously divided by any military escalation of the war."

For public consumption, Nixon made a show of ignoring the demonstrations and claiming they were of no avail. The movement, for its part, had no way of knowing what catastrophe it was averting, and thus felt helpless. Nixon, meanwhile, moved to split militants from moderates. He combined stepped-up repression, surveillance and press manipulation with a calming strategy that included markedly lower draft calls and, eventually, a draft lottery system that defused opposition by pitting the unlucky few against the lucky. Within the movement, the minority who faulted the Moratorium for its relative moderation began arguing that a new level of militancy was required: first came trashing, then sideline cheerleading for the newly organized splinter group, the Weathermen. The result was a general demoralization on the Left.

At the moment of its maximum veto power, much of the movement's hard core fell victim to all-or-nothing thinking. White House seerecy was one reason the movement misunderstood its own force; the intrinsic difficulty of gauging political results was a second; the third was the movement's own bitter-end mentality. Much of the movement succumbed to a politics of rage. Relatively privileged youth had been raised in child-centered families and conditioned by a consumer culture to expect quick results. An excess of impatience made it easy for them to resort to terrorism. Thus, the movement drove itself toward self-isolating militancy and, by 1971, away from most activity altogether. A desperately revolutionary self-image drove the hard core to disdain alliance with moderates, which, of course, was just what the White House wanted.

When Nixon ordered the invasion of Cambodia in the spring of 1970, hundreds of thousands poured into the streets in protest. But the old movement leadership had burned out or burrowed into underground fantasies, and the new activists lacked leadership. This new round of protest flared and disappeared quickly, especially as shrinking draft calls eliminated the immediate threat to many college students. At the same time the killings at Kent State stripped students of their feeling of safety. With their sense of exemption gone, results invisible and leadership lacking, it wasn't long before they subsided into inactivity. And yet, even then, the demonstrations convinced Nixon to limit the invasion's scope and cut it short. "Nixon's decision to limit the Cambodia offensive," Seymour Hersh concludes, "demonstrated anew the ultimate power of the antiwar movement." Even though the frequency and size of demonstrations declined over the next two years, their threat restrained Nixon's hand.

By this time, the movement's influence on the war was mostly indirect: a nudging of the elites whose children were in revolt, which paved the way for Establishment skepticism. Although radicals didn't want to think of themselves as "mere" reformists, they amounted to a small engine that turned the more potent engines that could, in fact, retard the war.

The movement continued to stimulate moderate antiwar sentiment in Congress, the media and churches even in later years, when demonstrations had become only a ghostly echo. As early as 1968, political, corporate and media elites grew disillusioned with the war. It wasn't "working." Although they accepted little of the antiwar movement's analysis, the elites capitalized on the movement's initiative and sometimes—as in the case of the McCarthy and Kennedy campaigns for the Democratic nomination in 1968—recruited troops as well.

The pivotal moment came just after the Tet offensive, when Johnson's top advisors decided that the war was costing too much in political, economic and military terms. Clark Clifford, Johnson's new secretary of defense, lost faith in the war effort and set out to mobilize influential opposition among the political elite that had represented foreign policy consensus since 1945. At the same time that the Joint Chiefs of Staff were requesting 206,000 new troops for Vietnam, Clifford was persuading Johnson to meet with the informal advisory group later known as the Wise Men: Dean Acheson, McGeorge Bundy, George Ball, C. Douglas Dillon, Cyrus Vance, General Maxwell Taylor and others, men who had occupied top positions in the Truman and Kennedy as well as Johnson administrations. If there was an Establishment, this was it.

Cyrus Vance said later, "We were weighing not only what was happening in Vietnam, but the social and political effects in the United States, the impact on the U.S. economy, the attitudes of other nations. The divisiveness in the country was growing with such acuteness that it was threatening to tear the United States apart." As guardians of America's world position, the Wise Men were sensitive to European doubts and frightened by the war's economic consequences—deficit financing, incipient inflation, a negative balance of payments and gold outflow. Some of them were also aware that American troops were becoming unreliable in the field and that, in an unanticipated echo of the antiwar movement, some soldiers were wearing peace symbols on their helmets.

"The meeting with the Wise Men served the purpose that I hoped it would," Clifford exulted later. "It really shook the president." Three days later, Johnson refused the Joint Chiefs' troop request, announced a partial bombing halt—and took himself out of the presidential race. Major new shipments of American troops became politically taboo for the duration of the war.

Nevertheless, the war went on for years, leaving hundreds of thousands of corpses as testimony to the movement's failure to achieve the peace it longed for. If it had been more astute, had cultivated more allies, it might have been able to cut the war shorter and reduce the general destruction. The largely middle-class antiwar movement could have broadened in several directions. If it had supported the growing GI antiwar faction more concertedly, had gotten over its squeamishness toward soldiers, the combination might have succeeded in frightening Johnson and Nixon earlier. A more serious alliance with antiwar veterans and working-class draftees might have broken the movement out of its middle-class ghetto, might have established before a hostile public and a cynical administration that the movement was more than a rabble of middle-class kids trying to preserve their privilege of avoiding combat. If the largely white movement had paid more attention to broad-based interracial alliances (as with the 1970 Chicano National Moratorium) and less to the glamour of revolutionary showmanship, it might have capitalized on high-level governmental fears of what Air Force Undersecretary Townsend Hoopes in his memoirs called "the fateful merging of antiwar and racial dissension." As we now know, the White House was terrified of black protest even into the Nixon years. A full year after Martin Luther King was assassinated, J. Edgar Hoover was sending memos on King's sex life to Henry Kissinger, who kept them on file, one National Security Council Staff member said, "to blunt the black antiwar movement."

If anything, the movement should be faulted for not being effective, ecumenical, persistent enough. It is even conceivable (history affords no certitudes) that a stronger movement might have kept the ferocious U.S. bombing from driving Cambodian peasants into the arms of the increasingly fanatical Khmer Rouge. All civilized people who are revolted by the Khmer Rouge mass atrocities should also remember that it was the Nixon administration, not the movement, that encouraged the overthrow of Prince Sihanouk and weakened opposition to this regime of mass murders. Moreover, whatever the movement's willingness to overlook authoritarianism in North Vietnam, a shorter, less destructive war might also have made postwar reconciliation easier in a unified Vietnam. And if the movement had survived to demand that the U.S. keep up its end of the 1973 Paris peace agreement, the promised American postwar aid might have overcome some of the austerity that later served Hanoi as a rationale for repression.

The movement left a mixed legacy. Even with most of its force spent, after the McGovern catastrophe of 1972, the phantom movement, coupled with the belated resolve of congressional doves, succeeded in keeping Nixon from a wholehearted new assault on Vietnam. Watergate was the decisive turn, though, that distracted Nixon from keeping his secret promises to Nguyen Van Thieu and short-circuiting the Paris agreements with a resurgence of American bombing. By the cunning of reason, Nixon's paranoia about the antiwar movement, among other bêtes noire, led him to such grossly illegal measures that he was ultimately prevented from continuing the war itself. And, of course, the antiwar feeling outlasted Nixon. As late as 1975, Congress was able to stop American intervention in Angola.

Even today, the memory of the movement against the Vietnam War works against maximum direct military intervention in Central America. Again, there's no cause for pure and simple jubilation: the doves failed to anticipate how easy it would be for later administrations to substitute heavy military aid and troop maneuvers for direct combat forces. The movement also failed to persuade enough of the country that democratic revolutionary change is often the superior alternative to hunger and massacre in the Third World, and that American support (what the New Left used to call "critical support") might soften the most repressive features of revolutionary regimes. The result of simplistic Cold War thinking is hardened revolutions and Third World dependency on the Soviet Union—which after the fact seems to confirm the Cold War notion that revolutions are nothing more than props for Soviet expansion. American troops en masse are not at this moment being sacrificed to unwinnable wars, but the same bitterend purpose is supporting Somocista guerrillas in Nicaragua, genocidal killers in Guatemala, death squads in El Salvador, a seemingly permanent U.S. base in Honduras—at a relatively cut-rate cost to American society.

The movement against the Vietnam War can be counted a real if incomplete success, even despite itself. But what happened to the movement in the process?

The movement sloppily squandered much of its moral authority. Too much of the leadership, and some of the rank and file, slid into a romance with the other side. If napalm was evil, then the other side was endowed with nobility. If the American flag was dirty, the NLF flag was clean. If the deluded make-Vietnam-safe-for-democracy barbarism of the war could be glibly equated with the deliberate slaughter of millions in Nazi gas chambers—if the American Christ turned out to look like the Antichrist—then by this cramped, left-wing logic, the Communist Antichrist must really have been Christ. Ironically, some of the movement anticipated the Great Communicator's jubilant proclamation that Vietnam was a "noble enterprise," but with the sides reversed. This helped discredit the movement in the eyes of moderate potential supporters—who were, in turn, too quick to find reasons to write it off. For too long the movement swallowed North Vietnamese claims that it had no troops in South Vietnam, even though, by the logic of the movement's argument that Vietnam was one country, artificially kept divided by American intervention, it should not have been surprising that northern troops would be in the south.

Romanticism and rage dictated that North Vietnamese and National Liberation Front heroism be transmuted into the image of a good society that *had* to exist out there somewhere. American activists who thought they were making a revolution, not a mere antiwar movement, borrowed their prepackaged imagery—their slogans and mystique—from Vietnamese cadres whose suffering and courage were undeniable but who had little to teach us about how to conduct a modern democratic society. In 1969, when zealots chanting "Ho, Ho, Ho Chi Minh" confronted other zealots chanting "Mao, Mao, Mao Tse Tung" and tore up SDS between them, both sides were surrendering political reason and curling up to father figures.

This kind of moral corrosion has become all too familiar in the 20th century: the know-it-alls explain away revolutionary abominations, try to corner the market in utopian futures and, in the process, become mirror-images of the absolutist authority they detest. In the end, the revolutionists have helped return moral title to conservatives.

Even today, we hear voices on the left conjuring rationalizations for crimes committed by left-wing guerrillas. A curious partial freedom is parceled out to state-sponsored socialism, as if revolutions are responsible for their accomplishments, while their brutality, if acknowledged at all, is credited to American imperialism. Why is it necessary to keep silent about the shutting down of newspapers in Managua in order to oppose American intervention on behalf of death squads?

There is no simple explanation why much of the antiwar movement leadership found it hard to criticize authoritarian socialism. Partly there was the fear of putting ammunition in the hands of the Right—as though if the Right were right about anything, it might be right about everything. Then, too, dressing up for revolution was easier than reckoning with the strangeness of being a radical movement, based on youth, spunk, marginality and educated arrogance, in a society that not only permitted dissent but made it possible to act in history without wholesale bloodshed. The heavily middle-class revolutionists tried to bull past their own isolation: they made themselves Leninists of the will. Others went the Yippie route, with toy machine guns and glib youth-cult gestures. The publicity loop boosted the most flamboyant leaders into celebrity and helped limit the movement's reach.

Caught in a maelstrom of images, the rest of the movement became massively demoralized by 1970. The vast, unorganized, indeed silent majority was appalled to watch SDS decompose into warring sects speaking in Marxist-Leninist tongues. They didn't think revolutionary Vietnam was the promised land. They hated illegitimate authority in all forms. If they were understandably sentimental about peasants shooting at fighter bombers with rifles from alongside their water buffalo, they also knew that by far the greatest bloodbath going on in the world came from American firepower—and that no halfway desirable objective could be worth it. And they were right. From their impulses, on top of the civil rights movement, came a more general refusal of unjust authority, which led, most profoundly, to the movement for the liberation of women. To choose political passivity today on the spurious ground that the antiwar movement of the '60s "failed" is to succumb to all-or-nothing petulance, to insist that history promise to bear out all one's dreams before one tries to stop a slaughter. We'll travel lighter now without the burden of revolutionary myths.

A final legacy of the antiwar movement is that it battered the unreflective anticommunism of the 1950s and made it possible to open new doors. Now it also becomes possible to think past the kneejerk anti-*anti*-communism of the '60s, and to oppose American interventionism on the ground that it violates the elementary rights of human beings, not that it obstructs the Third World's revolutionary emergence into the highest stage of social existence. Anyway, movements are compost for later movements. The Vietnam War bred succeeding wars, and so, in a sense, the meaning depends on what happens as we try to stop sequels in Central America and elsewhere. After throwing weight against a juggernaut once, and slowing it, the right lesson to learn is: Do it better and smarter next time. I like what William Morris wrote: "Men fight and lose the battle, and the thing that they fought for comes about in spite of their defeat, and when it comes, turns out not to be what they meant, and other men have to fight for what they meant under another name."

The Legacy of Choices

BY SAM BROWN

Council Bluffs, Iowa, was home to me. I was born there, went to school there, built hot rods there, and was for three years the outstanding ROTC cadet while in high school there. When I was growing up it never occurred to me that America could be wrong. The pattern of my upbringing and the texture of my day-to-day existence were solidly Midwestern and Republican; Dad belonged to the Rotary and everyone in the family went to church on Sunday. The world was an orderly, tidy place, and my place in it was secure. Even John Kennedy's death didn't upset that world. After all, his death was the act of a madman, not the result of structural defects in the American system. But other signs of the times began to erode my orderly world.

I was in college in Redlands, Calif., in 1962 when students began to question why the state imposed a ban on communist speakers. This struck me as a peculiar way to define a "free" society. I didn't see how it fit with what I had been taught in high school civics back in Abraham Lincoln High School, and it surely didn't fit my budding libertarian conservative political philosophy. This occurred about the same time as the Free Speech Movement was developing at Berkeley and the first Freedom Riders were taking buses through the South. The result was that I began to question everything I had believed about America. I questioned why the migrants who passed through Redlands lived the way they did. I questioned why the University officials at Redlands and Berkeley and the state officials in Sacramento were so virulent in their defense of order but unwilling to defend the First Amendment. Then came the fall of the Diem government, the initial U.S. combat presence in Vietnam and the U.S. intervention in the Dominican Republic. At that point, I was sure that everything the U.S. government supported abroad was wrong. By the time of the escalation of the war I knew without any very fundamental analysis of the facts that the war had to be stopped merely because it was our war. By 1969 my views would be codified in articles, essays and public debate, but in 1965 my thoughts were more visceral than intellectual.

For me it was an exciting time. Those of us who opposed the war all seemed to be young, wear our hair long, and at least some of my friends believed that legalizing marijuana and popularizing rock and roll were of the same degree of importance as ending the war in Vietnam. The press said we were doing exciting things (even the nearly universal editorial support for the war only convinced us that our work was important). Suddenly there were no unquestioned truths. Skepticism was the only acceptable intellectual posture, cynicism was almost always rewarded by an accommodating reality and paranoia, which seemed only trendy in 1967, turned out to be justified by 1973. Often after leaving the office of one or another of the antiwar organizations at midnight or 1 or 2 in the morning, we would continue our debate over Marcuse or Norman O. Brown or Marx or Freud for several more hours. They were heady times with a facade of sacrifice (long hours, little pay, a certain approbation among our elders) but with a taste of responsibility and seriousness far beyond our years.

It was not a time when people were particularly tolerant of each other. We were young, smart, intellectual (so we thought) and committed to a moral cause. We believed ourselves patriots defending America's ideals. They (and by that time "they" were almost always older) were, as far as we were concerned, narrow-minded, intolerant and unwilling to respect our patriotism. It was a time of intense certainty. The ideas espoused by either group were almost automatically opposed by the other. Each side held to its half-thoughts and unfounded assumptions. Each side hurt the other. My father and I grew apart even though he respected the seriousness of my intentions and endured late-night telephone threats and shunning from his fellow "Christian" churchgoers because of my activities.

I had little time to absorb the emotional impact of these events, but I knew that the orderly, tidy world of my Midwest past was not mine. I was on the outside. I wanted the political, economic and institutional status quo to be changed and that change had to come quickly. I distrusted big business and the big military and was skeptical about the capacity of the federal government to ensure both a measure of economic equity and civil liberties.

I also believed that with the right people, the political will and a few hundred thousand dollars, national policy could be changed for the better. I assumed that my generation, and specifically those of us who shared such a commitment to America in our efforts to end the war, could be a powerful influence for the better. With such certainty I began my public life.

Now, almost ten years later, my certainty has been tempered by events and experience. I have learned some lessons, one of which is plainly evident: My generation has not saved the world, nor has it yet changed the political topography of this nation. But the war that was so much part of our growing up continues to have an impact on our society and on how we shape our personal lives.

Even my way of thinking has been influenced by the war. The very structure and direction of the antiwar movement required a sense of direct response to events and an ordered process of getting there. Petitions had to be signed, candidates found to run for public office and demonstrations mounted to urge the end of the war. Things had to be done. In a way, the very organization of the antiwar movement was ironically similar to that of the military. The long-term consequences were also sometimes as mindlessly destructive as those of the war. Those on the fringe of the resistance to the war took up violence as an answer.

And, like the military, those who actively dissented developed a sense of camaraderie that grew from shared risks, values and experiences. If our reunions were never quite so structured as those at West Point, our identities have still been reaffirmed more than once by reminders of what we were doing during the war, the shared history has been used as a touchstone for future relations. The war became part of one's resumé.

The tag line "antiwar leader" has been as much a part of my name as an MD is of any doctor's. The tag line has been both something to be proud of and yet, at the same time, a very personal and sad reminder that the country was still divided. Memories have lingered.

I was not surprised, then, that when I was named the director of ACTION in 1976 my activities were closely scrutinized by some members of Congress. Even though I had spent two years being the state treasurer of Colorado, paying my dues, so to speak, I was typed by those who did not know me as the "radical 33-year-old," a phrase I once thought was a contradiction in terms.

President Carter's decision to swear me and Max Cleland, the Vietnam War amputee who became the head of the Veterans Administration, in on the same day seemed to signify a new tolerance, a willingness to find common ground for those of our generation who had been split apart by the decisions of another generation. But for a significant number of conservatives and indeed for some people on the left, my going to Washington to run ACTION did not change the context of how I was perceived. For those on the far right, I was suspect, the radical who was subverting the federal government from within. For those on the left, my commitment to the general principles which we had struggled to uphold had to be tested: Was I still one of them? Would I sell out?

After so many years of being on the outside, of being part of a political culture that was skeptical even of itself and often looked at the world in a "them" versus "us" dichotomy, being in public office was like stepping into a different culture with different customs, mannerisms, expectations, language and people. I felt comfortable and perfectly capable of being part of this culture, given my background and education, but my allegiance was split.

Intellectually, I remained rooted in the skepticism and outrage that had defined so much of my thinking. I looked for advice and counsel to the network of people who came to Washington at the same time as I did and had belonged to the antiwar movement. I felt a commitment to test the ideas of equity, citizen participation and community action that so many of us had talked about. Maybe "I" and "we" could hold power in a more responsible, sensitive and humane manner than the people whom we had criticized for so long. Yet I was equally bound and felt committed to the requirements of the office I held.

For four years I moved back and forth between these allegiances. At times, I felt like a translator interpreting conflicting attitudes and at times I felt compelled to deflate people's expectations of myself and what they thought the 1960s were all about. A mythology has grown up about the '60s, the sort of instant history reached sometimes by *Newsweek* or *Time*, that makes the record of that period seem too neat and tidy.

Clearly something happened. A generation came of age at a time of immense prosperity. Demographically we broke the charts. Economically our feeding, housing and need to be educated made work for almost everybody in America. The cultural epicenter of our country moved from one generation to another. Most importantly, our education and idealism led us to question America's post-World War II vision that all Americans were white, middle-class or soon going to be, and owners of a half-acre lot in the suburbs.

That we had the opportunity to question was surely a gift from our parents. We had the luxury to be idealistic, a luxury no doubt that we got because our parents never had that luxury when they were growing up. Blacks and other poor people, out of necessity and their commitment to the American ideal, had to question and then shatter America's contented image of itself. Those of us coming out of college in the early '60s could afford to do it. We could afford to go to Mississippi for Freedom Summer. We could afford to take a semester off and become Appalachian Volunteers. We knew that we could spend two years with the Peace Corps and indeed we were encouraged to do so. We were encouraged to be idealistic.

And so we were. One can look back a decade and say that we were truly a fortunate generation, maybe even spoiled. But one should also look back and say that we were patriotic and idealistic, young men and women of good intentions who wanted to make America better.

What really happened? Those of us who committed ourselves to a new and more democratic image of America soon found ourselves caught up in not one reform movement but many. Reform begat reform. Each movement spun off another. Everything was shared: tactics and strategy, office space and apartments, ideals and hopes. People coalesced around one cause only to go off to another. The movements innumerable became "The Movement." Capital M. America would move. America would be reformed.

No one can deny that Communists, Trotskyites and every other strand of leftist thinking had people participating in the Movement and in other reform efforts of the last decade, but so did large segments of the middle class and the business community. I remain convinced that the broad spectrum of people who supported the antiwar movement and other reform efforts, who wrote their congressmen, signed petitions and marched in support of causes wanted America to be the country we had been taught it already was.

I also cannot believe that we were duped or totally wrong in taking the positions we took during the war. More than once I have changed the opinions I held a decade ago. I find it impossible to be supportive of what Vietnam has done in Laos and what it did to the "boat people." I find it difficult to support Vietnam's domination of Cambodia, but find the alternative of supporting Pol Pot even worse. One cannot accuse America of being too militaristic without questioning what the Soviet Union has supported in Cambodia, what it did in Afghanistan and what it threatens to do in Poland.

But these changes reflect changes in attitude toward other nations, not toward America. Those of us who criticized America's involvement in Vietnam did so because we held America to a higher standard than that of the Soviet Union and Vietnam. That standard hasn't changed. Hans Morgenthau wrote in 1970 in *Truth and Power* that a country founded on Jeffersonian principles cannot long survive by using the methods of Bismarck to make its foreign policy succeed. The truth and power of that statement have not diminished in the last decade.

The legacy of Vietnam is easier to understand in terms of political reactions than it is in terms of the emotional upheaval the country endured and the sentiments that are held today by the American people about Vietnam. The loss of authority caused by the deception of the American people by two presidents is a source of distress for many, including myself. The possibility of a "lost generation" of voters seems very real and dangerous. No country can long survive if a significant portion of its citizens are unwilling to sanction the actions of its leaders.

How those in power come to terms with the issue of restoring that trust seems to me to be a critical issue of the 1980s. I see no indication that those now in power in Washington have any understanding of how to go about regaining that trust. Their desire to restore the old lines of authority without any sensitivity to the fundamental fracturing that took place seems to me to be at best a stopgap measure that is reassuring to an older generation but not to the country at large and to my generation in the specific.

The emotional wounds caused by conflict are more difficult to discern. One reads on occasion of the Vietnam veteran who suddenly goes berserk and one wonders whether it is a foreshadowing of something that the country at large has yet to go through. The Red Scare of the 1920s, the McCarthy purges of the 1950s and the Nixonian abuse of constitutional liberties, events that showed the worst side of the American character, were ugly political spasms that followed other conflicts that to some degree divided the country. At times I fear that an even larger spasm will be pushed upon the American public by conservatives determined to vindicate themselves. My nightmare is tempered by the knowledge that a majority of Americans have shown an extraordinary adaptability in coming to terms with the war. Reduced to cryptic statements about it being a "mistake" and a "waste," most Americans seem to have little desire to engage in witch-hunts.

I am also troubled by the sense of irresponsibility and cynicism which many people have about our obligations to freely serve others and to defend our common interests. As I traveled to college campuses in the fall of 1980, I frequently ran into people whose trip to the post office to register for the draft was their first act of citizenship and who were appalled when I told them that I favor not only registration but a military raised by equitable conscription and, moreover, that I believe in national service for both men and women.

My feelings toward members of my generation are different. We remain split from within and from the generations before and behind us. I feel a sense of separateness from those people of my age who simply responded to what they regarded as the nation's interest by going to war. I am pained by the personal stories of tragedy of Vietnam veterans. I do not think that they were foolish, stupid or criminals. Just used.

The split inherent in any generation between the classes, a split that our society has traditionally been able to keep indistinct, became pronounced and rigid, codified by the Selective Service classification system—I-A, 2-S, I-Y, 4-F. We all remember, don't we? Anyone who grew up during the war knows who went and who didn't. The poor, less-educated and lower-middle-class men went and those of us who were upper-middle-class and college-educated didn't. The fact that many of us didn't because we found it morally impossible does not negate the fact that one class of people was used while another remained privileged.

The knowledge that so many men of the upper middle class used the system to beat it only accentuates the divisions between men of my generation. I am saddened by the cynicism of the many people whose prime motivation for being involved in the antiwar movement was merely self-preservation. Once the heat of the draft had ended, they went on with the business of being stockbrokers or lawyers or whatever else they had hoped for in their lives

For many of us who fought to end the war, it has taken over a decade to sort out what happened. The sifting and sorting has been intensely personal. For some men who opposed the war, the fact that they used the country's repugnance toward it to avoid the draft has left a residual guilt of not facing one's obligations. Only a few, like James Fallows, have had the integrity to speak openly about what has been on the minds of many.

For other men, not joining the Army left them with the distinct feeling that they had missed a critical "rite of passage" in coming to terms with their manhood. Understanding the long-term consequences of missing that ritual passage is beyond my capacity. But the fact that this feeling came at a time when the very idea of manhood was rightfully being challenged by the feminist movement has to be factored into any new conceptualization by our culture of what it means to be a man. This is a task that seems to me to be as profound as any we will face in the next ten years.

But for many more of us the "rite of passage" was met. Moral choices had to be made. Reduced to the abstractness of the Selective Service System's draft categories, the choices were nevertheless full of distinctions that were difficult to articulate but full of moral meaning to those who faced them squarely: to serve or not to serve; to avoid the draft by faking a medical or becoming a CO; to leave for Canada or to become a draft resister and face the possibility of jail; to demonstrate or not to demonstrate; to practice civil disobedience and face arrest or to avoid it. Finally, to face one's parents and peers once a decision had been made. That choices of a different nature but of equal seriousness were made by those who went to Vietnam I have no doubt.

The legacy of having to make such choices so early in one's life seems to me to be a capacity for tolerance and empathy by members of my generation for anyone, regardless of what side they chose, who made such decisions. I have found that people of my generation show such a tolerance for each other, an empathy that does not reach beyond generational lines when talking about the war. 'Nam is a generational talisman that only we can touch.

For those of us who actively dissented, the war has been the point around which we have pivoted our lives during the last decade. It shaped our attitudes and personal lives more than we ever imagined. Some of us had to overcome a deep suspicion and at times the justified paranoia that those in authority were systematically disrupting our lives. Parts of our lives were delayed because we felt compelled to commit ourselves to each new facet of the Movement. It is only now that we have begun picking up those pieces—buying houses, getting married, having children and settling on careers. A few of us "burnt out" and rejected everything about the political process. But many more of us, if we had an adverse reaction to the power of the federal government to do harm, turned that reaction into a positive commitment to make government more responsive to people where they live and work, at the local and state level.

Looking back on those years I see two aspects of the Vietnam era that are fundamentally positive for the future of this country: the capacity for self-criticism and the tolerance that people within my generation have developed. Our ability to rebuild a core vision of what we want our society to be in the future rests largely on our ability to use these capacities in a positive way.

I see little indication that those who hold power now will do so. It may be that developing a new vision of what our society should be, one that encapsulates a richer understanding of patriotism, our obligations to each other and to the world, will have to wait until we are in our political majority a decade hence.

People have a tendency to look upon our generation as one that is already politically spent, to see us as part of history. I don't believe that to be the case. They forget that we were all in our early twenties when we did what we had to do in the '60s. Our real influence as a generation has yet to be felt.

A Young Pacifist

BY PAUL GOODMAN

I.

My son, Mathew Ready Goodman, was killed mountain-climbing on August 8, 1967, age 20. Burton Weiss, a close friend of his at Cornell, has sent me an account of Matty's political activities there—to which I will preface some memories of his similar activities before he went to college. Matty was essentially an unpolitical person; his absorbing intellectual interest was in sciences—in which he had gifts, and he wanted to live and let live in a community of friends—at which he remarkably succeeded. Nevertheless, he was continually engaged in political actions, against war and irrational authority. This pattern is common to many hundreds, and in increasing numbers, of brave and thoughtful young people these days; it is worthwhile to describe it in a typical example. In any case, the group at Cornell—Burt, Jerry Franz, Tom Bell, Bruce Dancis, and a few others whom I did not know personally—have managed to make that unlikely school one of the most radical in the country, with a strongly characteristic style: undoctrinaire yet activist, deeply communitarian and imbued with an extraordinary honesty and good faith. In this group, Matty was an important spirit.

Emotionally, from early childhood, Matty's pacifism was certainly related to his unusual protectiveness of his many animals. He identified with their lives. I remember him and his mother medicating and sometimes saving sick little turtles, tropical fish, white rats. Yet there was nothing squeamish or sentimental in his attitude. If he needed to feed his lizards, he calmly caught flies, tore their wings off and

Reprinted from *Drawing the Line: The Political Essays of Paul Goodman*, Ed. Taylor Stoehr, E. P. Dutton. Copyright © 1967 by Sally Goodman.

offered them; but otherwise he would not kill a fly but adroitly catch and let it out the door. He gave up fishing around age 10 and began to rescue the fish and return them to the river. Mostly he liked just to watch the fish and pond life, for hours, in their natural habitat.

More intellectually, he was an ardent conservationist, indignant at the spoliation, opposed to insecticides. The focus of his scientific interests (in my opinion) was ecology, the community of living things in the appropriate environment. And in method he strongly favored—so far as the distinction can be made—naturalistic observation, letting things be, rather than experimenting and imposing programs. These were also his political biases.

My first political recollection of him is when, in junior high school, he called my attention to corporation advertising being used in his class. He collected the evidence and we succeeded, temporarily, in having it expelled. This involved his being called down and rebuked by the principal.

During his first year at Bronx Science High School he wrote a report on the life of Gandhi, who impressed him deeply. For a reason known only to himself, he took to fasting one day a week—and continued this sporadically later.

He was active in the antibomb protests in 1960–62. He used to take part in the "General Strike For Peace" thought up by Julian Beck. Since people were supposed to leave off work for a day and picket for peace, Matty took off from school and picketed the Board of Education on Livingston Street. Naturally he was captured as a truant and I had to go and rescue him. This was one of the few moments of pure delight I have ever had in the peace movement.

He was at the Times Square demonstration against the bombtesting when the police rode their horses into the crowd. Matty was in the line of fire and came home shaken, saying, "This is serious."

As a junior in high school, he refused to take part in a shelter drill and he and three others who would not recant were suspended. But there was considerable newspaper publicity and they were reinstated and allowed to stand aside during the drills, which were soon discontinued. His reasons for nonparticipation were (1) the shelters were unscientific, (2) the drill was an insult to intelligence in its form and (3) it predisposed to accepting nuclear war.

When reinstated, he was told he had a black mark on his record. I wrote to Admissions at Harvard asking if this was a disadvantage; when we received the expected reply that it would rather be judged as a sign of critical independence, Matty had the letter copied off and distributed around Bronx Science—which sorely needed the nudge.

By now he was a seasoned radical and when he was again threat-

ened with punishment for pasting antiwar stickers in the school subway station, he faced down the administration by pointing out that
the subway was not in its jurisdiction.

At age 15 he and other high-school students formed a city-wide
association to protest against nuclear war. This came to nothing.

When he applied for admission to Cornell, Professor Milton Konvitz phoned me in alarm that he was likely to be rejected because he
had sent a photo of himself with uncombed hair. Matty said, "If they
don't want me as I really look, they can keep their lousy school."
They admitted him anyway, but sometimes they may have regretted
not following their routine impulse. Matty loved Cornell and therefore fought it tooth and nail.

At 18, he refused to register for the draft. I shall return to this
later, but I recall that, the following summer, he distributed antiwar
leaflets in front of the Army recruiting station in St. Johnsbury, Ver-
mont, near where we have a summer home. This made me anxious,
since of course he had no draft card. But he explained, "I can't live
in fear every day. I must act as I ordinarily would." My guess is that
he loved St. Johnsbury and wanted to redeem it for having a recruiting station.

II.

Burt Weiss writes as follows about Matty at Cornell (my own comments are in brackets):

"Students for Education, SFE, organized themselves in late February, 1965. Matty was in almost from the beginning. He was most
active in the Grading Committee, whose only proposal he and I ham-
mered out. The S-U option in it has since come to be offered in much
weakened form by most of the Cornell colleges.

[In fact, insisting on another option in the proposal, Matty got his
professors not to grade him at all, or to keep his grades secret from
him. Later, to his annoyance, he found his name on the Dean's list,
and crossed it out with a crayon and complained.]

"Astonishingly, Mathew attended all meetings and rallies of SFE
and its steering committee. Such an attendance record was unique
for him. He had little toleration for contentious political meetings,
especially when the contention was made by those he loved. When
he guessed that a meeting was likely to be angry and unfruitful, he
usually stayed home. If he went despite his guess, or if the angry
mood of a meeting took him by surprise, he left early. Several times,
when he stuck it out, he was moved to the point of tears or actually
cried. I loved him then very much, and respected his ability to

mourn. He mourned that people were acting stupidly, timidly, or dishonestly. He mourned the sudden vanishing of community spirit.

"Later that spring, Matty took part in the 24-hour vigil in the Arts Quad and in the walkout while Rockefeller was speaking at the centennial celebration. Nobody got in trouble for either of these actions. But then came the Harriman lecture and the resulting fracas was widely reported in the press. Before Harriman spoke, he received the enclosed letter written by Matty and Jerry Franz. [The letter complains that official spokesmen evade real questions and warns that the students will insist on real answers. Harriman's behavior did turn out to be insulting to college-level intelligence and the students sat down around him.]

"In May came the sitdown—to block the ROTC review in Barton Hall. All (70) participants were prosecuted by the University, but Matty and Jerry walked out of the hearing before the Faculty Committee on Student Conduct. Here, according to the Cornell *Sun*, is what they said: 'The members of the group made a definite commitment to stand by each other if there was anything like differential punishment. Tonight they went back on their commitment. The group agreed that it was necessary to have collective hearing so that past offenses could not be taken into account. Tonight the group agreed to let them take past offenses into account. Therefore we can no longer be associated.' They were summarily suspended, but reinstated when they appeared, just the two of them, at the next meeting of the Committee. They were placed on Disciplinary Probation.

"That was the exciting spring. We kept rushing about in no particular direction, although everything we did seemed to be of a piece. Most important things happened late at night, leaflet-writing, mimeographing, emergency meetings, passionate revelatory dialogue among friends.

"During our months in Europe—fall of '65—Matty had little to do with politics. One day in Paris—I think it was an International Day of Protest, Oct. 1965—he picketed the American Embassy. He had expected to meet others there. As it turned out, he was all alone, but picketed anyway. In Seville we went to see the American consul to register our protest against the Vietnam war. We did nothing to end the war, but did get a good idea of the sort of person who is appointed to American consulships.

"At Cornell in the spring of 1966, Matty and some friends founded the Young Anarchists. The group never did much, but it put out some neat broadsides. Nevertheless, as I later learned by accident, the very existence of a group of that name intimidated the administration and extensive files were kept, including glossy blown-up photos of every member.

[It is touching that I, a long-time anarchist, never heard of these Young Anarchists from my son.]

"In May a hundred students sat in at President Perkins' office to protest against Cornell's complicity with Selective Service. Matty was one of the first seven to get there and so was able to enter the presidential suite before the campus police locked the doors. The latecomers were kept in the corridor. Only the 'inner seven' were prosecuted by the University. The Undergraduate Judiciary Board, composed entirely of students, voted 'no action' and made us all proud. The Faculty Committee, however, changed this to 'reprimand.'

"The day after the sit-in, the University Faculty met in special session to discuss the relation between Cornell and Selective Service. As faculty members entered the meeting, they were handed 'A Plea Against Military Influence at Cornell,' written by Matty and Jerry.

"In the last year of his life, Matty was deeply involved with two groups, Young Friends and the Ithaca We Won't Go group. He was committed to the people in these groups and to the fraternal and community spirit among them. This was the only time since SFE that he was so committed.

"In the fall Matty helped organize the Five-Day Fast for Peace, explained in the enclosed leaflet that Matty helped to write. The fast was very successful in terms of the number who participated, the interest and sympathy roused on campus and in town, and the amount of money raised for medical aid [for North and South Vietnamese]. For some reason Matty gradually became the chief PR man for Young Friends. He was rather inept in that position.

[Again, I was surprised to learn of his Quaker connections. His mother and I had never been able to interest him in religion at all, even to read the Bible as literature.]

"Also that fall, Matty, Tom Bell, and I began talking about starting a local draft resistance group. The group grew slowly and beautifully, just as Tom Bell explained in *New Left Notes* last March. When Matty returned from inter-session in February, he was excited about the possibilities for mass draft-card destruction, and the desirability of starting on April 15 in New York. Everybody was interested, yet nobody seemed moved to action. Finally, Jan Flora and I were startled to realize how soon it would be April 15. We called Matty, rounded up a small meeting, and decided to go ahead. I was going to New York later that night and so I was asked to find out what people there thought. You were the first person I saw. The rest you know.

[I tried to rally help for them by a letter, to academics who had signed Vietnam ads in the *Times,* of which Matty distributed six thousand copies. On April 15, about 160 students burned their cards in the Sheep Meadow. Matty, who had no card, held up a sign—"20 Years Unregistered."

[And proud Matty would have been on October 16, that so many who were leaders of the 1500 who turned in their cards had been his fellows in the Sheep Meadow on April 15.]

"For Matty, the most painful occurrence in connection with the draft-card destruction was the breakdown of community spirit that it, and the Easter Peace Bridge demonstration, occasioned in Young Friends. SDS was soliciting pledges in the student union. The Proctor was citing those responsible to appear before the Judiciary boards and suspending those who refused to give their names. Matty and others tried to get Young Friends to solicit the same pledges at their own table, in solidarity with fellow war-resisters. At first Young Friends went along, but then began to talk about backing out. At about the same time, Matty saw the official 'instructions' for the Easter demonstration at the Peace Bridge, in which Young Friends, including Epi and himself, had planned to participate. This document had nothing to do with love, fellowship, or respect for the individuality and holy spirit in every person, what Matty conceived to be the essence of Quakerism. There were strict rules governing both the demonstration itself and the personal behavior and attire of the participation. Worse, the document advised male participants to bring along their draft cards to show at the border. The whole thing made Matty sick. Yet his feelings seemed to be shared by only a minority of Young Friends. The group was falling apart in front of his eyes. . . .

"Matty had planned to go to Brazil this summer as part of a Cornell anthropological project. His main purpose, as he explained at the first meeting, would have been to work politically with Brazilian students and thereby help to foster an international community of radical students.

[This project was abandoned when, at the disclosure of C.I.A. tampering with American students, the Brazilian students had to dis-invite the Cornellians. Matty told me that previous South American trips had been exciting and useful. He had worked hard learning Portuguese.

[When Brazil was closed off, Matty at once proposed that the en-

tire group should go to Cuba; this would be a reasonable and necessary retaliation to the C.I.A. system and was also worthwhile in itself. Dr. William Rogers, who was the director of the project, has
written me as follows: "I won't detail the debate that followed
Matty's proposal. It was the age-old struggle of the soul between the
single act of moral purity and courage, and the prudential and tactical considerations of effectiveness. We spoke of Jesus' parable of
the Pearl of Great Price. Was this act the pearl for which a man will
sell all that he has, in order to possess it? Matty, with an eschato-
logical sense akin to the New Testament, seemed to think so. Considerations of the future did not weigh heavily with him. The important thing was to be moral, thoroughly moral, now. How much
longer can we wait?" Unfortunately, Matty did not persuade them.]

"Early in the spring Matty took part—as who did not?—in the
riotous demonstration which defeated the DA when he came on campus to suppress the sale of the literary magazine. Matty's battle-cry
was entirely his own: 'Fuck you, Thaler,' he said to that unfortunate
man's face.

"Later in the spring he made it his business to operate the printing
press in the We Won't Go office. He intended, next year, to spend
considerable time there doing routine work."

On August 7, Matty and I drove down from Expo in Montreal,
where we had attended the Hiroshima Day youth rally. In his sleeping bag Matty had hidden some contraband, a book of short stories
bought at the Cuban pavilion as a gift for his teacher in a course on
Mexican revolutionary novels. However, we decided to declare it, in
order that the book might be seized and burned and we could com-
plain to Robert Kennedy. The Customs offices obligingly acted up in
the face of our high literary disdain, so we had fun planning our indignant letter. Next day Matty died on the mountain, but I have sent
the letter.

III.

Matty refused to register for the draft on general pacifist grounds—
the subsequent worsening of the Vietnam war merely confirmed
what he already knew.

His method of refusal was not to recognize the draft system at all
and to continue as usual, including, of course, his overt antiwar activity—now without a draft card. In fact, he stepped up this activity,
but I think this was because of Vietnam rather than to force a show-
down. I never saw any sign that he courted going to jail. He did not
regard himself as a Witness in any way. On the other hand, he was
entirely too open to live "underground." And the "tactical ap-

proach," of trying for C.O. or accepting II-S in order to carry on revolutionary activity, was also against his disposition: he could not live on an ambiguous basis. Besides, he believed it was bad politics; his enthusiasm for the mass draft-card burning meant that he believed in open massive noncooperation and active nonviolent resistance. His eyes twinkled at the idea of "nonviolent terrorism": if one is arrested, five others burn their cards on the courthouse steps.

The F.B.I. first got in touch with him in November 1966, purportedly about a classmate applying for C.O., for whom Matty had agreed to be a reference! (This was part of his "business as usual.") They visited him as a nonregistrant in March 1967 and set the wheels of prosecution going.

Matty's approach—to "do nothing"—is appropriate, in my opinion, only to young people who are sure of their own integrity and the human use of their own developing careers, who just need to be let be. Matty had this confidence. Besides, he was a balky animal: he would have found it impossibly humiliating, paralyzing, to try to move his feet toward anything he strongly disbelieved in, such as filling out a draft form. He was not, in my experience, "rebellious," defiant of authority as such. But he had learned that authority was very often irrational, petty, dishonest and sometimes not benevolent, so he was antiauthoritarian. (The school administrations he had dealt with were certainly not models of magnanimity, American democracy or even simple honor; and these are the only officials that a growing boy knows, unless he is a juvenile delinquent or on relief.) Matty was also unusually stubborn in general. He had to do things his own way, at his own pace, according to his own slowly developing concern or fantasy. This was often too slow for other people's wishes, including mine, but there was no hurrying him. Once he cared, he acted with energy and determination.

He refused to be a leader—at Cornell, as at Berkeley in its best days, leadership was regarded as a poor form of social organization. Yet it is clear in the above accounts that Matty often did lead. But this was because he acted according to his own inner belief, without ambition or ideology. He was frank, loyal and consistent, and his integrity was legendary. If, in an action, he was among the first, or seemed to be the most intransigent and unwilling to compromise, it was not that he was brash or doctrinaire, but because of some elementary human principle. Naturally, then, others found security in him and went along. So far as I can discover, he had no enemies. Even administrators liked him personally and have sent me touching letters of condolence. His lust for community seems to have been equal to my own, but he had more luck with it.

After he became seriously illegal at 18 he, like others in a similar plight, showed signs of anxiety, a certain tightness, a certain hardness. This roused my indignation more than anything else, that the brute mechanical power of the State was distorting the lives of these excellent youth. For nothing. For far worse than nothing—abstract conformity, empty power, overseas murder. Nevertheless, in Matty's case at least, his formula of dismissing fear and acting as he ordinarily would, seemed to work spectacularly. Once he had made the hard choice, he threw himself into all his activities with increased enthusiasm; new energy was released and during this period—whatever the causal relationship—he embarked on an uninterrupted and pretty happy love affair with Epi Epton, who shared his convictions; this of course must have immensely increased his security, assertiveness and courage.

As I said at the outset, Matty was not essentially political; he was politically active only by duty, on principle. Rather he was a daring swimmer, a good handball player. He ground his own telescopes. He jeopardized his nonexistent II-S deferment and took off for Europe for a semester. He had found a method of meditation that suited him. Hungry for music, he sat for hours at the piano and was in charge of selecting the records in the library. He was an Honors student in anthropology and he was, I am told by Professor Joseph Calvo and Dr. Elizabeth Keller, beginning to do original work in genetics. But his political activity also blessed him with friends and community.

My own hope was that, after he was arrested, he would—having fought through to the end—skip bail and go to Canada, since jail did not seem to be the best environment for him. He said he would make up his mind when it was necessary. He had looked into it and made connections so that it would be possible for him to work politically in Canada.

Every pacifist career is individual, a unique balance of forces, including the shared hope that other human beings will become equally autonomous. Most people want peace and freedom, but there are no pacifist or anarchist masses.

As I tearfully review my son's brief pacifist career, the following seems to have been his philosophy: He had a will to protect life in all its forms and to conserve the conditions for it. With this, he had a kind of admiring trust in the providence of natural arrangements and liked to gaze at them. He felt that human beings too could form a natural and wise community and he was daringly loyal to this possibility. He was astonished to see people act with timidity, pettiness or violence. Yet he was not naive. He knew that people in power and people bureaucratized are untrustworthy and one has to be prepared for their stupidity and dishonesty and confront them. (I don't know if he thought that people as such could be malevolent.) As for himself, he felt that there was plenty of time to brood and mull and observe and wait for the spirit; it did not delay, and there was no need for pressuring or forcing votes. What he himself could do to help was to be open to the facts, honest in speech and as consistent as possible. When a practical idea occurred to him, it was never complicated or dilatory, but always a simplication and a way of immediately coming across.

It is a beautiful soul we have lost, who behaved well and had a good influence.

What Did You Do in the Class War, Daddy?

BY JAMES FALLOWS

Many people think that the worst scars of the war years have healed. I don't. Vietnam has left us with a heritage rich in possibilities for class warfare, and I would like to start telling about it with this story:

In the fall of 1969, I was beginning my final year in college. As the months went by, the rock on which I had unthinkingly anchored my hopes—the certainty that the war in Vietnam would be over before I could possibly fight—began to crumble. It shattered altogether on Thanksgiving weekend when, while riding back to Boston from a visit with my relatives, I heard that the draft lottery had been held and my birthdate had come up number 45. I recognized for the first time that, inflexibly, I must either be drafted or consciously find a way to prevent it.

In the atmosphere of that time, each possible choice came equipped with barbs. To answer the call was unthinkable, not only because, in my heart, I was desperately afraid of being killed, but also because, among my friends, it was axiomatic that one should not be "complicit" in the immoral war effort. Draft resistance, the course chosen by a few noble heroes of the movement, meant going to prison or leaving the country. With much the same intensity with which I wanted to stay alive, I did not want those things either. What I wanted was to go to graduate school, to get married, and to enjoy those bright prospects I had been taught that life owed me.

I learned quickly enough that there was only one way to get what I wanted. A physical deferment would restore things to the happy state I had known during four undergraduate years. The barbed alternatives would be put off. By the impartial dictates of public policy I would be free to pursue the better side of life.

Like many of my friends whose numbers had come up wrong in the lottery, I set about securing my salvation. When I was not participating in anti-war rallies, I was poring over the Army's code of physical regulations. During the winter and early spring, seminars were held in the college common rooms. There, sympathetic medical students helped us search for disqualifying conditions that we, in our many years of good health, might have overlooked. Although, on the doctors' advice, I made a half-hearted try at fainting spells, my only real possibility was beating the height and weight regulations. My normal weight was close to the cut-off point for an "underweight" disqualification, and, with a diligence born of panic, I made sure I would have a margin. I was six-feet-one-inch tall at the time. On the morning of the draft physical I weighed 120 pounds.

Before sunrise that morning I rode the subway to the Cambridge city hall, where we had been told to gather for shipment to the examination at the Boston Navy Yard. The examinations were administered on a rotating basis, one or two days each month for each of the draft boards in the area. Virtually everyone who showed up on Cambridge day at the Navy Yard was a student from Harvard or MIT.

There was no mistaking the political temperament of our group. Many of my friends wore red arm bands and stop-the-war buttons. Most chanted the familiar words, "Ho, Ho, Ho Chi Minh/NLF is Gonna Win." One of the things we had learned from the draft counselors was that disruptive behavior at the examination was a worthwhile political goal, not only because it obstructed the smooth operation of the "criminal war machine," but also because it might impress the examiners with our undesirable character traits. As we climbed into the buses and as they rolled toward the Navy Yard, about half of the young men brought the chants to a crescendo. The rest of us sat rigid and silent, clutching x-rays and letters from our doctors at home.

Inside the Navy Yard, we were first confronted by a young sergeant from Long Beach, a former surfer boy no older than the rest of us and seemingly unaware that he had an unusual situation on his hands. He started reading out instructions for the intelligence tests when he was hooted down. He went out to collect his lieutenant, who clearly had been through a Cambridge day before. "We've got all the time in the world," he said, and let the chanting go on for two or three minutes. "When we're finished with you, you can go, and not a minute before."

From that point on the disruption became more purposeful and individual, largely confined to those whose deferment strategies were based on anti-authoritarian psychiatric traits. Twice I saw students walk up to young orderlies—whose hands were extended to receive the required cup of urine—and throw the vial in the orderlies' faces. The orderlies looked up, initially more astonished than angry, and went back to towel themselves off. Most of the rest of us trod quietly through the paces, waiting for the moment of confrontation when the final examiner would give his verdict. I had stepped on the scales at the very beginning of the examination. Desperate at seeing the orderly write down 122 pounds, I hopped back on and made sure that he lowered it to 120. I walked in a trance through the rest of the examination, until the final meeting with the fatherly physician who ruled on marginal cases such as mine. I stood there in socks and underwear, arms wrapped around me in the chilly building. I knew as I looked at the doctor's face that he understood exactly what I was doing.

"Have you ever contemplated suicide?" he asked after he finished looking over my chart. My eyes darted up to his. "Oh, suicide—yes, I've been feeling very unstable and unreliable recently." He looked at me, staring until I returned my eyes to the ground. He wrote "unqualified" on my folder, turned on his heel, and left. I was overcome by a wave of relief, which for the first time revealed to me how great my terror had been, and by the beginning of the sense of shame which remains with me to this day.

It was, initially, a generalized shame at having gotten away with my deception, but it came into sharper focus later in the day. Even as the last of the Cambridge contingent was throwing its urine and deliberately failing its color-blindness tests, buses from the next board began to arrive. These bore the boys from Chelsea, thick, dark-haired young men, the white proles of Boston. Most of them were younger than us, since they had just left high school, and it had clearly never occurred to them that there might be a way around the draft. They walked through the examination lines like so many cattle off to slaughter. I tried to avoid noticing, but the results were inescapable. While perhaps four out of five of my friends from Harvard were being deferred, just the opposite was happening to the Chelsea boys.

We returned to Cambridge that afternoon, not in government buses but as free individuals, liberated and victorious. The talk was high-spirited, but there was something close to the surface that none of us wanted to mention. We knew now who would be killed.

As other memories of the war years have faded, it is that day in the

Navy Yard that will not leave my mind. The answers to the other grand questions about the war have become familiar as any catechism. Q. What were America's sins? A. The Arrogance of Power, the Isolation of the Presidency, the Burden of Colonialism, and the Failure of Technological Warfare. In the abstract, at least, we have learned those lessons. For better or worse, it will be years before we again cheer a president who talks about paying any price and bearing any burden to prop up some spurious overseas version of democracy.

We have not, however, learned the lesson of the day at the Navy Yard, or the thousands of similar scenes all across the country through all the years of the war. Five years later, two questions have yet to be faced, let alone answered. The first is why, when so many of the bright young college men opposed the war, so few were willing to resist the draft, rather than simply evade it. The second is why all the well-educated presumably humane young men, whether they opposed the war or were thinking fondly of A-bombs on Hanoi, so willingly took advantage of this most brutal form of class discrimination—what it signifies that we let the boys from Chelsea be sent off to die.

The "we" that I refer to are the mainly-white, mainly-well-educated children of mainly-comfortable parents, who are now mainly embarked on promising careers in law, medicine, business, academics. What makes them a class is that they all avoided the draft by taking one of the thinking-man's routes to escape. These included the physical deferment, by far the smartest and least painful of all; the long technical appeals through the legal jungles of the Selective Service System; the more disingenuous resorts to conscientious objector status; and, one degree further down the scale of personal inconvenience, joining the Reserves or the National Guard. I am not talking about those who, on the one hand, submitted to the draft and took their chances in the trenches, nor, on the other hand, those who paid the price of formal draft resistance or exile.

That there is such a class, identifiable as "we," was brought home to me by comparing the very different fates of the different sorts of people I had known in high school and college. Hundreds from my high school were drafted, and nearly two dozen killed. When I look at the memorial roll of names, I find that I recognize very few, for they were mainly the anonymous Mexican-American (as they were called at the time) and poor whites I barely knew in high school and forgot altogether when I left. Several people from my high school left the country; one that I know of went to jail. By comparison, of two or three hundred acquaintances from college and afterwards, I can think of only three who actually fought in Vietnam. Another dozen or so served in safer precincts of the military, and perhaps five went through the ordeal of formal resistance. The rest escaped in one way or another. . . . There are those who contend that the world has always worked this way, and perhaps that is true. The question is why, especially in the atmosphere of the late sixties, people with any presumptions to character could have let it go on. . . .

First we should consider the conduct of those who opposed the war. Not everyone at Harvard felt that way, nor, I suspect, did even a majority of the people throughout the country who found painless ways to escape the draft. But I did, and most of the people I knew did, and so did the hordes we always ran into at the anti-war rallies. Yet most of us managed without difficulty to stay out of jail. The tonier sorts of anti-war literature contained grace-note references to Gandhi and Thoreau—no CO application would have been complete without them—but the practical model for our wartime conduct was our enemy LBJ, who weaseled away from the front lines during World War II.

It may be worth emphasizing why our failure to resist induction is such an important issue. Five years after Cambodia and Kent State, it is clear how the war could have lasted so long. Johnson and Nixon both knew that the fighting could continue only so long as the vague, hypothetical benefits of holding off Asian communism outweighed the immediate, palpable domestic pain. They knew that when the screaming grew too loud and too many sons had been killed, the game would be all over. That is why Vietnamization was such a godsend for Nixon, and it is also why our reluctance to say No helped prolong the war. The more we guaranteed that we would end up neither in uniform nor behind bars, the more we made sure that *our* class of people would be spared the real cost of the war. Not that we didn't suffer. There was, of course, the *angst*, the terrible moral malaise we liked to write about so much in the student newspapers and undergraduate novels. . . .

The children of the bright, good parents were spared the more immediate sort of suffering that our inferiors were undergoing. And because of that, when our parents were opposed to the war, they were opposed in a bloodless, theoretical fashion, as they might be opposed to political corruption or racism in South Africa. As long as the little gold stars kept going to homes in Chelsea and the backwoods of West Virginia, the mothers of Beverly Hills and Chevy Chase and Great Neck and Belmont were not on the telephones to their congressmen, screaming *you killed my boy*, they were not writing to the President that his crazy, wrong, evil war had put their boys in prison and ruined their careers. It is clear by now that if the men of Harvard had wanted to do the very most they could to help shorten the war, they should have been drafted or imprisoned en masse.

This was not such a difficult insight, even at the time. Lyndon Johnson clearly understood it, which was the main reason why the *graduate school* deferment, that grotesque of class discrimination, lasted through the big mobilizations of the war, until the springtime of 1968. What is interesting is how little of this whole phenomenon we at Harvard pretended to understand. On the day after the graduate school deferments were snatched away from us, a day Johnson must have dreaded because it added another set of nasty enemies to his list, the Harvard *Crimson* responded with a magnificently representative editorial entitled "The Axe Falls." A few quotes convey its gist:

"The axiom that this nation's tangled Selective Service System is bound to be unfair to somebody fell with a crash on the Harvard community yesterday. The National Security Council's draft directive puts almost all college seniors and most graduate students at the head of the line for next year's draft calls. Three-fourths of the second-year law class will go off to war. . . . Yesterday's directive is a bit of careless expediency, clearly unfair to the students who would have filled the nation's graduate schools next fall."

That was it, the almost incredible level of understanding and compassion we displayed at the time—the idea that the real victims of General Hershey's villainous schemes were *the students who would have filled the nation's graduate schools next fall.* Occasionally, both in the *Crimson* and elsewhere, there were bows to the discriminatory nature of the whole 2-S deferment system and the virtues of the random lottery which Edward Kennedy, to his eternal credit, was supporting almost singlehandedly at the time. But there was no mistaking which emotions came from the heart, which principles really seemed worth fighting for.

It would be unfair to suggest that absolutely no thought was given to the long-run implications of our actions. For one thing, there were undercurrents of the sentiment that another *Crimson* writer, James Glassman, expressed in an article early in 1968. "Two years ago, Harvard students complained that the system was highly discriminatory, favoring the well off," Glassman wrote. "They called the 2-S an unfair advantage for those who could go to college." But, as the war wore on, "the altruism was forgotten. What was most important now was saving your own skin—preventing yourself from being in a position where you would have to kill a man you had no right to kill."

Moreover, a whole theoretical framework was developed to justify draft evasion. During many of the same meetings where I heard about the techniques of weight reduction, I also learned that we should think of ourselves as sand in the gears of the great war machine. During one of those counseling sessions I sat through a speech by Michael Ferber, then something of a celebrity as a codefendant in the trial of Dr. Spock. He excited us by revealing how close we were to victory. Did we realize that the draft machine was tottering towards its ultimate breakdown? That it was hardly in better condition than old General Hershey himself? That each body we withheld from its ravenous appetite brought it that much nearer the end? Our duty, therefore, was clear: as committed opponents of the war, we had a responsibility to save ourselves from the war machine.

This argument was most reassuring, for it meant that the course of action which kept us alive and out of jail was also the politically correct decision. The boys of Chelsea were not often mentioned during these sessions: when they were, regret was expressed that they had not yet understood the correct approach to the draft. We resolved to launch political-education programs, some under the auspices of the Worker-Student Alliance, to help straighten them out. In the meantime, there was the physical to prepare for.

It does not require enormous powers of analysis to see the basic fraudulence of this argument. General Hershey was never in danger of running out of bodies, and the only thing we were denying him was the chance to put *us* in uniform. With the same x-ray vision that enabled us to see, in every Pentagon sub-clerk, in every Honeywell accountant, an embryonic war criminal, we could certainly have seen that by keeping ourselves away from both frying pan and fire we were prolonging the war and consigning the Chelsea boys to danger and death. But somehow the x-rays were deflected.

There was, I believe, one genuine concern which provided the x-ray shield and made theories like Ferber's go down more easily. It was a monstrous war, not only in its horror but in the sense that it was beyond control, and to try to fight it as individuals was folly. Even as we knew that a thousand, or ten thousand, college boys going to prison might make a difference, we knew with equal certainty that the imprisonment and ruination of any one of us would mean nothing at all. The irrational war machine would grind on as if we had never existed, and our own lives would be pointlessly spoiled. From a certain perspective, it could even seem like grandstanding, an exercise in excessive piety, to go to the trouble of resisting the draft. The one moral issue that was within our control was whether we would actually participate—whether, as Glassman put it, we would be forced to kill—and we could solve that issue as easily by getting a deferment as by passing the time in jail. . . .

Lord Jim spent the rest of his days trying to expiate his moment of cowardice aboard the *Patna*. The contemporaries of Oliver Wendell Holmes felt permanent discomfort that Holmes, virtually alone among his peers, had volunteered to fight in the Civil War. I have neither of those feelings about Vietnam, so they are not the reason I feel it important to dredge up these hulks. Rather, the exercise can serve two purposes—to tell us about the past, and to tell us about the present.

The lesson of the past concerns the complexities of human motivation. Doubtless because the enemy we were fighting was so horrible in its effects, there was very little room for complexity or ambiguity in the anti-war campaigns. On the black and white spectrum by which we judged personal conduct, bureaucrats were criminals if they stayed inside the government and politicians cowards if they failed to vote for resolutions to end the war; the businessmen of Dow and Honeywell were craven merchants of death, and we, meanwhile, were nothing less than the insistent voice of morality, striving tirelessly to bring the country to its senses. . .

Of course we were right to try to stop the war. But I recall no suggestion during the sixties that it was graceless, *wrong* of us to ask the Foreign Service Officers to resign when we were not sticking our necks out at the induction center . . . If nothing else, a glance back at our own record might give us an extra grain of sympathy for the difficulties of bringing men to honor, let alone glory.

The implications for the present are less comforting and go back to the question asked several pages ago. The behavior of the upper classes in so deftly avoiding the war's pains is both a symptom and a partial cause of the class hatred now so busily brewing in the country.

The starting point for understanding this class hatred is the belief, resting just one layer beneath the pro forma comments about the unfortunate discrimination of the 2-S system, that there was an ultimate justice to our fates. You could not live through those years without knowing what was going on with the draft, and you could not retain your sanity with that knowledge unless you believed, at some dark layer of the moral substructure, that we were somehow getting what we deserved. A friend of mine, a former Rhodes scholar now embarked on a wonderful career in corporate law, put the point more bluntly than most when he said, "There are certain people who can do more good in a lifetime in politics or academics or medicine than by getting killed in a trench"; in one form or another, it was that belief which kept us all going. What is so significant about this statement is not the recognition of the difference in human abilities—for that, after all, has been one of the grand constants of the race—but the utter disdain for the abilities, hopes, complexities of those who have not scrambled onto the high road. The one-dimensional meritocracy of Aldous Huxley's *Brave New World* is not so many steps away from the fashion in which we were content to distribute the burden of the war. . . .

The "movement" of the sixties extended from the civil rights struggle through the campaign to end the war, and there was continuity as well in its view of the lower class. By the end of the sixties, when the anti-war campaign was going full steam, it exhibited contempt for the white proles in three clear ways. One way paying so little attention to the rate at which the Chelsea boys were dying; we mentioned the casualty rates, but not the fact that it wasn't our type of people being killed. The second was the bullying, supercilious tone which said that to support the war was not so much incorrect as *stupid*. (Recall how quickly arguments about the war reached the pedant's level with the question, "Have you read. . . ? If you haven't read . . . how can you presume to say anything?") And the third, rivaling even the first in ugliness, was the quick resort to the phrase "pig" for the blue-collar, lower-class people who were doing the job they thought they were supposed to do. They had been the "pigs" holding down the black people in Mississippi, the children of the pigs were being sent off to die in Vietnam, and now "pigs" were clubbing our chosen people, the demonstrators, in Chicago. We hated the pigs, and let them know it, and it was no great wonder that they hated us in return.

Now that the war is over, there is a fourth demonstration of our contempt for the proles. Among any high-brow audience, it is scarcely possible to attract a minute's attention on the subject of Vietnam veterans. Ralph Nader sponsored a study of their predicament, written by Paul Starr, but apart from that the intelligentsia has virtually willed them out of existence. The indignities they suffer rival those of any other oppressed group, but the only magazine to give sustained attention to this fact is *Penthouse*. On television the veterans are painted with extremely unflattering strokes—as war-time junkies or pathological killers who keep re-enacting the massacres they took part in—but no protests are heard about this crude stereotyping. The most frequently offered explanation for the neglect of the veteran is the *kind* of war we fought, and our eagerness to forget it. No doubt that is partly true. But our behavior is also shaped by *who* the veterans are. They are the boys from Chelsea, and if we were embarrassed to see them at the Navy Yard, when their suffering was only prospective, how much more must we shun them now?

Why Protest?
(ADDRESS TO CLERGY AND LAYMEN CONCERNED ABOUT VIETNAM, APRIL 4, 1967)

BY MARTIN LUTHER KING, JR.

I come to this magnificent house of worship tonight because my conscience leaves me no other choice. I join you in this meeting because I am in deepest agreement with the aims and work of the organization which has brought us together: Clergy and Laymen Concerned about Vietnam. The recent statement of your executive committee are the sentiments of my own heart and I found myself in full accord when I read its opening lines: "A time comes when silence is betrayal." That time has come for us in relation to Vietnam.

The truth of these words is beyond doubt, but the mission to which they call us is a most difficult one. Even when pressed by the demands of inner truth, men do not easily assume the task of opposing their government's policy, especially in time of war. Nor does the human spirit move without great difficulty against all the apathy of conformist thought within one's own bosom and in the surrounding world. Moreover, when the issues at hand seem as perplexing as they often do in the case of this dreadful conflict, we are always on the verge of being mesmerized by uncertainty: but we must move on.

Some of us who have already begun to break the silence of the night have found that the calling to speak is often a vocation of agony, but we must speak. We must speak with all the humility that is appropriate to our limited vision, but we must speak. And we must rejoice as well, for surely this is the first time in our nation's history that a significant number of religious leaders have chosen to move beyond the prophesying of smooth patriotism to the high grounds of a firm dissent based upon the mandates of conscience and the reading of history. Perhaps a new spirit is rising among us. If it is, let us trace its movements well and pray that our own inner being

Reprinted by permission of Clergy and Laity Concerned.

may be sensitive to its guidance, for we are deeply in need of a new way beyond the darkness that seems so close around us.

Over the past two years, as I have moved to break the betrayal of my own silences and to speak from the burnings of my own heart, as I have called for radical departures from the destruction of Vietnam, many persons have questioned me about the wisdom of my path. At the heart of their concerns this query has often loomed large and loud: Why are *you* speaking about the war, Dr. King? Why are *you* joining the voices of dissent? Peace and civil rights don't mix, they say. Aren't you hurting the cause of your people, they ask? And when I hear them, though I often understand the sources of their concern, I am nevertheless greatly saddened, for such questions mean that the inquirers have not really known me, my commitment or my calling. Indeed, their questions suggest that they do not know the world in which they live.

In the light of such tragic misunderstanding, I deem it of signal importance to try to state clearly, and I trust concisely, why I believe that the path from Dexter Avenue Baptist Church—the church in Montgomery, Alabama, where I began my pastorate—leads clearly to this sanctuary tonight.

I come to this platform tonight to make a passionate plea to my beloved nation. This speech is not addressed to Hanoi or to the National Liberation Front. It is not addressed to China or to Russia.

Nor is it an attempt to overlook the ambiguity of the total situation and the need for a collective solution to the tragedy of Vietnam. Neither is it an attempt to make North Vietnam or the National Liberation Front paragons of virtue, nor to overlook the role they can play in a successful resolution of the problem. While they both may have justifiable reason to be suspicious of the good faith of the United States, life and history give eloquent testimony to the fact that conflicts are never resolved without trustful give and take on both sides.

Tonight, however, I wish not to speak with Hanoi and the NLF, but rather to my fellow Americans who, with me, bear the greatest responsibility in ending a conflict that has exacted a heavy price on both continents.

Since I am a preacher by trade, I suppose it is not surprising that I have several reasons for bringing Vietnam into the field of my moral vision. There is at the outset a very obvious and almost facile connection between the war in Vietnam and the struggle I, and others, have been waging in America. A few years ago there was a shining moment in that struggle. It seemed as if there was a real promise of hope for the poor—both black and white—through the Poverty Program. There were experiments, hopes, new beginnings. Then came the build-up in Vietnam and I watched the program broken and eviscerated as if it were some idle political plaything of a society gone mad on war, and I knew that America would never invest the necessary funds or energies in rehabilitation of its poor so long as adventures like Vietnam continued to draw men and skills and money like some demoniacal destructive suction tube. So I was increasingly compelled to see the war as an enemy of the poor and to attack it as such.

Perhaps the more tragic recognition of reality took place when it became clear to me that the war was doing far more than devastating the hopes of the poor at home. It was sending their sons and their brothers and their husbands to fight and to die in extraordinarily high proportions relative to the rest of the population. We were taking the black young men who had been crippled by our society and sending them 8,000 miles away to guarantee liberties in Southeast Asia which they had not found in Southwest Georgia and East Harlem. So we have been repeatedly faced with the cruel irony of watching Negro and white boys on TV screens as they kill and die together for a nation that has been unable to seat them together in the same schools. So we watch them in brutal solidarity burning the huts of a poor village but we realize that they would never live on the same block in Detroit. I could not be silent in the face of such cruel manipulation of the poor.

My third reason moves to an even deeper level of awareness, for it grows out of my experience in the ghettos of the north over the last three years—especially the last three summers. As I have walked among the desperate, rejected and angry young men I have told them that Molotov cocktails and rifles would not solve their problems. I have tried to offer them my deepest compassion while maintaining my conviction that social change comes most meaningfully through non-violent action. But they asked—and rightly so—what about Vietnam? They asked if our nation wasn't using massive doses of violence to solve its problems, to bring about the changes it wanted. Their questions hit home, and I knew that I could never again raise my voice against the violence of the oppressed in the ghettos without having first spoken clearly to the greatest purveyor of violence in the world today—my own government. For the sake of those boys, for the sake of this government, for the sake of the hundreds of thousands trembling under our violence, I cannot be silent.

For those who ask the question, "Aren't you a Civil Rights leader?" and thereby mean to exclude me from the movement for peace, I have this further answer. In 1957 when a group of us formed the Southern Christian Leadership Conference, we chose as our motto: "To save the soul of America." We were convinced that we could not limit our vision to certain rights for black people, but instead affirmed the conviction that America would never be free or saved from itself unless the descendants of its slaves were loosed completely from the shackles they still wear. In a way we were agreeing with Langston Hughes, that black bard of Harlem, who had written earlier:

O, yes,
I say it plain,
America never was America to me,
And yet I swear this oath—
America will be!

Now, it should be incandescently clear that no one who has any concern for the integrity and life of America today can ignore the present war. If America's soul becomes totally poisoned, part of the autopsy must read Vietnam. It can never be saved so long as it destroys the deepest hopes of men the world over. So it is that those of us who are yet determined that America will be are led down the path of protest and dissent, working for the health of our land.

As if the weight of such a commitment to the life and health of America were not enough, another burden of responsibility was placed upon me in 1964; and I cannot forget that the Nobel Prize for Peace was also a commission—a commission to work harder than I had ever worked before for "the brotherhood of man." This is a calling that takes me beyond national allegiances, but even if it were not present I would yet have to live with the meaning of my commitment to the ministry of Jesus Christ. To me the relationship of this ministry to the making of peace is so obvious that I sometimes marvel at those who ask me why I am speaking against the war. Could it be that they do not know the good news was meant for all men— for communist and capitalist, for their children and ours, for black and for white, for revolutionary and conservative? Have they forgotten that my ministry is in obedience to the One who loved his enemies so fully that he died for them? What then can I say to the Vietcong or to Castro or to Mao as a faithful minister of this One? Can I threaten them with death or must I not share with them my life?

Finally, as I try to delineate for you and for myself the road that leads from Montgomery to this place I would have offered all that was most valid if I simply said that I must be true to my conviction that I share with all men the calling to be a son of the living God. Beyond the calling of race or nation or creed is this vocation of sonship and brotherhood, and because I believe that the Father is deeply concerned especially for his suffering and helpless and outcast children, I come tonight to speak for them.

This I believe to be the privilege and the burden of all of us who deem ourselves bound by allegiances and loyalties which are broader and deeper than nationalism and which go beyond our nation's self-defined goals and positions. We are called to speak for the weak, for the voiceless, for victims of our nation and for those it calls enemy, for no document from human hands can make these humans any less our brothers.

And as I ponder the madness of Vietnam and search within myself for ways to understand and respond in compassion my mind goes constantly to the people of that peninsula. I speak now not of the soldiers of each side, not the junta in Saigon, but simply of the people who have been living under the curse of war for almost three continuous decades now. I think of them too because it is clear to me that there will be no meaningful solution there until some attempt is made to know them and hear their broken cries.

They must see Americans as strange liberators. The Vietnamese people proclaimed their own independence in 1945 after a combined French and Japanese occupation, and before the communist revolution in China. They were led by Ho Chi Minh. Even though they quoted the American Declaration of Independence in their own document of freedom, we refused to recognize them. Instead, we decided to support France in its re-conquest of her former colony.

Our government felt then that the Vietnamese people were not "ready" for independence, and we again fell victim to the deadly western arrogance that has poisoned the international atmosphere for so long. With that tragic decision we rejected a revolutionary government seeking self-determination, and a government that had been established not by China (for whom the Vietnamese have no great love) but by clearly indigenous forces that included some communists. For the peasants this new government meant real land reform, one of the most important needs in their lives.

For nine years following 1945 we denied the people of Vietnam the right of independence. For nine years we vigorously supported the French in their abortive effort to re-colonize Vietnam.

Before the end of the war we were meeting 80% of the French war costs. Even before the French were defeated at Dien Bien Phu, they began to despair of the reckless action, but we did not. We encouraged them with our huge financial and military supplies to continue the war even after they had lost the will. Soon we would be paying almost the full costs of this tragic attempt at re-colonization.

After the French were defeated it looked as if independence and land reform would come again through the Geneva agreements. But instead there came the United States, determined that Ho should not unify the temporarily divided nation, and the peasants watched again as we supported one of the most vicious modern dictators—our chosen man, Premier Diem. The peasants watched and cringed as Diem ruthlessly routed out all opposition, supported their extortionist landlords and refused even to discuss re-unification with the North. The peasants watched as all this was presided over by U.S. influence and then by increasing numbers of U.S. troops who came to help quell the insurgency that Diem's methods had aroused. When Diem was overthrown they may have been happy, but the long line of military dictatorships seemed to offer no real change— especially in terms of their need for land and peace.

The only change came from America as we increased our troop commitments in support of governments which were singularly corrupt, inept and without popular support. All the while the people read our leaflets and received regular promises of peace and democracy—and land reform. Now they languish under our bombs and consider us—not their fellow Vietnamese—the real enemy. They move sadly and apathetically as we herd them off the land of their fathers into concentration camps where minimal social needs are rarely met. They know they must move or be destroyed by our bombs. So they go—primarily women and children and the aged.

They watch as we poison their water, as we kill a million acres of their crops. They must weep as the bulldozers roar through their areas preparing to destroy the precious trees. They wander into the hospitals, with at least 20 casualties from American firepower for one Vietcong-inflicted injury. They wander into the towns and see thousands of the children, homeless, without clothes, running in packs on the streets like animals. They see the children degraded by our soldiers as they beg for food. They see the children selling their sisters to our soldiers, soliciting for their mothers.

What do the peasants think as we ally ourselves with the landlords and as we refuse to put any action into our many words concerning land reform? What do they think as we test out our latest weapons on them, just as the Germans tested out new medicine and new tortures in the concentration camps of Europe? Where are the roots of the independent Vietnam we claim to be building? Is it among these voiceless ones?

We have destroyed their two most cherished institutions: the family and the village. We have destroyed their land and their crops. We have cooperated in the crushing of the nation's only non-communist revolutionary political force—the unified Buddhist Church. We have supported the enemies of the peasants of Saigon. We have corrupted their women and children and killed their men. What liberators!

Now there is little left to build on—save bitterness. Soon the only solid physical foundations remaining will be found at our military bases and in the concrete of the concentration camps we call fortified hamlets. The peasants may well wonder if we plan to build our new Vietnam on such grounds as these? Could we blame them for such thoughts? We must speak for them and raise the questions they cannot raise. These too are our brothers.

Perhaps the more difficult but no less necessary task is to speak for those who have been designated as our enemies. What of the National Liberation Front—that strangely anonymous group we call VC or Communists? What must they think of us in America when they realize that we permitted the repression and cruelty of Diem which helped to bring them into being as a resistance group in the south? What do they think of our condoning the violence which led to their own taking up of arms? How can they believe in our integrity when now we speak of "aggression from the North" as if there were nothing more essential to the war? How can they trust us when now we charge them with violence after the murderous reign of Diem, and charge them with violence while we pour every new weapon of death into their land? Surely we must understand their feelings even if we do not condone their actions. Surely we must see that the men we supported pressed them to their violence. Surely we must see that our own computerized plans of destruction simply dwarf their greatest acts.

How do they judge us when our officials know that their membership is less than 25 per cent communist and yet insist on giving them the blanket name? What must they be thinking when they know that we are aware of their control of major sections of Vietnam and yet we appear ready to allow national elections in which this highly organized political parallel government will have no part? They ask how we can speak of free elections when the Saigon press is censored and controlled by the military junta. And they are surely right to wonder what kind of new government we plan to help form without them— the only party in real touch with the peasants. They question our political goals and they deny the reality of a peace settlement from which they will be excluded. Their questions are frighteningly relevant. Is our nation planning to build on political myth again and then shore it up with the power of new violence?

Here is the true meaning and value of compassion and non-violence when it helps us to see the enemy's point of view, to hear his questions, to know his assessment of ourselves. For from his view we may indeed see the basic weaknesses of our own condition, and if we are mature we may learn and grow and profit from the wisdom of the brothers who are called the opposition.

So, too, with Hanoi. In the North, where our bombs now pummel the land, and our mines endanger the waterways, we are met by a deep but understandable mistrust. To speak for them is to explain this lack of confidence in western words, and especially their distrust of American intentions now. In Hanoi are the men who led the nation to independence against the Japanese and the French, the men who sought membership in the French commonwealth and were betrayed by the weakness of Paris and the willfulness of the colonial armies. It was they who led a second struggle against French domination at tremendous costs, and then were persuaded to give up the land they controlled between the 13th and 17th parallel as a temporary measure at Geneva. After 1954 they watched us conspire with Diem to prevent elections which would have surely brought Ho Chi Minh to power over a united Vietnam, and they realized they had been betrayed again.

When we ask why they do not leap to negotiate, these things must be remembered. Also it must be clear that the leaders of Hanoi considered the presence of American troops in support of the Diem regime to have been the initial military breach of the Geneva Agreements concerning foreign troops, and they remind us that they did not begin to send in any large number of supplies or men until American forces had moved into the tens of thousands.

Hanoi remembers how our leaders refused to tell us the truth about the earlier North Vietnamese overtures for peace, how we claimed that none existed when they had clearly been made. Ho Chi Minh has watched as America has spoken of peace and built up its forces, and now he has surely heard the increasing international rumors of American plans for an invasion of the North. Perhaps only his sense of humor and irony can save him when he hears the most powerful nation of the world speaking of *his* aggression as it drops thousands of bombs on a poor weak nation more than 8,000 miles away from its shores.

At this point I should make it clear that while I have tried in these last few minutes to give a voice to the voiceless on Vietnam and to understand the arguments of those who are called enemy, I am as deeply concerned about our own troops there as anything else. For it occurs to me that what we are submitting them to in Vietnam is not simply the brutalizing process that goes on in any war where armies face each other and seek to destroy. We are adding cynicism to the process of death, for they must know after a short period there that

Cynicism

none of the things we claim to be fighting for are really involved. Before long they must know that their government has sent them into a struggle among Vietnamese, and the more sophisticated surely realize that we are on the side of the wealthy and the secure while we create a hell for the poor.

Somehow this madness must cease. We must stop now. I speak as a child of God and brother to the suffering poor of Vietnam. I speak for those whose land is being laid waste, whose homes are being destroyed, whose culture is being subverted. I speak for the poor of America who are paying the double price of smashed hopes at home and death and corruption in Vietnam. I speak as a citizen of the world, for the world as it stands aghast at the path we have taken. I speak as an American to the leaders of my own nation. The great initiative in this war is ours. The initiative to stop it must be ours.

Statement of Mr. John Kerry, Representing the Vietnam Veterans Against the War

(SENATE FOREIGN RELATIONS COMMITTEE, APRIL 22, 1971)

Mr. Kerry. Thank you very much, Senator Fulbright, Senator Javits, Senator Symington, Senator Pell. I would like to say for the record, and also for the men behind me who are also wearing the uniform and their medals, that my sitting here is really symbolic. I am not here as John Kerry. I am here as one member of the group of 1,000, which is a small representation of a very much larger group of veterans in this country, and were it possible for all of them to sit at this table they would be here and have the same kind of testimony. . . .

I would like to talk to you a little bit about what the result is of the feelings these men carry with them after coming back from Vietnam. The country doesn't know it yet but it has created a monster, a monster in the form of millions of men who have been taught to deal and to trade in violence and who are given the chance to die for the biggest nothing in history; men who have returned with a sense of anger and a sense of betrayal which no one has yet grasped.

As a veteran and one who feels this anger I would like to talk about it. We are angry because we feel we have been used in the worst fashion by the administration of this country.

In 1970 at West Point Vice President Agnew said "some glamorize the criminal misfits of society while our best men die in Asian rice paddies to preserve the freedom which most of those misfits abuse," and this was used as a rallying point for our effort in Vietnam.

But for us, as boys in Asia whom the country was supposed to support, his statement is a terrible distortion from which we can only draw a very deep sense of revulsion, and hence the anger of some of the men who are here in Washington today. It is a distortion because we in no way consider ourselves the best men of this country; be-

Reprinted from *Congressional Record—Senate*, April 23, 1971.

cause those he calls misfits were standing up for us in a way that nobody else in this country dared to; because so many who have died
would have returned to this country to join the misfits in their efforts
to ask for an immediate withdrawal from South Vietnam; because so
many of those best men have returned as quadruplegics and am-
putees—and they lie forgotten in Veterans Administration Hospitals
in this country which fly the flag which so many have chosen as their
own personal symbol—and we cannot consider ourselves America's
best men when we are ashamed of and hated for what we were called
on to do in Southeast Asia.

In our opinion, and from our experience, there is nothing in South
Vietnam which could happen that realistically threatens the United
States of America. And to attempt to justify the loss of one American
life in Vietnam, Cambodia or Laos by linking such loss to the preser-
vation of freedom, which those misfits supposedly abuse, is to us the
height of criminal hypocrisy, and it is that kind of hypocrisy which
we feel has torn this country apart. . . .

We are probably angriest about all that we were told about Vietnam and about the mystical war against communism. We found that
not only was it a civil war, an effort by a people who had for years
been seeking their liberation from any colonial influence whatsoever,
but also we found that the Vietnamese whom we had enthusiastically
molded after our own image were hard put to take up the fight
against the threat we were supposedly saving them from.

We found most people didn't even know the difference between
communism and democracy. They only wanted to work in rice
paddies without helicopters strafing them and bombs with napalm
burning their villages and tearing their country apart. They wanted
everything to do with the war, particularly with this foreign presence
of the United States of America, to leave them alone in peace, and
they practiced the art of survival by siding with whichever military
force was present at a particular time, be it Viet Cong, North Vietnamese or American.

We found also that all too often American men were dying in those
rice paddies for want of support from their allies. We saw first hand
how monies from American taxes were used for a corrupt dictatorial
regime. We saw that many people in this country had a one-sided
idea of who was kept free by our flag, and blacks provided the highest percentage of casualties. We saw Vietnam ravaged equally by
American bombs and search and destroy missions, as well as by Viet
Cong terrorism, and yet we listened while this country tried to blame
all of the havoc on the Viet Cong.

We rationalized destroying villages in order to save them. We saw America lose her sense of morality as she accepted very coolly a My Lai and refused to give up the image of American soldiers who hand out chocolate bars and chewing gum.

We learned the meaning of free fire zones, shooting anything that moves, and we watched while America placed a cheapness on the lives of orientals.

We watched the United States falsification of body counts. We listened while month after month we were told the back of the enemy was about to break. We fought using weapons against "oriental human beings." We fought using weapons against those people which I do not believe this country would dream of using were we fighting in the European theater. We watched while men charged up hills because a general said that hill has to be taken, and after losing one platoon or two platoons they marched away to leave the hill for reoccupation by the North Vietnamese. We watched pride allow the most unimportant battles to be blown into extravaganzas, because we couldn't lose, and we couldn't retreat, and because it didn't matter how many American bodies were lost to prove that point, and so there were Hamburger Hills and Khe Sahns and Hill 81s and Fire Base 6s, and so many others.

Now we are told that the men who fought there must watch quietly while American lives are lost so that we can exercise the incredible arrogance of Vietnamizing the Vietnamese. Each day to facilitate the process by which the United States washes her hands of Vietnam someone has to give up his life so that the United States doesn't have to admit something that the entire world already knows, so that we can't say that we have made a mistake. Someone has to die so that President Nixon won't be, and these are his words, "the first President to lose a war."

We are asking Americans to think about that because how do you ask a man to be the last man to die in Vietnam? How do you ask a man to be the last man to die for a mistake? But we are trying to do that, and we are doing it with thousands of rationalizations, and if you read carefully the President's last speech to the people of this country, you can see that he says, and says clearly, "but the issue, gentlemen, the issue, is communism, and the question is whether or not we will leave that country to the communists or whether or not we will try to give it hope to be a free people." But the point is they are not a free people now under us. They are not a free people, and we cannot fight communism all over the world. I think we should have learned that lesson by now. . . .

Suddenly we are faced with a very sickening situation in this country, because there is no moral indignation and, if there is, it comes from people who are almost exhausted by their past indignations. . . . The country seems to have lain down and shrugged off something as serious as Laos, just as we calmly shrugged off the loss of 700,000 lives in Pakistan, the so-called greatest disaster of all times.

But we are here as veterans to say we think we are in the midst of the greatest disaster of all times now, because they are still dying over there—not just Americans, but Vietnamese—and we are rationalizing leaving that country so that those people can go on killing each other for years to come.

Americans seem to have accepted the idea that the war is winding down, at least for Americans, and they have also allowed the bodies which were once used by a President for statistics to prove that we were winning that war, to be used as evidence against a man who followed orders and who interpreted those orders no differently than hundreds of other men in Vietnam.

We veterans can only look with amazement on the fact that this country has been unable to see there is absolutely no difference between ground troops and a helicopter crew, and yet people have accepted a differentiation fed them by the administration.

No ground troops are in Laos so it is all right to kill Laotians by remote control. But believe me the helicopter crews fill the same body bags and they wreak the same kind of damage on the Vietnamese and Laotian countryside as anybody else, and the President is talking about allowing that to go on for many years to come. One can only ask if we will really be satisfied only when the troops march into Hanoi.

We are asking here in Washington for some action; action from the Congress of the United States of America which has the power to raise and maintain armies, and which by the Constitution also has the power to declare war. We have come here, not to the President, because we believe that this body can be responsive to the will of the people, and we believe that the will of the people says that we should be out of Vietnam now.

We are here in Washington also to say that the problem of this war is not just a question of war and diplomacy. It is part and parcel of everything that we are trying as human beings to communicate to people in this country—the question of racism, which is rampant in the military, and so many other questions such as the use of weapons; the hypocrisy in our taking umbrage in the Geneva Conventions and using that as justification for a continuation of this war when we are more guilty than any other body of violations of those Geneva

Conventions; in the use of free fire zones, harassment interdiction fire, search and destroy missions, the bombings, the torture of prisoners, the killing of prisoners, all accepted policy by many units in South Vietnam. That is what we are trying to say. . . .

We are also here to ask, and we are here to ask vehemently, where are the leaders of our country? Where is the leadership? We are here to ask where are McNamara, Rostow, Bundy, Gilpatric and so many others? Where are they now that we, the men whom they sent off to war, have returned? These are commanders who have deserted their troops, and there is no more serious crime in the law of war. The Army says they never leave their wounded. The Marines say they never leave even their dead. These men have left all the casualties and retreated behind a pious shield of public rectitude. They have left the real stuff of their reputations bleaching behind them in the sun in this country.

Finally, this administration has done us the ultimate dishonor. They have attempted to disown us and the sacrifices we made for this country. In their blindness and fear they have tried to deny that we are veterans or that we served in Nam. We do not need their testimony. Our own scars and stumps of limbs are witness enough for others and for ourselves.

We wish that a merciful God could wipe away our own memories of that service as easily as this administration has wiped away their memories of us. But all that they have done all that they can do by this denial is to make more clear than ever our own determination to undertake one last mission—to search out and destroy the last vestige of this barbaric war, to pacify our own hearts, to conquer the hate and the fear that have driven this country these last ten years and more. So when 30 years from now our brothers go down the street without a leg, without an arm, or a face, and small boys ask why, we will be able to say "Vietnam" and not mean a desert, nor a filthy obscene memory, but mean instead the place where America finally turned and where soldiers like us helped it in the turning.

Thank you.

Part Five

THE CONTINUING CONTROVERSY: COMING TO TERMS WITH A CONFUSING WAR

These following selections complement the reading of Walter Capps's *The Unfinished War,* which offers insight into the deep and enduring effects of the Vietnam experience on American culture, conscience, and consciousness. The Capps book also provides a good, brief review of American history in Vietnam.

In "American Guilt," Richard Falk answers questions on a range of issues. He makes a clear distinction between guilt and responsibility, guilt being the failure to exercise responsibility, and suggests constructive ways of coming to terms with the moral pain experienced by those who feel corrupted by the war.

"Is American Guilt Justified?" is a sharp debate between scholars about a moral issue posed by the war. On the one side, a revisionist argues that immoral conduct must involve immoral intentions, regardless of the consequences. On the other side, opponents of the war argue that support for an immoral regime is immoral. For them, the morality issue does not have to do with American good intentions, but with whether or not we had a right to be in Vietnam in the first place.

"What Are the Consequences of Vietnam?" is another political discussion between thoughtful people with opposing viewpoints, arguing on different levels, using different values to interpret the same evidence. Those on the right want to come to grips with a military question. How does America effectively use her power abroad? Those on the left want to deal with a moral question. What should American foreign policy goals be? What objectives justify what costs?

American Guilt

AN INTERVIEW WITH RICHARD FALK ON VIETNAM

This interview was conducted by Executive Editor Donald McDonald during the Center's Pacem in Terris III convocation in Washington.

Q: Professor Falk, a Northwestern University student was recently quoted in the Christian Science Monitor *as saying, "I have spent ten years of my life reading about civil rights, Vietnam, and the environment. I want to start reading about happier things. I think most people want to start enjoying the pleasures of life again." Given that view, and it is probably typical, how can it be squared with the fact that we did something horrendous to the Vietnamese people and that we just cannot walk away from it now, forget it, pretend it never happened?*

FALK: People would like to be done with the whole Vietnam experience and with all the confusion and anguish it has occasioned. But it would be compounding the tragedy of that experience to ignore what we have done—and are still doing. We continue to uphold the Thieu regime with massive economic aid. Some of that aid is used directly to support the South Vietnamese internal security forces, which are holding a minimum of one hundred thousand and possibly as many as two hundred thousand political prisoners under cruel conditions. This has been attested to by a number of impartial groups.

As long as the U.S. government supports this kind of action, we continue to endorse the practices that led so many Americans to be appalled by our involvement in Indochina for the last ten years. A great many of those incarcerated in Thieu's jails are third-force people; prisoners of conscience—students, labor leaders, newspapermen—who acted out of their personal convictions in opposi-

Reprinted from *The Center Magazine*, January/February 1974, by permission of *The Center Magazine*, a publication of The Center for the Study of Democratic Institutions.

tion to what the Thieu regime is doing to Vietnam. The least that one can expect from our leaders at this point is that, instead of supporting the torture system in the South, we should honor the obligation we undertook in the Paris agreements to bring peace and conciliation to Vietnam, as well as to help rebuild all Indochina. That obligation pertaining to reconstruction aid has been conveniently forgotten by the President and Congress.

Q: Were there any conditions put on our aid?

FALK: Not really. And there was even a dollar figure evidently attached to the bargain; although not specified in the agreement, it was a part of the negotiations between Le Duc Tho and Henry Kissinger. Money cannot compensate of course for all the damage and suffering caused by the war, but at least it could represent a tangible contribution to the restoration of normalcy to Indochinese society. And it would indicate that we had acted in good faith in the Paris negotiations.

Another reason why the United States cannot turn away from the Vietnam experience is that there are still thousands of Americans who are suffering because of their opposition to the war. I refer to the amnesty question as it relates to those who evaded the draft and also to the large number of American military men who deserted or were given less than honorable discharges as a result of their experiences in Vietnam.

Robert Jay Lifton suggests in *Home From the War* that war resisters are not only people who acted out of ideological conviction against the war. Many servicemen engaged in irrational and deviant behavior because they found their combat experience in Indochina so appalling. I had hoped that, as an aftermath of the Paris agreements, our President would have encouraged rather than hindered the healing and reconciliation process in our own country. An essential step in that process is the grant of a general pardon covering all those whose conscience led them to draft evasion, desertion, resistance, and actions in the military which caused them to receive less than honorable discharge. And, of course, if one accepts the view that both the conduct of the war and our underlying involvement violated international law, then the real amnesty issue should concern the fate of American policy-makers, not draft evaders and other resisters.

Q: Have our policy-makers learned any lessons from Vietnam?

FALK: That brings me to a third reason why we cannot allow ourselves to turn away from the Vietnam experience. I do not feel we have yet learned its fundamental political lesson. The counterrevolutionary foreign policy that led us into Indochina in the first place still characterizes America's involvement throughout the Third World. We still interpret it as a geopolitical victory for ourselves if, in the name of anti-Communism or in the name of right-wing values, a government comes to power and represses its own people in a cruel and reactionary way.

I think our role in Latin America has been a successful variant of what we tried unsuccessfully to achieve in Indochina. Despite the horrible things that have happened to them, the Vietnamese at least take pride in knowing that to a great extent they succeeded in their struggle for national self-determination. By contrast, throughout much of Latin America the people are held captive by an alliance of indigenous military and privileged elites who are supported by the United States in substantial respects. The United States has been actively involved in counterinsurgency efforts throughout the hemisphere, especially through our role in training and orienting the elite officer corps. We continue to train Latin American police in torture methods to be used against political prisoners. These are activities that many Americans found so abhorrent during our involvement in Vietnam. They continue as an essential part of our policy in Latin America.

Q: It would seem that this last-named step—dissociating ourselves from all further counterrevolutionary activities in the affairs of other countries—would have to precede the other two actions: helping restore Indochina and granting general amnesty to draft evaders and war resisters. This third step would involve at least a tacit acknowledgement that the U.S. intervention in Vietnam was a moral and political transgression of the first magnitude. Until that acknowledgement is made, it is not very realistic to expect that the United States will begin rebuilding Indochina and grant amnesty to the opponents of that war.

FALK: I think that is right. There was a profound failure in Presidential leadership during and right after the period in which the cease-fire was negotiated in Paris. There was a great opportunity at that time for the President to come before the American people and say: "This war has been a horrible experience for our nation. Reasonable and decent American citizens have fought and suffered and died in this war. Others, no less reasonable and decent, have opposed it in a variety of ways. Let us move beyond this experience. Let us adopt an attitude of reconciliation which extends both to the participants in the war and to the opponents of the war." General Charles de Gaulle successfully pursued such a policy of reconciliation in France after the Algerian war of independence; he forgave all activities of O.A.S. resistance against the settlement of the struggle that he had negotiated with the F.L.N. in 1962.

Q: Do you think the parents of young men who were killed in the war would have accepted this?

FALK: No policy on an issue as broad as this would be acceptable to everybody, but I think it could have been made acceptable to the great majority of Americans. Such an approach would have created a very positive climate, particularly as it would have been coupled with the efforts of this Administration—which I think have been largely successful—to bring the Cold War to an end. It could have signaled a new era in American foreign policy, and at the same time inspired a new sense of hope for domestic America. Of course, all the wounds of Vietnam cannot be healed. But as long as you do not heal at least some of them, no recovery is possible; as it is, our country can only pretend to be healthy, like a patient who gets out of bed too soon.

Q: Can the United States do anything therapeutic or rehabilitative before the political dust settles in South Vietnam?

FALK: Because the world is so interdependent, there will inevitably be some American interference in the internal affairs of South Vietnam. But I think one can ask our government, at a minimum, to stop blatant violations of the Paris agreements and to dissociate itself from the most abhorrent policies and practices of the Saigon regime, thereby at least signaling our disapproval of such barbarism. The abuse of political opponents directly violates the Paris agreements in which Saigon promised to restore reasonable political freedom to the South Vietnamese people. Without such restoration it was meaningless for the N.L.F. (or P.R.G.) to agree to a shift of the unresolved civil conflict from the battlefields of South Vietnam to its political terrain.

Q: So, you are saying that if the United States would stop supporting the repressive practices of the Thieu regime that would pave the way for the United States to begin doing some rehabilitative work in Indochina?

FALK: Yes. Removing ourselves from the most horrendous features of the Thieu regime, and, for that matter, of the Lon Nol regime in Cambodia would be presently far more important than coming into these countries with our aid. What the Vietnamese people need above all is less American involvement in their lives. There are other countries in the world—for example, Japan or various European states—which have the resources to help the Vietnamese if we don't.

Certainly it would be good for us to give the aid; the whole domestic political process in America of justifying the congressional decision to appropriate funds for the Vietnamese people would be a clarifying experience for all of us. But I think that the Vietnamese could get along without it.

Q: Much of what you say must be done depends on a raised and realistic consciousness of the American people as to the nature and dimension of what American intervention has meant to the Vietnamese people for the last decade or more. But as the Northwestern University student suggests, the American people just do not want to think about that anymore.

FALK: True. The prevailing mood is to turn away from and repress that which is unpleasant, particularly now when very little that is pleasant seems to be happening in American political life at large. There is a connection between our Indochina experience and the Watergate events. But again, that connection, if imaginatively used by political leaders—both in the Administration and in the opposition—could be translated into an important learning experience for the American people.

Congressman Robert Kastenmeier has been talking about an initiative for legislation which would make government officials directly and explicitly accountable for conforming to international treaties during times of war. As I understand his proposal, it would bar from public office those officials who had failed to comply with internationally negotiated treaty obligations. The practical effect of this is not as important as its symbolic value, which suggests that the government and its elected officials acknowledge that they must take legal restraints on the exercise of power seriously. If they fail to restrain themselves, they not only expose others to great suffering, but they also bring it back home, into our domestic life.

It is impossible for a government to pursue a policy of lawless violence in foreign societies—however covert it is kept—without tending to behave the same way in dealing with its own population. What is done abroad sooner or later contaminates what is done at home. The Watergate disclosures confirm the view that the world of Watergate was the same world as that of the Pentagon Papers, that what an earlier Democratic administration in Washington did in Indochina set a pattern which became gross and blatant in the Nixon Administration.

Q: Do the American people know enough, with enough precision, about what we actually did in Vietnam: the numbers of tons of bombs we dropped and their effect; the extent to which we destroyed crops and poi-

*soned their irrigation system; the numbers of square miles of forest and
grass cover we destroyed? Do you know, for example, how many people
have bought your book,* Crimes of War, *which details this destruction?*

FALK: The book has reached only a very small number of people
directly. However, late in the war there was evidence in the opinion
polls that a fairly large percentage of the American people realized
that our involvement in Indochina was an immoral venture. Yet they
still did not want to be confronted with specific evidence of exactly
what was wrong with our involvement. This was due in part to a
cycle of systematic non-awareness that set in: the mass media created
boredom and then responded to it.

Still, I am opposed to confronting the public with further evidence
of atrocities in Vietnam unless it is also possible to indicate a constructive way of converting that negative experience into something
positive. All our evidence suggests that if you do not do this, then it
is not helpful to confront people with information about the terrible
things Americans have done. It frustrates and finally embitters them;
it provokes hostile responses.

Q: Somebody has to provide the vision of constructive possibilities.

FALK: Yes, and that is why political leadership is so important at
such a time. The United States has been relatively lucky throughout
its history in having outstanding leadership during periods of crisis.
We don't have it today and that is why we are so unable to fashion
appropriate responses to moral challenges. These challenges represent subtle but significant issues; they do not touch directly the nation's wealth or power, and yet they destroy its confidence and erode
its character.

*Q: Given the present mood and the present Administration in Washing-
ton, what do you think can be done, practically, to enable the American
people to make a morally healthy response to Vietnam?*

FALK: One thing that can be done is to relate current political hap-
penings to our Indochina experience. For example, it would be important to expose the direct and indirect roles played by the United
States in the overthrow of Allende in Chile. Such an exposure would
demonstrate to the skeptical liberal that our Vietnam pattern is
continuing. During the Allende years we trained and supplied the
Chilean armed forces, emphasizing counterinsurgency warfare and
the mission of the military to save its country from radical internal
enemies. After the junta seized power the United States government
was among the first major governments to recognize the military

regime. We have done nothing about the summary execution or mistreatment of Left leaders; we have made no offer of asylum to Chileans in jeopardy or to other Latin American political refugees who are threatened by the junta with deportation to such oppressive countries of origin as Brazil. Such American behavior discloses our reactionary preferences and our insensitivity to the minimal well-being of Third World peoples.

Q: A couple of years ago, Telford Taylor called for a national commission of inquiry which would have the power to compel testimony and grant immunity in order to discover and make public the military operational directives that we enforced in Southeast Asia during the Vietnam war. He wants to let the American people know what standards of training and discipline we followed with regard to observing the laws of war and the carrying out of military justice in dealing with war crimes. Do you see any "consciousness-raising" value in such a commission?

FALK: A commission like this could be desirable if it managed to clarify the way in which our military forces operate in war situations. If it were not successful, it would have a demoralizing effect on the people. But, more basically, I don't think the proposal goes to the fundamental question, which involves the kind of mission that American civilian leadership entrusts to the military.

Such an inquiry into military justice could actually create the wrong impression if it suggested that the real problem in Indochina was that our military was not sensitive enough to the guidelines of international law. Certainly, the military was not very sensitive. But it is even more true that the civilian policy-makers were giving the military certain priorities in the war which made it almost mandatory to adopt the indiscriminate and cruel forms of warfare that were practiced in Vietnam.

Q: You once said that although you were still opposed to having a war-crimes trial, you had changed your mind about the war-crimes question and that you had come to believe it "vitally important to appreciate the extent to which the Vietnam war has displayed the capacity of our government to operate beyond the restraints of law without provoking much of a negative reaction except among the young." How does one make the relevance of this war-crimes question more or less universal, rather than limit it to a fairly small group of scholars like you who have been studying such questions for a long time?

FALK: What is needed is vigorous opposition leadership; a voice above partisan politics which would bring to the attention of the people a clear recognition of the relationship between our Indochina-style operations and Watergate-style operations, which would make explicit the connections between the Pentagon Papers and the Watergate situation, which would show that if you have a government of unprincipled men rather than laws you cannot expect to restrain that government in its domestic affairs—and, as a consequence of that, the very survival of democratic society becomes jeopardized.

Q: Do you think that rules of war such as the Hague Convention of 1907, the Geneva Protocol of 1925, and the Geneva Convention of 1949 are still practically applicable to the conduct of war? Jerome Frank has said that a nation's war potential now depends heavily on its industrial capacity, that all productive citizens have become, in a sense, combatants, and so the inflicting of massive carnage on civilians has come to be viewed as a necessary part of a military struggle for victory. Dr. Frank thinks that "attempts to arrive at generally agreed-upon definitions of war crimes are doomed to futility."

FALK: The first thing our Indochina experience suggests is that there is an urgent need to revise the laws of war, based on the technological realities of modern counterinsurgency conditions. This applies to the way in which both the insurgents and the incumbent and its foreign allies conduct their operations. It is especially important in situations where the insurgency occurs in a low-technology society but the counterinsurgents, supported by a sophisticated foreign government, enjoy high-technology armaments.

Q: I recall Donald Kennedy, of the biological sciences department at Stanford, saying when the Stanford Biology Study Group completed its study of American destruction in South Vietnam that the United States was not fighting a war against an enemy. "Instead we are waging a war against a people and the land they live on."

FALK: I agree with his view. We engaged in such combat practices as saturation bombing, crop-denial and destruction programs, defoliation, the uprooting and forcible removal of massive numbers of civilians. It is clear that the burden of all those tactics was borne not by the North Vietnamese armies nor by the National Liberation Front, but by the Vietnamese peasants. The RAND Corporation, certainly not a hotbed of antiwar activism, studied the impact of our crop-destruction program and concluded that it had virtually no effect on the N.L.F.'s food supply, because wherever the N.L.F. had control, it obtained the food needed for its forces. Rather, whatever food shortages developed took food away from the very old and the

very young—that is, from those having least to do directly with the
war effort.

Q: You believe, then, that the rules of war must be revised.

FALK: Yes, there is urgent need for it. But perhaps even more fundamental is the moral crisis posed by the relationship between modern weaponry and the objectives for which those weapons are used.
In either a nuclear or a counterinsurgency context, it is very difficult
for me to envision a situation in which the ends being sought through
warfare justify the means used to reach them. We have, in my view,
come to the end of that road by which morally sensitive individuals
can regard war as a just means by which to pursue their ends.

*Q: That would apply to the insurgent or the revolutionary, too, wouldn't it?
If he knows that a high-technology, genocidal counterinsurgency effort will
be mounted against the revolution, in which vast numbers of people will
be wiped out, he, too, would be inhibited, for moral reasons, from seeking
a military solution to a political or social problem.*

FALK: These are complex moral questions. What I had intended to
suggest is not so much that every instance of recourse to political violence is disproportional to the goals being sought, but that in any
situation where it is necessary to rely on the massive application of
high-technology weaponry, the moral threshold of decency is trans-
gressed to such an extent as to throw in doubt any claim of justification and make the net effect likely to cause more harm than benefit.

I think a great deal more attention must be given to the whole
ethos and role of nonviolence in the modern world as a technique for
change and resistance. There are ways other than war to accomplish
political ends. I think that the Arab countries, for instance, could
have done a great deal over the past twenty or thirty years with the
creative use of nonviolence in the Middle East. The Israeli government would not be willing to do what Nazi Germany did or what
South Africa might do in the face of nonviolent resistance. Sending
Palestinians, for instance, peacefully across the Jordan River bridges
in large numbers, or calling some kind of general strike among Arabs
in occupied territories would have a strong effect, if well-planned
and executed.

We must direct our best thinking to practical alternatives to war.
But in addition it is imperative that we imagine, and then embody, a
world political system which will eliminate the war system. This involves, in the first instance, a revitalization of the disarmament
effort. A kind of sophisticated consensus has developed that says it is

bad form to talk about anything other than arms control, which involves only small adjustments. Arms-control thinking produces various pressures to develop weapons systems as "bargaining chips" or to agree that weapon x will not be developed, but justify this agreement as desirable because it frees up resources to develop weapons y and z on a more accelerated basis. Major governments devote huge budgets to build weapons that would be disastrous for all concerned if they were ever used. Beyond these issues of prudence and waste, is the possibility of starting a moral revolution based on the notion that relations in the post-state era we are now entering will have no place for a war system.

Q: In that connection, perhaps the deep and instinctive repugnance which youth in this country and elsewhere felt during the nineteen-sixties for our old-fashioned reliance on war and killing to resolve international differences will make that moral revolution more thinkable.

FALK: Yes. To an extent, our elites are entrapped in a set of obsolete values and beliefs. The question is whether their outmoded consensus can be penetrated by this new-generational perspective. These new perspectives will be resisted very strongly. The discouragement that young people of sensitivity and conscience feel with the American political process is based, in part, on the fact that, to participate successfully in the governing process, they realize they would have to surrender what they really believe.

As a result there is a kind of negative selection process: the government tends to recruit only those people who either lack any feel for American constitutional traditions or can easily acquiesce to whatever demands will advance their careers. This is particularly unfortunate today when we need the talents of the best young people to challenge the predispositions of a statecraft built out of an essentially obsolete nationalism.

Q: If enough young people said it is unthinkable to resort to weapons to solve problems, the governments could no longer rely on them to wage their wars. And isn't this, in effect, what we said to the German people after World War II: that they should have refused the Hitlerian government's orders to fight? I gather, from what you have written on the subject, that you considered the Nuremberg war-crimes trials a valid exercise of international law, that Nuremberg was not simply "victor's justice." If it was valid, why should it not apply equally to us with respect to what we did in Vietnam?

FALK: I guess my position on Nuremberg is somewhere between saying it is a valid precedent on the one hand and, on the other,

agreeing with critics that it is discredited because it partakes of vic- *Nuremberg*
tor's justice. I think Nuremberg was a weak precedent, flawed in certain fundamental ways; but it did state an essentially valid claim,
namely, that individuals who act on behalf of the state must be held
personally accountable for their failure to adhere to legal principles
of restraint which have been agreed upon and which reflect a minimum moral content. Further, injecting this minimum moral content
in statecraft is important as a source of guidance to those who would ✓
resist the state.

I have tried elsewhere to argue that Nuremberg may not have been
important in restraining Lyndon Johnson or Richard Nixon in Vietnam, but it has been important in providing an objective foundation
and some sense of energy and direction for individuals, like Daniel
Berrigan and Daniel Ellsberg, who were, I think, acting in part out
of the sense that they had both a right and a duty to resist governmental crime. My own feeling is that the renewal of America and
more generally the reform of world society will depend on a kind of
populism arising among people who lose faith in the capacity of their
governments to be the repository of legitimacy and to serve as the
valid expression and agency of national interests. Nuremberg is one
element in that process. It is very important that Nuremberg exists
as a historical fact, even though—and particularly in its application
to the Japanese leaders—it represented in many respects an arbitrary, one-sided effort to attach individual responsibility.

I think that the Japanese recourse to war was consistent with the
logic of the war system in human affairs as it was operating at that
time. The Japanese were not depraved in the way that the Nazi leaders were. Furthermore, Japan was the victim of some of the worst
war crimes in World War II. The two landmarks in that war which
one remembers as the ultimate expression of criminal or pathological
war-waging are Auschwitz and Hiroshima. These are the two symbols of depravity, so to speak, that have endured in international
conscience.

Q: At the time of the Nuremberg trials, Justice Robert Jackson said: "If ✗
certain acts in violation of treaties are crimes, they are crimes whether the ✗
United States does them or whether Germany does them, and we are not
prepared to lay down a rule of criminal conduct against others which we
would be unwilling to have invoked against us." I don't think I have ever
seen that quotation used in any recent or current discussions and arguments
concerning American military actions in Vietnam.

FALK: There is no question that we have not honored the reciprocal
side of Justice Jackson's pledge at Nuremberg. We have not accepted

the fact that it created a duty for the United States as well as a burden
for those Germans we indicted, prosecuted, and punished at Nuremberg. In fairness, it can be said that other governments also have not
accepted the Nuremberg precedent. So, before we become too guilt-
ridden, I think it is important to relate some of the analysis of this
problem to the way in which the war system operates in the context
of state sovereignty.

All governments continue to regard themselves as having the right
to use force when their national interests are at stake and virtually to
do militarily whatever will help them succeed. At the same time, I
think citizens have a responsibility to try to make restraints on political leaders more viable with regard to the conduct of practical politics.

*Q: Who was responsible for Vietnam? Who was guilty? Are we all guilty,
to an extent? You once said during the war that "these war crimes are
being committed in our name and in our behalf." Max Lerner has said
that the trouble with holding that everyone is guilty is that "you reduce the
idea of guilt to an absurdity." And Sartre has said that the unprovoked
killing of Vietnamese peasants, women, and children, "carried out every
day before the eyes of the world, renders all who do not denounce it accomplices of those who commit it." Is there something pathological about
those Americans who feel they are guilty for what was done to the Vietnamese people "in their name and in their behalf"? Or is there something
wrong with those Americans who feel no guilt whatever for what was
done in Vietnam?*

FALK: You are posing very complicated cultural questions. They
involve how we, as a country, given our whole spiritual, religious,
and moral tradition, feel about a failure to take risks in situations
where we feel a responsibility. I would make a strong distinction between guilt and responsibility. Lerner confuses the issue by linking
the two.

Certainly it is true that pointing the finger at one another is not the
way to respond creatively or constructively. On the other hand, it
seems to me to be equally true that those of us who had an awareness
and a capability to act had a certain obligation to follow our personal
moral directives. I would be reluctant to judge how far each individual should carry his conscience. No society is composed solely of heroes and martyrs. Given each person's whole psychic and spiritual
makeup, what is appropriate is essentially a question of each person's
fidelity to his own sense of responsibility. But I do think one must
pose this challenge of responsibility to the public so as to activate the
moral sensibilities of the public.

It was important for some Americans to point out what was taking place in Vietnam in the name of America and what Americans might do to stop the war. On such a basis leaders of the antiwar movement hoped, often in vain, that there would be a growth and intensification of a movement of opposition and resistance so that the claims would become more potent politically. I think the record of American antiwar opposition is not a bad record when it is compared with what other populations have done about immoral wars carried out in their name.

On the other hand, much more could have been done, had we had greater courage behind our convictions and a little more confidence in the effectiveness of the antiwar protests. The main failure of the large-scale antiwar movement was a lack of perseverance, an inability to sustain a massive oppositional presence beyond participation in sporadic events.

Q: The protests were more effective than the protesters knew?

FALK: Yes. The Pentagon Papers indicate that the antiwar demonstrations were having a much greater impact on the policy-makers than most of us believed at the time. Had we only persisted with what we were doing, and if we had looked upon opposition to the war as a continuing process rather than a quick-fix spectacular, it might have been more successful.

One of the things I have learned from the Vietnamese people over the years is the extent to which a struggle for what one believes is a process; it is not something you start one day and forget the next. It has to become an integral part of one's life and imagination. If there was failure in the antiwar movement, it was that it did not create in its ranks this understanding of the long range nature of the struggle.

Q: Why do you separate guilt and responsibility? I realize that guilt—its intensity and nature—is different in each person. But are you saying there is no relationship between guilt and responsibility?

FALK: No. There is a relationship. But to me guilt implies a kind of passivity in relation to certain behavior, whereas responsibility implies a recognition of one's duty to act in accordance with one's conscience. Guilt is a failure to exercise responsibility. The prior and more constructive claim is to have people acting responsibly at all levels of society—from the most ordinary citizen to the most prominent leaders. Our failures during the Vietnam war were failures to exercise responsibility in relation to moral and legal restraints.

Q: What about the consequences for grievous moral failure? Does punishment have any role to play?

FALK: I think that focusing on war crimes as a potential foundation for punishing other people is a misappropriation of energy. We have little evidence that punishment does any good, even in domestic affairs. People who are normally on the liberal or progressive side of issues now want to punish some of our leaders for what they did in Vietnam. I do not think that punitive efforts represent a fruitful way to proceed, especially when it is completely implausible from a political point of view.

We should direct our energy to trying to create a responsible America, not a guilty America. To search for scapegoats like Richard Nixon or William Calley whom we can blame and punish for the war is not the most productive course of action in terms of learning from our Vietnam experience.

Q: However, if the Nixons and the Calleys are not identified in some way—not necessarily isolated and punished, but identified—does that not imply that they were not acting irresponsibly?

FALK: It is a dilemma. All things being equal, I think it was important that Calley was convicted and sentenced.

Q: What about our top political leaders and the "war managers"?

FALK: I challenged the selection of William Bundy as editor of *Foreign Affairs*, not on the ground that I wanted to punish him but because it seemed to me important that a person who played an important policy role in the war and has not regretted playing that role should not be rewarded with such a symbol of intellectual leadership in American foreign affairs. I think it was legitimate on my part to impose some standards of accountability, or at least to expose the absence of a moral sensitivity on the part of those who selected Bundy for such a job while the war was still under way.

Q: You have said you are not interested in creating a "guilty America," but is there any part that guilt can play that is not neurotic and that would help people to arrive at a sense of responsibility? Should not one feel a little guilty? One does not advocate going around weeping all day and becoming pathological about one's guilt, but . . .

FALK: It's a hard thing to know. The whole Protestant background of so many Americans predisposes the country toward a sense of sin and guilt. At the same time, this seems to inhibit many Americans from acting responsibly in relation to our real potentialities for doing good, or better, in concrete human affairs. Guilt becomes a substitute for responsible action. I think I agree with the implication of your question: that there is a circular relation in which guilt can animate responsibility that, in turn, replaces guilt by real action. One acts to avoid being guilty. Obviously that can be constructive. Robert Lifton, in that book of his I referred to earlier, emphasizes what he calls "animating guilt" and the "animating relationship to guilt." Lifton discusses those antiwar veterans who were led into constructive forms of behavior because they wanted to absolve their guilt. His argument is that had they either wallowed in their guilt or not felt guilty at all, they probably would not have been able to deal with their own psychological problems arising out of their experience in Vietnam. I think that, to a lesser extent, this applies to all Americans who were passive witnesses to the war.

Now we are obliged, as I said in the beginning of our discussion, to act in certain ways—to end our support of the cruel police-state activities of the Thieu regime, to begin the process of reconciliation and healing at home, and to stop intervening in the affairs of other nations, such as those in Latin America. If we do not do these things now, then we are indeed guilty of wrongdoing. If we do not do something about the political prisoners in South Vietnam and about the candidates for amnesty and pardon in America, then we are guilty of being accessories to moral complacency.

Q: I remember Lifton saying once in a symposium with Leslie Farber that one way to rescue one's animating relationship to guilt is to become more sensitive in our response to our weaponry and our destructive technology. I think he said that we must recover the idea of guilt as the "anxiety of responsibility." One must be careful when using such terms, because one can begin to sound neurotic. Of course Lifton recognizes that. He said that as a psychiatrist he had been led to look upon guilt as a profound problem within the neuroses, but that in certain situations he had learned to value guilt as a needful process. I take it you would not disagree with that.

FALK: No, no. It's only when guilt becomes a kind of hermetic category that it is unhealthy. And, as I have said, I think there is a predisposition in a certain part, the Calvinist part, of the American temperament to make one's guilt a kind of passive reality that operates to excuse individuals from doing good works.

Q: Do you think the leaders of the major institutions in our society should feel a little guilty for their performance during the Vietnam war? I refer to the churches, the mass media, the universities, the professions, Congress, the courts.

FALK: There is no question that these institutions were acquiescent in the basic course of the war, particularly as long as it was reasonably successful or was perceived as being successful. If one wants to pass judgment on liberal Americans, many of them began opposing the war only after the Tet offensive in February of 1968. The wrongfulness of what we were doing was to be found in the intrinsic character of our actions, not with how successful or unsuccessful we were in defeating the N.L.F. insurgency in South Vietnam. The lesson one can learn from the role played by these institutions is that it would be healthy if they became more autonomous, if they began looking at such foreign-policy issues on their merits.

With the buildup of power in Washington, and with the concentration of mass communications control in so few hands, we need independent centers of sentiment and judgment. It is extremely important to have academic centers of thought and action with greater financial and political autonomy than universities now have. We hope such centers of national conscience will be established and endowed by men of good will.

Is American Guilt Justified?

GUENTER LEWY (*Professor of Political Science, University of Massachusetts, author of* America in Vietnam). The Vietnam war was perhaps the most divisive and most difficult war that this country has experienced. The impact of the war on American society was highly damaging. Among other things, it has resulted in an attitude of cynicism and distrust of government. Perhaps still more damaging, it has left the country with a tremendous sense of guilt, not only because the war was lost, but because, in the eyes of many, the entire enterprise was flawed, the war was criminal and immoral. *His Posca*

It is my position that the wounds suffered were largely self-inflicted, and that the American sense of guilt is not warranted by the facts about the war which we know today. What follows is a summary account of my argument, which is developed and substantiated in my book.

I hope that the passion of the public debate over Vietnam has subsided and cooled sufficiently by now so that my argument can be considered on its merits. Some of my critics have painted me as a kind of moral leper, comparing me to those who deny that the Jewish Holocaust happened, that six million Jews were murdered during that Holocaust. Others say my work is a revisionist job, useful, perhaps, in stimulating debate, but otherwise too extreme to be considered reliable. Of course, I disagree with both those appraisals.

Peter Berger, an opponent of the American involvement in Vietnam, has said my book is disturbing because it calls into question many of the moral judgments which he had made and which he had considered settled once and for all. I hope that, like Peter Berger,

Reprinted from *The Center Magazine*, July/August 1979, by permission of *The Center Magazine*, a publication of The Center for the Study of Democratic Institutions.

you, too, may be willing to rethink some of your assumptions and some of the conventional wisdom on the war.

I will touch briefly on three issues that bear on the question of American guilt. First, American military tactics and their legality and/or morality; second, the over-all impact of the war on Vietnamese society; and third, individual atrocities and war crimes.

Regarding American military tactics in Vietnam, critics have said that such actions as the bombardment of fortified villages, the creation of free-fire zones, the destruction of crops, and the defoliation of forests were illegal and/or immoral. Now, it is rather clear to me—and in this I do not adopt a position that is unusual—that reliance on these tactics, accompanied by the lavish use of fire power, ignored the political and social dynamics of a revolutionary war and the need to win the proverbial hearts and minds of the people in Vietnam. American reliance upon such heavy-handed tactics may, and probably does, help explain why we lost the war. But these tactics were not illegal under the international law of war. I will go further and say that for the most part, neither were they immoral.

The international law of war consists of treaties and conventions; it also includes certain customs and principles that govern the conduct of war, that seek to minimize the ravages of war. Because it codifies certain minimum rules of human decency in war, the international law of war has a moral dimension. Therefore, to abide by the law of war means to abide by certain elementary moral standards. Much of the vehement criticism of my book probably derives from the critics' acceptance of this link between legality and morality. Because I show that American military tactics were legal, I clearly also undermine their assertion that the American conduct in Vietnam was immoral.

Immoral conduct must involve immoral intentions. The context and the purpose of an action must be taken into account in evaluating it. For example, a motorist who, because he is a bad driver, accidentally kills a child has not committed the same moral evil as someone who abducts, rapes, and kills a child to satisfy his aggressive and sadistic impulses. The law recognizes this distinction. It distinguishes between homicide and murder.

Moral judgment, too, recognizes the crucial importance of intent. So moral judgment of military actions must consider intent. The terror bombing of civilian populations in World War II in order to break the morale of people was immoral. On the other hand, American military commanders in Vietnam who created free-fire zones and destroyed crops did not intend thereby to terrorize the civilian population. For the most part, they believed—however mistakenly—that these actions were essential to win the war, and indeed that they would speed up its successful conclusion. It is rather clear now that these tactics were shortsighted, if not downright stupid. They lose wars. But they did not constitute either illegal or grossly immoral conduct.

The Nuremberg tribunal in 1946 ruled on the legal aspect of this issue in the so-called hostages case. "It is our considered opinion," said the court, "that the conditions as they appeared to the defendant at the time were sufficient upon which he could honestly conclude that urgent military necessity warranted the decision made. This being true, the defendant may have erred in the exercise of his judgment, but he was guilty of no criminal act." And, in my view, such a person was also not guilty of immoral conduct.

With regard to the over all impact of the war, it has been argued that America committed genocide in Vietnam. However, it is not difficult to make the case that neither in terms of intent nor in terms of results did American actions constitute the crime of genocide. Again, intent is essential in the definition of the genocide code, as adopted by the United Nations. And, of course, results are similarly crucial. According to statistics developed by the United Nations, the population of South and North Vietnam, during the course of the war, increased at a rate roughly double that of the United States in a comparable period. That alone makes the charge of genocide—i.e., _Gʋ/ɔ cɒɒɛ_ intentional destruction of a whole people—rather grotesque.

It can be shown—and I try to do this with some care in an appendix of my book—that noncombatants were not killed in Vietnam in anything like the proportions that they were in Korea; and the proportion killed was probably even somewhat lower than the proportion in World War II. Civilian deaths were drastically lower in absolute numbers, despite the fact that the Vietnam war lasted such a long time. The proportion, in absolute numbers, between noncombatants and military deaths in Vietnam is roughly half what it was in the Korean war, and slightly lower than it was in World War II.

All of this casts doubt on the charge that was often heard during the course of the Vietnam war—that America was destroying a whole society. That charge remains unproven and must be rejected.

With regard to the third point—individual atrocities and war _Atrocities_ crimes—atrocities did occur in Vietnam. Every war has its atrocities. Atrocities happened in World War II also. They were largely ignored then because that war was seen as a crusade against evil, a crusade in which the Allies could do no wrong. But, after a careful examination of the record, I am convinced that atrocities in Vietnam were far less frequent than was alleged during the course of the war. Critics of the American war effort, like Telford Taylor and Daniel Ellsberg, agree with me that the My Lai atrocity was not typical. It was quite unusual.

We also know now that many alleged atrocities, which received considerable publicity in the media, did not occur, but were staged for a variety of reasons. We know of at least one instance where a dead body was thrown out of a helicopter, a soldier took a picture and forwarded that picture, with a suitable story, to his friend, who submitted it to the Washington *Post*. That became the proof of a practice that we all heard a lot about—although not a single case has been confirmed—namely, the practice of taking Vietcong captives up in a helicopter and throwing one of them out in order to scare the others into talking.

We know of at least one case where a C.B.S. cameraman provided a knife to an American soldier and asked him to cut off the ear of a dead Vietcong. That was filmed and was a big sensation on the Walter Cronkite evening news.

At the so-called winter soldier investigation of war crimes, held in Detroit early in 1971, alleged American atrocities were reported by alleged veterans. It turned out, upon examination and investigation, that these veterans had never been to Detroit. Some of them were able to submit sworn affidavits by their employers that they had never left their places of employment. What had happened was that someone had used their names and serial numbers in order to read charges of crimes into the record.

The Committee of Concerned Asian Scholars, at one of the sessions of the Bertrand Russell war crimes tribunal, heard a North Vietnamese investigator testify that American fliers who had been shot down had in their possession maps on which hospitals were marked. Now, that, of course, could be given a quite innocuous interpretation. Hospitals could be marked on aviators' maps so that the aviators would not bomb these hospitals. The Concerned Asian Scholars reported this testimony, slightly changed, namely, American aviators who were shot down had maps with hospitals marked as targets.

There *was* American laxity in enforcing the rules of engagement governing combat, and I make some rather severe charges against General William Westmoreland on that count. But violations of the law of war were known, and they were vigorously prosecuted by the Judge Advocate General's Corps. Between January, 1965, and March, 1973, 201 Army personnel were convicted by court-martial of

serious offenses against Vietnamese civilians. During that same period, seventy-seven Marines were similarly convicted. The United
States is the first country in history which tried its own military
offenders while a war was still going on.

The seriousness with which the Judge Advocate General's Corps
pursued the enforcement of the law of war is reflected in the following incident. In August, 1966, a Marine lance corporal had killed an
unarmed villager, allegedly for revenge. The accused was charged
with premeditated murder. He took the stand and testified that he
had been in heavy combat for several months, that he had seen many
of his buddies get killed and wounded, and that finally he decided,
"I had to kill a VC for those guys; I just had to kill one."

A psychiatrist had examined the accused, and he testified that as a
result of stress experience, the defendant's ability to adhere to morally licit behavior was significantly impaired. Another psychiatrist
testified that his ability was impaired to some degree. The prose-
cutor, backed up by the law officer of the court-martial, argued that
the accused had known what he was doing, and that there was not
enough impairment of his ability to exculpate criminal responsibility. "Gentlemen," he told the court, "life is not so cheap, even in
Vietnam, that indiscriminate killing of a defenseless Vietnamese can
be tolerated or condoned." The court found the Marine guilty as
charged, and sentenced him to dishonorable discharge, forfeiture of
all pay and allowances, reduction to the rank of private, and confine-
ment at hard labor for life.

The terror tactics of the Vietcong were morally more reprehensible
because, unlike American atrocities, they were officially condoned.
That included such things as what the Vietcong called the extermina-
tion of traitors; the best-known example of that is the massacre at
Hue. It included the mining of roads used by the villagers taking
their wares to the market. It included attacks on refugee camps, several of these attacks being with flamethrowers. It included the indiscriminate shelling of cities with rockets. And it included the torture
of American prisoners, both in the North and in the jungle cages of
South Vietnam.

Some French intellectuals, who earlier had been in the forefront of
the worldwide opposition to the American actions in Vietnam, have
since acknowledged that they were less than fair or objective in their
defense of the Vietcong and the North Vietnamese. One such is Jean
Lacouture, who had an important influence not only in France, but
on the American antiwar movement as well. In a recent interview
with a Milan newspaper, Lacouture acknowledged that "with regard

to Vietnam, my behavior was sometimes more that of a militant than a journalist. I dissimulated certain defects of North Vietnam at war against the Americans, because I believed that the cause of the North Vietnamese was good and just enough so that I should not expose their errors. I believed it was not opportune to expose the Stalinist nature of the North Vietnamese regime in 1972, right at the time when Nixon was bombing Hanoi. If we re-examine the dossier, it is true that I did not tell all that I knew about Vietnam."

Lacouture goes on to call people like himself "vehicles and intermediaries for a lying and criminal propaganda, ingenious spokesmen for tyranny in the name of liberty." He admits "my shame for having contributed to the installation of one of the most oppressive regimes history has ever known." The last reference is to the Pol Pot regime in Cambodia. But in Lacouture's review—and I agree with him— the Communist regime in North Vietnam is a close second.

I hope that American intellectuals may be willing to undertake the same kind of soul-searching demonstrated by Jean Lacouture. I hope that this reexamination will also include the conduct of the Americans.

BARTON J. BERNSTEIN (*Professor of History, Stanford University*): Your analysis, Professor Lewy, strips the historical context of the Vietnam war by not asking how and why it was that the United States got into that war in the first place. Your analysis talks of North Vietnam, but presumably there were those other people in the South. Was South Vietnam's government legitimate? What was the National Liberation Front? Who invited America to Vietnam? Was that invitation legitimate in any way, or was it fundamentally illegitimate?

What does one do with the 1954 settlement, the Geneva accords? What does one do with the systematic violation of that settlement? What does one do with the systematic dissembling by the American government—first under John F. Kennedy, and then under Lyndon Johnson—as to the nature of the war and the American commitments in that war? What about the secret war in Laos, a war that American leaders denied was being conducted all the while it was being conducted? What about the American bombing that was being done when American leaders were denying it was being done?

Your analysis can be faulted on at least three grounds. First, it eliminates history; and yet the basic questions I have asked are historical and their relevance is essential. Second, it looks only at the conduct of the war and eschews all questions about proclamations by U.S. leaders describing that war. Third, even in analyzing the

American conduct of the war, you rely, for your evidence of intent, on highly selected material from some military people when there is good reason to believe that they dissimulated, often upon at least implicit directives from above. By the criteria you use today, what would you do with, say, the Central Intelligence Agency's technique of plausible denial? People are instructed to deny what they are doing. How can you use, as genuine evidence, the documents of people who are told not to admit what they are really doing?

You use the example of the motorist killing a child to illustrate the importance of intent. It is true that if a motorist accidentally kills a child, society does not usually impute immorality. But let me offer you this scenario: a motorist is speeding across town at eighty miles an hour because he hankers for a lollypop. He races through two school zones, and kills a child. He did not intend to kill anyone, but we would make a particular moral judgment of that motorist based upon our sense of what constitutes reasonable and prudent driving conduct.

But going beyond that, you contend that bombing which to us in America looked very much like terror bombing, was not really terror bombing because it was designed to win the war. Indeed, the legitimation for terror bombing during World War II was that that war was total, that it was waged not simply against armies, but against the political economy of the German homeland; and so in order for the Allies to win, it was necessary, it was argued, to destroy the Germans' industrial base and the people's morale, which was essential both to that industrial base and to the Army. I contend that the same underlying conception is what accounted for the American activity in Vietnam and which led to the very acts you say are not illegal, and thus not immoral.

I say those acts in Vietnam were fundamentally immoral. Also, we will be able scrupulously to investigate each particular case, but only when complete documentation is available, not on the present basis of selective documentation through the Freedom of Information Act, which can deny as many things as it can grant. Only then will we be able to conduct a meaningful dialogue. To make a full judgment of American activity in Vietnam on the basis of selective documents provided by the government about its own conduct is to engage in an illusory, self-deceptive, fundamentally flawed pursuit.

Under the Freedom of Information Act and the mandatory declassification review—the two procedures under which most of these documents have become available—material which is said to be pertinent to national security can continue to be kept secret. One must expect, then, that a certain skewed evidential pattern will be made available by the government.

Having got some Vietnam material declassified, and having got a good deal of that declassified for the period from 1944 through the nineteen-sixties, having written more than five hundred letters to the American government over the last eight years, and having secured close to ten thousand documents, I am prepared to say, on the basis of watching the selective quality of that trickle and its relationship to politics, that one is not getting simply a random selection of documents bearing upon the Vietnam war, but documents made available according to political criteria for a particular purpose. That must be taken into account in judging the evidence on which Professor Lewy relies.

DAVID KRIEGER (*Political scientist and author*): Professor Lewy suggested that the war was damaging to American society because it generated cynicism toward the political system and guilt because the war was perceived to be criminal and immoral. But rather than seeing those as damaging outcomes of the war, I see them as positive outcomes. I do not think it is inappropriate to be cynical toward a political system which has demonstrated rather conclusively that government officials had little difficulty in lying to the American people about why we were in Vietnam and what we were doing there.

Professor Lewy talked about immorality and illegality in the context of the war, but he did not deal with some of the things that Mr. Bernstein talks about, i.e., the constitutionality of our presence in Vietnam. Also, he did not talk about the fact that the United States supported rather corrupt regimes in South Vietnam, and a case can be made rather well that supporting an immoral regime is immoral.

JAMES ROSENAU (*Director of the School of International Studies, University of Southern California*): Professor Lewy, if indeed there is a pervasive sense of guilt in the American people, what do you mean by guilt? Maybe it is a pervasive sense of something else, chastisement perhaps. Also, what kind of evidence demonstrates a pervasive sense of guilt, irrespective of whether its consequences are positive or negative?

LEWY: The sense of guilt is very pervasive in the intellectual community. The issues which gave rise to this sense of guilt should not be swept under the rug. We need the kind of re-examination which at least some French intellectuals are beginning to undertake.

How do we establish that there is this pervasive sense of guilt? I arrived at it largely on an impressionistic basis, simply having lived in the intellectual community for the last ten or fifteen years. I may be all wrong in my impressions, and you may have contrary data. If so, it would be interesting to get this data. But it is my sense, which seems to be shared by many others, that this feeling of guilt is indeed pervasive in the intellectual community. Of course, the intellectual community dictates, at least to some extent, the over-all *Zeitgeist*, as it were, of society at large. So if it is true that society feels guilty, then this is an important issue and it ought to be addressed in very substantive terms. Is the guilt warranted?

ROSENAU: We do not have data on that. We haven't even wrestled with what is meant by guilt. But at one point in your response, you sounded as though you equated guilt with a feeling of having engaged in immoral actions in Vietnam.

LEWY: Yes.

ROSENAU: Now, David Krieger is saying that guilt with respect to Vietnam is a positive thing. Do you interpret his remark as an expression of unwarranted guilt? In your view, is his judgment that Americans engaged in immoral actions in Vietnam the equivalent of a sense of guilt? If guilt is an appropriate judgment about this, I agree with you that it then has important consequences.

LEWY: There are two issues here. First, is there a sense of guilt in the American intellectual community today, because of past criminal and immoral conduct by this country? Second, how do we interpret and evaluate that? Is it something positive or negative?

A number of German Protestant theologians, to take a different example, looked with a sense of guilt upon the attempted assassination of Hitler in July, 1944. For them, the attempt was something almost positive; they felt that the assassination attempt, had it succeeded, might have been justifiable. Yet it still left them with a sense of guilt. They could condone the deed morally, and yet they felt somewhat guilty about it. So, the dimension of guilt and the sense of guilt are complex. I used only a shorthand expression for it here.

In reply to Professor Bernstein, I did not address the issue of how the United States became involved in Vietnam and whether it was

legal to become involved in what many regard as a civil war, because
it seems to me there is a clear distinction in the tradition of international law between what we call *jus ad bellum* and *jus in bello.* The
jus ad bellum does involve the question, was it right, was it legal, to
intervene in a particular conflict? Having intervened, *jus in bello* ad-
dresses the question, what was the conduct of the armed forces in
that conflict?

Conceptually the two are completely separate; they do not over-
lap. It is possible to engage in a just war under *jus ad bellum,* but
to conduct the war unjustly and illegally under *jus in bello.* And
vice versa. For example, we regard the German war effort in World
War II as an illegal and immoral war of aggression; yet we also know
that some German generals, including General Erwin Rommel, had
clean hands. Their conduct of the war easily passes muster by the
criteria of *jus in bello.*

So it is possible to evaluate how a country conducts its military
operations—that is, whether it does or does not violate canons of *jus
in bello*—without getting involved in the still more difficult questions
of why did the country become involved in the war. Was it justified?
Was it a civil war? What about the status of the Geneva accords? Is it
significant that South Vietnam was recognized by forty other countries in the world? Is it significant that at one time the Soviet Union
tried to get both Vietnams admitted to the United Nations? Does
that make South Vietnam legitimate, or does it not? The issues get
quite complex. But it seems to me there is no need to get into these
in order to discuss the issue of *jus in bello,* which is what I addressed
myself to.

Now, what is the nature of my evidence? I must tell Professor
Bernstein that hardly any of my documentation was acquired through
the Freedom of Information Act. Some was, but little of any significance. Most of my documentation was obtained on the basis of a
blanket clearance to examine military documents in possession of the
various offices of military history in the Army, the Air Force, and the
Marine Corps. This clearance was made possible on the basis of an
executive order, first issued by President Dwight Eisenhower, later
confirmed by, of all people, President Richard Nixon in 1972, and
recently somewhat watered down in a new executive order by President Jimmy Carter.

This executive order grants to the Secretaries of the military services the discretionary authority to admit scholars to classified defense documentation. Once you get this clearance—and I received it
not as a special favor, but simply because no one else had applied for
it—you can see anything, and I mean anything, up to your level of

clearance. My clearance included Confidential, For Official Use Only, and Secret. The only thing that I could not see immediately was Top Secret, and that was no more than perhaps four per cent of the total documentation. Even there, in some cases, I was able to ask for downgrading of the classification, and that was possible. So, for all practical purposes, I was able to work with the complete files that no one had sorted, and from which nothing had been removed.

I can tell you that the evidence that comes out of these files is sometimes devastating. This is not self-serving evidence; these are raw data. We do know that even raw data can be falsified. The most notorious instance is that of the body count in Vietnam. But in that case, I could check evidence from different elements involved in Vietnam. For example, there was an organization called the Pacification Studies Group, troubleshooters who had their own transportation and could go anywhere in Vietnam without asking anyone's permission. They could snoop around and report back to the head of the Pacification Program in Southeast Villages, who was, at one point, William Colby. The reports of these people have to be read to be believed. Much of my most devastating criticism of American military tactics—and there is plenty of that in my book—comes from that source.

It seems to me that one cannot, on the one hand, welcome internal evidence when it is damaging, and, on the other hand, reject the evidence that may be exculpating. That, of course, is what happened with the Pentagon Papers. Many critics accepted the veracity of the Pentagon Papers when it suited their political purposes, but rejected those same Pentagon Papers as "unreliable," when what they found there did not support their position.

BERNSTEIN: There are three issues. First, the Pentagon Papers were classified as Top Secret, and only a little more than a handful of copies was available. Second, the notion that you have seen almost everything because only four per cent was withheld from you strikes me, as a historian who has worked through archives for years, as naive. That is like going into a civilian agency, or a business corporation, and getting to see the files of all the secretaries in the outer offices who keep the blue copies of the marginal material, but not the files of the president and the chairman of the board. When you say that you have seen all but four per cent of the evidence, you beg a fundamental analytical question. If you have not seen four per cent of the evidence, then—unless you think that the security system is totally random in the most statistical sense—there is every reason to think that you have not seen the vital material.

THE 4% HE DON'T SEE MIGHT BE VITAL

Third, let us take one of the empirical conclusions upon which you have built an argument about both morality and legality. You say that the bombing was not designed to terrorize, but to win. But that kind of judgment is based upon material you have seen in the province of the office of chief of military history and the counterpart agencies for the other services. There is good indirect evidence to suggest that the most interesting material does not even reach those offices. So, what you have seen is only that part of the material which they are able to gather, or permitted to hold. Now, how can one make a judgment about the intentions behind our bombing if one cannot have access to the most classified material on bombing?

On the face of it, to reach the comfortable conclusion that you did—i.e., that this was bombing designed to win, but not to terrorize—runs contrary to common sense. It also relies upon a dubious distinction between winning and terrorizing.

And your conclusion runs contrary to earlier American military practices, about which we have more evidence. For example, we probably have more evidence on the Korean war in the public domain than we do on the Vietnam war. We certainly have more evidence on World War II than we do on the Vietnam war. Indeed, scholars having paid attention, as citizens, to the American adventures in Vietnam, have gone back and looked at earlier wars and discovered things which, at the time, scholars passed by because they seemed either uninteresting or irrelevant.

So let me ask you to stipulate, if you will, the kind of evidence that permits you to determine that our bombing in Vietnam was militarily essential and not part of terrorizing, that our free-fire zones were militarily essential, but not a part of terror tactics. Tell me about the nature of that evidence.

LEWY: Let me correct one misunderstanding. A lot has been said here about military documentation. I would not be worth anything if I were to build an analytical judgment on simply one type of document. I think I have used everything that anyone else has been able to use; but, in addition, I have been able to use military documentation, which I think is highly interesting and valuable. With regard to the bombing of both North Vietnam and South Vietnam, I have read my way through congressional reports, reports of journalists, and diaries of soldiers who have written about it. The military documentation is simply an added dimension; it is certainly not the only one.

Second, it is probably correct to say that the four per cent of the military documents that remain classified as Top Secret involve, for the most part, diplomatic issues; that is to say, our relationship with the Cambodian government, issues touching on relations with China, and the like. They have hardly any bearing at all on the issues that we are concerned with here.

You ask me how can I judge intent? Well, how do you judge intent? First of all, you examine what people themselves say; and that always has to be taken with a grain of salt. Then you check this against the account of others who have observed what was going on. And you look at consequences. In some way you arrive at a judgment.

As regards free-fire zones, the intent was to negate what Mao Tse-tung had called the secret of guerrilla warfare. Mao said guerrillas had to be like fish in the water; they derived their sustenance from the people among whom they lived. The American intent in establishing the free-fire zones was to isolate the guerrillas, to drive a wedge between them and the people. The tactic was to remove the civilian population from thvuu ureao, ɔu that all that would be left in these zones would be combatants who could then be attacked.

Now, we know that in practice the free-fire zone tactic did not work out that way. We know it was counterproductive. But the fact remains that the American intent was not to terrorize the civilian population. Quite the contrary; it was to remove the civilians from battle so that when, indeed, guerrilla forces were attacked, civilians would not be hurt. There is very little mystery about all that.

WALTER H. CAPPS (*Center Associate; Professor of Religious Studies and Director of the Institute of Religious Studies at the University of California at Santa Barbara*): Perhaps the reason for American guilt feelings is that the Vietnam war was unlike other wars; therefore, it does not help us very much to draw upon traditional categories of warfare to alleviate or eliminate those guilt feelings. In your book, you said, "A decisive reason for this growing disaffection of American people was a conviction that the war was not being won, and apparently showed little prospect of coming to a successful conclusion."

I am not sure that that is the case. Other literature suggests that the people involved in the war thought there was no way that the war could be won, because winning and losing did not mean what they once did. Since there were no analogues for the Vietnam war, traditional categories of warfare could not be tapped to explain what was happening. Therefore, the guilt probably cannot be dismissed in this way.

ALEXANDER DE CONDE (*Professor of History, University of California at Santa Barbara*): I find this discussion intellectually disturbing. Professor Lewy did not answer Professor Bernstein's questions about discerning the difference between terrorism and winning. Also, I have heard the fuzziest of generalizations. Professor Lewy has cited as evidence the opinion of one French journalist. Opinion is not evidence. Further, we hear that the American people felt this way or that way. That is utter nonsense. We do not know what the American people felt. We have an idea of what it might be, but no firm documentation on that. Regarding guilt, I don't know how one can analyze that, except in the context of an entire society, or within at least a segment of a society, and its philosophy.

As to Professor Capps' comment, I think there are numerous analogues to the Vietnam war in America's pre-Vietnam past. You can find one in the Mexican War. You can find one in the War of 1812. And all you have to do is read *Bury My Heart at Wounded Knee;* that is one "My Lai" after another. Guilt over the Vietnam war is one of the healthiest things that ever happened in the American society. It moved a number of scholars, as Professor Bernstein indicated, to look into our past and find black records that had been buried by earlier American scholars and intellectuals.

So, I don't see the Vietnam war as something unique in our history. Much of what happened in the Vietnam war is about as American as apple pie.

RICHARD FLACKS (*Professor of Sociology and Chairperson of the Department of Sociology at the University of California at Santa Barbara; founding member of Students for a Democratic Society*): One piece of data on American intellectuals is in the book *The American Intellectual Elite* by Charles Kadushin, an interview study of people identified by the author as leading figures in the American intellectual community. Much of Kadushin's study is focused on Vietnam. One of his conclusions is that there is relatively little basis for thinking that the intellectuals who strongly opposed the war did so on moral grounds. Their opposition was much more in terms of the cost of the war and the policy implications of the war, and the fact that we couldn't win it.

Professor Lewy, you said the word guilt was shorthand for something complex. I am wondering what it is shorthand for. From what I heard underneath your statement, I think it is shorthand for your distress that there is so much resistance among intellectuals and other Americans to repeating the Vietnam type of experience. I take it that you wish there was less public resistance to American involvement in foreign conflict. There is indeed resistance throughout society—a resistance based on guilt or some other emotion or consideration—to this country's moving in a direction that would lead to "another Vietnam." I take it that, either before you started the book or after you finished it, one of your intents—since you are interested in intention—was to try to overcome that resistance. So, it is not just a question of guilt, but also a question of the policy results of what you call guilt, namely, that it seems to reduce the flexibility in foreign affairs of some people in the American government, and you do not like that.

Some of us like that. We might like it on three distinct grounds. First, some of us are opposed to the institution of war, and we wish that the human race would make some progress in abandoning it. Therefore, a resistance by a population that previously had mixed feelings about its country's military posture seems like a healthy sign.

Second, some of us feel that the American empire ought to be dismantled, that we are past the stage when empires can guarantee anything decent for humanity. On that score, we find it healthy that there is resistance to further military adventures that seem to preserve the boundaries of the empire.

Third, there are people who react more particularly to the Vietnam war itself. They want to make sure that people do not forget it. It did happen, it was at least a thirteen-year involvement of the American people in an adventure which they regard, in one sense or another, as immoral.

Regarding the immorality question, during the war period I must have made several hundred speeches against the war. So I am one of your young intellectuals who was trying to shape public opinion on it. I never tried to rest my argument about the immorality of the war primarily on what the United States was doing in Vietnam. What we were doing in Vietnam was a by-product, a symptom, a necessary consequence, if you will, of the fact that we were in Vietnam. Therefore, the immorality issue, as well as the practicality issue, had to do with whether we ought to be in Vietnam in the first place. To try to define the immorality issue primarily in terms of America's conduct of the war itself bypasses the central and basic point of the debate during that period. It also bypasses what most people probably think was the lesson of Vietnam.

With regard to genocide, I am willing to grant that a cold analysis of the world does not lead to the conclusion that the United States destroyed a whole people. Samuel P. Huntington, in a quote often cited, spoke of America's policy of "forced urbanization" in Vietnam as being the real intent, or purpose, of our bombing. Forced urbanization means the movement of a whole people from the countryside to the cities. I think that when many people used the word genocide, they meant not just the physical destruction of human beings, but the total disruption of the Vietnamese people's way of life, which we carried out because we felt that that was in our policy interests.

In reading the Pentagon Papers, one of the people I always rely on to define American intent is the late John McNaughton, assistant to Robert McNamara in the Department of Defense. McNaughton was clear, perhaps for good reason; that is, he wanted to make some other American policy-makers see what their intent actually was. At one point, McNaughton, in listing the reasons why we were in Vietnam, said that it was primarily to preserve American power. It was not to save the people of Vietnam. Now, was it not at least bordering on the genocidal to uproot a whole people from the countryside and to use bombing to induce them to move, all for the purpose of preserving America's credibility as a world power?

LEWY: The crime of genocide, as defined in the unanimously adopted resolution of the United Nations General Assembly, on December 9, 1948, is committing acts with intent to destroy, in whole or in part, a "national, ethnical, racial, or religious group as such." Included are acts such as "killing members of the group, causing serious bodily or mental harm, deliberately inflicting on the group conditions of life calculated to bring about a physical destruction in whole or in part." So what is crucial is physical destruction, in whole or in part, and done with the intent to destroy, in whole or in part, a group for being what it is. Of course, the prototype of genocide is the "final solution," the destruction of European Jewry for no other reason than that they were Jews.

FLACKS: Deciding that a peasant society which harbors guerrillas should no longer exist, is that genocidal? This kind of debate does not make me particularly comfortable. Unfortunately, it is somewhat semantical. Maybe what we did is not genocide as defined under existing statutes. But it seems to me to be a very questionable moral posture for a great power to be in, that is, to decide that this present Vietnamese society is untenable for our purposes, and, therefore, we will force the urbanization of that society. That raises a serious moral question.

LEWY: I did not set out to write my book in order to prepare Americans for new Vietnams, even though some of my critics have suggested this to be the case. I do not want more Vietnams, any more than you do; nor do I like wars any more than you do. Nor do I have any desire to resurrect the American empire.

But that is not the issue. The slogan, "No More Vietnams," strikes me as inane and empty. It does not provide guidance for American foreign policy. That slogan is symptomatic of a mood of neoisolationism, which is why it has spread in this country because of Vietnam. I do not consider this a healthy phenomenon. I do not think that the world is a better place if the United States is weak.

Perhaps, Mr. Flacks, you may agree with me that, for example, American influence and strength are displayed rarely these days, but they were displayed in the Israeli-Egyptian negotiations. So, in the long run, our leverage may have some beneficial results. And there may be other areas of the world where American strength could lead to consequences that you and I would be willing to consider beneficial.

It strikes me, given the suffering of the people of Indochina today, that it is not completely stupid to think that the American intervention—even though it was based not only on that, of course—may have had some moral justification. It was always said, if only the United States would get out of Indochina, peace would be restored and the suffering of the people of Indochina would come to an end. You and I know—and this is, in part, what I think has led to the reassessment by Jean Lacouture—that the suffering of the people of Indochina today is in many ways infinitely worse than it was before. Peace has not come to Indochina.

BERNSTEIN: Let us compare, for a moment, the U.S. war experiences in Korea and Vietnam. Given the fact that each, it can be argued, was a civil war; that each involved massive American intervention; that in both wars many concluded that America could not win, at least not without violating alliances and ultimately escalating the danger—given those three salient similarities, we should ask, if we want to assess the impact of Vietnam, why did Korea produce in American society such a different impact, such a different set of values than did Vietnam?

Why didn't the Korean war raise questions about legitimacy in America and about the morality of authority? Why didn't it raise questions about the nature of the war? When Americans argued about the Korean war, they argued about whether to escalate or pull out, and whether the United States could conduct a limited war. There was almost no argument in the American body politic from 1950 to 1953 about whether this was a moral war and whether we were conducting it in the right way. Why does the massive intervention in Korea from 1950 to 1953 have one set of impacts upon American society, and the prolonged and seemingly more enervating intervention in Vietnam, roughly from 1961 to 1975, produce such a different set of responses?

One could say that the length of both interventions had something to do with it. But that is not terribly useful.

Was moral and legal and governmental authority questioned in the case of Vietnam because our intervention there occurred in a markedly different American culture, one prepared to receive and translate the evidence differently? Is it that the evidence, correct or not, was distinctive in the case of Vietnam? Did the media play a different role in the Vietnam era? Is it both of these, plus something else?

Going one step further, what has happened to the former consensus on anti-Communism, and to the narrowing of intellectual dialogue in the academies? If one compares 1950–1953 with 1961–1967, could it be that a major difference is the already various openings to a broader theory, to a Left, or radical, theory, as the Vietnam war heated up? Think back to the McCarthyite period; the whole construction of ideology had been precluded from American dialogue in that period. By 1950, there was no Left in America. By 1950, there was only a truncated dialogue in the academy, the sole issue being, who is a better anti-Communist?—a question which had everybody scurrying for his credentials. But Vietnam occurred in a very different climate. People were prepared to read evidence differently; also they received rather different evidence.

During the Korean war, even major American newspapers accepted the official military and political versions of our bombing. Twice in July and twice in August of 1952, we bombed Pyongyang, the capital city of North Korea. Three of those attacks were, until then, the largest bomber attacks in the war. Nevertheless, *The New York Times* reported that only military objects were targeted. The clear implication was that civilians did not get killed. But we know at least two things now: one, that surgical bombing has never been precise, the only question being the degree of imprecision; two, official military history documents the fact that we practiced terror bombing, we waged psychological warfare in Korea through bombing. But *The New York Times* did not tell us that at the time.

In contrast, when the bombing of cities and villages occurred in Vietnam at an early stage—certainly by 1965—the reporting in American news media included the fact that civilians were being killed. And there was at least the subtle, lurking attribution of intent in those dispatches; it was somehow made implicit that our bombing was designed to kill civilians. I suggest that that tells us something very critical about the differences in the American people's reception of the two wars.

OLE HOLSTI (*Professor of Political Science, Duke University; Visiting Professor of Political Science, University of California at Davis*): In its origins, Korea looked in some respects like World War II, something Americans were familiar with. Massive infantry and armored divisions crossed what was at least intended to be a temporary frontier.

Further, whatever one might think of the United Nations, the fact is that there was considerable international support for the American intervention in Korea. Sixteen nations became involved on behalf of South Korea. Whether that makes the intervention legitimate or not, it does lend something to the enterprise that was clearly missing in the Vietnam war. In Korea we had some client states providing some assistance.

Also, the world in 1950 was viewed rather differently by a whole lot of publics. What looked like a legitimate enterprise in 1950 looked less so by 1961. Why? One of the reasons is the international context. In 1950, the world was seen as bipolar: Communist and non-Communist, and there was a fair degree of solidarity within the members of the so-called Communist bloc. By 1965, when the U.S. bombing started in Vietnam, that assumption of bipolarity was clearly open to serious question. In other words, some of the assumptions about the nature of the international system had changed.

I am not arguing here against Professor Bernstein's view that American society had changed. I think it had. But other things had changed, too. We can go too far in seeing parallels between Vietnam and Korea. The world between 1950 and 1965 had really changed, and the perception of the world had changed. That was crucial.

LEWY: I think that in due time there will be the kind of reassessment I am asking for. When that is done, the sense of guilt and self-flagellation that has occurred will pass, or at least weaken, and that will be all to the good. I do not relish the idea of feeling guilty for something I have not done or my society has not done. I do not see anything positive in feeling guilty unless I am convinced that I have done wrong.

I will add two points with regard to the question, how different was Korea? Korea was different in the sense that it resulted in a stalemate, not a lost war. The old borders were reaffirmed, and South Korea remained a going concern. Today, South Vietnam no longer is a going concern. In that sense, the end of the war in Vietnam was a smashing defeat for the United States, which had tried to protect South Vietnam.

Also, the Vietnam war was the first war seen on television screens, and in living color, to boot. Blood is red, it doesn't look good, and when you see it every night, a cumulative effect develops. If World War II had been shown on the television screens every night, and if the Korean war had been seen on the screens every night, I think Americans might have felt somewhat different about those two wars as well.

On the Consequences of Vietnam

THE FOLLOWING FORUM IS BASED ON A DISCUSSION HELD AT THE HARVARD CLUB IN NEW YORK CITY. JAMES CHACE SERVED AS MODERATOR.

JAMES CHACE
was for many years managing editor of Foreign Affairs *and is currently an editor of the* New York Times Book Review. *His books include* Solvency: An Essay on American Foreign Policy *and* Endless War: How We Got Involved in Central America—And What Can Be Done.

PAUL M. KENNEDY
is Dilworth Professor of History at Yale. His books include Strategy and Diplomacy, 1870–1945 *and* The Rise and Fall of British Naval Mastery. *He is at work on* The Dynamics of World Power from 1500 to the Year 2000.

EDWARD N. LUTTWAK
is a senior fellow at Georgetown University's Center for Strategic and International Studies. His most recent book is The Pentagon and the Art of War: The Question of Military Reform.

FRANCES FITZGERALD
writes frequently for the New Yorker, *the* New York Review of Books, *and other publications. Her books include* Fire in the Lake: The Vietnamese and the Americans in Vietnam *and* America Revised.

PETER MARIN
is a novelist and essayist who has written on the moral and cultural issues raised by the Vietnam War for the Nation, Harper's, Psychology Today, *and other publications. He is currently at work on a book entitled* Conscience and the Common Good.

KEVIN P. PHILLIPS
is president of the American Political Research Corporation and editor of
American Political Report. *His books include* The Emerging Republican
Majority, Post-Conservative America, *and, most recently,* Staying on Top:
The Business Case for a National Industrial Strategy.

GEORGE GILDER
is author of Sexual Suicide, Visible Man, Wealth and Poverty,
and, most recently, The Spirit of Enterprise.

JAMES CHACE: Whether we like it or not, the American experience in
Indochina deeply affects the way we live now. Ten years after the last
Marine was lifted off the roof of our doomed embassy in Saigon, the
traces of that conflict are present everywhere in this country—in our
military's attitude toward foreign involvements, in the design of our
foreign policy, in the structure of our domestic politics, and, perhaps
most evidently, in the conflicting images Americans have of their
country's role in the world.

It was only a generation ago, when John F. Kennedy was president and our creeping involvement in Southeast Asia was scarcely
 noticed, that the United States seemed omnipotent. Then, Americans were truly the "watchmen on the walls of world freedom," as
the young president wrote in the speech he was to deliver in Dallas
on the day he was assassinated.

Today, when Americans speak darkly of the "lessons of Vietnam,"
that confident talk of American omnipotence seems very far away.
Most attempts to exert American power abroad in recent years—the
tentative intervention in Lebanon, for example, or the entire U.S.
policy in Central America—have been beset by controversy. Indeed,
Americans seem unable to agree on what the lessons of Vietnam *are,*
at least as regards the central question of where and under what circumstances the United States should use military force abroad.
While many see in the myth of American omnipotence a dangerous
illusion that might again lead us into futile adventures abroad, others
want to reconstruct the myth, or, in any event, to restore to America
the role of world leader it played before its failure in Vietnam.

Our subject today is not the lessons but the consequences of Viet-
nam. Our task is to search out the traces Vietnam has left on the
America of 1985. Where precisely do we find the consequences of
Vietnam in today's America? Have we overcome any of the effects of

Vietnam? Is America, in Ronald Reagan's words, "standing tall" again?

I thought we might begin by considering what would seem to be the most direct consequences of the Vietnam War—the military ones. From there we can move on to the larger social and moral questions of how the war has affected American behavior both at home and abroad, and how it is likely to do so in the future. Paul Kennedy, as a military historian, what do you see as the main military consequences of the Vietnam War?

PAUL M. KENNEDY: Well, it's difficult to separate the specific effects the Vietnam War has had on America's role in the world from the much larger, structural changes that have gradually transformed the international balance of power during the last twenty-five years. Of course the direct consequences of the war on our military are fairly clear. America now has a noticeably cautious Pentagon, a military establishment that nervously questions itself about when and in what circumstances it can intervene abroad without getting bogged down in an unpopular, divisive war. As is evident from Secretary of Defense Weinberger's speech last November on U.S. military policy, the Pentagon is demanding to know where it can fight and be *assured* of public support; which is to say, our military is submitting its strategy to a sort of "Vietnam litmus test." And the obvious consequence of *that* consequence is that the United States has become a very cautious imperial power.

That much is pretty straightforward. The problems arise when we try to separate the specific military consequences from other important changes that have tended to complicate America's role in the world, but that probably would have occurred in any event, even if the war had never happened. For example, in the last quarter-century or so we have witnessed an enormous change in Third World attitudes toward the United States. Many Third World governments have reacted strongly against what they consider an overwhelming American presence, against the growing influence of American capital and the American culture and mores that have come with it. During the same period our European allies have become stronger and more independent, and less willing to follow America's lead unquestioningly in matters of foreign policy. Finally, and perhaps most important, the Russians succeeded in closing the gap in strategic nuclear forces, and the United States lost its position as the clearly predominant superpower.

These gradual transformations, and others we could name, have combined to give Americans the very definite sense that the world is no longer their oyster. And all of them would have occurred even if Vietnam had never happened.

EDWARD N. LUTTWAK: Your analysis implies that the world after Vietnam has achieved a new equilibrium, an equilibrium that includes an inevitably diminished American role. My own assessment is quite different: I believe the war, and its effect on America's willingness to exert its power, has led to world disequilibrium.

Let's look more closely at the purely military consequences of the war. You mentioned the so-called Weinberger doctrine, which basically says that operations like Grenada represent a ceiling on the level of military action the Pentagon is willing to contemplate. Weinberger essentially declared to the world, "We will apply military force only if we know we're going to win quickly and easily, and only if we are guaranteed total support from the public." I think his statement accurately reflects the views of our professional military. I believe this is a wholly praiseworthy doctrine—wonderfully suited to a country such as Switzerland, which promises to come to the aid of no other nation, guarantees no order to the world, and in short, is content to live in a world in which events are dominated by others. But for a country such as the United States, the Weinberger doctrine is completely and absurdly unsuitable.

What are the consequences of this attitude—the consequences of the consequences of Vietnam? Consider the American performance in El Salvador. The American military, in supervising the war, is imposing its current preoccupation with its great rearmament program, a program that obviously must be sustained politically. The military believes it is very bad business indeed to get involved in Central America: let's not erode the political basis for our new weapons by getting enmeshed in what might become a very unpopular war in El Salvador—that's the Pentagon's attitude.

Hence the President's Central America policy is supported only most reluctantly by the military. It makes no effort to ensure that the pitifully few advisers we have in El Salvador are the very best men; fifty-five people are simply assigned to El Salvador as if it were Germany or Korea. The military makes no attempt to guarantee that the miserable amount of American aid is even applied to acquiring and maintaining suitable weapons. Instead, the military's standard-issue weapons, intended for the world's richest armed forces, are given to the world's poorest. This is just lack of professional attention.

My point is that America's military has been thoroughly corrupted. Not in the trivial sense of soldiers stealing or taking bribes—in that sense the American military is uniquely honest. The military has been corrupted in the classical Greek sense of having lost its essential virtue, its *arete*. The virtue of a knife, the *arete* of a knife, is its "cuttingness"; the virtue of a military force is its "fightingness." The U.S. military now stands ready to fight the imagined, pre-planned "real war"—that is, the war in Europe—but has no willingness to fight the wars that actually happen, such as that in El Salvador.

The consequence of this is world disequilibrium. International society today is characterized by a sort of perverted Gaullism. But de Gaulle, in his heyday, needed all the strength of his towering figure, and control of a truly major country, to assert a minimum of independence against two terrifically dynamic superpowers. The Soviet Union today, because of the decrepitude of its economy, has lost its dynamism. The Russians can't open new accounts. They can keep Cuba afloat but they can't take on Mozambique. And the United States, because of the consequences of the war that I've described, is mostly passive.

In this perverted Gaullist world, a country need not be led by a de Gaulle to assert its independence. Broad areas of the globe are left unmanaged, to be exploited by regional organizers like South Africa or Syria, which the superpowers can't control. And pirate states—St. Augustine's *magna latrocinia,* great thieveries—such as Qaddafi's Libya thrive. Only recently a ship chartered by the U.S. Navy was attacked by actual pirates in the Strait of Malacca. This is the disequilibrium of the world we live in today. This situation will not last. The question is whether it will be the United States that remedies it; if not, other forces will.

CHACE: While Paul Kennedy described an inevitable adjustment of and constraint on American power that followed the Vietnam War but only partly resulted from it, Edward Luttwak is implying that the United States could still function as a world policeman, could still *impose* a kind of *Pax Americana* on countries ranging from South Africa to Syria—if only it had the will. But is such a role possible for any nation any longer?

LUTTWAK: Apart from the United States, I see no power willing or able to play this role. The United States is in a transitional stage where the consequences of Vietnam are slowly being absorbed. But I see a clear and logical link between the 1,000 sorties flown each day in Vietnam—which, had they hit worthwhile targets, would have

ended the war in a day—and those Marines standing guard outside
U.S. battalion headquarters in Beirut who didn't have a single loaded
round in their M-16s.

FRANCES FITZGERALD: Whom exactly would you have bombed in
Lebanon?

LUTTWAK: To be an advocate of strategy is not quite the same as
being an advocate of frenzied bellicosity in every direction. As it
happens, I would not have intervened in Lebanon at all. My point is
simply that the United States made a minimum symbolic commitment
in Lebanon. During the Marines' mission, Secretary Weinberger ad-
vertised his displeasure with their deployment every time he appeared on television. The operational consequence of that reluctance
was that the 1,800 Americans were not seen as the point of a wedge
that would broaden into a 5,000- or 50,000-man force, if necessary.
They were not seen as merely the tangible manifestation of a greater
American power but as the affirmation of American impotence. That
was the pitiful, helpless giant of Nixon's immortal words, stationed
there in Beirut.

FITZGERALD: As a matter of fact, I consider that speech of Nixon's—
in which he announced the Cambodian incursion—crucial to an
understanding of American foreign policy after Vietnam. In that
speech, a certain vision of the world is clearly delineated. The alternatives set out are American control over the world, or anarchy and
totalitarianism. There is something metaphysical in this vision—
particularly as Nixon goes on to say that it is not our power but our
will and character that are being tested. Apparently, the United
States can restore world order by symbolic action, and by force of
character alone. This has now become a familiar theme in American
foreign policy; and it is hardly *Realpolitik*, though some present it as
such. Nixon is not discussing whether the United States really has
the capacity to project its power all over the world; rather, he is discussing the country's character, or virtue.

Mr. Luttwak, what would you prescribe for our policy in El
Salvador?

LUTTWAK: I believe the United States should help the Salvadoran
government, which is a democratizing regime, win the war. By "win"
I mean reduce the level of guerrilla activity to endemic banditry,
which is appropriate to a place of that sort. The United States can
permit the Salvadorans to prevail by using their traditional meth-

ods—which simply entail killing as many people as they can until there are no guerrillas left. Or, if we insist on imposing our own squeamish tastes on the Salvadorans in typical Yankee imperialist fashion, we must supply them with enough military aid to fight the war cleanly. American methods are clean, but very expensive, requiring helicopters and other sophisticated equipment. The traditional way requires only infantry battalions and plenty of sharp knives. At present we are imposing our mode of warfare on the Salvadorans without funding it sufficiently.

FITZGERALD: What is this nonsense about "endemic banditry" and "clean American methods"? It's absurd to look at a situation like that in El Salvador from a purely military point of view. The problem in El Salvador is not the guerrillas but the government—the military-dominated government that actually created the guerrillas and now can't get rid of them without American help. But the kind of help the United States can provide—greater troop mobility and vastly increased firepower—inflicts enormous damage and suffering on the civilian population. The destruction is "clean" only in the sense that it's impersonal.

Karl Marx once said that history repeats itself only as farce. From the point of view of American policy, El Salvador is a farcical replay of Vietnam. The difference is that the Salvadoran guerrillas are very, very vulnerable in a way that the Vietnamese were not, because El Salvador is a small country and it's possible to drive all civilians out of guerrilla-held areas, to drain the water and leave the fish exposed. The evacuation of the guerrilla-held zones is already half accomplished. But it does not solve the political problems of El Salvador.

LUTTWAK: Look, El Salvador is a tiny country with a few flea-bitten guerrillas. If our country was not traumatized by Vietnam, the whole affair would be concluded very quickly, I assure you.

KENNEDY: I wonder about that. If Vietnam had not occurred, and America never experienced the loss of morale and the feelings of insecurity the war brought with it, I still doubt that, at this point, the United States would be able to go in and *solve* the conflict in El Salvador, or *solve* problems in other Third World countries.

PETER MARIN: I think we're ignoring another significant constraint on American power emerging from the war: the political pressures that seem to restrict America's foreign, and especially military, policies. Something extraordinary and, I think, quite wonderful happened in this country during the Vietnam War—a large part of the population refused to accept the government's announced policy. What you take to be a loss of morale seems to me to be a kind of growing up. One must not forget that by the end of the war, elected officials were able to govern only by shooting people in the streets, or threatening to.

One of the major constraints on American policy is the lingering fear—conscious or unconscious—on the part of those in authority that a similar crisis could erupt if certain kinds of policies are implemented. We now have in the United States a military and political policy constrained, at least in part, by the feelings of its citizens, feelings based on remembered experience rather than on propaganda.

KEVIN P. PHILLIPS: I'm not sure American public opinion is the constraint you think it is. Let's look at some recent foreign-policy controversies to see if what you say holds true. First, there was the acrimonious debate over the Panama Canal Treaties in 1977 and 1978. The treaties were widely condemned in this country, and I think that was a measure of Americans' frustration with their country's diminished role in the world after Vietnam and their rejection of what appeared to be a retreat in Central and South America. Related feelings, I think, lay behind the public's anger with President Carter's inability to exercise American power effectively during the Iranian hostage crisis.

But consider the reaction to the Grenada invasion—Americans expressed enormous pleasure at this exercise of U.S. power, even though it was used only to invade a little tinpot country. Their pleasure was enough to kick up President Reagan's approval rating about ten points overnight. The public is completely amenable to an *effective* display of American power.

FITZGERALD: But at what cost? Grenada is a small, pathetic place; it was possible to "conquer" the island quickly with very few casualties. Would Americans support interventions where the costs were not quite so small?

The problem here is partly that, as Professor Kennedy said, during the last twenty years the United States has had to face revolutionary changes in the Third World. During the fifties, when most Third World countries were still governed by very small groups of elites and the great masses of people were uninvolved in their national politics, it was easy for the United States to overthrow what it considered an undesirable government. In 1954, the United States was able to overthrow the Arbenz government in Guatemala in a few weeks by means of a secret, inexpensive, and relatively painless CIA operation. In Iran, the year before, a single CIA agent was able to restore the Shah to his throne in a matter of three days.

But small-scale and painless interventions are practically impossible these days. The recent upheaval in Iran, in which a small, American-backed ruling elite was violently overthrown—and which was prefigured to some extent by the U.S. defeat in Vietnam—has been repeated in less dramatic form in many Third World countries. Even in a tiny country like El Salvador, the United States is finding it must exert an enormous effort and inflict hideous pain on the local population just to ensure that its allies remain in power.

I don't believe Americans are interested in such costly interventions, however much they enjoyed the symbolism of Grenada. But many in this country have not quite accepted the changes in the Third World as a part of reality, a part of the world as it is. They picture a bipolar world in which only the United States and the Soviet Union have any real power and Third World countries are essentially amenable to manipulation by whoever gets there first.

LUTTWAK: When we talk about the Third World, I think it's important not to replace the outdated conception of the 1960s—which saw the Third World as completely malleable when in fact it was becoming less so—with one that is already becoming outdated. Many Third World nations are again becoming receptive to American influence. U.S. forces in El Salvador, for example, don't evoke a negative reaction from people whose greatest ambition is to emigrate to the United States. For a good number of Salvadorans, McDonald's is an ideal.

Obviously there is greater resistance in more strongly defined cultures—like the Islamic culture—that are now in decay. If the young men in these countries desert the mosques, they do so to read *Playboy*, not *Pravda*. So it is perfectly rational for the Islamic fundamentalists to see the United States as their principal threat. Their very extremism stems from their sense of imminent cultural collapse. They fear that if they don't follow the Western model they'll simply rot, culturally and intellectually.

FITZGERALD: Given your analysis, one might wonder why it has proved so difficult for the United State to defeat "a few flea-bitten guerrillas" in El Salvador. On the other hand, the United States is not seen as the only threat to the Islamic world. In Afghanistan, the Russians are being resisted with great intensity, as is the Soviet model. The Third World's, and especially the Islamic world's, reaction to the Soviet invasion has been instructive. So it does seem to matter who gets there first.

LUTTWAK: Behind the Soviet helicopters there are no McDonald's. That is a consideration.

CHACE: It seems to me that Lebanon is a good example of a country, once strongly pro-Western, that has undergone some of the up-heavals Frances FitzGerald described. In his summary of the American public's reaction to recent foreign-policy controversies, I don't believe Mr. Phillips mentioned the Reagan Administration's intervention in Lebanon, which no one could perceive as a success, either strategically or in terms of public opinion.

PHILLIPS: But the failure in Lebanon was not held against the Administration. Why? Because Americans do not associate this Administration with the retreat of American power. However ineptly or ineffectively he may have applied that power in Lebanon, President Reagan was able to wrap the Star Spangled Banner around himself—simply because he has always opposed the idea that the United States should acquiesce to indigenous challenges in the Third World.

CHACE: In other words, the failure in Beirut was covered over by rhetoric.

PHILLIPS: Such failures often are. The point is that the political opportunities for blaming Reagan were virtually nonexistent because he had cultivated an image of strength.

MARIN: That Americans love an *image* of strength is not being contested here. Whether that means they would accept another 50,000 dead in a foreign intervention is another question. No one has mentioned those 50,000 dead. I don't believe the war can be fully understood if it is regarded only as a strategic defeat; the war was also a traumatic event in the lives of actual men and women. We have to consider the American people's perception of the suffering we inflicted on others and the suffering at least some Americans experienced directly. After all, the war was perceived by many Americans not just as a military defeat but as a moral defeat, or at least a moral error.

What do people do when they have not only been defeated militarily but also believe they have been defeated morally? How does a country like ours, with its mythical sense of itself as a force for good in the world, deal with a moral defeat, a moral tragedy? These questions have been pushed beneath the surface during the last ten years—and I believe the fact that they are there, unacknowledged, has colored our foreign policy much more than the military defeat *per se* has.

PHILLIPS: Actually, the United States has a long pathology of postwar reaction. After wars, Americans tend to blame dissidents, and political parties, for unpatriotic behavior. The Federalist Party was crushed after the War of 1812, in which it had been seen as giving aid and comfort to the British; the Whigs were undercut by their opposition to the Mexican War; after World War I there was a large-scale crackdown on antiwar dissidents and radicals. And McCarthyism was in some measure a means to allocate blame for the "loss" of Eastern Europe and China as a result of what were perceived to be weak Democratic policies.

MARIN: Yes, but when Americans are confronted with the *reality* of defeat, they tend to reassert their old myths. That is what seems to be happening under Reagan, who presents an *image* of power while avoiding those confrontations that might put it to a test—which, in my view, is precisely why Americans like him.

LUTTWAK: I would like to step back from this debate on public opinion to point out that the purpose of strategy in foreign policy is not to recognize and infinitely adapt to change, but to maintain a set of values and interests by *resisting* change. Any empire is a great machine of conservation against change—that is the nature of empire. Thus to say that because the Third World is becoming more independent, we automatically must do such and such is not strategy.

KENNEDY: Of course all great powers are essentially conservative—they've risen to the top and don't want to be thrown off. But it's necessary for them to find ways of responding to challenges to their position with some degree of subtlety. Sometimes, of course, such challenges must be resisted. But if an empire is completely ethnocentric, if all it can see is a world filtered through its own strategic concerns, then its chances of misreading the situation in a country—of standing firm where it isn't a good idea to stand firm, or of not standing firm where it is—are that much greater.

GEORGE GILDER: But the fact remains that support around the world for the American system has in fact increased since Vietnam. To see this clearly we have only to look at the world economically, instead of geopolitically. If we consider the economic consequences of Vietnam, I think we'll see that there's a real sense in which the United States won the Vietnam War. At least we won the one prize that was worth anything—the boat people. The boat people are now key figures in the high-tech companies in Silicon Valley and across the country, and are thus contributing substantially to American economic growth.

America's victory in Vietnam is more evident when we look at our economy's growing dominance in the world. At the end of the war, our gross domestic product was a quarter of the world's output; for 1984 it is estimated at almost a third. And the predominance of the capitalist system is nowhere more dramatic than in Asia. The communists may continue to dominate the pathetic small places, but less pathetic small places—Singapore, Hong Kong, Taiwan—are booming capitalist countries.

This massive shift in economic power from the communist world to the capitalist world, symbolized by the boat people, has been far more important than the tactical defeat the United States suffered in Vietnam. America's position in the world has steadily improved in the last decade. And it will keep improving if we continue the emancipation of our economy that President Reagan has begun—recapturing the momentum the Kennedy Administration began with its tax cut. The Vietnam War was a crucial factor in this economic development, because in the late 1960s, partly to pay for the war, the government started raising tax rates again. There was economic devastation for several years because of Vietnam. But as soon as the war was over, as soon as tax rates were cut, the United States began to demonstrate that it could again dominate the world economically—which is the way that counts.

Indeed, perhaps the most harmful consequence of Vietnam was that it helped reinforce the fallacy of geopolitics—the idea that the cold war is about real estate, that it really makes a difference to America's power that the Russians control Afghanistan or Angola or Ethiopia, all those pathetic countries you can't even visit without getting sick.

LUTTWAK: Such as Transylvania, where I happen to have been born.

GILDER: Well, maybe you have emotional ties to Transylvania. But in the long run you're probably much more valuable to the United States.

CHACE: Perhaps this is the point where, after discussing the war's effects on the American military, and after touching on its economic consequences, we should take up the question of America's "vital interests." In fact, Vietnam was always of marginal strategic importance to the United States. Another consequence of the war, surely, has been a continuing debate about what we actually mean by an American vital interest. President Reagan, for example, defined Lebanon as a vital interest, but our withdrawal from Beirut does not seem to have hurt the United States. How do we define what this country's vital interests are?

LUTTWAK: When an empire loses a vital interest, it's supposed to collapse. If the empire doesn't collapse, then what it lost wasn't a vital interest.

MARIN: I think the problem has to do with how we see ourselves. Everyone here keeps using the word "empire," assuming that the United States must intervene all over the globe or else fade into insignificance. There is obviously a lot of room in between; yet Americans don't have any images or theories to help them describe their country's role in the world—to explain themselves *to* themselves. We have a sense of defeat, I believe, not simply because the American empire seems to be falling apart, but because once we can no longer see ourselves as a great empire, we don't know how to see ourselves.

GILDER: I think the Vietnam War did vindicate a certain world view— that of the American right. No one talks about this much, of course, but our retreat from Vietnam led to a holocaust, a stream of atrocities that consumed all of Indochina—which was precisely what the right had warned would happen. That holocaust allowed the rest of the world to see clearly what happens when a country is lost to communism, and it is bound to make other countries more willing to resist communism on their own.

MARIN: That's much too simple a view. The effects of Vietnam are more tragic, and less ideological, than that. Many Americans are smart enough to realize that while our withdrawal from Vietnam had certain tragic consequences, our presence, had we remained there, would have led to a different, and equally tragic, set of consequences. This knowledge is the difficulty: we understand that both America's presence and its absence have had consequences of which we despair. And no one on the left or right has managed to do much with this knowledge, other than to assert over and over the weakness of the other side's position.

LUTTWAK: But empires shouldn't have to use military force to secure their interests in the first place. Empires secure their interests by *not* using military force; they rely on their reputation for using force only when it is absolutely needed, and then in an utterly implacable manner. If you're in the empire business, it is your duty to be implacable when somebody opposes you—especially when the conflict is on a small scale, and terminating it is nice and cheap. The problem is that the American people never really saw their country as an imperial power; the United States was not designed to manage an empire.

GILDER: America is not in the empire business; the Russians are. But the Soviet Union's economy is steadily declining. The Russians can't even feed themselves. The country is a total failure, a pitiful, helpless giant in every respect except the ability to build up military power. Everything outside the military sphere is going in the United States' direction, beyond the greatest expectations anyone had in the 1950s or 1960s. Today socialism is a joke. Nobody believes in it as a workable economic paradigm anymore. The dynamic has definitely shifted; soon our military strategies will develop to the point where they will properly complement the resurgence of American power and capitalist domination.

KENNEDY: But the war in Vietnam, along with the massive outpouring of *vox populi* to end the fighting, lent new prominence and seriousness to the ongoing debate over what the country's vital interests really are. Of course, many other countries, great empires and small, have asked these questions of themselves—What are our vital interests? When should we fight for them? But usually the debate has taken place secretly, within an elite group of rulers. It is much more difficult to define your vital interests in a public forum without at the same time letting your adversaries know where you will stand and fight and where you will not. I think that was a big part of the problem in Lebanon; Secretary of Defense Weinberger and the Joint Chiefs were afraid of getting bogged down—and the secretary said so publicly. Since Vietnam, the military has been hypercautious because it has not devised an effective way to analyze America's vital interests and priorities in public. The public debate—as well as the constant leaks about the private debates—makes managing a global system of influence and interests extraordinarily difficult.

LUTTWAK: A nation can overcome some of the problems you mentioned simply by advertising clearly to its people, and to the world, a general willingness to defend areas that are strategically or economically important to it. To point to specific places is to be *un*-strategical—an empire doesn't protect its interests by fighting all over the world; rather, it discourages other nations from taking action against it by responding decisively and implacably when it absolutely must.

KENNEDY: Yet it is much easier for a nation to be predictable and implacable in defense of its interests when it has a government and a military designed to carry out sustained overseas wars. A small professional army and a nondemocratic system of government enable a nation to maintain an empire. But a full-blown democracy with a conscript mass army—which is what America was at the time of the Vietnam War—will have an extraordinarily difficult time repeatedly going to war to keep recalcitrant natives down. For that, you need a quite different military structure and a quite different constitution.

MARIN: Which leads us to another important consequence of Vietnam: the war forced many Americans to recognize the caste nature of their army—who went to war and who did not. Americans began to notice that their country's conscript army was drawn from the lower middle class and the working class—the young men who didn't go to college. And this knowledge in turn made people most resistant to authority and suspicious of elites who might lead them to war. The war also showed Americans that one could refuse to fight without anything terrible happening. It's difficult to administer an empire if, in the midst of a war, people are able and willing to say: We don't want to fight.

CHACE: Mr. Phillips, how do you assess the war's effect on American politics?

PHILLIPS: Of course, the impact of Vietnam has dominated American politics for the last decade. The most obvious consequence of the war was the radicalization of the Democratic Party and the shift of the patriotic image to the Republicans. This has allowed the Republicans to control the political debate since 1968, except for the interval of Watergate. Watergate, which was clearly tied very closely to Vietnam, destabilized the Nixon/Ford regime and helped elect Jimmy Carter, who could have reached the presidency only after a scandal that enabled him to run as the Sunday school candidate preaching a government of love and trust.

I think Vietnam and Watergate together distorted the underlying political trends of the last fifteen years. Instead of the orderly advance of the moderate conservative political cycle that started in the late 1960s, there was an aberrant interruption of it—in the person of Jimmy Carter—followed by a more extreme repackaging of conservatism under Ronald Reagan. I say extreme because this Administration, in its foreign policy at least, appeals to Americans who long for the simpler days of overwhelming American power. But the country can't return to the good old days, so Americans glory in the conquest of Grenada—just as Britain, that old empire with *its* nostalgic government, gloried in its conquest of the Falklands.

MARIN: But here we come back to the social dimension of Vietnam that no one seems to want to discuss. American authority was exposed as incompetent and corrupt. Our soldiers refused to fight. Our intelligence agents denounced their government and revealed CIA crimes. Our leaders were shown to be scheming criminals. Day after day, the front page of the evening newspaper, the first few minutes of the evening news, told Americans about the stupidity and dishonesty of their government. Americans, in short, found themselves unable to see the emperor's clothes any longer, whether they wanted to or not. And what they did see, I believe, is still bothering them today, even though many of them seem to be struggling mightily to forget it.

LUTTWAK: Irving Kristol has a theory about this, which explains these events as part of the classic demoralization of the elites in power. According to Kristol, these elites were eventually undermined by another group—the so-called new class of journalists, publicists, academics, and advertising men.

MARIN: Look, I'm trying to talk about the effect of the Vietnam War on the American people. Define what happened as a result of a struggle among elites, if you like. But obviously the war had an enormous effect on the populace at large.

LUTTWAK: Sure it did. The populace at large reacted by shouting, "We want Ronald Reagan!"

MARIN: It is extraordinarily simplistic to treat the American public as if it were one great reactive animal. In order to understand the social effects of the war we have to examine the different groups in our society. For instance, the war had a different effect on the left than on the right. The odd thing was that the left was more demoralized by the cupidity of power than the right; it was as if those on the left learned that what they had been saying for so long about authority and power in America was true, and yet they found themselves unable to do anything with this confirmation.

PHILLIPS: It's true the war crippled the right and the left in different ways. Liberals and others on the left find it impossible even now to come to grips with the question of the effective use of American power. For the voters, the upheavals surrounding the war served to gather together a whole cluster of issues that were widely unpopular, at least in Middle America—what were considered permissive attitudes toward crime and education, and disrespectful attitudes toward patriotism—and to identify them closely with reform elements within the Democratic Party. That radicalization of the party, combined with the weakness of its old elites and the dramatic new assertiveness of minorities, tremendously enfeebled the Democrats.

The Republicans, meanwhile, have been able to use the patriotism issue effectively since 1968. But Vietnam crippled conservatives as well, in a different sense, giving them a rather warped, nostalgic view of American power and a simplistic view of recent American history. They cling to the belief that America can pull the world together again, as it did under Eisenhower. I think that's an illusion, with little basis in the political and economic facts of the world we live in today.

KENNEDY: But how long do you think these political effects will be felt? Today I see on the campuses a different generation, for whom the war and the bitter battles that were fought over it are ancient history. I wonder if we're not really talking about attitudes that are held strongly by one or two generations, but that have not been absorbed by the larger culture.

MARIN: Perhaps. It may well be that a couple of American generations experienced in this war, at least in a small way, something akin to what Europeans suffered in World War I. Vietnam drove home to Americans that war is *tragic*. Vietnam was as close as modern war has ever come to the United States. The number of men who served, the

embittered veterans, the nightly television news, the violent demonstrations in our streets—all this ensured that the war would have an
extraordinary impact on the American imagination. Hundreds of
books have been written about the war—not books about policy or
strategy, but books about horror, about terror, about shame.

GILDER: And that obsessive attitude toward the war so paralyzed the
Vietnam generation that it couldn't participate effectively in the
American economy for many years. These people just sat around
smoking pot and fantasizing about fascist "Amerika."
    The new generation on the rise sees not violence on our campuses
but the Chinese Communist leaders declaring that Marxism is dead—
which happens to be immensely more important than any consequence of Vietnam. It is clear by now that the notion that America
was losing authority in the world, that it was being overwhelmed by
some inexorable trend exemplified by Vietnam, was plain wrong.

MARIN: The Vietnam War was a moral event, and you're incapable of
providing anything but an economic response to it. Americans have
no means to describe the moral experience of Vietnam. This experience has been lost; or rather, it has become subterranean, and will
probably remain so because we have no language to bring it to the
surface. This failure of language was the great problem of the left—
whatever lessons it learned it turned into hysteria, rather than into
wisdom. And this explains, partly, the upsurge of the new privilege
George Gilder mentioned—the right simply had no other response
to the events that happened during the war. So the left remains
mute, and the right grows increasingly self-righteous and trivial in
its concerns. That's an immense waste. We could perhaps have become a wiser people. But the war is an experience that is not becoming part of the collective wisdom.

GILDER: Americans are getting on with their lives, in other words.

MARIN: Yes, but perhaps at the expense of our children. We must not
"get on with our lives" without coming to terms with what happened
in the war.

FITZGERALD: I believe that America's reaction to the war has been
solipsistic, in several ways. First, Vietnam veterans have a deep
sense that their government victimized them by sending them off on
a venture that the society, in the end, didn't approve of. The war was
undertaken to achieve aims that were totally unclear to those who

fought it, and which turned out never to have existed at all. I don't think this sense of victimization has been overcome. But it has remained a psychological issue for the veterans; it has never really been transformed into a politics. Look at the novels that have come out of Vietnam. They're all intensely personal. There has been no novel of any political scope about Vietnam since Graham Greene wrote *The Quiet American*. There's been no *Catch-22*, no attempt at such a comprehensive political understanding on the part of any veteran, or any novelist for that matter.

Americans still prefer to treat Vietnam as a psychological problem for veterans—post-Vietnam syndrome. We can't seem to *see* the war as a political problem. And the analyses of what post-Vietnam foreign policy should be seem to me similarly solipsistic. No one can come to grips with the fact that none of the objectives the United States imagined it had going into the war justified the size and the ultimate cost of the commitment. What finally happened when we were defeated, when we lost the war? Nothing. Our defeat left our vaunted national security interests in Asia essentially unharmed; indeed, the United States today is arguably in a better position in Asia than it ever has been.

So what *did* we lose? The right usually answers with more psychological propositions: Vietnam was a failure of will, a failure of nerve. Apparently their concern is that the American image was damaged. But what is that except a sort of narcissistic mortification? The war has not prompted a realistic, reasonable debate about what America's foreign-policy goals are; rather, it has prompted violent swings of emotion over ridiculous symbols. The Grenada invasion was a perfect example of such a symbol—an event of no real consequence that caused an enormous emotional outpouring in this country. So now America is "standing tall" again. The only serious foreign-policy question that has been asked as a result of Vietnam is "Where can the United States intervene militarily?" Surely there are more important questions to ask about the goals of American foreign policy than that.

LUTTWAK: The questions about American foreign policy after Vietnam certainly will not be answered by pondering Grenada. To answer those questions we have to look at Europe.

During the war, it was the hope of the left that America's eventual defeat would bring to an end the assertion of American power worldwide. The left hoped we would withdraw from Europe and Korea and our other primary commitments abroad, thus enabling the world to achieve a new equilibrium where good leftist regimes would run the show. But the mainstream consensus about America's role in the world was not smashed by our withdrawal from Vietnam; in large part the common sense of the American people prevailed, although there is more disagreement than before about peripheral interests. But when we talk about America's role in the world, we are talking first of all about Europe; and there the question is not military intervention but our presence in Germany, which continues to link the fate of America to what happens along the border between the two Germanys. That's why when we talk about America "projecting its power abroad," we are really talking about piddling little areas that are not central to the debate.

MARIN: We must not forget that there exists a realm between the political and the psychological. We need to define what the terms of a moral debate would be—that is, what consequences justify what costs? For instance, some estimates of the number of vets who committed suicide after the war are as high as 50,000. Americans have never confronted this fact. And it has not been ignored because of our wonderful economic situation and the rise of the yuppies. We have evaded it, because recognizing it would demand so much of us. What does it mean to America that after this war, 50,000 ex-soldiers committed suicide? And what does it mean that our nation won't confront this?

GILDER: There we have a vivid demonstration of the solipsism of the left on the subject of Vietnam—the notion that all Vietnam veterans are somehow traumatized by guilt. In fact, most of them are very proud of their participation in the war; it's the people who evaded the draft who are suffering traumas of guilt. By pointing to all this supposed psychological damage, the left is attempting to show that its opposition to the war has been vindicated.

LUTTWAK: The suicides were a result of the fact that the elite presented the war in a manner designed to humiliate those who fought in it, to make their sacrifice seem unworthy.

MARIN: It is truly corrupt to take this fact and turn it into a political argument. Why should we assume that all the vets committed suicide for precisely the same reason? What you describe was one reason, but there were many others.

GILDER: Such as drug abuse.

MARIN: Such as shame and humiliation. I know vets who think it was a wonderful war and were deeply enraged by the reception they got when they came home. But there are many vets, perhaps far more, who can't get over their guilt. Let me give you a very simple example: a vet who can't forget that at the beginning of the war, he threw cans of food to children from the backs of trucks because he wanted to feed them, and that by the end of the war, he was *pelting* the children with the cans, trying to *kill* them. He says he will spend the rest of his life trying to find a way to atone for that.

Now, he doesn't feel shame about America's role in the war or the loss of the war; he feels shame about what he himself did during the war. And our inability to recognize this adds to his shame.

KENNEDY: The argument I've been witnessing for the last few minutes seems to me a consequence of Vietnam: an almost unbridgeable divide has been created in the political culture of this country.

I recently attended a conference on Anglo-American relations. During the proceedings, one of the Brits mentioned the Suez intervention in 1956, whereupon another Brit jumped to his feet and violently disagreed with him. Then several others joined in. The entire conference stopped dead for ten minutes while this group of Brits of a particular generation quarreled about Suez. This explosion was a startling reminder of what the impact of Suez had been at the time; it was an event which sent shock waves through the British body politic.

The Vietnam War had an even more violent impact on the Americans who lived through it. It enormously intensified political and ideological feelings, and some Americans will never stop quarreling about it—about the appropriate use of military force, about whether it is moral or not moral for America to intervene abroad, about whether a democracy can truly manage an empire. All of these political disagreements extend outward from the sort of arguments we've heard around this table today.

MARIN: The quarrel, I fear, involves far more than political differences. It involves a disagreement about how men and women, and nations, ought to measure their actions. The vets I know best, for instance, are Catholics, the good boys who went to war because their leaders and priests told them to fight godless communism. Many of them now feel enormous guilt at having done things for which they find themselves unable to atone. The priests in Vietnam came to bless their guns rather than to give them counsel or comfort or genuine help in coming to terms with their actions. This turned many of these vets against the church in the end: they could no longer depend on it to guide them in their lives.

A crisis concerning the proper moral basis for actions and decisions was coming in America anyway, but the war precipitated it, brought it to the surface. The same kinds of complex ethical questions raised by the war are at work in the abortion controversy and the debate about Baby Doe. After all, what we are talking about here is *killing*. We are discussing when and where the state, or individual men and women, have a legitimate right to accomplish their ends by taking thousands of lives, or even, for that matter, a single life.

What we are talking about, in short, is the value of human life, and this is not merely a political or legal issue. It points, as do the other disagreements around this table, both to the complexities of moral choice now confronting us and to a tremendous confusion about the nature of moral life itself. This, I believe, more than any political controversy, explains the power the war still exerts upon us.

CHACE: Finally, we have to ask: Has the American myth, so damaged by Vietnam, really been reconstructed? Perhaps "reconstructing the myth" is a prejudicial phrase; it might be simpler to ask, Has the *idea* of America, pre-Vietnam America, been reconstructed? The America that can bless a war as it has in the past, that can take firm action in the belief that it is acting rightly, that formulates policy in the belief that it is fulfilling a right and proper mission in the world? Or has this America been set aside—and if so, for how long?

PHILLIPS: In all likelihood, the effects of Vietnam will be pervasive in the United States so long as the generation that was in its early and mid-twenties at the war's height holds sway in American society. And that generation is just assuming power. Through this generation, Vietnam will continue as a subliminal disability in American politics and American society—saddling the left with a paralyzing inability to come to grips with the use of American power abroad, pushing the right to pursue a nostalgic re-creation of an all-powerful America drawn from another era, and, in general, undercutting all attempts to achieve consensus in American foreign policy.

CHACE: We have certainly seen here today that while Ronald Reagan's America may be an assertive America, a resurgent America, it is not an undivided America. The foreign and domestic consensus that largely made possible the forceful exercise of American power after World War II was broken by Vietnam and has never been put back together again. Vietnam was the beginning of the end of the American dream of limitless expectations—we lost our first war.

Without such a consensus, managing a coherent and effective foreign policy is terribly difficult. More to the point, U.S. military intervention abroad, without a clear-cut threat to the United States proper, becomes nearly impossible to carry out. It is not simply a question of military power; the moral and political backing for such intervention, which is imperative in a country such as ours, is lacking.

Without a shared set of moral and political values, how can we agree on what should be defended and with what means? From what we have heard today, it is hard not to conclude that while the image of a self-confident America may well be in the making, the reality remains very different.

Epilogue

BY JAMES QUAY

I first went to the Wall in February 1984 during my first visit to Washington, D.C., in nearly 15 years. I had heard about the Vietnam Veterans Memorial, had seen photographs and film of it, and knew what an emotional impact it had on visitors.

As I walked along Constitution Avenue toward the Memorial, I kept looking for the black granite walls made familiar by photographs. When I couldn't see them, the landscape before me on the Mall became uncanny. Somewhere ahead of me I began to feel the Memorial as a specter that I would confront abruptly. The lightness of anticipation I had been feeling became weighted with a kind of dread.

Like all too many Americans, I was coming to the Memorial with a name to look for: Glendon Waters. He wasn't my comrade-in-arms, or a friend, or a relative. In fact, we had never met. Glendon Waters had been dead over two years when, on a cold November night in 1969, I carried his name on a placard around my neck in the "March against Death."

In that march, 45,000 people, each with the name of an American killed in action in Vietnam and a lighted candle, walked across the Arlington Memorial Bridge, past the west side of the Lincoln Memorial to 1600 Pennsylvania Avenue. There each marcher paused before the main entrance of the White House, stepped on a short wooden stand, and, one by one, said the name he or she carried, loudly or softly as they chose. It took nearly 40 hours to say all the names.

In November 1982 the names were spoken again in the Candlelight

Reprinted from *Reflections on the Wall: The Vietnam Veterans Memorial*, ed., Edward C. Ezell, with permission of Stackpole Books. Copyright © 1987 by Stackpole Books.

Vigil of Names that preceded the dedication of the Vietnam Veterans Memorial. This time the names weren't being shouted at the White House but were being intoned quietly in the National Cathedral. And this time it wasn't the war's opponents who spoke the names, but the war's veterans. Yet the spirit was the same. As we had once shouted the names to demonstrate that the war's individual costs were not to be forgotten, now the war's veterans were intoning the names, for the very same reason.

Suddenly, I turned a corner and there they were. There they were, all the names. They started at ground level and rose slowly as I walked down the path, rose until I felt I was descending into an open grave. At the center I stopped, in the midst of the names that now towered over me, closed my eyes, bowed my head, and just stood there, utterly overwhelmed. There are so very many names.

The names receded only when I walked up the path to the directory. Glendon Lee Waters: panel 23 East, line 33. Back down into the Memorial, I found the name of the man who had been killed just as I had publicly begun to oppose the war. What would we have said to one another if we'd met then in July of 1967? Or now? What would we say to one another now?

The Memorial makes meetings possible between the living and the dead. . . . Here, children meet fathers they never knew. Parents meet sons. Lovers are reunited. Comrades. Glendon Waters and me.

The names of the dead wait here for the living to come close and touch them. But as the Wall gives them to us, it also takes them away again, for touching the names only makes us feel how far away they are. They must remain there, united by their shared catastrophe, while we, the living, must leave, united by our shared grief.

It was this grief that made me climb the steps of another Memorial to gaze at the somber face of Abraham Lincoln. That face had known grief, and I felt that Lincoln, of all Americans living or dead, would understand what I was feeling. He too looks upon the Wall. Only when I read again the words he had used to heal a divided nation— "With malice toward none, with charity for all"—did I feel my pilgrimage was complete.

I am profoundly grateful to the dedicated men and women who built the Memorial, for they have given all who were hurt by the Vietnam War the shrine we need if we are ever to be healed. Like the war it recalls, the Memorial has been denounced and defended. But . . . it brings together the conscientious objector and the general, the protestor and the warrior. Important differences between us may remain, but the Memorial has given us something still more important—the common ground of grief. So long as such grief is heartfelt, shared, and remembered—always—there is hope for peace, and so for us all.

The generations wounded by the war will come to the Wall, bringing our scars and our memories with us, looking for healing. But to truly heal ourselves, we must ensure that when future generations look upon the Memorial, they will not have lost what we have lost to feel the absolute, silent sorrow embodied by the black walls, the American names that are on them, and the Vietnamese names that are not.

Notes on Contributors

Loren Baritz has served as the chairman of the History Department at the University of Rochester, acting chancellor of the State University of New York (SUNY), director of the New York Institute for the Humanities, and provost at the University of Massachusetts. He is currently professor of history at the University of Massachusetts at Amherst. He is the author of *Servants of Power*, *City on the Hill*, and *The Culture of the Twenties*.

Peter Braestrup is editor of *The Wilson Quarterly*. He was *Washington Post* Saigon bureau chief from 1968 to 1969 and national staff writer in Washington from 1969 to 1973.

Sam Brown was a student organizer for the "Dump Johnson" movement and founder and coordinator of the Vietnam Moratorium Committee. He served as director of ACTION, President Carter's federal agency in charge of all volunteer programs, including VISTA and the Peace Corps. He is now a businessman.

Cecil B. Currey ("Cincinnatus") is professor of history at the University of South Florida, Tampa. He has served as a chaplain in the National Guard since 1961. He is the author of *Self-Destruction: The Disintegration and Decay of the U.S. Army During the Vietnam Era*.

Robert Elegant is a former journalist who now writes novels. He is best known for *Dynasty*, set in the Far East.

Richard Falk is professor of international law, affiliated with both the Woodrow Wilson School and Princeton University's Political Science Department. His most recent books are *The Promise of the World Order* and *The Dual Fate of International Terrorism*.

James Fallows is Washington editor of *The Atlantic*. He was an editor of *The Washington Monthly* in the early 1970s and chief speech writer for President Jimmy Carter from 1977 to 1979.

Richard A. Gabriel is professor of politics at St. Anselm's College, in Manchester, New Hampshire. He is a retired career army intelligence officer and a coauthor of *Crisis in Command: Mismanagement in the Army*.

Todd Gitlin is professor of sociology and director of the Mass Communications Program at the University of California at Berkeley. He is the author of *The Whole World is Watching: Mass Media and the New Left* and *The Sixties: Years of Hope, Days of Rage*.

Paul Goodman was a novelist, poet, playwright, psychotherapist and social critic. He is best known for *Growing Up Absurd*, a critique of American education.

John Kerry is the junior senator from Massachusetts. He served with the navy in Vietnam.

Martin Luther King, Jr. was the leader and chief spokesman for the Civil Rights Movement during the 1950s and 1960s.

Phillip Knightley has been a feature writer for the *Sunday Times of London* since 1963. He is a coauthor of *The Philby Conspiracy* and the winner of the Overseas Press Club Award.

Myra MacPherson is a political writer for *The Washington Post*. She has worked for *The New York Times* and *The Washington Star*. She is the author of *Power Lovers: An Intimate Look at Politics and Marriage*.

Peter Marin is a culture critic who has contributed articles on the Vietnam War and Vietnam veterans to a number of journals, including *Harper's, The Nation,* and *Psychology Today*.

Thomas McCormick is professor of history at the University of Wisconsin in Madison and the author of *China Market* and numerous essays.

Charles Mohr is a *New York Times* reporter who, between 1962 and 1973, spent a total of four years covering the Vietnam War.

Norman Podhoretz is a political, social, and literary critic who is best known as the editor-in-chief of *Commentary Magazine*.

James Quay is executive director of The California Council for the Humanities. He was a conscientious objector during the Vietnam War.

Paul L. Savage is chairman of the Politics Department at St. Anselm's College, in Manchester, New Hampshire. He is a retired career army intelligence officer and a coauthor of *Crisis in Command: Mismanagement in the Army*.

James C. Thomson, Jr. is curator of the Nieman Foundation for Journalism and a coauthor of *Sentimental Imperialists: The American Empire in East Asia*. He served as special assistant to the assistant secretary of state for Far Eastern affairs in 1963–64 and as staff member of the National Security Council in 1964–66.

Howard Zinn is professor of government at Boston University. He went to North Vietnam to assist in the release of the first American POWs.

Index

Abortion: 298
About Face (underground newspaper): 175
Acheson, Dean: 20–22, 25, 28, 30, 189
ACTION: 197–98
Adams, Ian: 122
Adams, John Quincy: 7, 8, 11
Advisers, military: 107, 109, 145; as combat pilots, 111; killed at Ap Bac, 112; *see also* MAAG
Aeneid (Virgil): 54
Afghanistan, Soviet Union in: 199, 285–86
Agence France Presse: 108
Agent Orange: 55, 66–67
Agnew, Spiro: 127, 233
Aid, U.S.: 20, 29; *see also* advisers, military
Air America: 119
Air Force, U.S.: 115; refusal to fly combat missions by pilots of, 176
Alcohol: 62
Algeria, France and: 244
Ali, Muhammad: 166
Allende Gossens, Salvador: 246
All Quiet on the Western Front (Remarque): 53, 58, 61–62
Almanach de Gotha: 89
Almedina, Angel: 65
Alsop, Joseph: 114
America in Vietnam (Lewy): 257
Americal Division: 125, 128, 131; *see also* Calley, William L., Jr.; Haeberle, Ronald L.; My Lai

American Indians: 54
American Intellectual Elite, The (Kadushin): 270
American Legion: Vietnam veterans' contempt for, 65; Vietnam veterans as members of, 65; right-wing orientation of, 71
Americans: as "chosen people," 5–6, 8–9; affluence of, 14; *see also* United States
America's Army in Crisis (Hauser): 101
Amnesty, for U.S. antiwar activists/deserters: 242, 243, 255
Andrews, Bruce: 173
Angola: 191
Anticolonialism: 19
Anticommunism: 35, 274; as cloak for colonialism/conquest, 143; *see also* McCarthyism
Antiwar movement: 34–36, 53–54, 64, 163–237, 242; Vietnam veterans in, 63, 65 (*see also* Vietnam Veterans Against the War); on campus, 92, 170–72 (*see also* Kent State University, massacre at); after Tet offensive, 147; blacks in, 165–66; civil rights movement and, 165–66; intellectuals in, 168; Catholic Church and, 169–71 (*see also* Berrigan, Daniel; Berrigan, Philip); "common" citizens among, 173; U.S. servicemen as activists in, 173–78, 189; successes of, 184, 186–91, 193, 253; government *agents provocateurs* in, 185; as middle-class

(continued)

306 THE AMERICAN EXPERIENCE IN VIETNAM

melodrama, 190, 193; patriotic aspects of, 199–200; as draft-evasion ploy, 201; during World War I, 287; *see also* civil disobedience; demonstrations; draft, resistance to; Moratorium Day; pacifism; peace rallies; riots
AP (Associated Press): 108, 112, 123–24; coverage of Tet offensive by, 157, 161–62; *see also* Arnett, Peter
Ap Bac: 111–12, 147
Apocalypse Now (film): 58
Arab world: 249
Arbenz, Jacobo: 284
Arms control: 250; *see also* disarmament
Army, German: 88–91, 94, 97–98 n.; desertion from, 97 n.; noncombatants of, 98 n.
Army, North Vietnamese: *see* NVA
Army, South Vietnamese: *see* ARVN
Army, U.S.: 68; disintegration in, 51, 86–97; "Zippo brigades," 59; German army contrasted with, 88–91; and "buddy system," 94; Prussian influence on, 97 n.; effect of Vietnam War on, 99–103; post-Vietnam amnesia of, 99–103; theft from, 118–19; Criminal Investigation Division of, 119; and corpse mutilation, 122; and rape/murder, 130–31; withdrawal from Vietnam of, 134, 178–79; caste nature of, 291; *see also* advisers, military; atrocities; National Guard; officers, U.S. Army; Reserves; ROTC; veterans, U.S. Vietnam War
Arnett, Peter: 132, 143, 151
ARVN (Army of the Republic of Vietnam): 157; revolt in, 107; cowardice of, 112; humiliated at Ap Bac, 112; defections from, 160; incompetence at top of, 161
Associated Press: *see* AP
Atrocities: 128–32, 135–36, 259–260; cover-up of, 101; simulated, 141, 260; Vietnam veterans as witnesses to, 176; commission for addressing, 247; during World War II, 259; of Vietcong, 261; *see also* Calley, William L., Jr.; children, murder of; civilians, murder of; crops, destruction of; defoliation; hospitals, bombing of; irrigation systems, poisoning of; mutilation, corpse; My Lai; prisoners of war,

murder of; rape; torture; villages, destruction of
"Attrition," Vietnam as war of: 60
Auger, Anne M.: 59
Auschwitz: 251

Baby Doe: 298
Baldwin, Hanson: 159
Ball, George W.: 9, 40–41, 189
Baltimore, draft records burned in: 169
Baltimore Four: 181, 182
Bao Dai: 27, 28
Baritz, Loren: 3, 5–15, 303
Barthes, Roland: 75
Bauxite: 25
Bay of Pigs: 39
Beck, Julian: 205
Beikirch, Gary: 77, 78
Bell, Tom: 204, 208
Ben Suc: 129
Berger, Peter L.: 35, 257
Berlin, 1961 crisis in: 39
Bernard, Carl F.: 102
Bernstein, Barton J.: 262–75 passim
Berrigan, Daniel: 169–70, 251
Berrigan, Philip: 169, 182
Best and the Brightest, The (Halberstam): 187
Betrayal, The (Corson): 99, 101
Bigart, Homer: 108, 112, 149
Big Red One Division: 122, 123
Big Story (Braestrup): 146, 147
Bikers, 72
Black market: 80, 118–19
Black militants: 72
Blacks: 181; opposition to Vietnam War by, 165–66; U.S.-imprisoned, 170–71; antiwar bitterness among Vietnam-based, 176, 177; presidential fear of, 190; as disproportionate percentage of military, 226, 234; *see also* racism, in U.S. military
Bloodworth, Dennis: 108, 111
Boat people: 199; as U.S. citizens, 288
Body counts: 61, 65, 96, 115, 129, 235, 267; civilians used to beef up, 131
Bomb: *see* nuclear weapons
Bombing(s): 44–48, 115, 237, 245, 258, 262, 263, 266; saturation, 248; of civilians during World War II, 258; during World War II, 258, 263; of civilians, 274–75
Bond, Julian: 166

Born on the Fourth of July (Kovic): 178
Boston College, antiwar demonstration at: 171
Boston Five: 181
Boston Globe, and My Lai: 127
Boston University, antiwar demonstrations at: 174–75
Boyd, Jim: 126
Braestrup, Peter: 105, 146, 147 & n., 148, 153–62, 303
Bragg Briefs: 175
Braithwaite, Samuel: 182
Brave New World (Huxley): 222
Breaker Morant (film): 58, 59
Brehm, William K.: 68
Bribery: 119
Britain: 18; importance of Malaya to, 24; media of, 117, 183 and Falkland Islands victory, 191
Broder, David: 70
Brown, Norman O.: 196
Brown, Sam: 163, 195–203, 303
Browne, Malcolm: 108, 109, 112; and Thich Quang Duc suicide, 112
Brown University, antiwar demonstration at: 171
Brucker, Hubert: 55
Buckley, Kevin: 134–36
Buckley, William F.: 146
Buddhists: 112, 229
"Buddy system": 94
Bundy, McGeorge: 114 n., 189, 237
Bundy, William: 254
Bunker, Ellsworth: 160
Bureaucracy, detachment of: 44–45
Burma: 17; Communist threat to, 23
Bury My Heart at Wounded Knee (Brown): 270

Cable 1006: 110
CALCAV (Clergy and Laymen Concerned About Vietnam): 35, 163, 224
Calley, William L., Jr.: 58, 96, 125–27, 254, charged, 126
Calvo, Joseph: 212
Cambodia: 17, 134, 140, 244, 262; French puppet government in, 27; forcible repatriation to, 36; postwar tragedy of, 140, 199; invasion of, 162 n., 171, 179, 188, 282; secret bombing of, 187; Soviet Union and, 199; and U.S. "security," 234
Camden 28 (Camden, N.J.): 182

Canada: 174, 202
Candlelight Vigil of Names: 300–301
Cao Bung: 29
Capitalism: 3, 18–32; *see also* Keynesianism
Capps, Walter H.: 239, 269, 270
Caputo, Phil: 56, 68, 69
Carlson, Lynn A.: 122
Carter, Jimmy: 197, 266, 284, 292
Casualties of War (Lang): 130
Catch-22 (Heller): 295
Catholic Church: militant anticommunism of U.S., 78; antiwar movement and, 169–71, 182; antiwar demonstrations by clergy of, 182 (*see also* Berrigan, Daniel; Berrigan, Philip); soldiers/veterans and, 297–98
Catonsville (Md.), draft records burned in: 169
Catonsville Nine: 170, 181; *see also* Berrigan, Daniel; Moylan, Mary
CBS (Columbia Broadcasting System): 131; coverage of Tet offensive by, 154, 155, 161; simulated atrocities for, 260; *see also* Cronkite, Walter
Cedar Falls operation: 129
Center for the Study of Democratic Institutions, The: 241
Central America: 278, 280; as potential Vietnam, 146, 243; threatened U.S. intervention in, 191
Central Intelligence Agency (CIA): 30; and opium smuggling, 119; and student protesters, 209–10; and plausible denial technique, 263; in Guatemala, 284–85; in Iran, 285; crimes of, 292
Chace, James: 277–99 passim
Changing of the Guard, The (Broder): 70
Chaplains, bloodthirsty: 123
Chauvet, Pierre: 108
Cherne, Leo: 107
Chiang Kai-shek: 44
Chicago, antiwar protests in: 185
Chicano National Moratorium: 190
Children: as Vietcong militia, 58; murder of, 128–31, 252
Chile, U.S. intervention in: 246–47
China: post–World War II Japan and, 25; U.S. "loss" of, 36, 40, 287; *see also* Communist China
Chinese-Americans: 177
Chou En-lai: 171

Choy, Sam: 177
Christian Science Monitor: 119
CIA: *see* Central Intelligence Agency
Civil disobedience: 168
Civilians: murder of, 58–60, 80, 107,
    124–25, 129–32, 134–36, 179, 252,
    259 (*see also* My Lai); forced resettle-
    ment of, 111, 248; World War II
    bombing of, 258, 263
Civil rights movement and antiwar
    movement: 165–66
Civil War, U.S.: 13
Cleland, Max: 197
Clergy and Laymen Concerned About
    Vietnam (CALCAV): 35, 163, 224
Cleveland Plain Dealer, and My Lai
    photographs: 127–28
Clifford, Clark: 189–90
Clurman, Richard: 114
Cocaine, 63
COCOM (Coordinating Committee on
    Export Control): 25
Coffeehouses, antiwar-tilted: 175
Colby, William: 267
Cold War: 3, 11, 20, 22, 191, 244; 1950s
    escalation of, 107
Coles, Robert: 83
College(s): as draft-avoidance haven, 87,
    92, 94; antiwar demonstrations at,
    170–72; draft-evasion curricula of,
    215; need for improvements in, 256
Colonialism, U.S.: 18; *see also* France,
    in Vietnam; Philippines
Columbia Broadcasting System: *see* CBS
Committee of Concerned Asian Schol-
    ars: 260
Communism: 12, 23, 27, 35; John F.
    Kennedy and world, 39; U.S. Catho-
    lic Church vs., 78; and Vietcong, 230;
    as U.S. buzzword, 234, 235; *see also*
    anticommunism; Communists; Soviet
    Union
Communist China: nuclear capability
    of, 15; ascendency of, 22, 28; contain-
    ment of, 23, 38, 107; in Korean War,
    30, 38; and split with Soviets, 38;
    U.S. fear of, 38; "death" of Marxism
    in, 294; *see also* China
Communists: North Vietnamese, 36 (*see
    also* Vietminh); South Vietnamese (*see*
    Vietcong)
Concerned Officers Movement: 176

Conde, Alexander de: 269–70
Congo, U.S. bombing of: 170
Congress, U.S.: and dollar gap, 22; sup-
    port for war in, 47; and aid to Viet-
    nam veterans, 66–67; Cambodian
    adventure ended by, 179; presidential
    war-making powers limited by, 179;
    doves of, 191; *see also* House of Rep-
    resentatives, U.S.; Senate, U.S.
Congressional Medal of Honor: 77
Congressional Record, Hollingsworth
    story read into: 123
Conniff, Frank: 114
Conrad, Joseph: 84
Conscientious objection: 71, 202, 211,
    217, 218; during World Wars I and II,
    174; *see also* pacifism
Consequences of Vietnam War: 277–99;
    military, 279–84, 290; foreign-policy,
    282–86, 295; moral, 286–87, 294,
    296, 298–99; economic, 288, 294;
    and U.S. vital interests, 289–90;
    political, 292–93, 295–99; social,
    292–95, 298; for veterans, 294–97
Conservatives in United States: 10,
    12–13; religiosity of, 12
Coordinating Committee on Export
    Control (COCOM): 25
Cornell University: Daniel Berrigan at,
    170; radicals of, 204; *see also* Good-
    man, Mathew Ready; Students for
    Education (SFE)
Corpses, mutilation of: 122, 141; for
    TV, 141
Corruption: 118–19
Corson, William R.: 99, 101
Council of Economic Advisers: 21
Counterinsurgency: 39, 248, 249
Courts martial: 260–61; for perpetrators
    of U.S. atrocities, 130–31 (*see also* My
    Lai); for antiwar activists, 174; for
    Vietnam-era mutiny, 175
Cowan, Geoff: 126
Crane, Stephen: 53
Crawford, Kenneth: 113
"Credibility gap": 43
Crime and Punishment (Dostoyevsky): 84
Crimes of War (Falk): 246
Criminal Investigation Division, U.S.
    Army: 119
Crisis in Command (Gabriel/Savage):
    99, 101

Cronkite, Walter: 133, 155, 260
Crops, destruction of: 245, 248, 258
Crusades: 13
Cryptoracism: 45
Cua Viet River: 123
Cuba, U.S.-Soviet confrontation over: 14–15, 153
Currey, Cecil B.: 51, 99–103, 303

Daily Express: 117
Daily Mail: 111, 117
Daily Mirror: 117; *see also* Pilger, John
Daily Telegraph: 108, 111, 117; *see also* Nguyen Ngoc Phach
Dak To: 55
Dale, Edwin: 159
Da Nang: 162; Marine landing at, 119; antiwar sentiment at, 176
Dancis, Bruce: 204
Daniels, George: 174
Death of an Army (King): 101
Defense, U.S. Department of (DOD): *see* Pentagon
Defoliation: 246, 248, 258
De Gaulle, Charles: 243, 281
Dellinger, David: 167
Democratic Republic of Vietnam, formation of: 179
Demonstrations: 8; *see also* antiwar movement
Desertions: 87, 90, 97 n., 98 n., 174–75, 177, 242; in World Wars I and II, 174
Diem: *see* Ngo Dinh Diem
Dien Bien Phu: 9, 107, 228
Dikes, proposed destruction of North Vietnamese: 107
Dillon, C. Douglas: 189
Disarmament: 249–50
Discharge, military: 177; less than honorable, 242
Dispatch News Agency: 128
Dispatch News Service: 126
Dissent: *see* antiwar movement
DOD (Department of Defense): *see* Pentagon
Dodge, Father: 123
"Dollar gap": 19, 21; U.S. Congress and, 22; Third World markets as solution to, 23
Dominican Republic, U.S. intervention in: 196
Domino theory: 23, 38–39

DOS: *see* State, U.S. Department of
Dostoyevsky, Fyodor: 84
Draft: 71; resistance to, 57, 94, 163, 166–67, 202, 206, 208–11, 214–21, 242 (*see also* conscientious objection); Julian Bond *vs.*, 166; destruction of records relative to, 169–70, 182 (*see also* draft cards, destruction of); lottery version of, 188; inequities of, 201; as moral challenge, 202; physical unfitness–related evasion of, 214–17, 220, 221; adversarial technique of avoiding, 217; graduate school deferments from, 219
Draft cards, destruction of: 166, 185, 208, 209, 211
Draftees, Vietnam-based: 93, 94, 98 n.
Draper, Theodore: 44
Draw, John: *see* Nguyen Ngoc Phach
Dresden, fire bombing of: 60
Drugs: 87, 90–91, 98 n.; U.S. military use of, 62–63; Vietnam veterans and, 62–63, 296
Dulles, John Foster: 14, 30–31, 37
Duncan, David: 127

Eberhardt, David: 169
Economy, Vietnam War and U.S.: 189
Edison, Thomas: 13
Eisenhower, Dwight D.: 12, 14, 266, 293; commitment to Vietnam of, 39
Elegant, Robert: 105, 138–42, 146, 303
Ellsberg, Daniel: 115, 168–69, 251, 260; *see also* Pentagon Papers
El Salvador: 191, 280–83, 285
Emerson, Gloria: 82, 83
England: *see* Britain
Epstein, Edward J.: 154
Epton, Epi: 212
ERP (European Recovery Program): *see* Marshall Plan
Espionage Act, invoked against Ellsberg: 169
Esquire, and Xuan Ngoc account: 130
Europe: post-World War II poverty of, 19; imperialism of, 26; U.S. military deserters to, 174; U.S. "loss" of Eastern, 287
European Recovery Program (ERP): *see* Marshall Plan
Evans, Rowland: 179
Ewalt, Jack: 59–60

Executive fatigue: 42–43
Extortion: 119

Falk, Richard: 239, 241–56, 303
Falkland Islands: 292
Fall, Bernard: 111
Fallows, James: 163, 201, 214–23, 303
Farber, Leslie: 255
Far Eastern Affairs, Bureau of: 37–38
Fasts, antiwar-related: 208
Fatalism, Asiatic: 45
FBI (Federal Bureau of Investigation):
  bedeviled by Daniel Berrigan, 170;
  vs. Marty Goodman, 211
Federalist Party, War of 1812 and: 287
Fed Up!: 175
Felt, Harry D.: 109
Feminist movement: 201
Ferber, Michael: 220
Fern, Jack: 154
Fields of Fire (Webb): 60
Fire Base 6: 235
Fitzgerald, Frances: 277, 282–86,
  294–95
Five-Day Fast for Peace: 208
"Five o'Clock Follies": 132
Flacks, Richard: 270–73
Flora, Jan: 208
Fonda, Jane: 81
Ford, Gerald: 292
Foreign Affairs, W. Bundy and: 254
Fort Jackson (S.C.), antiwar turbulence
  near, 175
Fox, James: 123
Fraggings: 87, 90, 98n., 176
France: 18; defeat of, 29, 107, 229 (see
  also Dien Bien Phu); in Vietnam, 9,
  17, 19–20, 23, 26–29, 228; U.S. sup-
  port of, 25–29, 107; in Cambodia, 27;
  in Laos, 27; and Algeria, 244
Frank, Jerome: 248
Franz, Jerry: 204, 207
Freedom of Information Act: 263, 266
Freedom Riders: 195
Freedom Summer: 199
Free-fire zones: 60, 235, 237, 258,
  268, 269
Free Speech Movement: 195
French Indochina: see France, in
  Vietnam
Freud, Sigmund: 196
Fuerbringer, Otto: 113–14
Fulbright, William: 35

Gabriel, Richard A.: 51, 86–97, 101, 303
Galvin, John R.: 99, 100
Gandhi, Mohandas: 205, 218
Gellhorn, Martha: 124–25; blacklisting
  of, 125
General Strike for Peace: 205
Geneva Accords (Agreements) of 1954:
  231, 262, 266
Geneva Convention, 1949: 248; U.S.
  violations of, 236–37
Geneva Protocol, 1925: 248
Genocide: 259, 271–72
Germany: 296; rearmament of, 19; see
  also army, German
Giap, Gen. Vo Nguyen: 9, 160, 162
GI Bill, Vietnam veterans' version of: 66
Gilder, George: 278, 287–96 passim
Gilpatric, Roswell: 237
Gitlin, Todd: 163, 183–94, 304
Glassman, James: 219, 221
Goldwater, Barry: 12
Goodman, Mathew Ready: 204–13
Goodman, Paul: 163, 204–13, 304
"Gooks," enemy as: 58
Graffiti: 175
Great Britain: see Britain
Great Society, Asiatic version of: 8
Green Berets: 174
Greene, Graham: 295
Grenada, U.S. invasion of: 71, 280, 284,
  285, 292, 295
Griffiths, Philip Jones: 121, 125, 131
Gruening, Ernest: 185
Guardian: 117; and Gellhorn articles, 125
Guatemala: 191; CIA intervention in,
  284–85
Guerillas: 132, 269; El Salvadoran,
  282–83; see also Vietcong
Guilt: 239, 241–76; veterans and,
  56–57, 255, 296; and responsibility
  contrasted, 239, 253; Protestantism
  and, 254; animating, 255; see also
  shame
Gulf of Tonkin incident: 165, 180, 185

Hackworth, David: 100, 102
Haeberle, Ronald L.: 127, 128
Hagel, Chuck: 65
Hague Convention in 1907: 248
Hahn, Harlan: 173
Haiphong, bombings of: 179, 187
Halberstam, David: 112, 113, 187; JFK
  vs., 114

Hall, William: 113
Hamburger Hill: 235
Hamilton, Richard F.: 173
Hanoi, bombings of: 179, 187, 262; *see also* North Vietnam
Harassment interdiction fire: 237
Harriman, Averell: 38, 207
Harvard University, draft-evasion curricula of: 215
Harvey, Frank: 120, 121
Harvey, William: 174
Harwood, Richard: 162 n.
Hauser, William L.: 101, 102
Hawthorne, Nathaniel, 6
Heart of Darkness, The (Conrad): 84
Heilbroner, Robert L.: 35
Helping Hand: 175
Herbert, Anthony: 101, 129–30
Herndon, Ray: 100
Heroin: 62–63; South Vietnamese/U.S. authorities as entrepreneurs of, 91
Herr, Michael: 123
Hersh, Seymour: 126–28, 187, 188
Hershey, Gen. Lewis: 219, 220
Herz, Alice: 167
Higgins, Marguerite: 113
Hijacking: 119
Hill 81: 235
Hiroshima: 13, 251
Hiroshima Day: 210
Hitler, Adolf: as Ky hero, 118; attempted assassination of, 265
Ho Chi Minh: 28, 107, 192, 228, 231
Ho Chi Minh City: 179; *see also* Saigon
Ho Chi Minh Trail: 187
Holland, 18
Hollingsworth, James F.: 122–23
Holmes, Oliver Wendell: 221
Holocaust: 257, 272
Holsti, Ole: 275
Home From the War (Lifton): 242
Honduras: 191
Hoopes, Townsend: 190
Hoover, J. Edgar: 190
Hospitals, bombing of: 132, 179
House of Representatives, Georgia, Julian Bond and: 166
House of Representatives, U.S., antiwar sentiment in: 179
Hué: North Vietnamese occupation of, 36, 133; battle for, 146, 157–62; Vietcong massacre at, 261
Hughes, John: 119

Hughes, Langston: 227
Hughes, Richard: 108, 110
Humphrey, Hubert: 9, 168; as War apologist, 116
Huntington, Samuel P.: 271
Huxley, Aldous: 222

Idealism: 35; Wilsonian, 11
Imperialism: 26, 34; *see also* colonialism
India: 18
Indians, American: 54
Indochina: 17, 23; post-1975 suffering in, 36; French (*see* France, in Vietnam); *see also* Cambodia; Laos; North Vietnam; South Vietnam
Indonesia: 18, 31; U.S. interest in, 23; oil of, 24; mid-1960s power change in, 48
Intelligentsia, indifference to veterans of U.S.: 222
International law: 247, 258; U.S. violations of, 242; and *jus ad bellum* vs. *jus in bello,* 266
Iran: 18; U.S. hostages in, 65, 284; CIA intervention in, 285; revolution in, 285
Irrigation systems, poisoning of: 245–46
Islam: 285
Israel: 249; Egypt and, 273

Jackson, Robert: 251
Jacobson, George: 144
Janowitz, Morris: 97
Japan: 3, 18; in Vietnam, 17; post-World War II poverty of, 19; post-World War II China and, 24–25; post-World War II concerns of, 24 26; as "key" to "peaceful" Southeast Asia, 25, 26, 31 32; American peace treaty with, 31; Korean War-related prosperity of, 31; war guilt of, 251
Jaspers, Karl: 82
Jefferson, Thomas: 7
Jencks, Harlan: 99
Jihad: 13
Johnny Got His Gun (Trumbo): 178
Johnson, Lyndon B.: 8, 10, 34, 47–48, 155, 156, 184–85, 187, 189–90, 219, 251; and New Hampshire primary, 8–9; retirement of, 8, 133, 190; and Tet offensive, 133, 154, 181; and Gulf of Tonkin incident, 165; World War II record of, 218; dissembling of, 262
Jones, James: 53
Just, Ward: 120

Kadushin, Charles: 270
Kalb, Bernard: 115
Karnow, Stanley: 146
Kastenmeier, Robert: 245
Keegan, John: 62
Keller, Elizabeth: 212
Kennan, George F.: 8, 20, 22, 31
Kennedy, Donald: 248
Kennedy, Edward: 219
Kennedy, John F.: 6, 11, 34, 145, 278;
    and Cuban crisis, 14–15; and Nixon
    debate, 38; anticommunism of, 39;
    commitment to Vietnam of, 39; and
    Krushchev, 39; as Catholic, 78; de-
    ception of public, by, 110, 262 (see
    also Cable 1006); bullying of media
    by, 113; vs. Halberstam, 114; as-
    sassination of, 195
Kennedy, Paul M.: 277, 279–97 passim
Kennedy, Robert: 189, 210; as presi-
    dential candidate, 8–9; assassination
    of, 185
Kent State University, massacre at:
    171–72, 188
Kerry, John: 163, 233–37, 304
Keynesianism: 21; post-World War II
    Japan and U.S., 31
Khanh, Gen Nguyen: 180
Khe Sanh: 60, 157–59, 161, 162, 235
Khmer people: 140
Khmer Rouge: 140, 183, 190
Khrushchev, Nikita: 39
Kien Hoa, massacre at: 135
Kierkegaard, Sören: 84
King, Edward L.: 101
King, Martin Luther, Jr.: 163, 166, 185,
    224–32, 304; assassination of, 185;
    Hoover vs., 190; and Nobel Peace
    Prize, 227
Kissinger, Henry: 12–13, 141, 146, 151,
    187, 190, 242; shunned at Brown Uni-
    versity, 171; and peace, 179
Kitt, Eartha: 168
Klein, Edward: 135
Knightley, Phillip: 105, 107–36, 304
Komer, Robert: 124 & n., 136
Konvitz, Milton: 206
Korean War: 14, 29, 37, 107; effect on
    Southeast Asia of, 30–31; Communist
    China in, 38; "buddy system" in, 94;
    and rotation policy, 98 n.; official his-
    tory of, 100; and Vietnam War con-
    trasted, 273–76

Kovic, Ron: 177–78
Krieger, David: 264, 265
Kristol, Irving: 292
Krock, Arthur: 147
Kroll, Ray: 175
Ky, Nguyen Cao: see Nguyen Cao Ky

Lacouture, Jean: 261–62, 273
Laird, Melvin: 187
Landlords, murder of: 36
Lang, Daniel: 130–31
Lansner, Kermit: 136
Laos: 17, 134, 140, 236, 262; French
    puppet government of, 27; opium
    smuggling by generals of, 119; post-
    war tragedy of, 199; and U.S. "secu-
    rity," 234
Last Harass: 175
Latin America: see Central America
Lawyers, antiwar: 168
League of Nations: 11; failure of, 18
Lebanon: 71, 282, 290; U.S. interven-
    tion in, 278, 286; U.S. withdrawal
    from, 289
Le Duc Tho: 242
LeMay, Curtis: 12
Lerner, Max: 252
Levy, Howard: 174
Lewis, Anthony: 134
Lewis, Tom: 169
Lewy, Guenter: 257–76 passim
Liberals: 10–13
Libya: 281
Life, and My Lai: 126–28
Lifton, Robert Jay: 64, 82, 242, 255
Lincoln, Abraham: 301
Lipsitz, Lewis: 173
Literature: 67, 101
Loan, Gen. Nguyen Ngoc: 151
Lodge, Henry Cabot: 180
Lon Nol: 244
Look: 107; and My Lai, 126
Lord Jim (Conrad): 221
Lowell, Robert: 168
Lucas, Jim G.: 119–20
Luttwak, Edward N.: 277, 280–96 passim
Lynd, Staughton: 167

MAAG (United States Military Assis-
    tance Advisory Group): 108
MacArthur, Douglas: 25
McCarthy, Eugene: 9, 189; and New
    Hampshire primary, 133

McCarthy, Joseph: 200, 274
McCarthyism: 287; effect on Bureau of
Far Eastern Affairs of, 38
McCloskey, Jack: 61
McComb (Miss.), antiwar activism
in: 165
McCone, John: 180
McCormick, Thomas: 3, 17–32, 304
McCulloch, Frank: 128
McDonald, Donald: 241
McGovern, George: 191
McNamara, Robert: 43, 47, 111, 155,
237, 272; in praise of John Stennis, 165
McNaughton, John: 180, 272
MacPherson, Myra: 51, 53–73, 304
MACV (Military Assistance Command,
Vietnam): 134, 135, 144, 148 n.; on
Tet offensive, 160
Magazines: see media
Malaya: 18, 31; as British asset, 24
Manning, Robert: 110
Mao Tse-tung: 107, 192, 269
Marches, antiwar: 185; "March against
Death," 300
Marcuse, Herbert: 196
Marijuana: 62, 196
Marin, Peter: 51, 75–85, 277, 283–98
passim, 304
Marines, U.S.: at Da Nang, 119; gang
rape by, 130; murder of prisoners by,
130; burning of villages by, 131
Market(s): need for, 22–26; Southeast
Asia as, 31–32
Marketing, of War to American pub-
lic: 45
Marshall Plan: 19–21; Asian version
of, 21
Marx, Karl: 196, 283
Massachusetts, University of, antiwar
demonstrations at: 172
MDAP (Mutual Defense Assistance
Program): 21, 22
Meadlo, Paul: 128
Mecklin, John: 109, 112
Media: 105–62; and veterans, 68;
Washington pressure on, 113–15; at-
tempted seduction of, 116–17; Brit-
ish, 117–18; after My Lai, 133–36;
Vietnam War "lost" by, 138; power of
(see My Lai; Pentagon Papers; Tet of-
fensive); see also press; television
Medics: 64
Mekong Delta: 120

Melville, Herman: 5
Mengel, James: 169
Mexican War: Vietnam War and, 270;
Whigs and, 287
Military, U.S.: see Air Force, U.S.;
Army, U.S.; Marines, U.S.; Navy,
U.S.; Pentagon; veterans, U.S. Viet-
nam War
Military Assistance Command, Viet-
nam: see MACV
Miller, Arthur: 14, 83, 168
Milwaukee Fourteen: 181
Mission in Torment (Browne): 109
Mohr, Charles: 105, 113, 143–52, 154,
304; resignation from Time of, 114; in
combat, 114 n.; as antiwar hero, 115
Mongolia: 39
Morality, Vietnam War and: 239, 246,
249–50, 257–76
Moratorium Day: 176, 187–88
Morgenthau, Hans: 200
Morris, William: 194
Morrison, Norman: 167
Morse, Wayne: 185
Moses, Bob: 167
Moyers, Bill: 41
Moylan, Mary: 170
Moynahan, Brian: 118
Muller, Robert: 66, 77
Muste, A. J.: 42
Mutilation, corpse: 122, 141; for tele-
vision, 141, 260
Mutiny: 87, 90, 98 n.; 175; during Revo-
lutionary War, 174
Mutual Defense Assistance Program
(MDAP): 21, 22
My Lai: 59, 96, 123, 125–29, 132, 133,
136, 235, 260; repercussions of, 133–36

Nader, Ralph: 222
Napalm: 59, 75, 184, 234
National Broadcasting Company: see
NBC
National Committee for a Citizens Com-
mission of Inquiry on United States
War Crimes in Vietnam: 129
National Guard: 217; see also Kent State
University, massacre at
Nationalism: 11, 22; Puritan roots of
U.S., 10; Southeast Asian, 26; SEA,
27; Asian, 38–39
National Liberation Front (NLF): see
Vietcong

National security: 22
National Security Council: 22, 25, 30;
    and military aid, 29
NATO: 19–20
Navy, U.S.: 115; murder of civilians by,
    132; postwar purge of "undesirables"
    from, 177
Nazism: 13, 249; German army and, 88,
    89; see also holocaust
NBC (National Broadcasting Company):
    expulsion of correspondent for, 111;
    coverage of Tet offensive by, 154, 155,
    161
Newsmagazines: see media
Newspapers: underground antiwar mili-
    tary, 175; see also press
New Statesman: 116
Newsweek: 108, 111; on Diem, 107; sub-
    mission to official pressure by, 113;
    and My Lai, 128; on atrocities, 130;
    and Buckley/Shimkin exposé,
    135–36; coverage of Tet offensive by,
    154–55 & n., 158, 159, 161; see also
    Buckley, Kevin; Shimkin, Alec;
    Sully, François
Newton College of the Sacred Heart: 171
New Yorker: 129
New York Herald Tribune: 113
New York Post: 128
New York Review of Books: 34
New York Times: 107, 108, 118, 123–24,
    182; and My Lai, 126–28; Vietnam
    coverage by, 134 n.; dovishness of,
    155; interpretative reporting of,
    158–59; and Tet offensive, 161; and
    Pentagon Papers, 169; and North
    Korean bombings, 274; see also
    Bigart, Homer; Halberstam, David;
    Lewis, Anthony; Mohr, Charles;
    Reston, James; Sheehan, Neil;
    Sulzberger, C.L.
Ngo Dinh Diem: 44, 107–14, 180, 229,
    230; corruptness of, 108–109; vs.
    Saigon foreign press corps, 108–13;
    praised by Newsweek, 113; fall of, 196;
    U.S. conspiracy with, 231
Nguyen Cao Ky: 118
Nguyen Cong Hoan: 36
Nguyen Ngoc Phach: 117
Nguyen Van Thieu: 160, 162, 191, 244,
    255; political prisoners of, 241–42
Nhu, Madam Ngo Dinh: 113

Nicaragua: 191
Ninth Infantry Division: 135
Nixon, Richard M.: 12, 133, 141, 146,
    151, 155, 162 n., 186, 200, 218, 243,
    251, 262, 266, 282; and Kennedy de-
    bate, 38; and My Lai, 126; vs. Pen-
    tagon Papers, 169; and Cambodian
    invasion, 171; at 1972 Republican Na-
    tional Convention, 178; and antiwar
    protest, 181, 182, 187–91; and North
    Vietnam ultimatum, 187; patriotic
    hubris of, 235; guilt of, 254; and
    Watergate, 292; see also Watergate
NLF (National Liberation Front): see
    Vietcong; P.R.G.
Nolting, Frederick: 40
North Korea, U.S. bombing of: 274
Northshield, Robert J.: 154
North Vietnam: 140, 231; after defeat of
    French, 107; bombing of, 165, 167,
    185; and South Vietnam unified, 179;
    induced into naval battle, 184; Nixon
    ultimatum to, 187; Stalinist influence
    on, 262; army of (see NVA); see also
    Ho Chi Minh
Novak, Robert: 179
NSC (National Security Council): 124:
    32 n.
Nuclear weapons: 14; threat of use of,
    187; protests against, 205, 206
Nuremberg, war-crimes trials of:
    250–52, 259
Nurses, U.S. Army: 64
NVA (North Vietnamese Army): 59,
    138, 150

Oakland (Calif.), demonstrations in: 185
Oberdorfer, Don: 155 n.
O'Brien, David: 166
O'Brien, Tim: 65
Observer: 108, 111, 117
Obst, David: 126
Officers, German Army: 88–91
Officers, U.S. Army: 51; quality of, 80,
    86–87, 90–97; profiteering of, 91, 92,
    118; assassination of (see fraggings)
Offshore Islands: 38
Oil: 34; Indonesian, 24
Okamura, Akihiko: 130
Opium: 119
Orphans: 124, 229

Pacification Studies Group: 267
Pacifism: 163; see also Dellinger, David;
  Goodman, Mathew Ready; Morrison,
  Norman
Pakistan: 236
Palestinians: 249
Panama Canal Treaties: 284
Pan-Asianism: Japanese perversion of,
  26; Southeast Asia and, 26
Paris: peace negotiations in, 134,
  242–44; peace treaty at, 151, 179
Pathet Lao: 140
Patton, George, III: 122
Pauken, Tom: 70
Peace: negotiations for, 134, 242–44;
  treaty of, 151, 179
Peace Corps: 70, 83, 199; antiwar senti-
  ment in, 168
Peace movement: see antiwar movement
Peace rallies: 167–68
Pentagon: 21, 22; civilian control of,
  47; Vietnam as lab for, 111; victory
  assurances of, 133; in defense of
  operation Speedy Express, 136; dem-
  onstrations at, 185; postwar cau-
  tiousness of, 279, 280
Pentagon Papers: 110, 115, 169, 180, 181,
  245, 248, 253, 266, 272; see also
  Ellsberg, Daniel
Penthouse: 222
Pericles: 13
Perkins (Cornell pres.): 208
Perry, Merton: 113, 114, 144
Persian Gulf: 18
Petroleum: see oil
Philadelphia (Miss.), antiwar activism
  in: 165
Philippines: 18, 23
Phillips, Kevin P.: 278, 284–98 passim
Pilger, John: 117–18
Pines, Burt: 128
Podhoretz, Norman: 3, 34–36, 304
Point Four: 21, 23
Poirier, Norman: 130, 131
Poland, Soviet Union and: 199
Pol Pot: 199, 262
Poverty Program: 225
POWs: see prisoners of war
Press: role of, 105–62; vs. government,
  138, 154; underground antiwar mili-
  tary, 175; Nixon manipulation of, 188;

see also media, and individual publica-
  tions by name
P.R.G. (Provisional Revolutionary Gov-
  ernment): see Vietcong
Price of Power, The (Hersh): 187
Prisoners of war (POWs): U.S. soldiers
  as Vietnamese, 64; murder of, 130,
  237; war opposed by American, 177;
  torture of, 237
Profiteering: 80, 92
Propaganda: see media
Prostitution: 118, 229
Protest(s): see antiwar movement
Protestantism: 10; see also Puritans
Pueblo, U.S.S., seizure of: 156
Puppet governments, French: 27
Puritans: 5–7, 10

Qaddafi, Muammar: 281
Quakers: 208, 209
Quang Ngai: 131
Quay, James: 300–302, 304
Quiet American, The (Greene): 295
Qui Nhon, black market of, 119; hospi-
  tal at, 124

Racism: 26, 121–25, 139, 235; U.S.,
  165–66; in U.S. military, 176, 236;
  South African, 218; see also cryp-
  toracism; genocide
RAND Corporation: 168–69, 248
Rape: 129–31
Reagan, Ronald: 279, 284, 287–89, 292,
  298; defense of War by, 69; and Third
  World, 286
Red Badge of Courage, The (Crane): 53
Red Mountain, massacre of: 131
Red Scare, 1920s: 200
Referenda, re U.S. troop withdrawal:
  172–73
Refugees: 124–25, 134; Vietcong attacks
  on, 261
Regionalism, Pacific-area: 48
Rehyansky, Joseph A.: 99
Religion: 5, 10; U.S. conservatives and,
  12; technology as U.S., 15; Vietcong
  slaughter and, 123; see also Buddhists;
  Catholic Church; Clergy and Laymen
  Concerned About Vietnam; God;
  Islam; Protestantism; Puritans;
  Quakers

Remarque, Erich Maria: 53, 61
Repatriation, Cambodian: 36
Reserve Officers Training Corps:
    see ROTC
Reserves: 217; see also National
    Guard; ROTC
Reston, James: 158–59
Reuters (news agency): 108, 111, 112
Rheault, Robert: 129
Rhee, Syngman: 44
Ridenhour, Ronald: 125–26
Ridgway, Matthew: 30
Riots: 8
Robertson, Frank: 108
Roche, John P.: 146
Rock and roll: 196
Rockefeller, Nelson: 207
Rogers, William: 210
Roman Catholicism: see Catholic
    Church
Roman legions: 94
Rommel, Erwin: 266
Romulo, Carlos: 28
Roosevelt, Franklin D.: 34
Rosenau, James: 264, 265
Rostow, Walt W.: 146, 237
Rotation system: 87, 93, 95–96, 98 n.;
    in German army, 90; during Korean
    War, 98 n.
ROTC (Reserve Officers Training
    Corps): 92, 96; student protests
    against, 172, 184, 207
Rothwell, Bruce: 111
Rubber: 24, 25, 32 n., 34
Rumor of War, A (Caputo): 56
Rusk, Dean: 30, 180; as War apolo-
    gist, 116
Russell, Bertrand: 260
Russia: see Soviet Union
Russo, Anthony: 169

Sabotage, by antiwar activists: 168
Saigon: foreign press corps of, 107–15;
    U.S. mission in, 109, 111–13, 143–45,
    156; Vietcong in, 133, 144; fall of, 145;
    battle for, 151, 157–60, 162; North
    Vietnamese occupation of, 179; re-
    named Ho Chi Minh City, 179
Saint Cyr, Laurent de Gouvion: 101
St. Louis Post-Dispatch: 125, 127
Salinger, Pierre: 114 & n.
Samurai: 13

San Francisco Chronicle: 123, 127
Sartre, Jean Paul: 121, 252
Saturation bombing: 248
Sauvageot, Jean: 102
Savage, Paul L.: 51, 86–97, 99, 101, 304
Sayle, Murray: 118
Schell, Jonathan: 129
Schlesinger, Arthur, Jr.: 8
Schnall, Susan: 174
SDS (Students for a Democratic
    Society): 184, 185, 192, 209; dissolu-
    tion of, 193
SEA (Southeast Asia region): 18, 24
Search and destroy mission: 237
SEATO: 39
Seeley, John: 83
Self-Destruction (Currey): 101
Senate, U.S., Vietnam War hearings of:
    8; see also Congress, U.S.
SFE (Students for Education): 206
Shame: 294; draft evader's, 216, 223;
    among Vietnam War veterans, 234,
    297; of misled journalist, 262; see also
    guilt
Shaw, John: 110, 121, 130
Shawcross, William: 140
Sheehan, Neil: 112, 113, 132; and Pen-
    tagon Papers, 115
Shimkin, Alec: 134–35
Short Times: 175
Sideshow (Shawcross): 140
Sihanouk, Prince: 190
Simon, Ron: 72
Sit-ins: 208
Smith, Bob: 127
Smith, Clark: 57
Smith, Jack: 55
Smuggling: 119
SNCC (Student Nonviolent Coordinat-
    ing Committee): 166
Soldiers (Herbert): 101
Sophocles: 84
South Africa: 218, 249, 281
Southeast Asia region (SEA): 18, 24
Southern Christian Leadership Confer-
    ence: 226
South Vietnam: 262; after French de-
    feat, 107; collapse of, 179; and North
    Vietnam unified, 179; international
    recognition of, 266; army of (see
    ARVN)
Soviet Union: 10, 281; nuclear capability

of, 14–15, 22; containment of, 23; and split with Communist China, 38; and Afghanistan, 199, 285–86; and Poland, 199; and U.S. parity, 279; economic woes of, 290
Spanish Civil War, American correspondents in: 132 n.
Special Offshore Procurement Program: 19, 25
Speedy Express, Operation: 135
Spock, Benjamin: 220
Starr, Paul: 222
State, U.S. Department of (DOS): 21–22, 28–29, 39–40; dissent within, 40–42; "curator mentality" in, 43; and Saigon-based press corps, 109, 110; see also Acheson, Dean; Council of Economic Advisers, Dulles, John Foster; Far Eastern Affairs, Bureau of; Harriman, Averell; Kissinger, Henry
Steinke, Richard: 174
Stennis, John: 147, 165
Stimson, Henry L.: 46, 49
Stone, I. F.: 83
Strangers at Home (Smith): 57
Student Nonviolent Coordinating Committee: see SNCC
Student protest: see colleges, antiwar demonstrations at
Students for a Democratic Society: see SDS
Students for Education (SFE): 206
Student strike, Kent State-memorial: 172
Suicide: Vietnam War veterans and, 77, 80, 296; of Thich Quang Duc, 112
Sully, François: 108, 111; expulsion of, 111, 113
Sulzberger, C. L.: 114, 182
Sunday Mirror: 117, 118
Sunday Times (London): 108, 110, 117
Sunrise, Operation: 111
Supina, Philip: 167
Supreme Court, U.S.: and Julian Bond, 166; and Pentagon Papers, 169; and Vietnam War constitutionality, 179
Sutherland, Donald: 178
Syria: 281

Tarawa: 60
Taylor, Maxwell D.: 101, 189

Taylor, Telford: 247, 260
Teach-ins: 185
Technology: 13–14
Television: 59, 138, 140, 141; after Tet offensive, 133, 153–56, 158–60; nature of U.S., 156; treatment of Vietnam War veterans on, 222–23; Vietnam War on, 276
Terry, Wallace: 176
Tet offensive: 8, 36, 132–34, 143–47, 150–62, 181, 186, 256; press coverage of, 105–106; Johnson after, 189
Thailand: 17; Communist threat to, 23; anticolonialism of, 27
Theft: 119; from U.S. army, 118–19
Thich Quang Duc: 112
Thieu: see Nguyen Van Thieu
Thin Red Line, The (Jones): 53
Third World: 279, 284–87; Vietnam as part of, 17; as potential market, 22–26; U.S. and, 243
Thomas, Norman: 42
Thomson, James C., Jr.: 3, 11, 15, 37–49, 304
Thoreau, Henry David: 218
Time: 108, 110; on Diem, 107; submission to official pressure by, 113–14; and My Lai, 128; hawkishness of, 155; and Tet offensive, 158, 161; see also Mohr, Charles
Times (London): 111, 117; and My Lai, 127
Tin: 24, 25, 34
Tolstoy, Leo: 84
Tomalin, Nicholas: 122, 123
Tonkin, Gulf of: see Gulf of Tonkin incident
Torture: 130, 237; by U.S. military, 129; by South Vietnamese police, 242; in Latin America, 243; U.S. instructors of, 243; of American prisoners, 261; by Vietcong, 261
Truman, Harry: 20, 21; and military aid to French, 25–26, 29
Trumbo, Dalton: 178
Truth and Power (Morgenthau): 200
Turner, Carl C.: 119 & n.
Turner, Nicholas: 108, 111, 112

Udall, Morris: 126
UFO (GI coffeehouse): 175; see also antiwar movement

Uganda: 171
Unamuno, Miguel: 167
Unfinished War, The (Capps): 239
United Kingdom: *see* Britain
United Nations: Southeast Asian camps
    of, 36; genocide code of, 259; Viet-
    nams and, 266; and Korean War, 275
United Press International: *see* UPI
United States: as "city on a hill," 6–15;
    technological preeminence of, 13–14;
    wars of, 13; invulnerability myth of,
    14; Philippines and, 18; as world
    policeman, 18, 48, 281–82; and com-
    mitment to colonial France, 19–29; as
    Japanese occupier, 24–25; and "loss"
    of China, 37, 40; *see also* Americans
United States Information Agency: 116
United States Information Service: 109
United States Military Assistance Ad-
    visory Group: *see* MAAG
UPI (United Press International): 108,
    112; and Tet offensive, 157, 161
Urbanization, forced: 271–72
USSR: *see* Soviet Union

Vance, Cyrus: 189
Vann, John Paul: 112, 149
VC: *see* Vietcong
Vet Centers: 55
Veterans, U.S.: Vietnam War, 51,
    53–73, 222; on campus, 54; shame
    of, 56–57, 234, 297; and combat,
    57–61, 73 n.; on trial, 58–59; relative
    youth of, 61–62; and homecoming,
    63–66; as former POWs, 64; and me-
    dia, 68; public attitude toward,
    68–69; militance of, 72; lesson to be
    learned from, 75–85; psychological
    problems of, 79–80; antiwar, 176,
    233–237, 255 (*see also* Vietnam Vet-
    erans Against the War); on television,
    222–23; disabled, 234, 237; confu-
    sion of, 294–95; and suicide, 296;
    Catholic, 297–98
Veterans hospitals: 234; brutality in, 178
Veterans of Foreign Wars: *see* VFW
Veterans organizations: 65
VFW (Veterans of Foreign Wars): Viet-
    nam War veterans as members of, 65;
    right-wing orientation of, 71
Vietcong (National Liberation Front
    [NLF]): 40, 43, 102, 110, 138, 150,

184, 186, 225; victory at Ap Bac of,
    112; mutilation of dead, 122; as "ani-
    mals," 123, 124; and Tet offensive,
    133, 154; in Saigon, 144; losses of,
    148 n.; as scapegoats, 234; crop de-
    struction ineffective against, 248;
    atrocities of, 261
Vietminh: 19, 27, 28; Soviet recognition
    of, 28; victory at Cao Bung of, 29
Vietnam, Democratic Republic of, for-
    mation of: 179
Vietnam: A History (Karnow): 146
Vietnam: A Television History: 146
Vietnam GI: 175
Vietnam Inc. (Griffiths): 125
Vietnam Veterans Against the War
    (VVAW): 65, 163, 176, 233; *see also*
    Kovic, Ron
Vietnam Veterans Leadership Program
    (VVLP): 67–68
Vietnam Veterans Memorial: 55, 145,
    300–302; message of, 75–76, 85
Vietnam Veterans of America (VVA):
    66, 76–77
Vietnam Year (military tour of duty): 62
"Village of Ben Suc, The" (Schell): 129
Villages, destruction of: 111, 131, 235;
    see also Cedar Falls operation
Virgil: 54
Voorhees, Tracy: 22
Vought, Donald B.: 102
V.V.A. (Vietnam Veterans of America):
    66, 76–77
VVAW (Vietnam Veterans Against the
    War): 65, 163, 176, 233; *see also*
    Kovic, Ron
VVLP (Vietnam Veterans Leadership
    Program): 67–68

Wall Street Journal: 146; criticism of
    War by, 168
War and Peace (Tolstoy): 84
War crimes: *see* atrocities
Warner, Denis: 108, 111
War of 1812: Vietnam War and, 270;
    and Federalist Party dissolution, 287
War Powers Resolution: 179
Washington, George: 7
Washington (D.C.), marches in: 185
Washington Daily News: 133
Washington Post: squeamishness of, 123;
    and My Lai, 127; interpretative re-

porting of, 158, 159; coverage of Tet offensive by, 161; simulated "atrocity" story in, 260

Watergate: 169, 191; relationship of Vietnam and, 245, 248, 292

Waters, Glendon: 300, 301

Wayne, John: 81

Weather Underground (Weathermen): 184, 188

Webb, James: 60

Wehrmacht: *see* Army, German

Weinberger, Casper: 279, 280, 282, 290

Weiss, Burton: 204, 206

West, Richard: 116

Westmoreland, William C.: 99, 105, 146, 151, 260; Vietnam command assumed by, 115; after Tet offensive, 137, 161

West Point, antiwar sentiment at: 176

We Won't Go: 208, 210; *see also* antiwar movement

Weyand, Gen. Frederick C.: 160

Wheeler, John: 162

Whigs, Mexican War and: 287

White, John: 111

White House Years (Kissinger): 187

White Jacket (Melville): 5

Why Vietnam (Thomson): 42

Wicker, Tom: 36

Wilde, Jim: 108

Wilson, John P.: 61

Wilson, Woodrow: 11

"Winter Soldier" investigations: 176

Winthrop, John: 5–6, 7, 8, 13

Wire services: *see* press

Wisconsin, University of, Army Mathematics Research Center of: 184

Women's Strike for Peace: 42

World War II: 18; as inspiration to Vietnam War soldier, 57; official history of, 100

Xuan Ngoc: 130

Yippies: 193

York, Robert H.: 112

Young Anarchists: 207–208

Young Friends: 208, 209

Yugoslavia, Vietminh overtures to: 28

Yuppies: 296

Zinn, Howard: 163, 165–82, 304

Zorthian, Barry: 117